THREE WHO MADE A REVOLUTION

VOLUME TWO

THREE WHO MADE A REVOLUTION

A BIOGRAPHICAL HISTORY

BERTRAM D. WOLFE

WITH A NEW INTRODUCTION
BY ALLEN DULLES

RTP TIME Reading Program Special Edition
TIME INCORPORATED · NEW YORK

TIME-LIFE BOOKS
EDITOR *Norman P. Ross*
TEXT DIRECTOR *William Jay Gold*
ART DIRECTOR *Edward A. Hamilton*
CHIEF OF RESEARCH *Beatrice T. Dobie*
ASSISTANT TEXT DIRECTOR *Jerry Korn*

EDITOR, TIME READING PROGRAM *Max Gissen*
RESEARCHER *Ann S. Lang*

PUBLISHER *Rhett Austell*
GENERAL MANAGER *John A. Watters*

TIME MAGAZINE
EDITOR *Roy Alexander*
MANAGING EDITOR *Otto Fuerbringer*
PUBLISHER *Bernhard M. Auer*

COVER DESIGN *Norman Green*

CONTENTS

LIST OF ILLUSTRATIONS

CHAPTER TWENTY

THE TRIAL OF VLADIMIR ILYICH

Is everything that is gathering force, underground, in the dark, in the night, in little hidden rooms out of sight of governments and policemen . . . is all this going to burst forth some fine morning and set the world on fire? Or is it going to sputter out and spend itself in vain conspiracies, be dissipated in sterile heroisms and abortive isolated movements?

—THE PRINCESS CASAMASSIMA

Men cannot live forever at fever heat. Even in victory, as the years after 1917 would prove, the fever of social unrest has a way of burning down and leaving the frame exhausted. Those who are dedicated to the single goal of revolution may continue with their self-appointed tasks, though even they will show signs of lassitude. But the common man who lives for the day's bare existence must return to his personal cares.

While the wave was rising it swept all before it, bringing together the most diverse classes, groups, factions, temperaments. As it receded, spent swimmers found themselves in ridiculous postures far from their accustomed or intended haunts. Only the most determined and powerful could feel themselves being swept away by the current, yet still face upstream and keep thrusting toward the receding goal.

Lenin was an unusual compound of revolutionary temperament with an acute sense of actual reality. He was more reluctant than the Menshevik leaders, and slower by many months, to realize that the fortress could not be taken by storm. When he did recognize it, he found himself almost alone in his own camp. For several years he had to conduct a struggle with the majority of his colleagues to make them grasp the true state of affairs and abandon slogans, tactics, gestures, appropriate only to a time of open warfare.

All through 1906 and early 1907 he vacillated between sturdily realistic appraisal and too easily reviving hope. A big Socialist faction in the Second Duma (although almost three quarters were Mensheviks); strikes among backward workers who had not participated in the earlier ones; peasant riots, more numerous in the spring of 1906 than in 1905; a belated mutiny of peasants-in-uniform at Kronstadt and Sveaborg; all the lingering fires that flared in the peripheral regions of the great empire when the blaze at the center had died—each of these in turn was taken by Lenin as a sign of renewal. By temperament, by creed, by obligation, he would rather err on the side of hope than miss an opportunity because of too easy despair.

Revolutionary Social Democracy—he wrote in the middle of 1906—must be the first to enter on the path of the most decisive and relentless struggle, and the last to have recourse to methods which are more roundabout.

So his creed. But still his sense of reality bade him prepare for the resumption of the roundabout path.

It is not hard, with benefit of hindsight, to note the main steps in the reconsolidation of governmental power. The ending of the war with Japan freed the government for war with its own people. The abortive eight-hour strike by the workers and the promise of Duma and Constitution by the Tsar, combined to separate liberals and moderates from revolutionary socialists. The arrest of the Executive Committee of the Soviet and the crushing of the Moscow uprising gave the officials new confidence, strengthening the physical force wing in their camp as against the moderate constitutional tendency represented by Witte.

As Russia's greatest industrializer and financier, and as a constitutional monarchist, Count Witte alone enjoyed the confidence of foreign banking circles. With a devotion to his sovereign worthy of a better fate, he now negotiated a foreign loan to make the Tsar independent of the coming Duma. The bankers demanded constitutional forms as a means of conciliating public opinion in France and guaranteeing greater stability to the régime. It was Witte's mistake to believe that such forms of government would make him indispensable to the Tsar. He was a sort of "Menshevik" of government circles, too much the "Westernizer," too alien to Russia's historic peculiarities, to win out at Court, any more than the Mensheviks could in the long run win out with the Russian masses.

Secretly, with false passport, M. Noetzlin of the Banque de Paris et des Pays-Bas came to Petersburg during the October days to discuss terms for a 2,250,000,000 gold franc loan. The last act of the Soviet before its dispersal was to warn prospective creditors that a loan to the government for war on its own people would never be honored by the latter should they come to power. Fair warning! But the Banque de Paris was playing for bigger stakes than could be measured in per cent. The Algeciras Conference was in session. "Our representatives," recorded Count Witte, "were directed to vote for France."

Thus Witte was able to dump a huge pile of gold at the Tsar's feet, and the Tsar was enabled to dispense with Witte and ignore the coming Duma. Yet the loan was to be fateful for the dynasty. Its negotiation completed the long process begun when Bismarck chose Austria as against Russia in his scheme of alliances and instructed the Reichsbank to accept no more Russian bonds as collateral for loans. Now the last strand was broken which, for a full century—since their common complicity in the partition of Poland—had tied Russia to Prussia and Austria. Instead, a new chain of gold was forged to link millions of Tsarist bayonets to billions of French francs for a war which, narrowly averted at Algeciras, was less than a decade away. That war would give Lenin the chance which the Russo-Japanese War had fallen short of providing.

During the autumn and winter of 1905, Bolsheviks and Mensheviks had been almost indistinguishable. Lenin had moved closer to the Mensheviks by abandoning his opposition to the non-party soviet, to broad, non-controlled, mass organizations, to local autonomy and initiative, to democratic process in the movement that had conquered legality in despite of the law. The Mensheviks, for their part, forgot their distrust of conspiracy and of "planned" uprising, their misgivings about power's falling into their own reluctant hands, their eagerness to avoid clashes with the bourgeoisie before the latter had become the ruling class. While the masses were storming forward with irresistible *élan,* Mensheviks were swept along and as much attracted as Bolsheviks by the "Russian" as against the "Western" way of political struggle.

But at the beginning of 1906, Axelrod, who had stayed abroad during the great year and was thus exempt from its contagion, noted with a sense of shock what Lenin had already recognized with satisfaction: that Mensheviks and Bolsheviks had been fighting side by side in ways that implied the unconscious acceptance of a number of Lenin's views and tactical methods. In the cold outer darkness after the flames had died down, many a Menshevik decided that the Revolution of 1905 had failed because the working class had gone too far with its own independent tactics (strikes and the Moscow uprising), with the arbitrary dictation of its class will (the eight-hour decree of the Petersburg Soviet), with its own special demands as against those of the opposition as a whole. Thus it had frightened away the bourgeoisie, which, according to the Menshevik formula, should have been inspirited, encouraged, if necessary pushed, into taking power. The crisis in menshevism was the deeper for the fact that it was the Petersburg Soviet, an organization which they dominated, that had carried them away with it into pressing the extreme program. And it was their own daily, *Nachalo,* under the dynamic editorship of Parvus and Trotsky, which had advanced the wholly un-Menshevik idea of immediate working-class seizure of power and proletarian-socialist dictatorship—an idea still combatted even by Lenin. What could be more demoralizing than the fact that the Menshevik organ had advanced ideas which Lenin could praise and the Mensheviks could not choose but condemn. Martynov, as Menshevik spokesman at the unity congress of the two factions, summed up their conduct in 1905 in this fashion:

> We said to ourselves then: *Le vin est tiré, il faut le boire.*—Since the wine is poured, it will have to be drunk.—At decisive moments one is forced to act firmly, with no time to analyze. ... The difference, however, was that we considered our situation as one forced upon us, while the Bolsheviks strove for it and regarded it as natural.

A strange spirit in which to have entered into general strikes, an uprising, and a struggle for power! So deeply did they repent now of their ideological sins, committed when the revolutionary tide had swept them off their feet, that henceforth the Mensheviks were to become increasingly passionate pedants in their insistence that the working class must thrust the power into the hands of the bourgeoisie, though the latter was losing its appetite for rule without the security of a Tsar. The active paralysis of the will which the Mensheviks were to show in 1917, the dogmatic, even frantic way in which they would fight off power with both hands and feet when there was no other real center of power in the country, are largely attributable to the inner crisis of remorse which they went through during the years of reaction.

Martov no less than Axelrod was oppressed by a growing uneasiness as soon as he saw the proletariat—in the eight-hour strike and Moscow insurrection—fighting in isolation from the bourgeoisie and frightening and enraging the very ones who, according to Menshevik theory, were their natural allies and the legitimate claimants to power. As early as February, 1906, Martov wrote in a tortured letter to Axelrod:

> For two months now I have been unable to finish any of the writing I have started. It is either neurasthenia or mental fatigue —but I cannot gather my thoughts together.

Trotsky for his part drew his conclusion from the phenomenon of close Bolshevik-Menshevik unity in the time of actual revolution. The differences that had grown up in more peaceful times between the two factions had thus proved artificial and unreal. Whenever there was a chance for action, their common program, their common desire for socialism, their common loyalty to the working class would sweep aside all the pedantic and dogmatic cobwebs of their differences. For most of the next decade, from 1907 to 1917, he berated them both for quarreling so furiously with each other, and sought to make himself the champion of unity between them. Since Lenin was invariably the aggressor in the splits, he directed his main fire against the latter. After he became a Bolshevik in 1917, however, he thought otherwise. "Martov did not know what to call his illness in 1906," Trotsky wrote after 1917, when the private letter to Axelrod had become public, "but it has a quite definite name: menshevism."

At first, Lenin drew the same conclusion as Trotsky from the union of Bolsheviks and Mensheviks in 1905, for, like Trotsky, he was impressed by the way the Mensheviks had accepted the Trotsky-Parvus thesis of general strike, armed uprising, proletarian dictatorship.

Indeed—wrote Lenin in April, 1906—if we look at the matter from the point of view of the departure of the Social Democrats from their "normal" road, we will see that a period of "revolutionary whirlwind" shows *more* and not less closeness and ideological unity in the social democracy. The tactics of the epoch of "the whirlwind" did not increase the distance between the two wings of social democracy but brought them closer together. In place of the former differences there arose unity of views on the question of the armed uprising. The Social Democrats of both factions worked in the Soviet of Workers Deputies, those unique organs of embryonic revolutionary power. They appealed together to the soldiers, the peasants, to enter into the Soviets. They issued revolutionary manifestoes together with the petty-bourgeois revolutionary parties. The previous controversies of the pre-revolutionary epoch gave way to agreement in practical matters. The rise of the revolutionary wave removed the differences, compelling the acceptance of fighting tactics, brushing aside the question of the Duma, placing the question of an uprising on the order of business. . . . In the *Northern Voice,* Mensheviks and Bolsheviks together called for a strike and an uprising, together called upon the workers not to give up the fight until the power was in their hands. The revolutionary situation itself suggested the practical slogans. Differences of opinion concerned only details in the estimate of events. For instance, *Nachalo* regarded the Soviets as organs of revolutionary self-government, while *Novaya Zhizn* looked upon them as embryonic organs of revolutionary power, uniting the proletariat and the revolutionary democrats. *Nachalo* inclined to a dictatorship of the proletariat; *Novaya Zhizn* stood for the democratic dictatorship of the proletariat and the peasantry. [Lenin: *Collected Works,* Third Russian Edition, Vol. IX, pp. 123-4. This article was originally published legally in Saint Petersburg in April, 1906.]

That was the high point of friendliness on Lenin's part. But the same actions which had called forth Lenin's enthusiasm had awakened Axelrod's chagrin, Martov's abulia, Plekhanov's doubts and Martynov's remorse.

Whatever Bolshevik and Menshevik leaders may have thought, the demand for unity in the ranks had acquired so great a momentum that neither side dared oppose it. Both factions had been overwhelmed by an inrush of new members who knew nothing of the ancient quarrels. All over Russia, the organizations fused without waiting for the leaders. Around them was the whole newly awakened working class, demanding that their would-be leaders stop quarreling over bygones and "fine points." If we cannot get together, they said, how will we lick the Tsar?

Despite misgivings as to recent tactics, the Mensheviks were by conviction and dogmatic formula responsive to the popular will, and therefore they became champions of unification for the next decade. They did not renounce their theoretical position, but proposed to argue it out in a united party. Unlike the Bolsheviks, they even permitted their separate faction organization to disintegrate. Not so Lenin. At all times he strove to keep his faction apparatus tuned up for possible rupture, or alternatively, for the more effective imposing of his views upon the united party. Yet he too felt the force of the demand for unity, and became for the nonce in his own fashion that, to him, most detestable of political beings: a "conciliator."

By the end of 1905, finding their lower units everywhere fused, the two leaderships set up a provisional "Parity Executive Committee" with an equal number from each side, to prepare a joint unification congress. Krassin, Lalayants and Rykov represented the Bolsheviks; Krokhmal, Taresevich and Jordanski the Mensheviks. When the government suppressed their two daily papers, they set up a common daily with a joint editorial board: Lunacharsky, Bazarov and Vorovsky, Dan, Martynov and Martov.

Inside the fused locals Bolshevik and Menshevik leaders presented rival platforms and ran rival sets of delegates for the unification congress. Thus they would determine its decisions, and their relative shares in the united leadership.

But now a new sector of "public opinion" appeared on the scene, not sewed up in either faction. The special language groups, and the socialist parties of the subject nations and borderlands, seeing the prospect of a united party, sent fraternal delegates to see if they too could not enter into one all-Russian body. These included the Jewish Socialist Bund, the Social Democratic Party of Poland and Lithuania; those of Latvia, Armenia, and the Ukraine. Significantly, the overwhelming majority of the Georgians were in the Russian Menshevik faction as an integral part of its leadership, and the minority, in which Djugashvili was soon to figure as a leader, was an integral part of the Bolshevik faction. Other Georgian parties, more nationalist than socialist, did not apply for affiliation.

The fraternal delegates from the borderland parties came to the 1906 Stockholm unification congress empowered only as observers, but by the London Congress in 1907 they were full-fledged members. This time, it almost seemed as if the process of forming a single, All-Russian Social Democratic Party, which had miscarried in 1903, would be brought to completion. For the next four or five years, Bolsheviks and Mensheviks were on the whole so evenly balanced in the united organization, that the Poles under the leadership of Rosa Luxemburg and Jan Tyszka, the Latvians, and the Jewish Socialist Bund held the balance of power in the united committees and sought to exert it now this way now that, to keep the precarious see-saw in balance and themselves at the fulcrum as balancing force. Though the Poles and Latvians inclined toward Lenin most of the time, it infuriated him to be so dependent upon forces which he did not control and which might fail to see eye to eye with him on matters which seemed to him most precious. At the Stockholm Congress of 1906 he was in a minority. It elected a Central Committee of seven Mensheviks and three Bolsheviks. Hence he secretly kept his faction apparatus alive, though he had just voted for the motion to dissolve both factions. At the London Congress in 1907, where, with the aid of the Poles he got a majority on the Central Committee, five Bolsheviks, four Mensheviks, and two each from the Poles, Bund and Latvians, he felt the majority to be so slender and unreliable that still he kept his caucus. Too often when he was sure that he was right (a conviction that was always with him), the Poles, Letts and Bundists, holding the balance of power, voted against him, or sought a "despicable compromise." As we know his character, we need not be surprised to find that this ultimately became intolerable to him. For, whatever he was thwarted in was likely to assume the guise of a shibboleth, distinguishing Ephramites from the true followers of Gilead. This was one of the reasons why in 1912, after six or seven years of uneasy unity, he would once more split the united organization and proclaim his own faction to be the Party.

After the two unity congresses, the movement was to decline so rapidly that it would become incapable of holding another. All its subsequent quarrels, growing more ferocious as the movement dwindled, were fought out in lesser conferences, joint central committees, joint editorial boards, rival faction papers.

Indeed, there were signs and omens of disunion from the outset. Professional politicians differ considerably from the constituents who elect them. Though they bear the latter's mandate, they bear, too, longer memories, completer systems of views, more deeply ingrained attitudes. A young delegate named Voroshilov (future Commissar of War) came to Stockholm bearing the pseudonym Volodya Antimekov, a cryptogram for Anti-Menshevik, while Katerina Samoilova sported the *nom de guerre* of Natasha Bolshevikova. Though the local elections had been held under joint party auspices, the credentials committee of the Congress became a battlefield. Krupskaya, for instance, sought to enter as a delegate from Kazan but, in her own words, "was short a small number of votes," i.e. her comrades had attempted to set up an *ad hoc* local but could not show enough members. She was accepted as a "consultative delegate," with voice but no vote. But, at the end of four additional days and nights of wrangling in the credentials committee, when a Georgian calling himself Ivanovich presented himself as a fictitious delegate from Tiflis, where the Bolsheviks had no organization at all, the credentials committee was so exhausted and the Mensheviks so sure of their majority that the Transcaucasian delegation (Mensheviks all) declared: "For the sake of peace and unity, we will not challenge Comrade Ivanovich's mandate." As victors foreseeing the difficulty of leading so ill united a party, they were inclined to be generous. Upon the defeated would fall the burden of reluctant subordination, or of finding the means to keep the fires of faction smoldering. At the Stockholm Congress, the Georgian Ivanovich attracted no further attention, but we shall soon have reason to keep an eye on him.

The final count of delegates to the Stockholm Congress was sixty-two Mensheviks to forty-six Bolsheviks. The Bolsheviks had lost the main working-class center of the country, Saint Petersburg, largely because of the inglorious role they had played in the Petersburg Soviet. They were hurt, too, by their opposition to taking part in the Duma elections. As the question of attitude toward the Duma was long to be a critical one, let us examine it in more detail.

During the General Strike of October, 1905, when the Tsar had issued his Manifesto promising a legislative Duma, all socialist parties had impulsively decided to boycott the elections. They did this because they were under the excitement of the October days, because they did not trust the Tsar to carry out his promise, and because they did not like the undemocratic electoral procedure of plural voting for the wealthier classes, and of indirect elections. The electoral law was drafted by S. E. Kryzhanovsky, then modified by Witte to give more representation to the "tsar-loving" peasant. After the October Manifesto, suffrage was extended to all males. But this suffrage was hedged by a plural weighting of the vote of the propertied classes, and by indirect elections. Following medieval Russian traditions, the voting was to be done by estates or classes. Peasants and workingmen voted in separate bodies, apart from landowners and urban property owners. Perhaps this division of the population into *soslovie* was intended to separate the masses from the influence of the radical intelligentsia. Moreover, Witte believed that the Zemstvo liberals were too radical and the peasants were by nature conservative. He hoped to bind them still closer to the throne by a sweeping program of land reform, but Witte's influence with the Tsar was too weak to get this part of his program through. All that remained was a voting scheme admirably adapted to promote class consciousness among workers and peasants. In factories employing more than fifty, the workingmen voted directly in their factory, an arrangement which tended to bring out a maximum working-class vote and develop a maximum of working-class consciousness. In each such factory (or group of smaller workshops), they chose delegates to a higher voting body, which in turn chose delegates to the "Workers' Curia" of the general electoral college of the city, which in turn chose deputies to the Duma. Thus the famed system of the Soviet Government, with voting by classes, "functional" representation by factories, and three- or four-stage voting, which was offered to the world in 1918 as something new under the sun, was really an invention of Kryzhanovsky, based on Russia's medieval heritage. But in 1906, Lenin joined with all other democrats and socialists in denouncing this indirect three- or four-stage voting as undemocratic. He denounced, too, the unequal representation of different classes, not according to their numbers but according to their "political reliability" or "stake in the state." Instead, he demanded what he called the "four-pronged democratic formula: *universal, direct, equal, and secret suffrage.*" Which did not prevent him in 1918 from adopting unequal, indirect, limited, and unsecret suffrage, as devices to maintain a Bolshevik majority in the Soviets though they were a minority in the country.

Both Mensheviks and Bolsheviks had accepted the idea of boycotting the elections when the Tsar first spoke of a Duma, but the Mensheviks soon decided that they had made a mistake. When the Bolsheviks, more stubborn and ardent boycotters, tried to use this "treason" as a talking point in the elections to the Stockholm convention, the Mensheviks registered gains instead of losses. For the rank and file of the Petersburg party membership, sensing that the period of direct assault was over, were beginning to turn their hopes to the Duma.

The Bolsheviks and the Social Revolutionaries, and—at the other extreme of the social spectrum—the Black Hundreds and the Union of the Russian People, continued to urge the masses to refuse to vote. Neither of these political extremes wished to accept the compromise of a constitutional monarchy, the Black Hundreds because they opposed any concessions by the Tsar, the Bolsheviks and Social Revolutionaries because they still hoped to overthrow him and call their own constituent assembly.

By the time the Stockholm Social Democratic Congress was assembling, voting for the Duma had already taken place in most parts of the country. To Lenin it was obvious that the Mensheviks had been right, and he and his group wrong. Ignoring the cries of boycottists, both of the Right and of the Left, the masses had voted in overwhelming numbers. In default of Social Democratic and Social Revolutionary candidates, they had voted for the most advanced personages available: for Constitutional Democrats, independent liberals and radicals, non-party labor men, individual Social Democrats who ran in defiance of party instructions, and (in the rural areas) for peasant and agrarian intellectuals who pledged themselves to demand a redistribution of the land. Thus the Constitutional

Democrats (popularly known as Kadets from the initials *Kah Deh*) had changed overnight from an insignificant group of doctrinaire intellectuals into the largest party in the Duma, with 190 mandates. No less revealing to Lenin was the news that there was a group of 94 agrarian laborites, calling themselves Trudoviki (from *trud*, meaning "labor"). As the Kadets under the leadership of Miliukov had swept the cities in default of Social Democratic candidates, so the Trudoviki under the leadership of Kerensky had swept the countryside in default of Social Revolutionary candidates.

When the Stockholm Congress assembled to take stock of this staggering news, elections were still to be held in Transcaucasia. The Menshevik delegation proposed that the Party give up its boycott and nominate candidates there. Indignation possessed the Bolshevik faction at this "betrayal" of the "revolutionary" position, but the indignation changed to consternation when Lenin deserted his faction and cast his vote for the Menshevik motion. The motion carried. Instructions to nominate a ticket were telegraphed to Transcaucasia, with the result that the Social Democratic Party carried not only the Workers' Curiae but the whole of Transcaucasia. All of its deputies to the Duma were Social Democrats of the Menshevik faction.

For several years—the next four, to be exact—the Duma question would overshadow all others, and would put Lenin into opposition both to the majority of his own faction and, for different reasons, to the Mensheviks. His faction were in love with that splendid moment when they had appealed to the masses to ignore the Tsar's concessions and, by insurrection, convene a constituent assembly. In Trotsky's tart words, they had observed that lightning is accompanied by thunder, and therefore concluded that if they kept making a noise like thunder, the lightning would strike again. Lenin's stern sense of realism told him that the days of direct storm were over, which alone could justify the departure from the Marxist tradition of participating in parliamentary elections. Hence he voted with the Mensheviks for participation, though it threatened to separate him from the faction he had formed.

Yet he could not agree with the Mensheviks either, for it seemed to him that they set too high a value on the Duma. He would make it a mere sounding board for revolutionary propaganda, a forum where revolutionists, clothed with special immunities and powers of attracting national attention, could denounce the Tsar's "parliamentary comedy" and could talk over the heads of fellow-deputies and ministers to the masses outside the Duma, rallying them to extra-parliamentary actions, strikes and demonstrations. The Mensheviks, however, took the "parliamentary comedy" as serious drama. They wished to propose genuine legislative measures in the interests of the working class; they sought to form a bloc with all oppositional parties, including the Kadets, against absolutism; they hoped to win genuine powers of legislation for the Duma, perhaps even a responsible ministry, which would take its instructions from the legislature and not from the Tsar: in short, they hoped to convert the Duma into a "Western" parliament. They ascribed to the Duma potential revolutionary significance, too, looking forward to the day when it might rally the whole nation behind it against absolutism, as once the French Estates General had rallied the French nation against Louis XVI. Finally, they saw in the Social Democratic Duma deputies one more chance to get out of the to them hateful blind alley of underground, conspirative revolutionary parties. The Social Democratic deputies, openly and democratically chosen by the masses, would provide, they hoped, a democratically elected socialist leadership to replace the self-appointed professional-revolutionary leaders.

Lenin held these views to be opportunistic, as he held the views of his own faction to be foolish and self-defeating. His own comrades' boycott would isolate the Party from the masses, who were interested in the Duma, and would voluntarily relinquish a weapon useful to expose "the parliamentary comedy." But Menshevism would lead the masses into the false path of parliamentary illusions, and away from the path of revolution.

A party such as he believed in, a self-chosen "vanguard" of underground conspirators and professional revolutionaries, could not develop primarily out of peaceful election campaigns, nor nominate its real leaders for public office, nor permit the "backward mass" to choose its leadership for it. If any Bolsheviks were elected, he thought they would be simple workingmen and not career leaders. His underground committee, or he himself, would draft speeches for them, and tell them what to say so that the parliamentary rostrum could become a splendid sounding board to train the masses and summon them to struggle.

Even in 1905, when the boycott tactics were first adopted, Lenin was reluctant to accept them. But at the Bolshevik Conference which was held at Tammerfors, Finland, in December, 1905, he was startled to find his whole faction lined up against him! Here is Joseph Stalin's report of that episode, as given to a little party in 1920 to celebrate Lenin's fiftieth birthday:

> The debate—at Tammerfors—opened, and the provincial members, Siberians and Caucasians, led the attack. What was our astonishment when, after our speeches, Lenin intervened and declared himself in favor of participating in the elections. But then he saw his mistake and took his stand with the faction. We were stupefied. The effect was electric. We gave him a great ovation.

Lenin did not reply at his birthday party but during the course of that same year, 1920, he took occasion to make it clear in a pamphlet that he thought that not he but "the Siberians and Caucasians" had been mistaken at Tammerfors.

Why then had he gone along? Was it because he feared to be cut off from his followers? That was part of it. For the next four years that fear would make Vladimir Ilyich tread warily, until he had mustered enough strength for his conception of Duma activities so that he could expel (and he actually did expel) all the recalcitrant revolutionary romanticists from his faction.

But in December, 1905, at Tammerfors, there had been special reasons for yielding to the "Siberians and the Caucasians." At that moment, the Duma was to Lenin a very secondary matter. He let himself be persuaded by the very unanimity of his conference delegates that they were expressing—how he longed to believe it!—the temper of the masses themselves. If it were but so that the masses had no faith in the Tsar's Manifesto, with its promises of Duma, Constitution, and civil liberties! Perhaps his followers were so unanimous because they had come right from the localities where the masses were planning, arms in hand, to overthrow the Tsar and write their own constitution. This attractive idea was the easier to accept because, even while the Tammerfors Conference was in session, the Moscow insurrection began. It was the crack of pistols and rifles there, and not the "attack of Siberians and Caucasians," by which Lenin had let himself be seduced. But by the time he got to Stockholm for the unity Congress he knew he had been mistaken to yield.

First he had noted with chagrin that the Black Hundreds, too, were for boycott. Next, that all the efforts of himself and his faction had failed to persuade the masses from voting. The Kadets and Trudoviki were benefiting thereby, while the Social Democrats were isolated. Moreover, his own followers showed him the dangerously undemocratic abyss toward which the boycott tactics led, when they came to him with a proposal that the Bolsheviks should use force against the "unheeding" masses to disperse the electoral meetings in which the workers were to choose their electors to the Workers' Curiae. The Bolshevik resolution on the First Duma, voted over Lenin's protest, read:

> . . . to declare everywhere a general political strike, hold manifestations, demonstrations, and utilize every means to the end of preventing elections from taking place, not hesitating if necessary even at the violent breakup of the electoral meetings. . . .

It was impossible for Lenin to imagine then that he too would one day use similar tactics against a constituent assembly, called into being by a successful revolution.

Most disconcerting of all to Vladimir Ilyich was the realization that he had utterly misjudged the peasantry. Unconsciously he had assumed—as had the government itself—that the "petty-bourgeois" peasant as voter would choose conservative rural leaders to represent him. But with simple, single-minded doggedness, they everywhere voted for the spokesmen who promised the most radical solution of the land question. Since the Social Revolutionaries, although they had a better understanding of the peasant, had also made the mistake of boycotting the Duma, the muzhiks were voting for unattached and independent village radicals, for the more articulate of their own people, or for radical members of the local *zemstvo* intelligentsia. Thus the Trudovik Party suddenly appeared in the Duma with ninety-four deputies, spiritually close to the Social Revolutionary Party.

> We are told—said one of the new peasant spokesmen in his maiden speech in the Duma—that property is sacred, inviolable. In my opinion it cannot possibly be inviolable; nothing can be inviolable, once the people will it. . . . Gentlemen of the gentry, you have stolen our land. . . . This is what the peasants who sent me here say: "The land is ours, we have come here not to buy it, but to take it."

What a golden opportunity for Lenin, who had been looking everywhere for a peasant movement with which to negotiate his alliance for a "Democratic Dictatorship of the Proletariat and the Peasantry"! This was not the Social Revolutionary Party, which also appealed to the working class and therefore had to be fought. This was a true peasant party such as he had dreamed of. And here he had left it alone in the Duma with the Kadets! Only four months had elapsed since Tammerfors, where, according to Stalin, he had "seen his mistake and taken his stand with the faction." But everything that had happened in those four months had convinced him that the Tammerfors Conference had been wrong and that he had been wrong to yield to it. That is why, at whatever risk, he broke with his faction at Stockholm, and voted with the Mensheviks on the Duma question.

The next six months were a particularly difficult time for Lenin. Never did he seem more irresolute, inconsistent, specious. On the one hand he was trying to hold onto his followers and maintain the prestige of the Bolshevik faction, on the other to force them toward the viewpoint which he felt was the only right one. In the face of his own better judgment, he continued stubbornly to maintain that the boycott, up to that very moment, had been correct. (Not until 1920 did he make public acknowledgment that the Bolsheviks had been wrong from the outset when they boycotted the First Duma. Then he did so for pedagogical purposes in the pamphlet *"Left" Communism: An Infantile Disorder,* directed against a faction in the Communist International that was in favor of boycotting parliamentary elections in imitation of the Bolshevik "model.")

The greater Lenin's logical entanglement, the more fiercely did he attack as "parliamentary opportunism" every utterance and action of the Mensheviks in connection with the Duma. The secret doubt that enmeshed him was whether he could or should risk an all-out attack on the stand of his own faction, so long as there was the slightest chance that the period of armed uprising was not over. If it was not over, the Duma was secondary and not worth a scrap with his faction. If it was over, then such a scrap was unavoidable. It was the government that finally resolved Lenin's difficulty by dissolving the First Duma.

Lenin had been expecting quite another outcome. He had calculated that the Tsar would ask the Kadets to form a ministry and that the Kadet Duma majority would make its peace with tsarism as a contrived deception of the masses. In this Lenin misjudged both the Kadets and the Tsar. The former were not unwilling to compromise with tsarism, but only on their own terms: a responsible cabinet government, limitation on the monarchy's powers, parliamentary control of budget, taxes, and legislation, end of the arbitrary régime of police violence and *ukaz*. If the Mensheviks overestimated the fighting spirit of this moderate democratic party, Lenin was no less wrong in imputing to them lack of principle and a mere desire to contrive maneuvers to cheat the masses. Now that the full record is available, it is clear that Miliukov and his associates in the leadership of the Kadets were a would-be loyal opposition to His Majesty within the framework of a limited monarchy. On the one hand they feared the people, the revolution and socialism; on the other they opposed absolutism and arbitrary government by camarilla. In short, they cherished a doctrinaire belief in moderate constitutionalism as that narrow strait between the twin rocks of absolutism and "anarchy" through which the ship of state must be cautiously steered to bring it into the safe harbor of "Western" ways.

Still wider of the mark was Lenin's estimate of the mentality of the other party to the anticipated "deal." Lenin always regarded the governing apparatus too schematically as a conscious, united and coldly calculating instrument of a conscious and united ruling class. It never occurred to him that the gulf between Black Hundreds and Kadets might be as wide as the gulf between Kadets and Bolsheviks, or that the Tsar's opposition to the responsible parliamentarism the Kadets worshipped might also be a matter of principle.

"One of the last of the Narodniki," G. P. Fedotov has shrewdly called Nicholas II, mindful of the fact that *narodnichestvo,* more than a definite economic-political program was a philosophical-emotional attitude toward "Holy Russia" and her destiny and toward the Russian muzhik as the primitive and undefiled repository of all Christian and Holy Russian virtues. The modern bourgeois world of Western Europe, worshipped by the Kadets and yearned for by the Mensheviks, was deeply repulsive to Nicholas. All that Lenin himself called backward, barbarous, Asiatic in Russia, was sacred to this romantic on the throne. The "dark peasant" whose entry on the stage of history inspired terror in Plekhanov, Miliukov, Martov, even in Maxim Gorky, was to Nicholas the guarantor of the throne and the source of Russia's strength and peculiar mission. Not even the shocks of peasant riots and mutinies could shake his faith in them. His "democratic" bearing with servants, grooms, common soldiers and muzhiks, testified to by all who were close to him, was undoubtedly genuine and spontaneous. But with advisers like Witte, Rodzianko and Stolypin he was always ill at ease. As his reign drew to a close he would increasingly dispense with such would-be councillors to take counsel with upstarts sprung from the folk, ignorant muzhik monks and "holy fools." In the end he would reject even the advice of reactionary nobles and grand dukes of the royal house, putting instead the fate of his family and the destiny of his empire into the hands of a coarse, lewd, mad, magnetic, "holy muzhik," whose shrewd and earthy judgments on matters of state were to the Tsar at once the voice of the people and the voice of God. The few courtiers whom he really trusted were men who shared his romantic, inverted-Narodnik views, or assumed the pose of sharing them. This brought him in principle and conviction far closer to the Union of the Russian People and the Black Hundreds than to the moderate reformers, the Wittes and Stolypins and Guchkovs, who sought to become his ministers and advisers, or the liberals who sought to set up a constitutional monarchy to limit his powers. And the Black Hundreds, as we have already noted, were as irreconcilable boycotters of the First Duma as were the Bolsheviks.

If the Tsar had no intention of letting the Duma control his policies or appoint his ministers, yet he had given his solemn word to permit its existence and he had no intention of going back on it. When the First Duma ventured to take up the land question in July, 1906, the Tsar ordered it dissolved. The entire opposition wrongly imagined that he was returning to the pre-1905 state of affairs. Haunted by reminiscences of the famous French Tennis Court Oath of 1789, the democratic and socialist deputies fled to Vyborg, Finland, the autonomy of which was still respected by the Russian police. From there they issued a manifesto calling upon the people to refuse to pay further taxes or furnish military recruits until the Tsar should permit them to reconvene. For good measure, the Social Democratic Party (led at the time by the Menshevik Central Committee Majority) followed this up with a call for a general strike to defend the Duma.

What should the Bolsheviks do who had just been denouncing the Duma as a government device for deceiving the people? And how would the masses themselves react to an appeal to defend the institution of which they had heard so much denunciation? To Lenin this exposed in a more glaring light than before the impossibility of the tactics his faction had forced upon him.

As was to be expected, the workingmen, exhausted and confused, remained passive. But again the peasants, and above all the peasants in uniform, furnished the surprises. They had set high hopes on the big Trudovik delegation, and on the land reform proposals of Kadets and Trudoviks, which had led to the Duma's dissolution. They responded with riots in many provinces and mutinies in the fleet and garrison at Sveaborg and Kronstadt.

The government was strong enough, however, to keep the initiative. It suppressed the disturbances, executed a few of the ringleaders, "pacified" the insurgent rural areas by punitive expeditions, disbarred the signers of the Vyborg Manifesto from running for office, and then—contrary to expectation—issued a call for elections to the Second Duma.

> History has shown—wrote Lenin in October, 1906—that the convening of the Duma brings with it the possibility of useful agitation . . . that inside we can apply the tactics of an understanding with the revolutionary peasants. It would be ridiculous to close our eyes to reality. The time has come now when the revolutionary Social Democrats must cease to be boycottists.

"History has shown"—that was Lenin's way of admitting that he had been proved wrong and learned something. But his followers were never so ready as he to go to school to Mistress History. Once more he had to fight on two fronts: against the irreconcilable among his followers (and that meant most of them), to drag them, reluctant, into the election campaign; and against the Menshevik-controlled Central Committee, which proposed an electoral bloc with the Kadets against the Rightist parties.

After the Unity Congress at Stockholm, Lenin had lost not a day in trying to mobilize the Party membership against the new Menshevik-controlled Central Committee. Now, when it was time to nominate Duma deputies from Saint Petersburg, he found himself with a majority in the capital, but not in the Petersburg Province as a whole. As so often happens, matters of principle got inextricably tangled with a petty organization question—whether Petersburg city should hold a nomination convention separate from the Province as a whole, or whether there should be a single, inclusive provincial convention. In the one case the Bolsheviks would control the city nominations, in the other the Mensheviks. We could well afford to ignore this squabble were it not for the fact that it nearly wrecked the new-found "unity" of the Party, and elicited from Lenin one of the most self-revealing documents that ever came from his pen.

In secure control of the city convention, Lenin put through a proposal there for "a Left Bloc" in the elections, a bloc of Social Democrats, Social Revolutionaries and Trudoviki *against* the Kadets. Obeying the instructions of the Menshevik-controlled Central Committee, thirty-one Menshevik delegates walked out of the city convention and held a separate provincial convention, which decided for a bloc *with* the Kadets as well as the more Leftist parties against absolutism and the parties of the extreme Right.

"Good-bye to unity," thought Lenin, whose mind was ever attuned to the idea of split. He proceeded on the assumption that the rift in Saint Petersburg was the beginning of a fresh split in the Party as a whole. Always ready for the offensive when battle was to be joined, Lenin promptly issued a pamphlet accusing the seceders of negotiating with the Kadets "for the purpose of selling the votes of the workers" and "bargaining to get their man into the Duma in spite of the workers and with the aid of the Kadets." This was not merely a charge against the seceders but also against the Central Committee of the Party, to which Lenin owed disciplined obedience according to his own theories of organization.

But the Party was not ready for a split, so that Lenin's calculations miscarried. Before long he found himself on trial before a democratically set-up Party court, charged with "conduct impermissible in a Party member." Lenin was allowed to name three judges, the Central Committee three judges, and the Lettish, Polish and Jewish Bund organizations, as neutrals, named one judge each. This was a species of democracy in Party trials which Lenin never allowed in the organization when he had majority control. The trial itself need not concern us, since it was interrupted by a new Party congress which upset the Menshevik majority and put Lenin in control.

But Lenin's remarkable speech in his own defense must concern us, for it throws a glaring light on his entire conception of how to conduct polemics with rival working-class groups and parties.

As the trial opened, Lenin calmly acknowledged that he had used "language impermissible in relations *between comrades* in the same party." He confessed that there were politically more accurate ways and more fraternal ones of designating the efforts of the Central Committee to unite all oppositions against the Tsar than that of charging them with "selling workers' votes." His choice of obnoxious phrases, he admitted, was

... calculated to evoke in the reader hatred, aversion and contempt ... calculated not to convince but to break up the ranks of the opponent, not to correct the mistake of the opponent but to destroy him, to wipe his organization off the face of the earth. This formulation is indeed of such a nature as to evoke the worst thoughts, the worst suspicions about the opponent and indeed, as contrasted with the formulation that convinces and corrects, it "carries confusion into the ranks of the proletariat." [The words in quotes are taken by Lenin from the Central Committee accusation against him.]

I may be asked [he continued], Well, do you admit that such formulations are *impermissible?* I shall answer: Yes, certainly, *but only with the following little proviso:* impermissible among members of *a united party.* . . .

A split means the rupture of all organizational ties, the shifting of the struggle of ideas from the ground of influencing the organization from within to that of influencing it from without, from the ground of correcting and persuading comrades to that of destroying their organization, to the ground of inciting the masses of the workers (and the masses of the people generally) against the seceded organization. . . . It is wrong to write about Party comrades in a language that systematically spreads among the working masses hatred, aversion, contempt, etc., for those who hold different opinions. But *one may and must write* in that strain about a seceded organization.

Why must one? Because when a split has taken place it is one's duty to *wrest* the masses from the leadership of the seceded section. I am told: you carried confusion into the ranks of the proletariat. My answer is: I purposely and deliberately carried confusion into the ranks of the section of the Saint Petersburg proletariat which followed the Mensheviks who seceded . . . and *I shall always act in that way whenever a split occurs.* . . . Against such political enemies I then conducted—and in the event of a repetition and development of a split *shall always conduct*—a fight of extermination. . . .

Are there any limits to permissible struggle based on a split? There are no limits to such a struggle set by any Party standards, nor can there be such, for a split implies the cessation of the existence of the Party. . . . The limits of the struggle based on a split are not Party limits, but general political limits, or rather general civil limits, the limits set by criminal law and nothing else. . . . [All italics in the original speech as published by Lenin. Full text in English in *Selected Works,* Vol. III, pp. 486-498.]

Three times, in a speech that could not have lasted an hour, did Lenin pledge himself that he should *always act thus,* whenever a split was in prospect. It must be recognized that he kept his word! Hence we shall always have to bear in mind this frankly avowed view that all things are permissible in polemics between competing parties. It will help us to understand the polemical documents from Lenin's hands, directed against

Mensheviks and Social Revolutionaries, against the Second International and its parties after he split from it to form the Third, against Bolsheviks differing from him sufficiently to secede or be expelled from his faction. But this will not exempt us, in any case, from a concrete analysis of his polemical writings to determine how much of each is objective truth, and how much deliberately "calculated to evoke hatred, aversion, and contempt . . . to evoke the worst thoughts, the worst suspicions about the opponent . . . not to correct his mistake, but to destroy him, to wipe his organization off the face of the earth . . ."

We shall have to bear in mind, too, that Lenin is not always as "rock-hard" as he would like to appear. There were times when he would restrain his polemical language out of other considerations than "the limits set by criminal law." Chief of these other considerations would be the feeling, often neglected but never fully abandoned, that the working class must in the long run be educated by political controversy to a deeper understanding of its position and tasks. As for the restraints of the criminal law, these would vanish when his party became the government and made the law. We shall have to ponder then what would happen to this doctrine, especially when the doctrine was taken up by lesser men with less ingrained humaneness and less concern for the long-run effect of polemics upon the understanding of the masses. Or when it was adopted by the leaders of other Communist parties, lacking the counterbalancing humane tradition of the old Russian revolutionary intelligentsia.

CHAPTER TWENTY-ONE

LENIN
AND
STOLYPIN

What they want is great upheavals; what we want is a great Russia.

—PETER ARKADYEVICH STOLYPIN

In party politics as in statecraft generally, the sovereign can do no wrong, nor be sued without consent. Lenin's trial for "conduct impermissible in a Party member" came to an abrupt end when, at the London Congress of the United Party (April-May, 1907), Lenin achieved a slender numerical majority. The new Central Committee simply forgot the charges against its now dominant figure.

But that did not put an end to the nagging Duma controversy. All through the years from 1906 to 1912 Lenin had to continue his war on two fronts: with the Bolshevik boycotters for their "infantile leftism"; with the Mensheviks for their "parliamentary opportunism." His need to keep the boycotters with him sharpened his fight against the "non-revolutionary" use of the Duma by the Menshevik deputies, while his need to join with the Mensheviks against his own boycottist faction embittered relations inside the Bolshevik group. In the years of lowest ebb in the revolutionary movement (1909 to 1911) this tangled controversy, conjoined with other issues, called forth splits in both factions. The general confusion was fantastic. Everyone became short of temper and long on vituperation.

In the year elapsing between the Stockholm (1906) and the London (1907) Congresses, it looked as if Lenin's authority would win over, or at least overawe, the majority of his faction on the Duma issue. But in the summer of 1907, just as Lenin seemed to be making decisive progress, the government under Premier Stolypin reopened the whole question in a much more drastic form. On June 16, 1907, Premier Stolypin peremptorily dissolved the Second Duma, using as a pretext a circular planted by a police agent, and the revolutionary speeches concerning armed insurrection in which Lenin and his fellow-Bolsheviks had indulged at the London united party congress. Duma deputies had participated in these conspirative discussions, Stolypin declared (they happened to be Menshevik deputies, opposed to Lenin's viewpoint!), and he demanded that these conspirers be expelled from the Duma. When the latter body hesitated to deprive them of their mandates and immunities, Stolypin dissolved it. Then, by simple *ukaz*, the government revised the electoral laws so that they would not again give a majority to the oppositions, as they had in the First and Second Dumas. The new *ukaz*, known as the *Coup d'état of June 16, 1907*, cut the value of a peasant's vote in half. Labor electors were cut by one-third. Poles and other deputations from the border countries were greatly reduced. The Third Duma was thus packed with landowners and their agents, priests, great-Russian nationalists, state officials, and other conservatives. All the radical oppositions: Kadets, Poles, Social Democrats, Social Revolutionaries, Trudoviks, etc., were cut to an insignificant minority.

A new cry arose for boycott of the Duma. The Social Revolutionary Party reverted to boycott, while Lenin's faction overwhelmed him once more. This was a "cardboard, comic-opera Duma," they cried, and the Constitution was now a mere fraud. What self-respecting revolutionary could so humiliate himself and so deceive the masses as to participate in such undemocratic elections, play a role in such a farce, pretend that anything could be accomplished in such a travesty on the idea of popular representation?

But Lenin knew no finical pride as to the kind of institution in which he would work if he could thereby serve the revolution. "In a pig-sty if necessary," he told his comrades. Moreover, he had been studying Stolypin and his maneuvers with increasing respect. Here was an opponent worthy of his steel, a man who, with opposite intentions, but from similar premises, was doing much what Lenin would have done had he been a champion of the existing order and an enemy of the revolution.

Stolypin's policy as Premier combined measures to diminish the franchise of "unreliable elements" and to repress open revolutionary activity, with a series of bold positive schemes for modernizing Russian life, reforming agriculture, and stabilizing the tsarist régime. As if he had studied Lenin's *Development of Capitalism in Russia* and all Lenin's writings on the agrarian question, Stolypin proceeded now to foster capitalism in agriculture, to promote class differentiation in the village, to break down the communal *mir*, to secrete out a new class of property-minded individual peasant proprietors as a rural support for the existing order. ("I put my wager not on the needy and the drunken, but on the sturdy and the strong.")

The trouble with the Emancipation of 1861, reasoned Stolypin, was that it actually preserved and fostered the peasant commune instead of setting up a class of individual proprietors. Each communal village had received the entire area of land allotted to its members as a communal holding under a system of collective responsibility for the redemption payments of all its members. The commune itself then divided the land for tilling among its members according to the size of the families, fresh subdivision taking place every few years to keep up with population changes. Hence there was no inducement to improve the land, and no sense of private ownership such as characterized Western farmers and tended to make them socially conservative. The system conserved communal or corporate ideology. It preserved the memory of serfdom, and reminded the former serfs that they had gotten on the average only half of the land they had tilled for their lords before emancipation. Thus it kept alive the idea that the halfway job might be completed by adding the rest of the land of the big landowner to the communal village land fund.

Now Stolypin set about to create in Russia a class of individual small proprietors. He abolished the *zemski nachalnik* who kept the village in tutelage; he instituted equal civil rights for peasants with the rest of the population; he inaugurated a series of land and loan laws which would encourage all the more energetic to withdraw from the communes and become individual owners of their share of the land. "The natural counterweight to the communal principle," he said, "is individual ownership; the small owner is the nucleus on which rests all stable order in the state." In short, he tried to create the conservative, property-minded class that the Marxists had wrongly imagined the Russian peasant to be. This was sound reactionary politics, Lenin told himself with ungrudging admiration.

And no less sound was Stolypin's *ukaz* limiting the voting power of elements opposed to the régime while he enlarged the voting power of its supporters. So Lenin, too, would act in 1918, when he made a worker's vote equal to that of five peasants.

Between 1907 and 1914, under the Stolypin land reform laws, 2,000,000 peasant families seceded from the village *mir* and became individual proprietors. All through the war the movement continued, so that by January 1, 1916, 6,200,000 families, out of approximately 16,000,000 eligible, had made application for separation. Lenin saw the matter as a race with time between Stolypin's reforms, and the next upheaval. Should an upheaval be postponed for a couple of decades, the new land measures would so transform the countryside that it would no longer be a revolutionary force. How near Lenin came to losing that race is proved by the fact that in 1917 when he called upon the peasants to "take the land," they already owned more than three-fourths of it. According to Nicholas S. Timasheff, "the increase in the area tilled by the peasants (after the revolution) did not exceed 8 per cent; for an additional 8 per cent, the peasants no longer had to pay rent. The rest was not arable land." (*The Great Retreat,* p. 107.)

The Stolypin Constitution—wrote Lenin in 1908—and the Stolypin agrarian policy mark a new phase in the breakdown of the old, semi-patriarchal and semi-feudal system of tsarism, a new movement toward its transformation into a middle-class monarchy.... If this should continue for very long periods of time ... it might force us to renounce any agrarian program at all. It would be empty and stupid democratic phrase-mongering to say that the success of such a policy in Russia is "impossible." It is possible! If Stolypin's policy is continued ... then the agrarian structure of Russia will become completely bourgeois, the stronger peasants will acquire almost all the allotments of land, agriculture will become capitalistic, and any "solution" of the agrarian problem—radical or otherwise—will become impossible under capitalism. [*Proletarii,* April 29, 1908, reprinted in *Collected Works,* Third Russian Edition, Vol. XII, p. 193.]

Thus the two men had opposing purposes, but in premises, in analysis of the possibilities, in tactical methods, they understood each other. It almost seemed as if Premier Peter Arkadyevich were addressing Bolshevik leader Vladimir Ilyich directly when, from the rostrum of the Duma, he made his famous declaration:

"What you want is upheavals, what we want is a great fatherland."

Would a fresh upheaval come before the new régime could complete its self-reform and consolidate its new foundations? "I do not expect to live to see the revolution," said Lenin several times toward the close of the Stolypin period.

But the dark forces which Plehve had created and which Stolypin continued to use to spy upon the revolutionary movement were the forces which struck him down. On September 14, 1911, in the presence of the Tsar and two princesses, at a gala performance in the best theater in Kiev, an assassin's bullet put an end to the career of Peter Arkadyevich Stolypin. The murderer was a Jewish lawyer named Dmitri Bogrov, who seems to have been simultaneously an agent of the police and of the terrorist wing of the Anarchist movement. The assassination was never fully cleared up. Circumstances pointed to the possible complicity of the Department of the Interior, whose secret police were guarding the Tsar, or, at the very least, to the guilty negligence of the Kiev police authorities. The specters of the *agents provocateurs* like Ryss and Azev must have haunted Stolypin as he lay dying. The Tsar and Tsarina did not mourn the loss of the man who had tried so hard to save them. They never even understood what he was doing. The great state that he had hoped to reinforce and modernize by the combination of police force, legislative manipulation, and enlightened economic and political measures was taken over increasingly thenceforward by the dark and backward forces around Rasputin. Yet so well had Stolypin done his work that the agrarian reform continued to develop after his death. It was the sudden coming of war, and not the failure of his plans, which brought the fresh upheaval in time for Lenin.

The Central Committee (under Lenin's control since the London Congress) called an All-Russian Conference in July 1907 to consider Stolypin's coup d'état and prepare for the elections to the Third Duma. Though he had just captured the Central Committee, Lenin again lost control of his own faction. Out of fifteen Bolshevik delegates, fourteen were for boycott! The lone dissident was Lenin. They deposed him as spokesman and chose Bogdanov to report for them. Once more, as at Stockholm, Lenin voted with the Mensheviks. Poles, plus Bundists, plus Mensheviks, plus Lenin, outvoted the Bolshevik delegation.

All through 1908 the conflict smoldered in the faction, in forms too complicated to follow in detail. At times it seemed as if Lenin had persuaded a majority to participate in the elections. But then the fight broke out in a new form because they wanted to recall those Deputies who were chosen (14 of the 18, Mensheviks) for not acting in a sufficiently intransigent fashion. This trend Lenin dubbed *o zovism* ("recallism," from the Russian word for recall). Or they wanted to present an ultimatum to the socialist Duma Deputies, which could only lead to the resignation of the Deputies either from the Party or from the Duma. This trend received the name of "ultimatism."

All these boycottist and semi-boycottist trends rallied around the personality of the philosopher Bogdanov, who had succeeded Krassin as the number-two man in Lenin's *troika,* and who now threatened to oust Lenin from domination in his own faction. Among those who sided with Bogdanov were Lunacharsky, Gorky, Krassin, Bazarov, former Bolshevik Duma leader, Alexinsky, the historian, Pokrovsky, the future GPU chief, Menzhinsky, the historian of the Party, Lyadov, the future Comintern leader, Manuilsky, and many others whom we shall meet again. Not until the middle of 1908 did Lenin win a slender majority (eighteen to fourteen) in Moscow, and as late as 1909 he was still in a minority in Petersburg. Only when he felt strong enough and had built himself a new *troika* (the first three-man leadership had been Lenin-Krassin-Bogdanov; then Lenin-Taratuta-Dubrovinsky;   Lenin-Malinovsky-Zinoviev; Lenin-Zinoviev-Kamenev; then, in wartime, Lenin and Zinoviev), did he expel without ceremony or any constitutional warrant all the boycottists, recallists and ultimatists from his faction. Under what conditions we shall see in a succeeding chapter (Chapter XXIX, "Lenin as Philosopher").

Ultimately, all but two of these dissenters returned to the fold as more unconditional followers than before. Only Bogdanov remained aloof because of his independent temperament and deep differences on philosophical matters. The other permanent loss was Alexinsky, who became a bitter enemy of Bolshevism. However, at the high tide of the boycottist movement in 1907, Lenin had been so alone that even the future constituents of his *troika,* Zinoviev and Kamenev, were lined up for a while against him.

Once more, in this uncanny ability to appraise Stolypin correctly and to adapt his tactics to the hard realities of revolutionary decline, Lenin proved so superior to his faction that, as one by one, they returned rather sheepishly to the fold, they were more like sheep than before in their readiness to follow the leader. Here, for instance, are the words of the outstanding Marxist historian M. N. Pokrovsky:

> There was above all, his enormous capacity to see to the root of things, a capacity which finally awakened in me a sort of superstitious feeling. I frequently had occasion to differ from him on practical questions but I came off badly every time. When this experience had been repeated about seven times, I ceased to dispute and submitted to Lenin even if logic told me that one should act otherwise. I was henceforth convinced that

he understood things better and was master of the power denied to me, of seeing about ten feet down into the earth.

If we bear this strange, freely made confession in mind, bear in mind, too, that it is the utterance of an original thinker whose histories are monuments of research and rational and logical interpretation, we get an insight into the mind of the Russian intellectual and into some of the sources of Lenin's power over his followers. We get some insight, too, into how the power of Lenin came to be transformed into the quite different power of Stalin.

If the Duma question had been the only controversy at the Stockholm and London Congresses, Lenin would scarcely have dared to side with the Mensheviks on it, since it would have meant rupture with his faction. But, actually, it was overshadowed in all minds by a number of other issues which were to keep the united party in turmoil until it split forever six years later.

At the Stockholm Congress of 1906, as we know, the Bolsheviks were in a minority. Yet, except on the Duma and on the ticklish business of revolutionary holdups of banks and merchants, Lenin managed to retain the offensive and, in no small measure, impose his views upon the majority.

The Mensheviks were still too much under the spell of 1905 to say straight out what they thought of the Moscow uprising and of armed insurrection in general. Lenin pressed his advantage.

On the land question, too, as always throughout the history of Russian Social Democracy, he took the initiative. He it was who had written for the original Party program of 1903 the demand for the return of the *otrezki*—the pieces of common land cut off from the peasant estates at the time of the Emancipation. He had thought that a realistic, "immediate demand," but 1905 had taught him how inadequate it was and how little in tune with the mood of the peasantry.

Our mistake—he declared boldly—consisted in underestimating the breadth and depth of the democratic, or rather bourgeois-democratic, movement among the peasantry. It is stupid to persist in this mistake now when the revolution has taught so much.

Lenin thus criticizing his own errors, Lenin learning from "History"—here is Lenin at his best and greatest. Once more he caught the Menshevik majority at Stockholm off guard by proposing a new agrarian program, with two sweeping alternative or complementary proposals: support of the peasants in any attempts they might make at direct seizure of the land, or, as a more desirable variant, complete nationalization of the land by a victorious revolutionary government, which might then rent it, or if need be distribute it, to the peasantry. Lenin's predilection for strengthening the future revolutionary state power made him prefer nationalization to disorderly seizure from below, and state control to general distribution. Yet he knew—better than any other leader except Rosa Luxemburg—that a revolution is infinitely more complicated and disorderly and chaotic than any preconceptions and tidy formulae for channeling its torrents. Hence he thought of these alternative proposals not as in sharp opposition to each other, but as varying aspects of one general process which should break the power of the landowners, smash the old régime, win the support of the peasants for the workers' party. In mid-1917 it would be charged against him that he suddenly "stole" the land program of the Social Revolutionary Party; but those who made the charge were too short of memory. The program on which the Social Revolutionaries claimed exclusive copyright was one of the related alternatives which he kept in mind from 1906 onward.

Russian Marxists, both Bolshevik and Menshevik, tended to view the peasantry with strong reserve as a backward, property-loving, potentially hostile "petty bourgeoisie." In this all Marxists, Lenin included, differed from the Social Revolutionaries. But, unlike his comrades, Lenin could not forget that the peasants were in a majority and discontented, and that no revolution could be made without them or against them in the Russian land. Moreover, deep within him there was a substratum of peasantophile tradition inherited from the older Narodnik fighters. In the peasant question as in the terror, there was something, hard to put one's finger on, which distinguished his interpretation of their common formulae from that of all the rest of his Marxist brethren—including those in his own faction.

Instinctively, the Menshevik majority at Stockholm felt an aversion to Lenin's plan for seizure and nationalization or division of the land. Instead, Maslov and Plekhanov offered a proposal for "municipalization." Lenin's nationalization assumed a victorious revolution; his proposals for peasant seizure of the land were calculated to promote such a victory. But on what was their "municipalization" based? It reflected their longing for local self-government and their fear of centralization. It assumed somehow the emergence of democratic local governments. It was silent on the status of the national government during this period of emergence. And it was insistent that the peasants should wait in orderly fashion until the properly constituted municipal authorities were ready to rent the land to them. But behind this utopian plan lay not so much positive vision as instinctive dread. These men feared the peasantry in action, dreaded the prospect of anarchic, uncontrolled uprisings of the "dark folk." They sensed that Lenin's plan was tied to the heretical doctrine of seizure of power by the Party. Above all they feared—and this was a truly brilliant premonition on Plekhanov's part—that nationalization of the land would bind the peasant to the state afresh, to any state that might hold in its hands the weapon of overlordship of the soil, thus continuing the age-old servile "Asiatic" tradition which had always bound the rural masses to the ruling power. And if the peasant majority were bound, could the urban population be free?

The situation in our country—ran Plekhanov's prophetic warning—is such that the land, together with the tillers, was held in servitude to the state. And on the basis of that servitude, Russian despotism developed. . . . There is not, and cannot be, any guarantee against restoration. Remember the history of France, remember the history of England: in each of them, the wide sweep of the revolution was followed by restoration. . . . True, not the restoration of the remnants of feudalism. But in our country we have something that resembles these remnants, to wit, the fact that the land and the tiller of the soil are tied to the state, our own peculiar form of "land nationalization"! And, by demanding the nationalization of the land, you are making the return to this type of nationalization easier, for you are leaving intact this legacy of our old, semi-Asiatic order. . . ."

Thus was lifted for a moment the curtain that obscured the future. It was a prevision as brilliant as that of Lenin when he warned Trotsky of the consequences of an undemocratic revolution and minority party government, and that of Trotsky when he warned Lenin of the dangers inherent in his hierarchical, centralized, undemocratic party structure. They were like the three blind men who grasped three different parts of an elephant. Marxists contend that their method of sociological analysis enables them to predict the future. If these three Marxist prophecies could but have been added together, and acted on together, they would indeed have constituted a brilliant example of foresight and forewarning.

The curtain that was lifted a moment dropped again, for Plekhanov was no match for Lenin in debate on the agrarian question. Both camps were divided internally. Most Social Democrats knew so little about the countryside that the issues eluded them. The debate became more and more confused. Most Bolsheviks, too, faced the muzhik with ignorance, and a vague, unconscious dread, or with contempt, enclosed in the formula: "property-minded, petty bourgeois." Some delegates thought that the whole question of land proprietorship was alien to the workers. Others that nothing could be done until "after the revolution," and then there would be "immediate and total socialization of the land" in the form of big "agricultural factories" owned and controlled not by the vast majority of peasants but by the small class of hired help or "rural proletarians." Some abstained from voting. Others held that the question was "a bridge to be crossed when you come to it." Yet others thought up *ad hoc* motions, new and fantastic alternatives, which might satisfy their revolutionary feelings and give them something for which to cast their vote and yet evade the issue which eluded their understanding. In the end, Lenin's resolution, although in a diluted form, was the only one with a solid bloc behind it. He emerged once more as the expert on the question which was the key to popular revolution in Russia, and to the kind of state which would emerge from it. After all, Lenins were as rare in the Social Democratic camp as were Stolypins in the camp of tsarism.

At Stockholm, too, and more sharply at the London Congress, emerged the first outlines of two additional controversies which would tear the Party once more asunder. They were concerned with the two extremes of the variegated spectrum of popular organizations which had sprung up during the Days of Freedom in 1905: the open or legal mass organizations on the one hand and the illegal fighting companies or armed guerrilla bands on the other.

As we have already noted, the Mensheviks were inclined by temperament and conviction toward the trade union, the mass organization, the broad party *of* the working class; the Bolsheviks toward the conspirative underground, the armed group, the uprising, the narrow, self-selected vanguard party *for* the working class. The difference in attitude of the workingman toward his union, and of the outlawed conspirator toward his underground and his armed band, would determine real differences in spirit, relative staying power in the period of reaction, aptness for legality and for conspiracy, varying loyalties and degrees of devotion, attitudes toward autonomy, Party control, labor democracy, and a host of other divergencies. If we keep this fundamental difference of approach in mind, then many of the controversies which we are to consider in the next few chapters lose their apparent hair-splitting character and fall into place as parts of a pattern.

Outwardly the Stockholm Congress was full of confidence, in the spring of 1906, for the Party membership was still growing. But already the wider world of open and public activity and independent mass organization was being cut to pieces by the sabre blows of triumphant reaction. How the Mensheviks shuddered at the prospect of being driven back once more into the narrow cellars of the conspirative, "professional" underground! To stave it off, they revived Axelrod's proposal: the calling of a broad, non-partisan or multi-partisan labor congress, which should absorb all existing parties and mass organizations into a federated party of the entire working class.

Lenin was no less saddened than the Mensheviks by the disappearance of one after another of the new mass organizations. But he thought of it chiefly as the loss of the wider arena in which the Social Democratic Party had been able to operate, win converts, influence and control. Reluctantly, but with no severe jolt, he reverted now to his older conception that such open organizations as might still be maintained or set up should serve as mere "covers" or spheres of operation ("front organizations"—to borrow the terminology of a later day). In Axelrod's proposal he saw a heretical attempt to dilute socialist doctrine from the highly developed theoretical system of élite specialists in Marxism to the confused and "anti-proletarian" (i.e. incompletely socialist or anti-socialist) notions of an ignorant and backward working class. Against Axelrod's talk of control of the proposed new party by the mass organizations, he favored the control of the mass organizations by the vanguard party. Axelrod's "broad labor party" would be a "bourgeois labor party," he maintained, amorphous in structure, eclectic in doctrine, reformist and unrevolutionary in aim, and even— he was convinced—incapable of existence under an autocratic government. In the "right of the working class to self-determination" as urged by the Mensheviks, he saw only a "democratic superstition" that heads should be counted regardless of their individual capacity for determining matters which could be properly determined only by those who devoted their lives to the study of Marxist theory.

Even before the Mensheviks were quite sure what they were proposing, Lenin was denouncing its proponents as "liquidators" of the revolutionary party. Every time the proposal bobbed up, in whatever protean form, Lenin was ready with his epithet of scorn. As with other cherished phrases, he would hammer away at it for five years, until the entire Party began to feel the overtones of betrayal with which he endowed it, and until some of the "liquidators" defiantly accepted the epithet.

On the question of the Soviet, too, Lenin now reverted to his older conception, never altogether surrendered:

> The Party—he wrote in a polemic against the Stockholm majority—has never renounced its intention of making use of certain non-party organizations like the Soviets in order to extend the influence of the Social Democrats in the working class. At the same time the Social Democratic organizations must bear in mind that if social democratic work among the masses is properly and widely organized, such institutions may actually become superfluous. . . .

"Actually become superfluous!" This single statement, even if not matched by others of similar import, should be enough to destroy the sedulously nourished official legend that Lenin "instantly appreciated" the Soviets from the day the first Council of Workingmen's Deputies was formed in 1905. In the above quotation there is no room for the conception of the Soviet as a broader, more democratic workers' parliament, superior to the Party because more inclusive and more representative. Rather does such language foreshadow the wasting away of the Soviets once the growth of the influence and power of the Party might make them "actually become superfluous."

At that very moment, Trotsky in prison was writing:

The Soviet was in reality *an embryo of a revolutionary government.* . . . Prior to the Soviet, there had been revolutionary organizations among the workingmen. . . . But these were organizations *in* the proletariat; their immediate aim was to *influence the masses.* The Soviet is an organization *of* the proletariat; its aim is to fight for *revolutionary power.* At the same time, the Soviet was an organized expression of the will of the proletariat as a class. . . . The Soviet is the first democratic power in modern Russian history . . . the organized power of the masses themselves over their component parts. This is a true unadulterated democracy, without a two-chamber system, without a professional bureaucracy, with the right of the voters to recall their deputy at any moment and to substitute another for him. . . . There is no doubt that *the first new wave of the revolution will lead to the creation of Soviets all over the country.*

In this remarkable passage from Trotsky's *The Year 1905,* rather than in anything that Lenin was writing at the time, is the germ of the doctrine concerning the Soviet as labor parliament and proletarian government, which Lenin and Trotsky were to expound jointly in the autumn of 1917. Thus the Soviet idea has a peculiar history. It was conceived in the matrix of the Menshevik "autonomous local revolutionary self-administrations" and Axelrod's "broad, non-partisan (or rather, multipartisan) labor congress." It was nourished by Trotsky's and Parvus's doctrine of "permanent revolution." In 1917 it was to mature, as Trotsky had predicted, from "an organization of the proletariat fighting for revolutionary power" into "the organized power of the masses themselves over their component parts . . . and the embryo of a revolutionary government." And it was to go into decline after 1918, in accordance with the Leninist formula of a single party that controls all mass organizations and ultimately renders "such institutions actually superfluous." Thus the Menshevik conception was closest to the origins of the Soviet of 1905; Trotsky's to the high role assigned by him and Lenin to the Soviets in the autumn of 1917; and Lenin's to their ultimate destiny as mere instrument or transmission belt of the controlling party. Once more, three blind men, each gifted with a highly developed sense of touch, had grasped three parts of the elephant, and each described it as if it were the whole.

CHAPTER TWENTY-TWO

ARMS
AND
THE
MAN

An oppressed class which does not strive to learn to use arms, to obtain arms, deserves to be treated as slaves.

—V. I. LENIN

During the storms of 1905, all parties had sanctioned defensive arming: for the protection of meetings, leaders, racial minorities. But there agreement ended. The Mensheviks were slower to advocate the formation of armed bands when the tempest was rising, more insistent on their purely defensive function once they came into existence, swifter to demand their dissolution as soon as calm returned. But for Lenin they were an object of passionate absorption, central to his whole idea of revolution.

Not that he was one to play with armed insurrection in season and out. Yet, as soon as events permitted him to think—or hope—that an uprising might be on the order of business, he would give to the question of arms first place. From the day that the followers of the priest Gapon fell bleeding upon the snow, arms and armed bands or fighting companies were never absent from his thoughts.

"The arming of the people," he had written in his very first article after the news of Bloody Sunday reached him in exile, "the arming of the people has become an immediate task . . ."

Martov had spoken of arms, too, but Lenin had only scorn for Martov's twice-removed formula for "arming the people with the burning desire to arm themselves." Martov soon ceased to speak of arms even in such fashion. After the ill-prepared Moscow uprising of December 1905, he and his associates became convinced that it had been a mistake to form little armed bands for insurrection, or "conduct the struggle for democratic demands within the framework of a political conspiracy."

"They should not have taken up arms," said Plekhanov categorically.

On the contrary—answered Lenin—they should have taken to arms more resolutely, energetically and aggressively. . . . Those who do not prepare for armed uprising must be ruthlessly cast out of the ranks of the supporters of the revolution and sent back to the ranks of its enemies, traitors or cowards. . . .

In the exciting weeks and months after Bloody Sunday, Lenin had spent day after day alone in the library in Geneva, studying military tactics and translating General Cluseret on barricade fighting. In the summer and autumn, he had sent from Switzerland endless streams of instructions:

> I see with horror, real horror, that we have been talking of bombs for more than a half year and not one single one has been made. . . . Don't demand any formalities, for God's sake spit on all schemes, send all "functions, rights, privileges" to the devil. Don't demand of people entrance into the Party—in an armed uprising that's an absurd demand . . . the only condition, dependability against the police and readiness to fight against the Tsar's troops. . . . [Letter of October 16, 1905.]

He had worked out the most detailed practical directions:

> Give every company short and simple bomb formulae. . . . They must begin their military training immediately in direct connection with practical fighting actions. Some will immediately kill a spy or blow up a police station; others will organize an attack on a bank, in order to confiscate funds for the uprising. . . .

That last sentence was to open a gulf between him and the Mensheviks over which there would never be a dependable bridge again!

A few days later he had written on weapons: "rifles, revolvers, bombs, knives, brass knuckles, clubs, rags soaked in oil to start fires with, rope or rope ladders, shovels for building barricades, dynamite cartridges, barbed wire, tacks against cavalry . . ."

There were further precepts concerning passwords, the value of mobility and surprise, relations with friendly officers and soldiers, use of women, children and old people, duties of unarmed contingents, who might disarm a lone policeman or climb roofs and shower troops with stones, acid, boiling water.

No other leader, not Trotsky, who was to organize the Red

Army, nor Rosa Luxemburg, who was to lead the Spartacan uprising in Germany, and certainly no Menshevik spokesman, could conceivably write such instructions. If we would understand Lenin as revolutionist, we must never let them slip out of our mind. Such letters might alienate, indeed did alienate, many leading Bolsheviks, but in compensation the faction began to attract all the fighting types, of which this land of extreme passivity and bursts of sudden energy had so plenteous a share. During 1906 and 1907, Lenin would gather unto himself those who had put themselves outside the law by engaging in insurrection or acts of terror, and those hardy persons who hoped by supreme acts of individual will to hold back the ebbing tide and reverse its flow. This was what it meant to be a "hard" in a time of open combat. At the Bolshevik Conference in Tammerfors in December, 1905, news came that Moscow had risen. To express their feelings and continue the discussion in practical fashion, the delegates used the intervals between sittings in revolver practice (Krupskaya: *Memories,* Vol. I, p. 157). A year later, in defiance of the decisions of the Stockholm Congress and the instructions of the Central Committee, Lenin called a second conference at Tammerfors, this time a secret "military-technical" conference of a few kindred spirits, together with delegates from fighting companies and from sympathetic groups inside the armed forces. The government learned more than the Central Committee about what transpired there, since once more it had an agent among the participants.

The fighting companies or guerrilla bands were not Lenin's exclusive monopoly nor invention. They had sprung up spontaneously in all parties and factions and among many nonparty groups. They became most numerous in the borderlands: in Poland, where they were affiliated with Pilsudski's Polish Socialist Party and distinguished themselves by the great numbers of police officers and government officials that they killed; in the Baltic countries, where they produced crack riflemen and snipers and merged with such Robin Hood bands as the "Forest

Brothers"; in the Urals and the Caucasian mountains, where they had roots in an ancient heritage of banditry, smuggling, guerrilla warfare, and blood feud. In all these border lands they were sustained by the populace and nourished by general nationalist movements for independence.

But in Saint Petersburg after the general strikes, and in Moscow after the insurrection, armed bands began to grow, too, just as the revolutionary wave was beginning to recede. Workmen who had left homes and jobs to participate in barricade fighting; strikers blacklisted by their employers or sought as ringleaders by the police; revolutionaries who had been away from home when the gendarmes called, and who no longer dared to return; men who had acquired arms by attacking police posts, robbing sporting goods stores of rifles, breaking into arsenals; soldiers and sailors who had deserted; escaped mutineers; all the hunted and proscribed who had been thrust by circumstance or had thrust themselves by fearless deeds outside the law; energetic men of the people for whom life had, for the first time, taken on broader scope and deeper meaning—such were the recruits who swelled the ranks of the fighting bands at the very moment when the great grey mass was returning to sullen quiescence.

And, precisely because other forms of public activity were diminishing, the armed bands assumed a new importance to Lenin's movement. Funds were dwindling to a trickle when funds were needed more than ever. The working class was too new, the Party too little rooted in the masses and too little belonging to the masses, for them to finance it by regular dues. The well-to-do liberals, oppositional manufacturers, parlor pinks, who had contributed most of the funds up to now, were losing their taste for revolution. Insensibly, the fighting detachments began by financing themselves and ended by financing the Party, or rather Lenin's faction. The money came from raids on state and private banks, holdups of mail coaches and trains, and, since it was easier to "expropriate" individuals than well-guarded institutions, the robbery of merchants and manufacturers. Having failed to expropriate the bourgeoisie wholesale as a class, they began "expropriating" it at retail, using the word quite solemnly and unhumorously, until in Party literature and debate such robberies came to be known for short as "exes." This method of financing was to make the Party leadership more than ever independent of the rank and file.

The armed bands began to attract all sorts of men who had a stomach for such things. Moreover, even the most idealistic were forced to keep increasing sums from the holdups for themselves—how else could one live in this illegal underworld?—and to seek relaxation from the strain of such a life in carousal and the pleasant, protective cover of personal luxury. If one dressed well, one was safer from police suspicion than a ragged man haunting the slums. Besides, there is something in the hunted man's way of life which makes a moment's respite and physical ease seem intensely precious. Thus the dual process—from above, the incipient degeneration of idealists; from below, the recruiting of submerged, demoralized, declassed and criminal elements, the "Lumpen" or "slum proletariat." These last joined now the Church-blessed, pro-tsarist Black Hundreds, now the revolutionary fighting *druzhini* or *boyeviki*,* finding in both extremist movements ideological banners and moral sustenance for activities which formerly had been shamefaced and desultory, and had been frowned upon by the decent men and women who now gave warmth and significance and the courage of conviction to such deeds.

> Ordinary bandits—wrote Rosa Luxemburg in the recoil of horror—stand side by side with revolutionary workers before the courts-martial. They attach themselves to the class movement of the proletariat, enter into the common statistical figure of the victims of the counter-revolution, fill the same prison cells and die on the gallows with the song of the "Red Flag" on their lips. A large part of the bandits consist of former revolutionary workers and members of the various socialist

* *Druzhini* means "companies," "bands," "brotherhoods"; *Boyeviki* are "fighters."

parties. . . . How could this community arise between the drama of the proletarian revolution and the guerrilla struggle of the Lumpenproletariat against private property, a community so hurtful to the revolution?

Lenin, too, was not unaware of the danger. Yet, in autumn, 1906, after the Stockholm Congress had specifically forbidden armed bands and "exes," he wrote:

> The partisan struggle is an inevitable form of struggle at a time when the mass movement has already matured for an uprising and longer or shorter pauses occur between great battles.

And in 1907, when he already rejected the boycott of elections on the ground that there was no longer any prospect of an early "widespread revolutionary revival," he still continued secretly to direct "armed actions" and "expropriations," permissible only on the basis of the expectation that a "widespread revival" and a "major engagement of civil war" were imminent. How shall we explain this glaring contradiction? I think psychologically rather than logically. For his attitude toward parliamentarism he held as a derivative of the formulae of his international Marxism, while his attitude toward the terror was an unconscious heritage from the tradition of Russian conspirative technique and organization. Not in the realm of logic, but in the realm of practical organization, there was a connection between these two tactical measures. For Duma elections it was necessary to reach great numbers, and the "exes" gave him the wherewithal. When he thought of parliamentary activity he predicated it on the end of the period of direct assault. But when he thought of the armed bands, he estimated the same period as one of a "longer or shorter pause between great battles." A fascinating example of how the most logic-worshiping mind can harbor logic-tight compartments.

If it were indeed a pause between great battles, he reasoned, then the evil excrescences would be sloughed off. A growing social movement would bring them under control, the armed groups would coalesce, enlarge, be joined by contingents of the Tsar's armies and whole layers of the civilian population, merge into a general struggle for power. But if the revolution were on the downgrade . . . ?

The Mensheviks grew more and more alarmed and indignant. Sensational robberies, played up in the press of the world, began to compromise the Party in the eyes of a public opinion already weary of strife. The government used the holdups as a pretext for raids on unions and it added a fabricated conspiracy of its own to dissolve the Second Duma. Thus the whole system of open and legal organization was jeopardized by this return to the terror. Nor was their indignation lessened by the fact that the "exes" secretly directed by Lenin brought funds to the Bolsheviks, enabling them to maintain newspapers in the field, to pay the expenses of delegates to the united congresses, thereby giving Lenin's faction the upper hand. Henceforth the secret Bolshevik Center, and the still more secret "military-technical" center, became far richer and more powerful than the regular Party committees.

At Stockholm in the spring of 1906, the Mensheviks, with the support of great numbers of Bolshevik delegates, put restrictions upon Lenin's armed bands. The Congress forbade "expropriations," ordered the dissolution of all bodies engaged in such activities, and the expulsion of all "expropriators." Lenin was not afraid to face the issue, but was astonished to meet strong opposition in his own camp. He withdrew his own motion, the prohibition passing by a vote of sixty-four to four, with twenty abstentions. The twenty were Lenin's diehards. He himself stayed away from the session in which the vote was taken!

But the majority, still under the spell of the great year, felt obliged to accept his amendments to their resolution. The amendments sanctioned defensive actions against the Black Hundreds and the governmental terror. That was all Lenin needed. When the new Central Committee, with its Menshevik majority, set up a "military-technical bureau" to handle these confidential matters, Lenin easily won control of it. Was it not his special field and the field of men who would naturally be attracted to his position? In defiance of Congress decision and Central Committee discipline, he now used the military-technical bureau to call a conference in Tammerfors in November, 1906. Thenceforth the Party possessed a legal Central Committee, with a Menshevik majority and an almost nonexistent treasury, an extra-legal Bolshevik Center, and an illegal secret finance and military affairs committee of three: Lenin, Krassin and Bogdanov, which was more powerful than either of the other two, since it alone possessed funds. Even the Bolshevik Center, which was financed by it, did not control it or receive reports on its activities. Lenin's reasons for this were simple: the fewer there were who knew about such confidential matters, the less the danger of police agents getting in on the secrets. He picked "men of confidence" and they in turn other men of confidence, who engaged in the preparation and procurement of arms, and in border smuggling. These in turn chose traveling agents and regional agents, who selected local men of confidence to plan and execute the hazardous deeds for which the arms were supplied. Once more, Lenin was in possession of a complete apparatus built from the top downward. It was a party within the Party and a faction within his faction: the faction of the desperate, the hardy and the reckless. When Party members prepared to engage in big holdups, disciplinary requirements were met by the simple expedient of having them resign from the Party. But they continued, nonetheless, to receive instructions from the secret finance committee. By the time the second congress of the unified party was held in London in the spring of 1907, Lenin's financial resources were such as to give him the upper hand. The Mensheviks were outraged. They had a majority in the trade unions and mass organizations and official Party bodies, but Lenin turned up with a slight majority of the delegates. Part of the secret was the support of the border parties, and part his ability to pay the expenses of delegates for the journey.

The famous "majority of the London Congress"—Martov wrote—was manufactured. . . . "Voting units" were hastily formed with the aid of enormous pecuniary resources acquired by the editorial board of *Proletarii* [organ of the Bolshevik Center] in part by expropriations, in part by "confiscation" of funds intended for the general aims of the Party—and these "voting units" each gave the right to send a delegate.

When Martov first made his charges concerning the "enormous pecuniary resources" obtained "in part by expropriations, in part by confiscation of funds intended for the general aims of the Party," he did not have the details to prove his accusations. Lenin guarded secrets well, and it would take a better sleuth than the solitary theorizer Martov to disentangle them. During the next few years, however, the evidence slowly leaked out: the complaints of the female heirs of a wealthy manufacturer whose estate was left to the Party but confiscated by Lenin for his faction; the arrest of prominent Bolsheviks abroad trying to cash a huge quantity of five-hundred-ruble notes stolen in a celebrated bank robbery in Tiflis; the charges of fighting bands in the Urals, who had paid Lenin's secret committee for arms out of the proceeds of their holdups and then failed to receive the arms; finally a break of the other two members of the secret committee of three, so that Krassin and Bogdanov, who knew all that Lenin knew, could bear witness against him. By 1910 the scandal had grown so great that confidential committees of the Socialist International were forced to concern themselves with it, and Lenin had to hand over certain "dirty monies" (the phrase is that of his friend and admirer, Klara Zetkin, one of the founders and leaders of the Communist International) to a "Committee of Honor" of three German Marxist leaders, Franz Mehring, Karl Kautsky and Klara Zetkin. In 1910, too, Lenin had to face a "Court of Honor" in his own party, a conference of the leaders of all factions, which ordained a cleanup in the organization. When Lenin was thus brought to bay, the final split into two parties became inevitable.

In 1911, when Martov saw that Lenin was not abiding by the

agreement of the 1910 "disarmament" conference, he published all the patiently gathered evidence—as far as it was available and might safely be revealed to the police. His *Spasiteli ili uprazdniteli* ("Saviors or Destroyers," Paris, 1911) is one long documented indictment of Lenin's "fund-raising" methods. Its truth was never challenged by Lenin. In general, in all his fights against Martov on strategy and tactics, Lenin never cared to challenge the latter's personal honesty and veracity.

The pamphlet, given Lenin's temperament, made a final split inevitable. Yet, in 1912, when the split did occur, it was, as usual, on Lenin's initiative. He coolly summoned a conference of his faction in Prague and called it a Party Congress. It "expelled" Martov and his associates for refusing to recognize its discipline, and for "plotting to liquidate the Party." Ideological and political issues were so intertangled with moral ones, and the rank and file in the dispersed underground knew so little of the facts, that Lenin's separate party did not fare badly. On the contrary, his sense of timing and of issues, and his choice of the organizational form for the break enabled the Bolsheviks to forge ahead of the Mensheviks at the moment of rupture, although all through the years 1906 to 1911 the latter's supporters were in a majority in trade unions, legal organizations, Duma elections, and all tests of strength.

In *Saviors or Destroyers* Martov told, among other sensational things, the tangled story of the "expropriation" by Lenin of funds intended for the general Party treasury. In 1906, Nicholas Schmitt, member of the millionaire Morozov family and owner of a Moscow furniture factory which had served the insurrectionists as a fortress, was jailed on the charge of financing the purchase of arms for the Moscow uprising. In prison he committed suicide, leaving his estate to the Party. Since this occurred between the Stockholm and London Congresses, while the Mensheviks controlled the Party machinery, Lenin attempted to arrange the diversion of the sum to the "Technical Military Committee," where he did have a majority. The "legal heirs" were two unmarried sisters. Lenin's first emissary, a Bolshevik lawyer, married the older sister to establish a legal claim, but then handed over to Lenin only a small portion of her share. Vladimir Ilyich now sent one of his boldest and most unscrupulous agents, "Victor" (Victor Taratuta). Seeking a legal counterclaim to pose to that of the older sister, he became the lover of the younger one. But, being himself "illegal" he could not marry her to acquire a legal claim on her heritage. So he arranged a fictitious marriage between his mistress and Ignatiev, another member of the Bolshevik fighting detachments who somehow had escaped a police record. Mr. and Mrs. Ignatiev now claimed her share, and handed it over to her lover. But Taratuta was not satisfied. He threatened the older sister and her husband with a visit from the Caucasian fighting detachments unless they, too, handed over the remainder.

It was at this point in our novelesque tale that the Mensheviks became sufficiently aware of the whole "confidential" operation to put in a claim on behalf of their section of the Party. This was the "dirty monies" to which Klara Zetkin had reference, and which Lenin was compelled in 1910 to turn over (insofar as it was unspent) to the Court of Honor of the International Socialist Bureau, Mehring, Kautsky and Zetkin. But in 1912, when Lenin's rump convention in Prague declared itself to be "the Party," he managed to persuade the Court of Honor to turn the remainder over to him.

> The Bolshevik Center—wrote Dan in the Martov-Dan *Geschichte der russischen Sozialdemocratie*—supplied each month to the Petersburg Committee 1000 rubles and to the Moscow Committee 500 rubles. During the same period the Central Committee of the Party did not have an average income of so much as 100 rubles a month.

This assertion is confirmed by a number of Bolshevik documents. Thus, in the summer of 1908, when the movement had so far declined that income from dues had ceased, Lenin wrote to Vorovsky, living in Odessa:

We absolutely count upon your coming as a delegate. . . . We will send money to all the Bolsheviks for the journey. . . . We beg you to write for our paper. We can pay now for articles and will pay regularly.

To this letter Lenin's wife, Krupskaya, appends the explanation that the funds came from the fictitious marriage which Victor Taratuta had arranged between his lover, Elizaveta Pavlovna Schmitt, and the Bolshevik Ignatiev (*Memories of Lenin,* Vol. II, p. 25).

And there are the memoirs of Sulimov, who participated in the Ural "exes" or holdups. In *Proletarskaya Revolutsia* (Moscow, 1925, No. 7), published under Bolshevik auspices, he writes:

During the years 1906 and 1907, we sent to the District Committee of the Party (Bolshevik) some 40,000 rubles and to the Central Committee—i.e. Lenin's Secret Center—some 60,000. With these resources the District Committee issued three papers: *The Russian Soldier, Proletarii,* and a paper in the Tartar tongue. Besides, money was provided for the journey of the delegates to the London Congress, for the support of the school for military instructors in Kiev and the Bomb-throwing School in Lemberg, as well as for the arrangement of border crossing for the smuggling of publications and fugitives.

Lenin himself, though he might use deceit freely against the police and his comrades in rival factions, was never one to shrink from the defense of the things he believed in. Hence his writings give more than one hint on the source of his funds. In a remarkable theoretical defense of *Guerrilla Fighting* (not available in English but translated into German under the title *Der Partisanenkampf, Saemtliche Werke,* Band X, pp. 113-26), written just prior to the London Congress, he declared:

The armed struggle pursues two *different* goals . . . in the first place the goal of the killing of individual persons, higher officials and subalterns in police and army; second, the confiscation of funds both from the government and from private persons.

The funds seized go in part to the Party, in part for the arming
and preparations of the uprising, in part for the support of the
persons who conduct the struggle. The funds which have been
seized in the great expropriations—more than 200,000 rubles
in the Caucasian, 875,000 rubles in the Moscow expropriation—
have gone in the first place to the revolutionary parties. Lesser
expropriations have served above all, sometimes even exclusively, for the maintenance of the expropriators.

This he published in his underground paper *Proletarii,* No. 5,
in the issue of October 13 (Old Style, September 30), 1906. The
statement must have been as interesting to the police as to the
Mensheviks, who, with much Bolshevik support, had prohibited just such operations only a few months before, at the
Stockholm Congress. At the London Congress, scheduled for
the spring of 1907, the Mensheviks would demand a reckoning.
But at the London Congress, aided by just such funds, Lenin
was to have a majority of the delegates!

The London Congress (April-May, 1907) marked the highest point ever reached by the "united" Party. Not one delegation appeared but five: Bolsheviks, Mensheviks, Polish Social
Democrats, Lettish Social Democrats, Jewish Bund. Leon Trotsky, just escaped from Siberia, tried to form yet another faction
of the "non-factional" but he could find only three. Almost
everyone was already lined up in a disciplined caucus. On most
issues, his four votes swelled Lenin's majority. The student Angelica Balabanoff, future secretary of the Communist International, and the writer Maxim Gorky, each visiting a Party congress for the first time, saw a festive and brilliant gathering: the
venerable but still vigorous founders, Plekhanov, Axelrod, and
Deutsch; their renowned disciples who had laid the cornerstone
inside Russia, Lenin, Martov, Dan; the disciples of these in
turn, young men of the generation of Trotsky and Stalin; the
founders of the Jewish Bund and the Polish and Lettish Social
Democracy; and, most impressive of all, a great flux of newcomers, genuine workingmen who had been brought to the

surface by the storms of 1905. The Congress statistics listed 116 workingmen and 196 intellectuals and professional revolutionaries, further noting that 118 delegates were "living at the expense of the Party," a truly impressive officer apparatus. With no less pride the delegates recorded the number of centuries of prison and exile that they had already collectively undergone. As we shall not again be able to see so many and such distinguished revolutionists assembled together, we might take advantage of the occasion to look at the Congress as it appeared to the eyes of Angelica Balabanoff and Maxim Gorky.

Around Lenin were gathered many of his present and future lieutenants: the philosopher-economist-scientist Bogdanov, who in 1904 had replaced Krassin as second man in Lenin's inevitable *troika;* Zinoviev and Kamenev, who would make up the *troika* after he had broken with Bogdanov; Tomsky, who would lead Bolshevik trade union work from 1905 until the purges of 1937; Litvinov, who would one day be Foreign Commissar; Voroshilov, who would be Commissar for War; Bubnov, who would be Commissar for Education; Yaroslavsky, future leader of the Atheist League; Pokrovsky, the historian; Alexinsky, Bolshevik spokesman in the Second Duma; Rykov, who would be Vice-Chairman of the Council of Commissars while Lenin was its Chairman, and Chairman of the Supreme Council of Economy; Nogin, who would lead the Moscow uprising of November, 1917; Victor Taratuta, who had just brought the Bolsheviks a pretty penny through the Schmitt legacy.

Besides the Mensheviks whom we have already met, there was a large and brilliant delegation from Transcaucasia, henceforward to be the chief popular base of Menshevism and of its block of Duma deputies. At the head of that delegation were Tseretelli of Georgia, leader of the Social Democratic Fraction in the Duma; Zhordania, who would one day be President of the Democratic Georgian Republic; and Noah Ramishvili, future Minister of the Interior.

And yet another Georgian, with whom we must concern ourselves from now on, appeared in the humble role of fraternal delegate, silent because he was not yet quite sure of himself in these fine-spun debates, without a vote because in all of Georgia he had not been able to muster the five hundred Bolshevik supporters, or major fraction thereof, which would have entitled him to a voting mandate. As at the preceding Stockholm Congress, the Menshevik Transcaucasian delegation again challenged his credentials, this time successfully because they showed that the Borchalo District, from which he professed to come, did not have a functioning branch. He attracted the notice of neither Balabanoff nor Gorky nor Krupskaya nor any other memorialist of the Congress. Official legend today makes him out to have been Lenin's right hand since the beginning of the century, but as late as this Congress in 1907 he was not yet important enough to be named as member or alternate for the Central Committee (the Bolsheviks named five members and ten alternates)* nor one of the secret committee of seventeen which was set up as an extra-legal Bolshevik Center to run the affairs of the supposedly dissolved faction. Yet, for reasons which will appear later in this chapter, he was beginning to attract Lenin's attention as a trustworthy lieutenant for some particularly difficult and dangerous tasks which required the highest secrecy and conspirative skill.

There were 91 Bolsheviks and 89 Mensheviks at the Congress (according to other accounts, 106 and 99), of whom we have named but a few of the outstanding. And there were 55 representatives of the Bund, of whom we must note at least Rafael Abramovich and M. I. Lieber (real name Goldman), who would be elected by the Congress as the two Bundist members of the Central Committee. Long after Martov was dead and Martynov had become a Bolshevik and Dan a "Menshevik fellow-traveler," Abramovich would become the outstanding leader of menshevism in the days of its post-1917 exile, when it had been reduced by defeat and persecution and de-

---

* Those named by the Bolsheviks as their members and alternates on the Central Committee were Lenin, Bogdanov, Krassin, Zinoviev, Rykov, Nogin, Dubrovinsky, Goldenberg, Roshkov, Teodorovich, Shantzer, Zommer, Leiteisen, Smirnov and Taratuta.

spair to a pitiful remnant, dispersed to the far corners of the earth.

Of the forty-four Polish Social Democrats, the most impressive were Rosa Luxemburg, frail and dynamic, fresh from prison, and her close comrade in leadership and personal companion, Jan Tyszka (Lev Grozowski or Leo Jogiches), who had just escaped from Siberia. He was the organization man of the Polish Social Democracy and she was the strategist and theoretician, as if Lenin's two roles in the Bolshevik faction had gotten incarnated into two separate persons forming one indivisible union. Though she might excoriate Lenin for his excessive centralism, his penchant for splitting and expelling and his "night-watchman discipline," her co-leader Tyszka ran the Polish Party with a similar hand of iron, drawing her into the complicity of justifying his acts with her pen. Both internationalists in a sense that the Russian leaders were not, they were active in three parties and they would ultimately lead the Spartacan uprising in Germany and perish in it. Around them in the Polish Party had already gathered an able group, of whom we must note at least Warski (real name Adolf Warshawski), who would be elected to the Central Committee in London along with Tyszka; Dzierzynski, Unschlicht, Radek, and Hanecki. All of these would become Bolsheviks in 1917. Dzierzynski would lead Lenin's Cheka and later Stalin's GPU while Unschlicht would become its Vice-Commissar. Radek, like Tyszka and Luxemburg, would be active in three parties and become an outstanding journalist for the Comintern and the Stalin régime, only to end up in the purge trials. Warski would become the leader of the Communist Party of Poland and would be killed along with all other leaders of that party who sought refuge in Russia, during the same great purges. Hanecki we shall meet again because he figures in the celebrated charges that Lenin was a German agent during the war.

Of the Letts we need note only Comrade "Hermann" (real name Danishevsky), one of the two elected to the Central Committee, to become celebrated later in connection with the crackshots of the Lettish Rifle Corps, which furnished such important contingents to the Cheka and GPU and to the Bolshevik armies in the period of civil war. Danishevsky was to become an important aide of Trotsky's when the latter was Commissar of War.

So vast an assemblage, so noisy and quarrelsome, including Caucasians in sheepskin hats and bearded workingmen in Russian blouses and ten Deputies from the Second Duma, over 300 delegates in all, representing over 150,000 members, could not contrive to meet in secret in some tiny cellar hole, unbeknown to the police. First the whole variegated army filtered into Denmark with the intention of meeting in Copenhagen. But the democratic city fathers took fright and banned their meeting out of deference for Denmark's ruler, who was uncle to Russia's Tsar. London was their next choice, but how to get funds to transfer three hundred-odd people to England? Angelica Balabanoff and Gorky proved to be more than interested spectators now, for the former secured a substantial donation from the German Social Democratic Party and Gorky raised additional funds in London.

The ousted Congress found shelter in the Brotherhood Church in Whitechapel belonging to a Christian Socialist group under the leadership of Ramsay Macdonald, a church—as Gorky noted—"unadorned to the point of absurdity."

Having lent their building for what they conceived to be a convention after the British fashion—two or three days to settle all issues—the congregation spent the next three weeks trying to get this convention-in-permanence to adjourn, if not *sine die*, at least long enough for Wednesday evening prayer meeting and Sunday service.

But these Russians had never had an opportunity to talk themselves out. Now they were going to say all that the censorship and the vicissitudes of prison and exile had forced them to leave unsaid. They were going to settle all the past; appraise the experiences of two years of revolution; apportion the blame for defeat; resolve all the problems of the unforeseeable future. The debate was a full-dress affair, alternately on a higher level than that of any other movement in the world, then as suddenly on the lowest plane of faction bitterness and calculation. To make matters worse, the heart of the Congress, the Russian delegation proper—180 strong—was almost evenly divided between Bolsheviks and Mensheviks: of the former 91 to 89 of the latter. Every debater had not only to pour out all that was on his heart, even if it meant repeating what a score had said before him; he must also say that unsaid word which he hoped would convince and reconvince the last man in his faction, win away some waverer from the opponent group, persuade the little reservoir of neutrals, Poles, Bundists, Letts, whose votes would break the deadlock. Every resolution had to be dickered over in caucus, compromised, blurred, until it could command somehow a slender majority. Everyone who abstained from voting felt an irrepressible urge to explain his abstention.

The election of chairman (Lenin won over Plekhanov by a few votes) "provoked a debate that covered practically every issue with which the Congress itself was to deal . . . raged for over a week with a ferocity which I felt sure must have exhausted the entire stock of polemics as well as the strength of the delegates" (Memoirs of Angelica Balabanoff).

Naturally, the funds ran out once more. Maxim Gorky was pressed into service to convince some wealthy London admirers to finance the further deliberations. A Mr. Joseph Fels (whose name the reader may recognize in the Fels-Naphtha soap trademark) was prevailed upon to make a loan of three thousand pounds sterling against a note signed by all the leading delegates. The Party would soon fall on evil days and be unwilling or unable to honor its note, but when the Bolsheviks took power Mr. Fels would dig it out of his bank vault and present it, and it would be paid. When last I was in Moscow, it lay on velvet in a glass case, a curious memento of an infinitely remote and incomprehensible day when the Revolution was not a state power but an inspiration.

Gorky had come from self-imposed exile in Italy, hungry for a Russian face, the sound of the Russian tongue, a glimpse of the "giants" of the movement.

> My festive mood lasted only until the first meeting when they began wrangling about "the order of business." The fury of the disputes chilled my enthusiasm. . . .
>
> When we were introduced, Lenin shook my hand heartily and looking me over with his keen eyes and speaking like an old acquaintance, he said jocularly: "So glad you've come. I believe you're fond of a scrap. There's going to be a fine old free-for-all here."
>
> I hadn't expected Lenin to be like that. Something was lacking in him. He rolled his *r*'s gutturally, and had a jaunty way of standing with his hands poked up somehow under his armpits. He seemed too ordinary, did not give the impression of a leader. . . .
>
> He began at once to speak about the defects of my book, *Mother*—evidently he had read it in the manuscript in the possession of S. P. Ladyshnikov.* I was hurrying to finish it, I said, but did not succeed in saying why. With a nod of assent, Lenin himself offered the explanation: Yes, I should hurry up with it, such a book was needed, for many workers who take part in the revolutionary movement do so unconsciously and confusedly, and it would be very useful to them to read *Mother*. The very book for the moment.

Thus began a friendship which, thanks to Lenin's special attitude toward literary talent and Gorky's admiration of a man in whom his soft, romantic temperament sensed strength and greatness, was able to outlast many bitter differences.

Martov, too, made an admirable impression on Gorky, as he did on everybody. But not so the rest of Lenin's opponents:

> Plekhanov, in a frock coat closely buttoned up like a Protestant pastor . . . spoke like a preacher confident that this ideas are incontrovertible, every word, every pause, of great value. . . .
>
> Little Theodor Dan spoke like a man whose relationship to the authentic truth was that of father to daughter. . . .

---

* Probably an error on Gorky's part for *Ivan* (not S. P.) Ladyshnikov.

Martov, this amazingly attractive man, spoke with the ardor of youth and was evidently most deeply affected by the tragic drama of the dissension and split. He trembled all over, swaying backward and forward spasmodically, unfastening the collar of his starched shirt and waving his hands about. . . . Martov did not give so much the impression of arguing as of urging and imploring. . . . At times he sounded almost hysterical. . . .

But now Vladimir Ilyich hurries to the pulpit and cries *Comrades!* in his guttural way. He seemed to me to speak badly, but after a minute I and everybody else was absorbed in his speech. It was the first time I had heard complicated political questions treated so simply. . . . No striving after eloquent phrases . . . but every word uttered distinctly, and its meaning marvelously plain. . . .

He was interrupted by shouts of hatred. One tall, bearded individual kept jumping up from his seat and stuttering: *Little p-plots . . . p-playing at little p-plots! Blanquists!* These hostile thrusts had no noticeable effect on him. I learned what this external calm had cost him a few days later. . . .

The debate which Gorky remembered so vividly two decades after it occurred was the one dealing with armed uprising, armed bands, "expropriations." As we have already seen, the bearded heckler had some grounds for excitement. The supreme body of the Party, the Congress at Stockholm, in the spring of 1906, had forbidden the "exes"; but all through that year notorious robberies continued. And in the autumn, Lenin had written the defense of such actions which we have already quoted. He had even hinted that he knew where the funds were going. ("The funds which have been seized in the great expropriations, more than 200,000 rubles in the Caucasian and 875,000 rubles in the Moscow expropriation, have gone in the first place to the revolutionary parties. Lesser expropriations have served above all, sometimes exclusively, for the maintenance of the expropriators.") There is a curious vagueness about one of the two large sums mentioned which tempts us to pursue the subject a little farther.

The Moscow "ex" referred to was the work of Maximalist

Social Revolutionaries, the Caucasian "ex" of Federalist Socialists; yet Lenin's secret bureau undoubtedly had a hand in the
second and probably in the first. At any rate, it is a matter of
Bolshevik record that Lenin's group did help the Social Revolutionaries in two other resounding exploits of the same year
1906. We can find evidence of this in the memoirs of Leonid
Krassin, and in recollections concerning him published shortly
after his death. Typical is this sentence from the essay of the
Communist party-historian Lyadov:

"The contrivance which blew up Stolypin's villa and the
bombs thrown in the Fonarny Pereulok [Fonarny Alley] were
made under Nikitich's supervision. Nikitich was a party pseudonym of Krassin."

Before we go into these celebrated holdups—and others still
more celebrated—we must look into this peculiar *de facto* alliance between Lenin's secret bureau and the Social Revolutionary Maximalists. The Social Revolutionary Party, the reader
will remember, was an offspring of the old Narodnaya Volya,
inheriting along with the latter's devotion to the peasantry and
democracy its inclination toward acts of terror. In an undemocratic land where the government employed organized violence
against all dissent, violence must be met by violence. Thus assassination and, by extension, "expropriation" were matters of
principle.

At the other extreme of the socialist spectrum were such men
as Axelrod and Martov, who favored "European," "civilized"
mass and class methods, and rejected acts of terror by individuals and small bands—also as a matter of principle. They looked
on holdups and assassinations as demoralizing adventurism,
unworthy, degrading, self-defeating for an idealistic movement
that was seeking to raise the level of social life. Such acts would
give supremacy inside the movement to the desperate, secret and
conspiratorial, and would alienate the broad mass of workingmen and all liberal and democratic public opinion.

In between these "Westernizing" Mensheviks, who thought
their movement should, politically speaking, learn to "talk Ger-

man," and the Russian Social Revolutionaries, who wanted their movement to "talk Russian," stood Lenin. In periods of lull he would have it "talk German" and in periods of storm "French" (France has more of a tradition of violent insurrection). But, more than he was himself aware, at all times he was building a movement that would "talk Russian"—the Russian of the old Narodnaya Volya and the Maximalist wing of the Social Revolutionary Party. He rejected individual terror only and exclusively on the basis of expediency. The main point of his article on *The Partisan Struggle,* from which we have quoted his figures on the size of certain "expropriations," is that a movement which aims at nothing less than the overthrow of the autocracy and the social order cannot be choosy about the means it employs, nor reject on theoretical or moral grounds any means of fighting which arise out of the struggle and seem to further it.

In the autumn of 1905, the Tsar's promise of a constitution had caused a division of the various revolutionary groups according to temperament and principle. The Social Revolutionaries, in love with democracy, had always said they would abandon the terror if a democratic way of transforming Russia were offered. When the elections to the First Duma were being held, they publicly renounced the use of terror. Only after the Duma was dissolved did they resume it as a method of political agitation. But Lenin deduced from the same Manifesto of the Tsar that the autocracy was feeling weak and was therefore engaging in a deceptive retreat, a mere maneuver. Hence the use of direct force and the blows of the armed bands should be redoubled. Thus Lenin became more "terrorist" than the terrorist Social Revolutionaries. Both the Social Democrats and the Social Revolutionaries split on this issue. While the Mensheviks and Social Revolutionary majority were for giving the Constitution and the Duma a reasonable trial, and avoiding acts which might give the government an easy pretext for return to unlimited absolutism, Lenin chose this moment to issue his precise and detailed instructions to the armed bands. At the same time, a

Left Wing group of the Social Revolutionary Party, calling themselves Maximalists, decided to continue the terror in defiance of their party's decision. The secret fighting groups of Lenin and of the Maximalists moved closer together. All through 1906 they cooperated in the manufacture of bombs (in Krassin's laboratory) and in a series of holdups and assassinations. In return for Krassin's preparation of the munitions of war, Lenin's group received some of the proceeds from Maximalist "exes." More than has been generally realized, this rapprochement paved the way for the united action of Leninists and Maximalists or Left Social Revolutionaries in 1917. The first Soviet coalition government was an alliance of these two tendencies.

The Moscow "ex" which Lenin referred to was one of a series of celebrated robberies of the years of 1906 and 1907. Twenty Maximalist *boyeviki* held up the Bank for Mutual Mercantile Credit in March, 1906, disarmed four guards and made off with 875,000 rubles. In October, the Maximalists held up the Mutual Credit Bank on Fonarny Pereulok in Saint Petersburg, and a treasury truck laden with funds for the State Bank. The explosives for Fonarny Pereulok and for Stolypin's villa came from Krassin's "Technical Bureau."

By virtue of his duties as an engineer, Leonid Krassin found it easy to travel. During 1906 he took several trips to Baku and Tiflis to "activate" the work of seizing funds in the Caucasus. At the same time, the third member of Lenin's secret *troika,* the philosopher Bogdanov, was given charge of operations in the Ural Mountains. There the guerrilla chieftain was a daring, capable fighter named Lbov, and the proceeds, as we have seen from Sulimov's memoirs, were for a while considerable. However, one of the chief confidential gun-runners recruited by Krupskaya, Kommissarov, turned out to be a man who had been planted in Lenin's immediate circle by the secret police so that when Kommissarov's wife transported guns to the Urals the entire shipment was seized there together with everybody with whom the police agents had contact (Krupskaya: *Memories of Lenin,* Vol. I, pp. 173-4).

But it was the Caucasus, with its mighty mountain ranges, embattled races and peoples, and long tradition of banditry, smuggling and guerrilla warfare, that proved to be the ideal center for these activities. The *boyeviki* could count on the sympathy of the common people and even of men in high official position. According to the memoirs of the Bolshevik Makharadze (*Twenty-Five Years of the Struggle for Socialism,* Tiflis, 1923) published by the Soviet Government while Lenin was still alive, 1150 acts of terrorism, large and small, were carried out in the Caucasus between 1904 and 1908.

Though the Bolsheviks were not numerous in Transcaucasia, they possessed a few men exceptionally qualified for the conspirative planning and execution of this kind of enterprise. These cooperated at first with other groups. Then, appetite whetted by some small successes, they organized on their own the most active and celebrated fighting band of all. Krassin conferred with them in Baku and Tiflis. The actual captain of their armed band, known as Kamo, made several trips in 1906 and 1907 to see the *troika* in Saint Petersburg and Finland. He came back with his head full of limitless admiration for the wisdom of Lenin, Bogdanov and Krassin, and with his suitcase full of dynamite, revolvers, munitions and bombs. For reasons which have never been clarified, Kamo's immediate superior, Joseph Djugashvili, also made two trips to see Lenin during 1907 and 1908, trips on which, despite his efforts to prove an early kinship with Lenin, he has been virtually silent.* We can only conjecture that they dealt with the question of continuing the "exes" after two Party congresses had forbidden them. (Since many details of these operations are to this day shrouded in mystery, our parenthetical notes and footnotes in

---

* The only mention of them came in his interview with Emil Ludwig: "Whenever I visited him abroad —in 1907, 1908 and 1912—I saw heaps of letters he had received from practical workers in Russia." (English language edition of the interview, Moscow, 1932, p. 18.)

this chapter are fuller than elsewhere, and the reader will be well advised to note where the sources are Bolshevik publications, where those of the police or partisan opponents, and where there is an element of conjecture. One of the unusual features of the passage from Lenin on the Caucasian "expropriation" (quoted above) is that he is both vague and incorrect as to the amount involved, though the daily papers were full of stories on the matter. He writes, as if with purposive inexactitude, "more than 200,000 rubles." Other Bolshevik sources specifically state: 315,000 rubles.* This raid on the Dushet Treasury was not carried on by Bolsheviks, yet according to the memoirs of the Bolshevik historian Lyadov both Krassin and Kamo had a hand in it. The actual holdup was the work of six Federalist Socialists (a Caucasian revolutionary party) disguised in the uniform of soldiers of the 263rd Regiment garrisoned there. They deposited the huge sum with a "reliable person," whence, according to a later complaint, it somehow found its way not into their party's, but into Lenin's coffers.†

So skillful and secretive was Stalin that few Bolshevik memoirs, even those of eyewitnesses and participants, recognize his directing part in these celebrated affairs. All of them, however, are aware of the exploits of Kamo, and the remoter superintendence of Krassin and Lenin. The first to give direct credit to Stalin is Tsintsadze, who knew whereof he spoke because, like Kamo, he was a leader of the Caucasian guerrilla bands. But

---

* See for instance note 71 in Vol. X of Lenin's *Collected Works*, German translated from the Second Russian edition.

† Souvarine: *Stalin*, p. 93. The reader will find the following partial studies of the question of expropriations readily available in English: Souvarine: *Stalin;* Levine: *Stalin;* Pope: *Litvinov;* Trotsky: *Autobiography* and *Life of Stalin.* The best of these is Souvarine's. All of them make use of original Soviet sources. To fortify the reader's belief in these fantastic facts, I have, wherever possible, traced their statements to the original sources, and, except for Martov, have given in general only sources published under Bolshevik auspices. My chief debt—a matter of lesser interest to the reader—is to Souvarine, who, in the French edition of his work, gives an excellent bibliography. He failed, however, to document the most striking statements by specific notes, merely giving references *en bloc* at the end of the chapter. The American publisher, without his consent, made the matter much worse by throwing out the bibliographical notes altogether, thus weakening the authority of a really solid and carefully documented work.

the real connecting link between the "exes" and Stalin is to be found in the person of Kamo.*

The *boyevik* known as Kamo was the proto-hero of all these holdups. Brave as a lion and crafty as a fox, simple, big-hearted, sentimental, worshipful of those whose leadership he accepted, ruthless in action and saintly in his selflessness, Kamo was a type of Robin Hood revolutionary scarcely to be conceived of in the Socialist movements of Western Europe and America. (The nearest comparable figure is the German revolutionary, Max Hoelz.) Even the Bolshevik historian Lepeshinsky expresses a sense of strangeness in paying tribute to him as a "medieval hero."

His real name was Semyon Arshakovich Ter-Petrossian. He was the son of a moderately well-to-do Armenian merchant of the town of Gori, which is also Stalin's birthplace. The two were chums in boyhood, Stalin, as the older and brighter, being the leader even then. When Semyon was early expelled from school for some "offense against religion," Djugashvili was engaged to tutor him. The ascendancy intensified: he converted his pupil to socialism, taking him along in due course into the Bolshevik faction. The very nickname, "Kamo," came from Stalin. One day when Semyon came for orders, speaking in Russian with his strange Armenian accent, he asked: *"Kamo?"* (meaning *komu?,* "to whom?") and Stalin teased him, "Hey you, *kamo, kamo!"* The name stuck and he became known by it throughout the movement.

When a bodyguard was required, or a spy was to be done away with, when heroism and loyalty and tight-lipped secrecy was needed, Kamo could always be depended on. His first suc-

* The memoirs of Tsintsadze were published in *Revoliutsiis Matiane,* Tiflis, 1923 and 1924, Nos. 3, 4, 9, 10. Most of the documents out of which the details of this obscure matter are pieced together were published during those two years either in Tiflis or Moscow (i.e. in both cases under Soviet auspices) as part of the voluminous literature attendant upon the celebration of the twenty-fifth anniversary of the foundation of the Russian Social Democratic Party. All the material was written in 1922 and 1923 and has the special authentication of having been approved for publication by the Soviet Government while both Lenin and Krassin were alive as well as many of the active participants in the events described.

cessful "ex" at Kutais netted fifteen thousand rubles, but he continued to allow himself and the members of his band exactly fifty kopeks (twenty-five cents) a day for maintenance. When he was caught after several such exploits, he made a daring escape from the Tiflis jail and went to Lenin, then in hiding in Finland. Lenin sent him to Belgium to aid "Papasha" (Litvinov) in gun-running. The future Commissar for Foreign Affairs, posing as an officer in the Ecuadorian Army, then as a Belgian, ordered arms from the State Munitions Factory of Denmark (Denmark's King was the uncle of Nicholas Romanov!) and from Schroeder and Company of Germany. Thence the dij̇ inutive Litvinov and his giant Armenian companion went to Bulgaria, where they let on that the arms were intended for Macedonian and Arj̇ enian revolutionaries fighting for freedom from Turkey. Litvinov purchased a small yacht in Fiume and engaged its entire crew to sail from Varna across the Black Sea to the Caucasus. But the yacht ran aground, Rumanian fishermen stole the arms, and Kamo and three associates were arrested and sent to Constanza. The sources for this strange story are Litvinov's own memoir on Kaj̇ o for a biography written by Bibineishvili and published in Moscow in 1934, and an entry in the archives of the tsarist secret police which reads:

> With money stolen from the revenue department of Kvirili in 1905, Kamo and the emigrant Meyer Wallach (Litvinov's real name) ... bought arms abroad and wanted to bring them on the yacht *Zara,* bought for this purpose, from Varna to Russia....

How the police department knew about it we shall learn later. Released from the Rumanian jail, Kamo returned to the Caucasus, stopping on the way to get bombs from Krassin. The bombs could not have been very good, for Kamo's wife, Medvedyeva Ter-Petrossian, records that they were serviceable only for a few days, so that he had to rush into holdups without proper planning. He made two unsuccessful attempts. In the second, one of his own bombs wounded him in the face so badly that he nearly lost his sight in one eye. Securing fresh explosives, he began planning more carefully what turned out to be the most famous of all revolutionary robberies.

On the morning of June 26, 1907, a cashier and a bank clerk drove through Erivan Square accompanied by a guard of two policemen and five Cossacks. In the carriage, according to an advance tip received by Kamo (the revolutionaries had spies in the government just as the government had spies among the revolutionaries) was more than a quarter-million rubles from Saint Petersburg, destined for the State Bank in Tiflis. Ten members of his band, two of them women, stationed themselves at various points in the Square. He himself, in the uniform of an army officer, had been circulating around the populous Plaza all morning, warning bystanders away in cryptic commands. On one side was his own coach. As the government mail coach drove in, bombs were hurled. Two policemen and a Cossack were killed and about fifty persons wounded, most of them but slightly. The frightened horses dashed off with the money still in the carriage till a bomb hurled at their legs put an end to their flight. The "army officer" Kamo, shouting and uttering fierce oaths, dashed up and "arrested" the member of his band who had seized the bags of money. The booty turned out to be 341,000 rubles,* nearly all of it in 500-ruble notes. Kamo hid it in a couch in the study of the director of the Tiflis Observatory. The hiding place assumes a special interest when we find that a few years back a police report had contained the following entry: "Joseph Djugashvili, employed at the Tiflis Observatory, intellectual, has connections with railwaymen . . ." (The police reports published in this chapter and throughout the work are those published by the Soviet Government after it opened the tsarist police archives.)

Four weeks later, once more disguised as an army officer and carrying a hat box crammed with 500-ruble notes, Kamo set out for the frontier. High in Lenin's confidence in Berlin was a

* The above figure, higher by almost a hundred thousand rubles than that given in most accounts, is taken from Lenin: *Collected Works,* Vol. XII, Third Russian Edition, 1936, p. 566.

Russian police spy, Dr. Jacob Zhitomirsky, entrusted by Lenin with all sorts of "confidential" tasks. He it was who notified the Russian and German police when Kamo arrived in Berlin, arranging that the Armenian should be arrested when he was carrying a suitcase laden with dynamite. In December, 1907, Lenin set a given day on which various agents should try simultaneously to exchange the 500-ruble notes in banks scattered all over northwestern Europe. Dr. Zhitomirsky was in charge of the agents entrusted with the "hot" money! Police and state banks in each country were supplied with a list of the serial numbers and descriptions of the persons involved. A Lettish Bolshevik was arrested in Stockholm; Olga Ravich, future wife of Zinoviev, and two Armenians, were taken with part of the *corpus delicti* in Munich; Maxim Litvinov, future Foreign Commissar, was picked up by the Paris Security Police with a huge sum in these stolen bills on his person.* There is a touch of irony in the fact that the new Minister of Justice in France, Aristide Briand, saved him from extradition to Russia by a decision that his crime was "political." Most unjust was the arrest of N. A. Semashko, future Commissar of Health in the Soviet Government, who had bitterly fought against Lenin on the question of the robberies. He fell under suspicion because some woman wrote a postcard to one of the would-be passers of the stolen funds, and addressed it care of Semashko. "It was the most absurd event in my life," he would write in his memoirs.

Further raids on addresses supplied by Dr. Zhitomirsky resulted in the capture of a supply of fresh banknote paper. From photographs, the paper firm identified the purchaser as the dignified representative of the Allgemeine Elektrische Gesellschaft, the engineer Krassin. Part of it had already been shipped to Lenin while he was still in Finland, through the transport facilities of the German Social Democratic daily, *Vorwaerts*. They

---

* For confirmation of these arrests and the reason for them see Krupskaya: *Memories of Lenin*, Vol. II, pp. 11-14. As this volume was published while Litvinov was Foreign Commissar, it omits his name. But Litvinov's own memoir on Kamo and other Bolshevik documents of the twenties give him a leading role in the attempt to dispose of the 500-ruble notes, as do the tsarist police archives and the records of the French police.

thought they were handling Russian underground literature, and were furious to learn that they had been made unwitting accomplices in a counterfeiting ring.

The scandal in Social Democratic circles was enormous. The Swiss party adopted a resolution protesting the abuse of their country's cherished right of political asylum by "common criminals." Men high in the Swedish and French parties rallied to the defense of the arrested. Axelrod wrote to Plekhanov suggesting that this was the time and the issue for discrediting Lenin once and for all. Yet, despite their indignation, the Mensheviks were too decent in their common feud with the tsarist police to arrange for any but highly secretive party investigations. From the standpoint of party welfare as they understood it, and certainly from the standpoint of elementary party discipline, they had grounds enough. Had not the Stockholm Congress of 1906 ordered the dissolution of the bands and the termination of the "exes"? And in 1907, had the vote not been even more overwhelming in London, where on most matters Lenin had a majority? Lenin, taking advantage of his place in the Chair, had avoided registering his vote. But a majority of Bolsheviks had voted with the Mensheviks. And, when delegates shouted from the floor: "What does Lenin say? We want to hear Lenin!" he only chuckled, "with a somewhat cryptic expression." (Trotsky: *Autobiography*, p. 218.)

Then, only a month later, with the Mensheviks still smarting at their defeat, due in part to his "superior finances," his secret committee had carried off the Tiflis holdup, provoking a scandal which cost the whole movement dear in public sympathy. By the year's end, with the arrests all over Europe of the stolen banknote passers, the scandal had become international.

Several investigations were set on foot at once: one by the Central Committee, which named a tribunal under the upright chairmanship of Chicherin (Litvinov's future chief as Foreign Commissar); another by the Transcaucasian Party Committee; a third by the International Socialist Bureau. Chicherin's probing began to point to the conclusion that Kamo had been planning to rob the banker Mendelssohn in Berlin (Bolshevik writers have denied this and assert that Kamo was planning to take explosives with him to the Caucasus), and that the banknote paper had been ordered by Krassin for counterfeiting Russian rubles. (This last takes on a special interest in view of the seizure of GPU agents in the United States in the nineteen thirties, when they were transporting counterfeit American dollars so perfectly printed that only the duplication of serial numbers confirmed their falsity. And still in 1946 the same story repeated itself when the Korean Communist Party was caught counterfeiting money in the American zone of occupation.*)

To block further exposure, Lenin managed to use his majority in the Central Committee to transfer the investigation from Chicherin's court of honor to a more "confidential" and more malleable sub-committee. In Baku and Tiflis, where the members of Kamo's band were found to have "resigned" from the Party prior to the raid, the finger of suspicion now began to point a little higher, at Kamo's superior, Joseph Djugashvili. Here it was impossible for Lenin to block the investigation, since the Mensheviks completely controlled Transcaucasia. The local committee continued to press its inquest until Djugashvili was either expelled, or else circumvented the dishonor of expulsion by timely resignation.†

But neither resignations in the Caucasus nor the sidetracking of the Chicherin Committee abroad could stop the slow accumulation of knowledge by Lenin's opponents. By the beginning of 1910 the scandals concerning the Schmitt estate, the "expropriations," the counterfeit banknote paper, and the arrests for attempting to convert the proceeds of the Tiflis "ex" into foreign currency, made such a clear picture that Lenin at last was brought to bay. The Mensheviks and those Bolsheviks who were shocked by the things done against their will and behind their backs by Lenin's secret committee, forced him to

---

* New York *Times,* May 11, 1946.
† For the evidence on this matter see Chapter XXVII.

agree to a joint party conference (held in January, 1910), which attempted to bring order out of chaos, disarm the factions, restore the Party as a united organization, abolish the faction organs, set up a single paper with a joint editorial committee of Bolsheviks and Mensheviks, and, in general, clean up an unhealthy mess. One of the first acts of the conference was to compel Lenin to burn the remaining 500-ruble banknotes (over 200,000 rubles' worth) and all the blank banknote paper intended for counterfeiting. But, even while he was at bay and on the defensive on these "technical" matters, Lenin pressed as best he could the beginnings of a fresh political offensive against the "boycotters, recallists and ultimatists" from his own faction, and against the "liquidators" in the Menshevik camp, who wished to liquidate the underground party in favor of legal trade unions and a legal party.

On February 1, 1910, Lenin wrote from Paris to his sister Anna:

> Darling Anyuta,
> We have had a very "stormy" time lately, but it has ended in an attempt at peace with the Mensheviks. Yes, yes, strange though it may seem; the factional organ *(Proletarii)* had been closed down and we are trying hard to move towards union. We shall see whether we shall succeed. I freed myself recently from very urgent matters in view of these changes. . . .

But we are running a little ahead of our story. . . .

In his German prison, Kamo's lawyer brought him a secret message from Krassin giving him a fresh assignment: he was to say nothing, but feign insanity. With amazing fortitude he carried out the order. Here is Souvarine's moving summary of what followed:

> He stamped, shouted, tore his clothes, refused food, struck his keeper. He was shut up naked in an icy cell . . . put under observation, subjected to horrible tests; he stood upright for four months, refused food, was forcibly fed at the expense of

several broken teeth, tore out his hair, hanged himself counting
on intervention at the last moment, opened blood vessels with
a sharpened bit of bone and lost consciousness in a flood of
blood. . . . To test his pretended insensibility, needles were stuck
under his nails and he was touched with red-hot irons. . . .

At last the German Government deported him to Tiflis, where
he underwent a fresh series of tortures. In August, 1911, after
four years, he achieved a perilous escape, aided by his fellow
boyevik, Tsintsadze. We cannot follow his incredible career
further, except to note that he was heartbroken to find that the
revered *troika* had broken up, that Krassin had dropped out
and that Bogdanov and Lenin were fighting each other on incomprehensible political and philosophical issues.

Lenin's repentance, or caution, did not prevent his sending
Kamo once more from abroad in 1912 to attempt another highway robbery in the Caucasus. Caught and sentenced to death,
his sentence was miraculously commuted to life imprisonment
as a result of a general amnesty order issued that year, as part
of the tercentenary celebration of the Romanov dynasty. Released by the Revolution of 1917, he died when an automobile
driven by a Soviet official struck his bicycle on a mountain road
in Tiflis. In Tiflis today this loyal and gentle and formidable
bandit of the Revolution has a street, a hospital, a steamboat,
and a children's park named after him. Not to know the career
of this twentieth-century Robin Hood Bolshevik is to miss an
essential element in the understanding of the Russian movement
and the Caucasian scene, out of which Joseph Stalin emerged
to leadership of an empire.

The expulsion, or resignation under fire, of Djugashvili in
connection with the Tiflis "ex" did not lower him in Lenin's
eyes. Rather was it dating from this time that Vladimir Ilyich
began to take note of him as an agent at once circumspect and
audacious. In 1912, while the Party was still ringing with the
scandals that Martov had just made public in his *Saviors or
Destroyers*, Lenin coopted "Koba" (Stalin's nickname at that
time) onto the Bolshevik Central Committee. In 1913, he called

Koba to him in Cracow, Austria, for training. He needed some spokesman of one of Russia's minority nationalities to present the Marxist—or better, the Leninist—view of the national question. To Gorky, who had just rebuked him for neglect of that burning issue, Vladimir Ilyich replied:

> As to nationalism, I am fully in agreement with you that it is necessary to pay more serious attention to it. We have here a wonderful Georgian who is writing a long article for *Prosveshchenie,* for which he has gathered all the Austrian and other material. We are applying ourselves to the question....

CHAPTER TWENTY-THREE

THE YOUTH OF SOSO DJUGASHVILI

If there are no separatist tendencies at present on the part of
the various nationalities, neither are there any on an all-Caucasian scale, because all the nationalities of the Caucasus are
at loggerheads with one another and submit to cohabitation
only under the influence of the Russian Government, without
which they would plunge at once into bloody rivalry.

—REPORT OF VICE-ROY VORONTSOV-DASHKOV
TO NICHOLAS II, OCTOBER 1912.

The Black Sea is half European, the Caspian all Asiatic. Between them lies a broad peninsula that would be a natural bridge uniting the continents, were it not for the Caucasian range, one of the mightiest mountain chains in the world. West of the range lies Turkey; east, the desert-steppe; south, the tableland of Iran; southwest, Asia Minor. Thus on three sides lies Asia, but on the northwest, Europe begins.

From before the dawn of history innumerable waves of migration, conquest, flight, have broken over these crests, leaving in high-hung valleys and inaccessible gorges fragments of all the passing peoples. There they have remained lost to time in little pocket-worlds of their own.

When the third of our protagonists was born in the mountain town of Gori, in the most important of these little "pockets," the ancient Kingdom of Georgia, this region was, as it still is, a veritable museum of history. The Soviets found it necessary to divide the area into some seventeen Autonomous Areas, Autonomous Regions and Autonomous Republics: the North Caucasian; the Adygeisk; the Cherkess; the Karachaevsk; the Kabardino-Balgar; the Northern Ossetian; the Southern Ossetian; the Chechen-Ingush; the Abkhaska; the Adzharskaya; the Nagorny Karabagh; the Yakhichev; the Orjonikidze; the Armenian; the Daghestan; and the Georgian. Nor does the above list complete the complexity of this patchquilt of peoples. Thus, to take only one of the Autonomous Republics: in 1945 the Council of People's Commissars of the Daghestan Republic included among its twenty-two members three Avars, five Kumyks, four Laks, two Lesghians and two Darghins. Stalin in *Marxism and the National Question,* written in 1913, would poke much fun at the Austrian Marxist notion that the way of maintaining the integrity of a multi-national state was the way of "cultural autonomy," but that is the solution he has adopted today for his homeland, insofar as there is any autonomy at all.

In 1913, too, he had the notion that there was no such thing as Georgian nationalist antagonism toward the Great-Russian rulers, only toward the neighboring nationalities:

> There is no serious *anti-Russian* nationalism in Georgia [he wrote] primarily because there are no Russian landlords there or a Russian big bourgeoisie to supply fuel for such nationalism among the masses. In Georgia there is *anti-Armenian* nationalism; but this is because there is an Armenian big bourgeoisie there which, beating the small and still unconsolidated Georgian bourgeoisie, drives the latter to anti-Armenian nationalism.

But the formation of a separate Georgian Republic in 1918, the repeated revolts against Soviet rule in the twenties, the vast numbers of soldiers of Georgian origin in displaced persons camps after World War II who refused to return to their homeland, tell a different story.

In his childhood, Joseph (Iosif) Djugashvili* rubbed shoulders with representatives of all these peoples, as well as with Turks, Tartars, Persians, Greeks, Kurds, Jews, Moldavians, Esthonians, Czechs, Poles, and, of course, the Ukrainians and Great-Russians who dominated the administrative centers and made up the majority of the newly forming industrial proletariat and technicians in the oil and machine industries. A perfect living laboratory for a future Commissar of Nationalities to be born into!

A child born in Transcaucasia might be born historically into almost any century, culture and code, or, indeed, into several at once. On feast and market days tribesmen came down to Gori from the higher ranges, resplendent in silver filigree, a slotted cartridge belt and a long-tongued dagger in a silver sheath. Hidden in the wilder gorges were such "museum" peoples as the Svanethians or Khevsurs (from the Georgian *Khevi*, "gorge" or "cleft"), numbering perhaps eight thousand, who,

---

* Pronounced *Jugashvili.* I have used the *Dj* instead of plain *J* merely because this has become conventional in English, but the Russian *Dzh* is exactly equivalent to our *J* in *Joseph.*

on festal occasions, still dressed in helmets, chain mail, greaves, shields, swords, the full panoply of the medieval crusaders who left this little time capsule as they passed through on their way to or from the Holy Land.

Nansen in 1925 found all these mountain peoples quarrelsome and quick-tempered, addicted to blood feuds in which a man's relatives and friends were subject to vengeance for his deeds. Feudists went armed even when they worked in the fields. "Just think," Stalin was to write in the polemic of 1913 from which we have already quoted, "just think of 'preserving' such 'national peculiarities' of the Transcaucasian Tartars as self-flagellation; or 'developing' such 'national peculiarities' of the Georgians as the vendetta!"

The legends of innumerable nations cluster round these peaks. On Ararat (16,916 feet high) on the Turkish slope, the Ark of Noah came to rest. Where the flank drops to the Black Sea is Colchis' strand, where Jason sought the Golden Fleece and modern Argonauts found oil. On Kazbek (16,531 feet) the father of the Greek Gods chained the revolutionist Prometheus. On the summit of Elbruz (18,480 feet above the level of the sea) there is today a statue of Joseph Stalin, bearing the legend: "On the highest crest of Europe we have erected the bust of the greatest man of our time."

When the boy Soso (diminutive for Joseph) chanced to lift his eyes above the roofs of Gori, he beheld Kazbek thrusting its peak more than 16,500 feet into the sky. Along its flank lay the famous military highway through the Dar-y-al Gorge (*Dary-al*, "Gate of the Alans"), reminding us that before the beginning of history the Alans from the Russian steppes went through this high-flung pass. To note the armies which have traversed it since would be to list almost all the conquering peoples of Eurasia. The tale of endless clashes would continue into Soso's childhood, when Slav and Turk fought south of the Caucasus wall; into his manhood, when in the winter of 1915, the Turks tried to force the frozen passes, leaving behind them

30,000 frozen corpses; on to 1921, when his friend, Sergo Orjo-nikidze, would lead a ragged band of the Red Army over the Dar-y-al Highway in a surprise attack upon the Socialist Republic of Georgia; and on to the year 1943, when the Wehrmacht stormed through to hold for a while the key town of Vladikavkaz, "Lord of the Caucasus."

Georgia is a land of ancient civilization. From Egypt and Mesopotamia, the smelting and forging of metals spread to Armenia and Georgia more than two thousand years before the Christian Era, while the Eurasian plain lived, for many centuries more, in the Stone Age. Two of the oldest Christian kingdoms in the world, Armenia and Georgia, were converted more than a half-millennium before Kievan Russia forsook its heathen gods.

But if Georgia entered earlier than Russia into history, it left it earlier too. From the late Middle Ages until the spouting of the oil gushers at the beginning of the present century, the land almost ceased to develop. Lying for centuries "between the hammer of the Turk and the anvil of the Persian," it had finally sought protection from Russia, which, converting "protection" into conquest, had detached it from Asia and incorporated it into Europe. Yet this age-old connection with Turkey and Iran was deeply to influence the Russian foreign policy of the Georgian who is today ruler of Russia. Few aspects differentiate more sharply the days of Lenin from the days of Stalin than the differences in their attitudes toward Turkey and Iran. Lenin was tireless in his denunciation of the tsarist government for its drive toward the Dardanelles and its efforts to subject northern Iran. Against the Kerensky government one of Lenin's bitterest accusations was that it still coveted these areas.

> The Provisional Government—he wrote in July, 1917—has not even published the secret treaties of a frankly predatory character, concerning the partitioning of Persia, the robbing of China, of Turkey, the annexation of East Prussia, etc. . . . It has confirmed these treaties concluded by tsarism, which for several centuries has robbed and oppressed more peoples

than all other tyrants and despots . . . disgracing and demoralizing the Great-Russian people by transforming them into an executioner of other peoples.

When Lenin came to power, one of his first acts was to renounce all claims to those areas of Iran and Turkey which Stalin is pressing for at this moment. Thereby he won the support of Turkey and Persia, an admiration and gratitude and close alliance which outlasted all vicissitudes of Soviet relations until the moment of the Stalin-Hitler Pact of 1939.

Transcaucasia is a Mohammedan stronghold too. Two decades before Djugashvili's birth there came to an end a twenty-year-long Mohammedan holy war of the Cherkess (Circassian) Moslems against the Russian conqueror. A year before Soso was born, they rose again.

On January 5, 1943, in the midst of the Second World War, the Soviet army journal, *Red Star,* startled many of its readers by announcing with approval that the Moslem Ingush tribe of the Caucasus had proclaimed a "holy war" against the Germans, and *Red Star* reported a rush of volunteers from the mountain heights—a report with a strange sound in a land that had had two decades of anti-religious campaigns and military conscription. That there was more to the story than appeared in *Red Star* became obvious later when an *ukaz* of October 17, 1945, revealed the summary extinction of both the Chechen-Ingush Autonomous Socialist Soviet Republic and the Karachaev Autonomous Region, their "self-determination" having been cancelled and their remains apportioned to the Georgian and other republics. It was reported that this was a punishment for "collaborationist tendencies in these districts at the time of their occupation by the German army." (New York *Times,* November 30, 1945.) To wipe out the very memory of their "autonomous" existence the names of some of their principal towns were changed from their tribal language to the Georgian tongue. As I write, eighty thousand former Soviet soldiers of Caucasian origin in displaced persons camps refuse to return to their homeland and families. They are all that are left after battle and labor battalion loss, forcible return, and execution of some four hundred thousand Red Army Caucasian troops who surrendered to the Germans and in some instances fought on their side (New York *Times,* December 15, 1946).

Stalin's later life, spent in industrial centers and among Russian Marxists, has not fully obliterated the marks left by his boyhood mountain home upon his character and thought. In his youth he assumed the nickname of Koba, derived from a celebrated guerrilla fighter for Georgian freedom. Says his schoolmate, Iremashvili:

> Koba became a divinity for Soso. He wanted to become another Koba, a fighter and a hero as renowned as Koba himself. . . . His face shone with pride and joy when we called him Koba. Soso preserved that name for many years, and it became his first pseudonym when he began to write for the Party. . . .

Like all revolutionists, he took many names to cover his traces: David, Nizheradze, Chichikoff, Besoshvili, Ko., K. St., K. Kato, Vasilyev, Totonyantz, Ivanovich, and others. But those which remained his favorites throughout were revealing: that of the romantic guerrilla fighter-bandit Koba and that of Stalin, Man of Steel. When the writer met him in the twenties, though Djugashvili had been using the name of Stalin officially for over a decade, he still delighted in having his intimates call him Koba. His most important theoretical work, *Marxism and the National Question* (1913), was signed K. Stalin, combining the two names.

It was this mountain background with its tiny pockets of national or tribal feelings which caused Lenin to encourage him to write on the national question in 1913, and to report on it at many subsequent Party conferences. This led to his appointment as Commissar of Nationalities in the first Soviet Government. If, as head of the state, this man from anti-Russian Georgia was to become more of a Russian nationalist than

the Great-Russian Lenin, the sources of that transformation
are to be sought in the same psychological well-springs that
made Napoleon, the Corsican, the symbol and architect of
Imperial France; Hitler, the Austrian, the protagonist of the
greater German Reich; Charles, the Fleming, the greatest instrument of Spain's world empire.

It would be false to look for a one-to-one correspondence
between a given aspect of Stalin's character and the characteristics of the peoples among which he was born, yet again and
again we will get sudden insights if we bear those Georgian
origins in mind. The difference between Stalinism and Leninism is as much explainable in terms of their differing back-
grounds as in their differing personal characters. Without that
key, the whole trend of Stalin's independent leadership after
Lenin's death is incomprehensible. The successive displace-
ments in leadership from 1917 on are a symbolic epitome of
the long struggle between Russophiles and Westernizers that
marks the dualism in the Russian soul: first Kerensky, Miliukov and the Mensheviks, extreme Westernizers all; then Lenin,
the Great-Russian from the Middle Volga, blend of Westernizer and Slavophile; finally the elimination of all of Lenin's
westernizing comrades by this Georgian from the Caucasian
mountain ranges.

By Lenin the word "Asiatic" was frequently used as a term
of opprobrium concerning Russia's past and institutions:
"Asiatic despotism," "Asiatic bureaucracy," the "Asiatic hu-
miliation of the individual." But by his Georgian disciple,
except in the one article he wrote under Lenin's direct personal guidance in 1913, the word is never used thus. And it would
be strange if it were.*

In April, 1941, when Matsuoka for Japan and Stalin for

---

* It is interesting to note that the classic Marxist classification of societies into "Asiatic, Ancient,
Feudal and Capitalist" has been completely abandoned in all present-day Stalinist literature. Since
Russia has taken on afresh some of the essential aspects of "Asiatic Despotism," the very words have
disappeared from historical and sociological literature published by Stalinist "Marxists." For the pro-
found social implications of this omission, see the forthcoming work: Russia's Asiatic Restoration, by
Karl A. Wittfogel.

Russia signed the non-aggression pact that set Russia free to face the West and Japan free for the attack on Pearl Harbor, Matsuoka raised his glass to express the hope that the treaty would be kept. "If not," he added with the institution of hara-kiri in mind, "I must give my life, for, you see, we are Asiatics."

"We are both Asiatics," was Stalin's retort.

Strange fact: in none of Stalin's biographies does he come to life! Whether official and authorized like Yaroslavsky's, Beria's, Barbusse's and that of the Marx-Engels-Lenin Institute, objective and critical like Souvarine's, or frankly hostile like Trotsky's and those of the Georgian Mensheviks who were the companions of his youth, there is a shadowy and insubstantial character to them all. So silently did he rise to power that he seems hardly to have attracted the attention of his contemporaries until he was already in the Kremlin. We know nothing about his father, of whom he has always been reluctant to speak. We have no such accumulation of memories from wife, brothers, sisters, neighbors, childhood friends, as in Lenin's case; no such collection of intimate and revealing personal and political letters; no self-revealing autobiography as with Trotsky; nothing to tell us what manner of boy, and little beyond public actions and dictated documents to tell us what manner of man he was. Every foreign observer has commented upon the secretiveness that envelops him. On his fiftieth birthday even *Pravda* took notice of this in an article entitled: "Stalin the Enigma." Official biographers, men who have worked and feasted with him (Enukidze, Beria, Yaroslavsky) write strangely as if they were reconstructing the life of a man long vanished from the scene. Their works are more notable for what is left out than for what is put in, and what is put in has the studied air of being manufactured to fit a prescribed pattern. We are beset with obscurities and contradictions at every step. The succession of "memoirs" and official biographies published since the "enigma" article of 1929 have served not to dispel but to increase the mystery, and to blot out the few fixed points of the earlier framework of fact.

When one writes of a still living man it would surely seem a simple matter to put moot points up to him, and then, since no man is to be fully trusted as to his own opinion of himself, to check his answers against records, the testimony of neighbors, friends, associates, opponents. But in Stalin's case this is not as simple as it sounds. The versions he himself has dictated sometimes contradict each other concerning even elementary facts. Records have been destroyed, altered, suppressed. Many of those in a position to speak—not only opponents but even comrades of a lifetime—have been silenced by fear or purge, or made to say what on the face of it cannot be so. Stalin has been made the object of an amazing cult which leaves no room for fallibility or common humanity. Mountains of documents, general histories, Party histories, memoirs, have been banned and burned. There was more barbarous bravado about German book burning, but far less thoroughness in the elimination of essential records. In the Soviet Union, state agencies are the sole publisher, entrust the task, direct the writing, dictate the approach and conclusions, censor, edit, correct, publish, market at wholesale and retail, purchase for schools, libraries and institutions, reward, recall, condemn, replace, destroy. Account after account has received the *imprimatur* and been declared official, only to be publicly denounced, or quietly withdrawn in favor of a different version within a year.

In 1935, to give only a single instance, the Ninth Congress of the Communist Party of Georgia concerned itself at some length with the rewriting (and not the first official rewriting nor the last!) of the history of the Transcaucasian revolutionary movement.

> Noting the distortions of the history of the Party and of the revolutionary movement in Georgia and Transcaucasia occurring in the works of a number of Communist historians, the Congress deems it necessary to concentrate still greater attention against attempts to falsify the history of Bolshevism.

On July 21 and 22, 1935, Lavrenti Beria—shortly to become head of the All-Russian *GPU*—delivered a two-day-long address on the execution of that instruction. The address was later printed in many languages under the title *On the History of the Bolshevik Organizations in Transcaucasia,* alternately titled *Stalin's Early Writings and Activities.* Previous histories and memoirs, many published when Stalin was already the head of the state, or as faction documents serving his rise to power, were declared by Beria to be false. He publicly warned the aged Philip Makharadze, until then regarded as the leading Communist historian of Georgia, that he had better revise all his writings afresh:

> As for the expositions of the struggle of the Transcaucasian Bolsheviks given in the writings of Ph. Makharadze . . . they contain a number of errors in principle and of a historical nature, distort historical facts and events and present a number of points in the history of the Party *dishonestly.*
> So far [added the future head of the GPU ominously] Comrade Makharadze has not taken the trouble to revise his works and correct the mistakes and distortions they contain.*

The meaning of Beria's admonition is made clearer by a sentence inserted at this point in a later edition:

> A. Enukidze and M. Orakhelashvili, since exposed as enemies of the people, smuggled deliberate distortion and falsification of the history of the Transcaucasian organization into their books.

Enukidze was executed; Orakhelashvili has disappeared

---

* It is interesting to note the dates of the various writings of Makharadze referred to by Beria. These dates reveal the length of time that some of them were considered authoritative and the fact that the later ones were actually written for the exaltation of Stalin. But, alas, Stalin's stature continued retroactively to grow! *The Dictatorship of the Menshevik Party in Georgia* (Moscow, 1921) and *On the History of the Communist Party of Transcaucasia* (Tiflis, 1923) were written while Lenin was still alive. *Outlines of the Revolutionary Movement in Transcaucasia* (Tiflis, 1927), *The Best Disciple of Lenin* (an article in *Zarya Vostoka,* No. 293, Tiflis, December 21—Stalin's fiftieth birthday—1929) and *Outlines of the History of the Workers' and Peasants' Movement in Georgia* (with G. Lachapuradze, Moscow, 1932) were faction documents serving the cause of Stalin's rise to power. But these, too, had lost their virtue by 1935!

without a trace. Yet Enukidze had been for over a third of a century an intimate friend of Stalin's. By 1930 he had sufficiently revised his always Stalin-loyal memories concerning the early history of the Transcaucasian movement so that he was selected by his Leader to be one of the four official birthday memorialists whose collective *Life of Stalin* was printed by the government in all the tongues of the Soviet Union and in many other languages for distribution by the Comintern throughout the world. (The other three co-authors were Kaganovich, Voroshilov and Orjonikidze.) To make matters worse, essential sections of Enukidze's earlier memoirs, now officially declared false, are confirmed precisely where they had been challenged—confirmed, that is, by a host of earlier published documents and by the memoirs of Krupskaya and Krassin, which are still officially declared true.

In view of this difficult state of affairs, we shall have to have recourse to the methods of the "archaeologist," who, by collating successive layers of myth and legend, seeks to arrive at the historical truth. Where there is doubt, we shall simply range the versions side by side, with due attention to antiquity, surrounding circumstances, and presumptive social meaning of each, leaving it to the reader to evaluate the evidence and draw his own conclusions as best he may.

Iosif or Joseph Vissarionovich Djugashvili was born at Gori, Georgia, on December 21, 1879. Leon Trotsky was then a month old, and Lenin a boy of nine. Gori was a town of perhaps five thousand, pleasantly situated on the River Kura. Soon after Soso's birth, the railroad was to link it to Tiflis, changing its ways, uprooting many of its inhabitants, the boy's family among them.

Soso, as he was called throughout his childhood, was born in a modest two-room house, now a national shrine, with walls and floor of rough native brick and a large window running the length of one side, as in an old-fashioned country store. The larger room, with its small table, rope-seat stool, sofa and built-

Lenin as a student in Samara 1893

Trotsky at eighteen

Trotsky when arrested
as chairman of Petersburg Soviet

Trotsky at the time
of his last exile by Stalin

Father Gapon, the Police Chief
of St. Petersburg, and members of Gapon's labor union

Stalin's mother

Stalin as a boy of fifteen

Bukharin in 1917

Stalin in 1917

in bunk covered with a straw mattress, served as living room, bedroom for the whole family, and cobbler's shop. The other room was a kitchen. Poverty and disease were familiar visitants. Soso's three brothers died in childhood, leaving him the only child. At seven he contracted smallpox, which left his swarthy skin oily and pockmarked. According to police records of 1903, which noted the pockmarks, his other distinctive mark was the joining together of two toes of one foot. In addition, some accounts say that his left arm was slightly atrophied. Leon Trotsky has suggested that the atrophy was a degeneration of congenital alcoholic or syphilitic origin, but this is pure speculation. It is too suspiciously frequent a phenomenon, this attributing of syphilis, congenital or otherwise, to detested men: a kind of folkloric vengeance. At the time of Lenin's death a number of circumstantial stories as to the "syphilitic origin" of the latter's final paralysis were spread, yet all the evidence, hereditary and medical, is to the contrary. Trotsky has also written that in sessions of the Political Bureau, to which they both belonged, Stalin frequently wore a warm glove on his left hand, alleging rheumatic pains. I have watched Stalin at close range, in meetings and in more intimate conversations, but aside from a comparative immobility of the left arm and a tendency to thrust it into the breast of his jacket—which may be a mere habit of posture—I never noted anything unusual. Its supposed immobility and imperfect growth, if such exist, suggest a mild attack of infantile paralysis in childhood more than anything else. It is a matter of record that in 1916 either this deficiency or the imperfect foot caused him to be pronounced physically unfit for military service after he had been called up in general mobilization. The police records, so far as I have been able to examine them, say nothing about an atrophy of the arm.

Joseph's father, Vissarion Djugashvili, is listed in police accounts as a peasant from the nearby town of Didi-Lilo. In biographical notes stemming from Stalin himself in the early twenties, he set down his father as "of peasant origin." Later, when the faction fight for the succession to Lenin was at its height and great store was being set by the "social origins" of the candidates for leadership (these origins were supposed to determine the "hereditary" social psychology and even the propensity to "deviations"), Stalin recorded himself as the "son of a factory worker."*

At the end of the thirties, when his leadership was secure and when social classes and class distinctions had been "abolished," a biography issued by the Marx-Engels-Lenin Institute combined the two versions. Actually, both are correct. Vissarion was a hereditary peasant, but, like so many of that class, he belonged to the category of peasant-artisan. For generations his family had engaged in cobbling. He intended his son Soso to be a cobbler, too, but died before he could instruct the boy in the trade. During his last years, the elder Djugashvili took employment in the Adelkhanov shoe factory, thus becoming "proletarian," without ceasing to be a peasant in the records of the state. Beyond that we know little concerning Vissarion Djugashvili. According to Iremashvili, boyhood friend and later political opponent, Soso's father was given to drinking and to beating the boy unmercifully. Stalin himself said to Emil Ludwig: "My parents did not treat me badly by any means." Beyond that he has never mentioned his father unless the following solitary passage may be regarded as a mention:

> Imagine [Stalin said] a shoemaker who once had his own tiny workshop, but being unable to stand the competition of the big man, is forced to close down and take a job, let us say with Adelkhanov. But he goes to work in Adelkhanov's factory, not with the idea of becoming a permanent wage worker, but in order to pinch and squeeze and save up enough money to open his own workshop again. As you see, the status of this shoe-

* At Party congresses it was the custom for delegates to fill out questionnaires in which they gave a brief *curriculum vitae:* date of birth, social origin, date of entrance into the movement, posts held, arrests, length of time in prison and exile, etc. Such information then served as the equivalent of a Russian *Who's Who* and for biographical footnotes in other publications. There are in addition a number of brief biographies of Stalin, written by men close to him or by men who were permitted to interview him to secure some of their material. Finally, there are two brief autobiographical speeches in which he told the assembled hearers the story of his life, a biographical chronology prepared by Stalin for his *Collected Works* and an official biography issued by the Marx-Engels-Lenin Institute, all of which derive their frequently contradictory data from Joseph Stalin.

maker is already that of a proletarian; his mentality, however, is not yet proletarian, but thoroughly petty bourgeois. . . . It is the external conditions, the mode of life of men, that changes first; then their mentality changes in conformity with the changed conditions.*

Vissarion Djugashvili died when Soso had reached eleven. Thereupon, his mother, devoutly religious and with no one to devote herself to but her sole surviving child, determined to prepare him for the priesthood. In Georgia, the ambitious were likely to select that career, for there was no other in which a non-Russian plebeian might easily rise. Along with service to the Church, it was, of course, a career of service to the Russian state.

Ekaterina Djugashvili (*née* Geladze) came from a family of peasant serfs of the village of Gambareuli. Soso, her fourth and last child, was born when she was twenty. Until he left her side as a grown man, widowhood was consecrated to supporting him and giving him the chance to prepare for something better in her eyes than the trade of cobbler. She was strong and industrious. Even while her husband lived she had eked out the family income by taking in washing and hiring out for housework by the day. She kept the boy from physical want, and it was not her fault that he did not realize her ambition.

At seven, according to one of the latest official biographies, that of Yaroslavsky, Soso "began to study the alphabet, and within a year was able to read, first in Georgian and then in Russian." Here, as throughout Yaroslavsky's account, the writing seems purposively or ineptly obscure. It is doubtful whether his mastery of Russian followed immediately, "within the year," his mastery of Georgian. More likely it came only with arduous study in the church school, where Georgian was forbidden as the language of instruction. Certainly, the latter tongue remained his language of preference and the one in which he habitually thought on homely topics for many years. The fact

* E. Yaroslavsky: *Landmarks in the Life of Stalin*, p. 38. Yaroslavsky uses the quoted anecdote not to throw light on Stalin's father but to exhibit the young Soso's ability "to explain the most difficult and intricate questions to the workers in a clear and comprehensible way."

that his power to express himself in Russian got its first development in the theological seminary left a life-long mark upon his style, which tends to dry, categorical and dogmatic assertion and the brief question-and-answer method of the catechism. To this day his Russian is spoken slowly with a distinct Georgian accent. A certain bareness of vocabulary and lack of imaginativeness remind us that it is not his native tongue, nor the language of his childhood thoughts and dreams.

In the autumn of 1888, when he was nearly nine, he enrolled in the church-controlled four-grade elementary school of Gori, where he remained until 1894. Then, being nearly fifteen, he entered the Tiflis Theological Seminary on a free scholarship providing uniform, clothing, meals and lodging. The studies were dull, dogmatic, repetitive. The discipline was that of a spiritual barracks, loyalty to God and the Tsar (the order is not certain) being the overriding consideration in determining the content of all subjects. The students were immured within the walls except for a brief leave on Sunday afternoons, were spied upon and regimented from matins to lights out. Stalin thus described his seminary life in his interview with Emil Ludwig:

> *Ludwig:* What drove you to become a rebel? Was it, perhaps, because your parents treated you badly?
>
> *Stalin:* No. My parents were uneducated people, but they did not treat me badly by any means. It was different in the theological seminary of which I was then a student. In protest against the humiliating régime and the jesuitical methods that prevailed in the seminary, I was ready to become, and eventually did become, a revolutionary, a believer in Marxism. . . .
>
> *Ludwig:* But do you not grant the Jesuits any good qualities?
>
> *Stalin:* Yes, they are methodical and persevering in their work. But the basis of all their methods is spying, prying, peering into people's souls, to subject them to petty torment. What is there good in that? For instance, the spying in the dormitory. At nine o'clock the bell rings for tea, we go to the dining hall, and when we return we find that a search has been made and all our boxes have been turned inside out. . . . What is there good in that?

Whatever freedom of spirit might be instilled was by reaction against the régime and studies. The faculty were wont to express contempt for the Georgian language and culture. This was a frequent source of disorder in nationalistic Georgia. In 1873, six years before Soso's birth, students had been expelled for Georgian nationalism. Again in 1885, a decade before his matriculation, circles sprang up among the students, mixing nationalism and socialism. When the rector expressed contempt for the national heritage, Sylvester Jibladze, who was to be one of Stalin's first Marxist teachers, arose from his student bench and struck the rector, to the fiery applause of his fellows. He was condemned to three years in a military disciplinary corps, and the seminary was closed. A year later, in true Georgian fashion, the rector was stabbed to death. The seminary was closed again. From the dispersed and expelled divinity students sprang up the first circle of Georgian Marxism, tinged with the colors of the national independence movement. Their spirit still hung over the place when, in 1894, young Soso entered.

In the 1930's, the seminary still stood, though put to other uses. On its façade was a plaque recording that Joseph Stalin had studied there "from September 1, 1894, to July 20, 1899," that is to say from a little before he turned fifteen until he was going on twenty. Those dates, presumably based on the school records, raise the first of a series of obscurities in Stalin's early career.

According to the Lenin Institute biography (1939), Djugashvili was expelled not on July 20 but on May 29, 1899, for "secret revolutionary activities." The date is almost two months earlier, and does not coincide with the end of a school year. In 1931, Stalin wrote in a questionnaire, after the word: *Education?*: "Turned out of a theological seminary for propagating Marxism." Henri Barbusse, who did an authorized biography in 1935, based on interviews with Stalin, declared that his protagonist was expelled for "a lack of 'political balance.' " Kaganovich, Voroshilov, Orjonikidze and Enukidze in their joint *Life of Stalin* state that he was expelled "as politically un-desirable" (1930). Earlier, Enukidze had written in an adula-tory biographical note that he "flew out of the seminary." In a series of tributes on the occasion of his sixtieth birthday (1939), Kalinin says: "He turned his back on the seminary." The *Small Soviet Encyclopedia,* in its article "Stalin" (Vol. VIII, 1930), writes: "In the seminary Stalin became 'suspect' and was soon expelled for 'infidelity.' " Other accounts, no less official, have him expelled for reading forbidden books. Yaro-slavsky (1940) grows prolix on this point, as if he were try-ing to reconcile all the variants into a concordance. In direct quotation marks he gives a number of synthetic-sounding and mutually contradictory "entries in the conduct book of the Theological Seminary" concerning the offenses of pupil Dju-gashvili. The first, dated September 29, 1898, reads:

> At 9 P.M. a group of students gathered in the dining hall around Joseph Djugashvili, who read them books [*sic*] not sanc-tioned by the seminary authorities.

Yaroslavsky does not tell us how many books nor which ones Djugashvili read to them on that occasion, but other "entries" charge the boy with belonging to the "Cheap Library," possess-ing a library card, being caught reading Hugo's *Toilers of the Sea* and *Ninety-Three,* and Letourneau's *Literary Evolution of the Nations.* Two entries deal with defiance of authority:

> In the course of a search of students of the fifth class made by members of the board of supervision, Joseph Djugashvili tried . . . to enter into an argument with them . . . declaring that such searches were not made in other seminaries. Djugashvili is gen-erally disrespectful and rude towards persons in authority and systematically refuses to bow to one of the masters. . . .

When one Father Dmitri entered Stalin's room, reports Yaro-slavsky, the student kept on reading. " 'Don't you see who is standing before you?' the monk demanded . . . 'I don't see anything except a black spot before my eyes.'" As this is not quoted from the records, the account of demonstrative rudeness must have come from Stalin himself.

Finally, on May 27, 1899, this Father Dmitri proposed to the seminary council "to expel Joseph Djugashvili as politically unreliable."

The proposal—continues Yaroslavsky, interspersing his own comment with quotations from the records—was approved. Officially, Comrade Stalin was expelled from the seminary for failing to pay tuition fees and for "not attending examinations for reasons unknown." But the real reason was his political activities. He was expelled from the seminary as a person who harbored views dangerous to tsardom.

Not paying his fees, not taking the examinations, rudeness, political manifestations, religious infidelity, reading forbidden books, to himself, to others, harboring dangerous views, actively propagating Marxism—that would seem to be at least a half-dozen reasons for being expelled, some mutually contradictory and most of them put into direct quotation as from the "records" of the school. Yaroslavsky advances all these reasons within two pages (English Edition, printed in Moscow by the Foreign Languages Publishing House, Moscow 1940, pp. 15-17). The more we collate the successive and simultaneous versions, the less certain we are whether Stalin left without taking his examinations or failed to pay tuition fees (he was a free scholarship student!) or was expelled. To add to our bewilderment, we have his mother's statement, made to reporters in the year 1930:

Soso was always a good boy. . . . I never had occasion to punish him. . . . His father, Vissarion, wanted to make of Soso a good shoemaker. But his father died when Soso was eleven. I did not want him to be a shoemaker. I wanted only one thing, that he should become a priest. . . . He was not expelled. I brought him home on account of his health. When he entered the seminary he was fifteen and as strong as a lad could be. But overwork up to the age of nineteen pulled him down, and the

doctors told me that he might develop tuberculosis. So I took
him away from school. He did not want to leave. But I took him
away. He was my only son. . . .

In 1946, all these contrary versions having been subjected to
merciless textual criticism by Souvarine and Trotsky in their respective biographies of Stalin, the protagonist set about to produce some order out of the chaos by preparing his own biographical notes to his *Collected Works*. According to these, he
entered the Gori, "Four-year church-run elementary school" in
September, 1888, and graduated in July, 1894, "in the first category," i.e. with high marks, among those of the uppermost section of the class (*Collected Works,* I, 415). As no light is shed by
Stalin on the apparent contradiction between graduating "in
the first category" and taking six years for a four-year course,
we may conjecture that he was either held back by his early difficulties with the unfamiliar Russian tongue or by illness.

On September 2, 1894, according to the same note, he entered
the Tiflis Priestly Seminary, where he claims to have, from 1896
on, "led Marxist study circles of the students," himself studied
Marx's *Capital,* the *Communist Manifesto,* "and other work of
K. Marx and F. Engels." In January, 1898, he "began to lead a
workingmen's circle in the main Tiflis railway shops." In August, he "entered the Georgian Social Democratic organization
Mesame-Dasi," where, apparently at once, "I. V. Stalin, V. Z.
Ketskhoveli and A. G. Tsulukidze formed the kernel of the revolutionary minority of Mesame-Dasi." It is Stalin himself that
puts his own name first as against that of Ketskhoveli, whom he
had earlier acknowledged to have been one of his teachers in
Marxism. On May 29, 1899, the account continues, "I. V. Stalin
was excluded from the Tiflis Priestly Seminary for the propaganda of Marxism."

Except for the light it throws on formative influences and on
the difficulties of our "archaeological" research, the whole matter would seem to be of small importance. A little earlier or a

little later, in one form or another, for one reason or another, Soso Djugashvili did undoubtedly break with the seminary and all it stood for. Whether he left or whether he was expelled, whether he lost interest, failed to present himself at an examination without excuse, read forbidden books by Marx or Victor Hugo, or both, whether he read them by himself or to others, did not pay his fee, was withdrawn for reasons of health, was expelled for holding undesirable views or teaching undesirable views or for being rude or irreligious or politically unreliable, does not alter that fundamental fact. His life would seem to be full enough of the honors that accrue from being expelled, jailed, hunted, persecuted, so that expulsion from a seminary would be a minor increment to the sum.

But if we try to represent him as "the best disciple of Comrade Lenin" and to present all other leading "disciples" as weaklings and foul and unfaithful traitors; if further we wish to portray him as "Lenin's closest collaborator throughout the history of our Party . . . from the very inception of bolshevism, Lenin's co-worker in the building of the Party" (Molotov); if, despite the ten years of difference in their ages, we would picture Stalin as advising Lenin from the start and "having no little influence on Lenin" (Kalinin); if, moreover, he is indeed "the greatest of our contemporaries" (Barbusse, Mikoyan, Beria, and others); "the most profound theoretician of contemporary times" (Beria); "no one so able to penetrate into the most secret recesses of the human heart" (Shvernik); "the God-appointed leader of our military and cultural forces" (Patriarch Sergius); "the father of us all" (Yaroslavsky); "the greatest man of all times, of all epochs and peoples" (Kirov)—then the need to establish the precocity of his genius and the vast sweep of his early rebelliousness becomes more understandable.

If we arrange all his successive official, officious and authorized biographies and birthday eulogies in chronological order, we observe a persistent process of enlargement of the precocity and scale of his theological seminary rebellion, along with a steady pushing back of the date when he first became active in the revolutionary movement and a continual enhancement of the scope of that early activity.

In the earliest editions of Lenin's *Collected Works,* the mention of Stalin brings a footnote, presumably stemming from his Party questionnaires, which records him as "member of the Party since 1898." In 1932, he told Emil Ludwig: "I joined the revolutionary movement at the age of fifteen (i.e. in 1894), when I became connected with certain illegal groups of Russian Marxists in Transcaucasia." Of course, these two accounts are not necessarily incompatible since he might have entered an illegal study circle at the first date and a membership organization on the second, and not left the seminary for yet another year. But soon after the Ludwig interview, Yaroslavsky and Beria went to work on the enlargement of the idea that Stalin became a Marxist at fifteen and they produced a number of improvements. Thus Yaroslavsky writes that in Gori (i.e. before he entered the seminary):

> While still a schoolboy he would explain to the workers and peasants the causes of their poverty . . . and got his first acquaintance with Marxist ideas. . . . When he left the seminary he already had had four years of experience in secret Marxist circles and had published his first illegal periodical.

Yaroslavsky, Beria, and the Lenin Institute all quote a memoir which pictures him as having read his first Lenin article in 1898 while a student at the seminary, and having said: "I must meet him at all costs." According to Beria, young Djugashvili was then "conducting two revolutionary Marxist circles of the students" and eleven or more "Social Democratic workers' circles" outside the school. The text, as so often in Beria's and Yaroslavsky's accounts, seems deliberately vague. On page 21 Beria writes, referring to "the period of 1898-1900," that "Comrade Stalin alone conducted more than eight Social Democratic workers' circles." But a footnote lists "two student circles . . . in 1896 and 1897" and "at the same time in 1898" eleven workers'

circles plus others "at small workshops, printing plants, etc."
It seems likely that activities of the years 1901 and 1902 are here
condensed and set back several years. Both Yaroslavsky and Beria picture the eighteen-year-old seminarist as having led a big
railway strike in Tiflis in the last years of the nineties, while he
was leading all these classes and study circles. More than mere
precocity of genius, this begins to suggest an astonishing ability
to get around, the more astonishing when we consider that he
himself has recorded that he and his fellow-students lived in a
barracks atmosphere, spied on in all their movements.

> Life in the school was sad and monotonous—writes his class-
> mate Iremashvili—Locked in day and night within barrack walls,
> we felt like prisoners obliged to spend years there.

Iremashvili's memoirs, more than a decade earlier than Beria's second-hand account, speak of one such circle in place of
Beria's dozen. His account tallies closely with one given by Stalin himself in 1926, nine years before Beria's lecture on "Stalin's
Early Writings and Activities." It is interesting to compare the
statements of the two classmates concerning the same episode.
Writes Iremashvili:

> One evening Koba and I secretly made our way from the
> seminary to a small house, which stood leaning against a cliff
> and which belonged to a worker of the Tiflis railway. After us,
> secretly arrived others from the seminary who shared our views.
> There also met with us a Social Democratic labor organization
> of revolutionary workers.

Said Stalin, speaking in Tiflis in 1926:

> I recall the year 1898, when the first circle from the railway
> shops was assigned to me. I remember how in the home of Com-
> rade Sturua, in the presence of Sylvester Jibladze—he was at the
> time one of my teachers—and of other advanced workers of
> Tiflis, I received lessons in practical work. . . . Here in the circle
> of these comrades, I then became a pupil of the revolution. . . .

The words "assigned to me" would give more importance to Stalin than Iremashvili's account written three years earlier, but neither version squares with the idea that the young student was conducting two student and eleven or more workingmen's Marxist circles at the time. Nor does it square with the picture Yaroslavsky gave to the Academy of Sciences of the USSR on Stalin's sixtieth birthday when he said:

> Beginning with the end of the nineties, Lenin and Stalin became for the development of the revolutionary movement of the new epoch . . . what Marx and Engels were for the previous century.

Finally, there is yet another version of Djugashvili's break with the seminary. According to Dr. Gogokhia, another classmate of Soso's whose memoirs received the official accolade of quotation by Yaroslavsky in the latter's biography of Stalin:

> Joseph stopped paying attention to his lessons, studied no more than to get passing marks, so as to pass examinations. The ferocious monk Abazhidze guessed when the talented, well-developed Djugashvili, who possessed an incredibly rich memory, studied only for passing marks and he (the monk) succeeded in obtaining a decision to expel him from the seminary.

With this passage we leave to the reader the problems and a consideration of the documentation. More interesting to us than the actual facts is the phenomenon of their retroactive "editing" and the social meaning of that method of writing history.

CHAPTER TWENTY-FOUR

BIRTHPANGS OF GEORGIAN BOLSHEVISM

O if the World were but to recreate,
That we might catch ere closed the Book of Fate,
And make the Writer on a fairer leaf
Inscribe our names.

—OMAR KHAYYAM

When Djugashvili left the seminary, he tried private tutoring. It was as a tutor that he won his influence over Kamo, the Transcaucasian Robin Hood. So miserable were his earnings that he had to be helped by comrades still at the seminary. This is affirmed both by Iremashvili, who was a fellow-student, and by Barbusse. But his poverty did not trouble him. Then as later, he lived simply and dressed modestly.

> He was not in the least concerned with his personal welfare
> —testifies the politically hostile Iremashvili—He demanded
> nothing from life, for he thought such demands incompatible
> with socialist principles. He had enough integrity to make
> sacrifices for his ideal.

Even when he had become lord of the Kremlin, he continued to dress plainly: an unobtrusive semi-military tunic, trousers stuffed into soft knee-high boots, peaked cap, alike for every day and state occasions. Only in the forties, when he had introduced gold braid and epaulettes for civil officials as well as military, to set the hierarchy once more apart from common mortals, did he don a marshal's uniform, shoulder-wide golden epaulettes, gold-braided cap, self-bestowed medals, decorations, ribbons, orders, a jeweled star. In the Teheran and Yalta Conferences, though his power was never greater, his rugged figure seemed somehow to have lost in magnitude now that the trappings had enlarged.

To his brief period of tutoring attaches the first of many evil rumors concerning his relations with comrades. According to the Social Revolutionary, Vereshchak, who was soon to be Stalin's cell-mate in prison and would one day be chairman of the Tiflis Soldiers' Soviet:

> Stalin's comrades in the seminary circle say that soon after
> his expulsion, they were in turn expelled [as] the result of a de-
> nunciation made by Stalin to the rector. He did not deny the
> accusation, but justified the deed by saying that the expelled
> students, having lost their right to become priests, would be-
> come good revolutionaries.

What credence shall we give to this? *Pravda* has set a perilous example in two articles by Demyan Bedny on Vereshchak's memoirs, under the title "Certified Correct," in which Bedny extracted all items favorable to Stalin. Still, the charge does not seem to be justified. It is contradicted by the declaration of Iremashvili that Stalin's fellow-students contributed to the expelled Djugashvili's maintenance. Moreover, if it were true, some official account would surely have boasted that Soso "took a group of students with him" when he was expelled from the seminary.

In December, 1899, Soso got his first and only "respectable" job. Vano Ketskhoveli, also a former seminary student, was about to resign from a minor post in the Tiflis Observatory, and apprised Djugashvili. The position required a literate person with a bit of education, but, as it paid poorly, was open to unskilled Georgian intellectuals. For the better part of a decade it was a monopoly of such "unfrocked" seminary students: first Ketskhoveli, then Djugashvili, then Davitashvili, then Berdzenishvili. Such was the continuity of the succession, that in 1907 Kamo was able to hide his booty of more than a quarter-million rubles in the couch of the director of the observatory.

Djugashvili's duties were not arduous. He had to make observations at night with the help of various instruments. But he did not last long as a scientific worker. On May 1, 1901, some two thousand Tiflis workingmen paraded through the streets in defiance of the police. They were fired upon, fourteen being wounded and fifty arrested. Then the police went round the city arresting all Social Democrats on the lists supplied by their spies. When they visited the observatory to pick up Djugashvili, he was not there. Nor did he report again for work, but hid in his native Gori. Thus began his career as professional revolutionary.

When the excitement blew over, he returned to Tiflis, where he lived, like a lay preacher in some poor sect, on the hospitality of comrades. He lasted thus for a year before the police got him and set him down as "without written documents or definite occupation and without lodgings of his own." Of his life during that year we have only sketchy indications, but they suggest that he was a center of Party quarrels and labor demonstrations, first in Tiflis, then in Batum, where he was staying at the time of his arrest.

In the autumn of 1901 he became a member of the Local Committee of the Tiflis Social Democrats. After attending only two sessions, he left for Batum. Official accounts picture him as having been "sent there" by the Tiflis Committee. *Brdzolis Khma* ("Echo of the Struggle"), a Georgian Menshevik paper published in Paris (No. 3, 1930) paints a less flattering picture of the motives for his journey:

> From the earliest days of his activity among the workmen, Djugashvili attracted attention by his intrigues against the outstanding Social Democratic leader, Sylvester Jibladze. He was warned but took no notice, continuing to spread slanders with the intention of discrediting the recognized representatives of the local organization.... Brought before a Party tribunal, he was found guilty of unjust slander and was unanimously excluded from the Tiflis organization.

But, as if made to order to refute this charge, Lavrenti Beria in the middle thirties published a newly discovered letter purporting to be from the chief of gendarmes of Tiflis to the assistant chief in Kutais, dated July 1, 1902: "At the end of 1901 Djugashvili was sent to Batum for propaganda work . . ." Beria's *Stalin's Early Writings and Activities* (1935) contains a number of such pat finds of old police records which fit like hand to glove for the refutation of the unfavorable memoirs of Georgian Mensheviks in exile, or of Georgian Bolsheviks whose reminiscences had been published by the Soviet Government while Lenin was still alive. Among such newly discovered police entries, we find:

> As a result of Djugashvili's activities Social Democratic organizations headed in the beginning by the Tiflis Committee began to spring up in all the factories of Batum.

> Djugashvili has always occupied extremely prominent posi-
> tions. . . .
> Djugashvili headed the Batum, Tiflis and Baku Social Demo-
> cratic organizations at various times. . . .

One wonders why these reports were not discovered in the
twenties when the police archives were opened and every scrap
of paper bearing on Party history was duly published. One is
moved to wonder, too, that these new finds tell a different story
and even speak another language from all police documents and
Bolshevik reminiscences published in the years 1919 to 1923,
while Lenin was alive and the memoirs of countless old Bolsheviks were still fresh and free.

The language sounds uncommonly like Beria's own. The
Tsarist Secret Service is actually exhibited as no less anxious
than the GPU to make clear the young Djugashvili's unique
leading role and to confound all his critics. Indeed, the excerpt
which makes Djugashvili "head" all three city organizations
proves too much, since it overlooks the fact that there was no
"head" to any Social Democratic organization in those days.
If outstanding leader was meant by the term, then there were
men like Zhordania, Khetskhoveli, Jibladze, Isidore and Noah
Ramishvili, Chkheidze, Topuridze, Shaumyan, and others who
were more prominent than Djugashvili, not to mention members in Transcaucasia of the All-Russian Central Committee
like Krassin and Nogin. The very idea of a personal and individual "head" is an anachronism borrowed from the language
and thought of a later day, when Stalin had had himself proclaimed *Vozhd,* or Leader (the Russian analogue of Duce and
Fuehrer) of Party, Army, Government, Comintern, the peoples
of the Soviet Union and of the World.

To be sure, the authenticity of any particular document can
be neither proved nor disproved in any final sense so long as
free research is not permitted. Such research would require an
examination of the paper, ink and type, a comparison with other documents from the same hand, the use of X-ray, and all
other methods that are employed when the authenticity of a

painting has been called in question. Until such an opportunity presents itself, we are limited to such tests as are offered by comparisons of style and subject matter, collating of earlier and later reminiscences, and occasional check against objective fact.

To return to the charges of intrigue against Djugashvili which the police record so patly refutes, we must note that such charges surround his personality at many points in his life. So far we have seen that he was accused of denouncing fellow circle members to the rector of the theological seminary and of having been forced to leave Tiflis because of intrigues against Jibladze. The same *Brdzolis Khma* makes yet a third charge to the effect that after he got to Batum he became jealous of the more prominent Shaumyan there and was suspected by the workers of denouncing Shaumyan to the police. His own arrest and exile is supposed to have prevented an investigation. Beyond the assertions of the Georgian Mensheviks in exile, there is no evidence that any of these grave charges are true. Still there are so many accusations against him (there are more to follow in our story) that it is important to note that men who worked with Stalin should have thought him capable of framing up his comrades to advance himself or his party's interests as he conceived them. Lenin and Trotsky, too, made bitter enemies and were subject to savage attacks by the defeated and the exiled. Yet in all the polemical literature against them, there is a notable absence of charges such as these.

"Before Stalin came to Batum," writes Beria, "there was no workers' Social Democratic organization whatever." On his arrival, he called a conference disguised as a New Year's party, at which he "delivered four or five brilliant talks" and set up "a leading Party group headed by Comrade Stalin." Within the next two months "eleven Social Democratic workers' circles began to function actively under the leadership of Comrade Stalin." On February 27, a strike broke out in the Rothschild plant in which "Comrade Stalin himself led the work of the strike committee, drew up the demands . . . wrote the

leaflets and organized the printing and distribution of them."
On March 8, thirty-two strikers were arrested for deportation
to their native villages. "Comrade Stalin retaliated" with a
demonstration which ended in three hundred arrests. An attempt was made to storm the jail: fifteen workers were killed,
fifty-four wounded, five hundred arrested.

Yaroslavsky's account, less dry than Beria's, treats us to a
vivid picture of the storming:

> Comrade Soso stood in the midst of the turbulent sea of
> workers, personally directing the movement. A worker named
> Kalanadze who was wounded in the arm during the firing was
> led out of the crowd and afterward taken home by Comrade
> Stalin himself. . . .

During all this feverish activity, according to Beria, "Comrade Stalin maintained close contact with the Tiflis organization, often visited Tiflis, and directed the work of the Tiflis Social Democratic organization." Such remarkable labors could
not go unnoticed forever, least of all in the hitherto somnolent
Batum. On April 18, 1902, Djugashvili "together with others"
was arrested "at a meeting of the leading party group." Thus
began his first prison experience.

An *Iskra* account of the Rothschild strike and storming of
the Batum jail, printed at the time, makes it appear more spontaneous and fails to make the usual claim to socialist leadership. It mentions two workingmen by name as having led the
affair; Stalin does not figure by implication or under any of
his aliases. Menshevik sources, however, confirm Beria's assertion that he was the secret promoter of the attack on the prison,
nay more, they reproach him for the "senseless adventure and
useless shedding of blood." Without accepting the officious
and official version which makes the young Djugashvili do everything, lead everybody, be everywhere at once, we can be
sure that the twenty-two-year-old professional revolutionary
took as active a part as he could in the turbulent strikes and
demonstrations that shook sleepy Batum shortly after his ar-

rival. We can be certain, too, of the date of his arrest, though not of the manner. Beria makes it "at a meeting." The Lenin Institute has him picked up during a general search. Barbusse pictures him as calmly facing the police during a raid on another's home, while "talking to Kandelaki and smoking a cigarette." These discrepancies are the more puzzling in that all three versions are based on the research of those who had the benefit of personal guidance from their protagonist.

For a year and a half Djugashvili was in the prisons of Batum and Kutais awaiting an administrative disposition of his case. Then he and fifteen others were exiled to Eastern Siberia. Among them were Lenin's friend Kurnatovsky and another veteran Social Democrat from Central Russia, Franchesky. These were given four years each. Djugashvili and the remaining twelve, possibly as first offenders or as natives "misled" by the two Russians, were given only three years. At the end of November, 1903, the exiles started out in slow stages for the long journey to Eastern Siberia. Soso's destination proved to be the lonely outpost of Novaya Uda, a tiny village in Irkutsk Province, not far from Lake Baikal. Quite a hard journey in the dead of winter, yet, within a month and eight days of his arrival, on January 5, 1904, he escaped, reappearing in his accustomed haunts in Tiflis and Batum in February.

While Djugashvili was still in prison, according to the inimitable Barbusse, he heard "a great piece of news": that the congress called to found an all-Russian party had not ended in the longed-for unification, but in a split. To most, this was a bewildering calamity. The differences, so far as anyone yet knew, turned about a single clause in the statutes and the personnel of the Editorial Board of *Iskra*. All the memoirs of old Bolsheviks concerning that period testify to their dismay when the tidings first reached them. Thus, the future Commissar of Education, Lunacharsky, remembers his "embarrassment at the insignificance of the reasons which led to the split." Piatnitsky, Lenin's faithful man Friday, "could not understand why

such petty differences should keep us from working together."
Krzhizhanovsky "found the idea of Martov's opportunism
far-fetched." Trotsky saw "nothing more than Lenin's desire to
get Axelrod and Zasulich off the Editorial Board." Plekhanov
took Lenin's part but was sure that the issues were too small to
keep the groups separated. When he came to the conclusion
that Lenin's stubbornness concerning the composition of the
Editorial Board was the chief hindrance to unity, he forced the
admission of the candidates of the other side. Even Lenin himself, as we have seen, did not consider it "great news" but a
matter for doubt and anguish. The very Bolshevik majority
he set up in the Central Committee soon deserted him in favor
of reunification ("conciliation"). The upsurge of 1905 forced
reunification, a unity which Stalin hailed as the principal
achievement of the London Congress of 1907. "The actual unification of the advanced workers of all Russia into a single all-
Russian party under the banner of revolutionary Social Democracy," wrote Stalin in 1907, "that is the significance of the
London Congress."

The period of decline after 1907 brought new squabbles,
but not until 1912 was the split made permanent, and even
after that Lenin sought unity, now with Plekhanov, and again
(more than once) with Martov. Yet Barbusse pictures the twen-
ty-three-year-old Djugashvili as seeing far beyond Lenin and
welcoming the unexpected split as "a great piece of news," not
"hesitating for a moment when, like Hercules at the beginning
of his career, he was compelled to choose between vice and
virtue." Without Barbusse's ornaments of style, all subsequent
biographers, not excluding Stalin himself, have sought to give
the same impression, which brings us to another problem re-
quiring "archaeological" investigation.

I first became acquainted with Lenin in 1903—Stalin declared
in 1924, one week after Lenin's death, in a memorial address to
the students of the military academy in the Kremlin.—True,
it was not a personal acquaintance; it was made by correspondence. But it left an indelible impression upon me, one which

has never left me throughout all my work in the Party. I was an exile in Siberia at the time. My knowledge of Lenin's revolutionary activities since the end of the nineties, and especially after 1901, after the appearance of *Iskra,* had convinced me that in Lenin we had a man of extraordinary caliber. I did not regard him as a mere leader of the Party, but as its actual founder, for he alone understood the inner essence and urgent needs of our Party. When I compared him with the other leaders of our Party, it seemed to me that he was head and shoulders above his colleagues—Plekhanov, Martov, Axelrod and the others; that, compared with them, Lenin was not just one of the leaders but the leader of the highest rank, a mountain eagle who knew no fear in the struggle and who led the Party boldly forward along unexplored paths. . . . This impression took such deep hold on me that I felt impelled to write to a close friend of mine who was living as a political exile abroad, requesting him to give me his opinion. Some time later, when I was already in exile in Siberia—this was at the end of 1903—I received an enthusiastic letter from my friend and a simple but profoundly expressive letter from Lenin to whom, it appeared, my friend had shown my letter. Lenin's note was comparatively short, but it contained a bold and fearless criticism of the practical work of our Party, and a remarkably clear and concise account of the entire plan of work of the Party in the immediate future. Only Lenin could write of the most intricate things so simply and clearly, so concisely and boldly that every sentence did not so much speak as ring like a rifle shot. This simple and bold letter strengthened my opinion that Lenin was the mountain eagle of our Party. I cannot forgive myself for having, from the habit of an old underground worker, consigned this letter of Lenin's, like many other letters, to the flames. My acquaintance with Lenin dates from that time.

The more we examine this spiritless memorial address on the beloved leader but a few days dead, the more questions it raises. Stalin assures the military cadets that he burned the letter: but where is Krupskaya's copy? It was written at a time when the Ulyanovs had a settled address in Geneva, and during the period immediately following the split, a period for which Krupskaya has conserved complete copies of all letters and notes which Lenin dictated to her, or wrote himself, including even letters drafted but not sent. And "this profoundly expressive letter contained a remarkably clear and concise account of the entire plan of work of the Party for the immediate future." Neither in Krupskaya's files, nor in her memoirs, is there any trace of this letter to Djugashvili in Siberia.

A more cogent question: by his own account, Stalin did not get to Novaya Uda until November 29, where he stayed a month and eight days, fleeing on January 5, 1904. There was thus no time for a letter from Geneva, or even from Russia proper, to reach him there in the dead of winter. As prisoners were never told their final destination until they were deep in Siberia, he could not even have had time to send his address home, still less to a friend abroad. In short, the facts as given are self-refuting, as Trotsky has fully demonstrated in his posthumous *Stalin.*

By now it should be clear to the reader that we are dealing with the most striking example in all history of a man who has succeeded in inventing himself. The entire governmental apparatus, the printing press, cinema, textbooks, schools, paintings, etc., of a great and centrally directed nation have been employed in the task of remolding its ruler's past closer to his heart's desire. There is none to challenge, for textual criticism is "treason" and challenger and evidence are destroyed together. This retroactivity concerns itself even with minuscule details, for the larger facts—that he early became a Leninist, early became important in Caucasian bolshevism, that his importance grew steadily until he became the most powerful man on earth—these facts are beyond dispute. It is fruitless, therefore, for us to follow this process in detail. It will interest us only where it throws, as it sometimes does, a strong light on the real events of Stalin's life and the social meaning of one or another emendation. As we shall see, his self-created or imagined life is usually a projection backwards in time of his real place in later life. Thus the biographer is faced with the unprecedented task of translating shadow into substance. In some ways this shadow life becomes as important a key to this man's true place in history and actual character as the real life that it retroactively transforms.

If we look into Krupskaya's records of Lenin's correspondence and literary activity during the period in question, we do find a document having a possible connection with Stalin's tale to the military cadets. At the moment to which Stalin's speech refers, Lenin was republishing in Geneva as a printed pamphlet a prior "Letter to a Comrade on Our Organizational Tasks." Written originally in September, 1902, to A. A. Schneierson, Lenin considered it important enough to circulate to other comrades in hectographed form. Then, in June, 1903, it was republished in Siberia by the Siberian Committee of the Party. It is not impossible that the Siberian hectographed copy was given to Stalin in exile by a fellow-deportee. It does indeed "contain a remarkably clear and concise account of the entire plan of work of the Party for the immediate future." If this conjecture—and it is no more than a plausible conjecture on my part—is correct, it would suggest that from that period dates Stalin's discipleship.

However that may be, the problem remains: what were Stalin's motives for predating his first *personal* acquaintance with Lenin, a predating accomplished exactly one week after Lenin was dead? One reason will become abundantly clear when we come to examine the strained relations between Lenin and Stalin during the last year or so of Lenin's life. And another when we examine the ensuing struggle for the succession. We cannot help but be struck by the long-range planning and meticulous attention to detail which Stalin showed thus early in the struggle for power.

A motive of a different order may possibly be supplied by an examination of the one police entry concerning Joseph Djugashvili which neither Beria nor any other official biographer has ever referred to:

> According to information recently received from our agents
> —reads a report of the Tiflis Chief of the Secret Police, Karpov

—Djugashvili was known in the Organization under the pseudonyms of Soso and Koba. He has been working in the Social
Democratic Party since 1902, first as a Menshevik, then as a
Bolshevik, as propagandist and director of the first section
(railways).

This item, like all the police archives in Georgia, fell into
Bolshevik hands in 1921, after the Red Army overthrew the
Georgian Republic headed by Zhordania. It was published for
the first and last time in the Soviet Union, in the Georgian
Bolshevik paper *Zarya Vostoka* ("Dawn of the East"), journal
of the Communist Party in Tiflis, on December 23, 1925. It was
one of a number of items from police records, reminiscences
of old Georgian Bolsheviks, etc., published to honor Stalin on
his forty-sixth birthday. For reasons which may not seem too
clear to a disinterested Western reader (one would think that
more than two decades of unquestioning discipleship as a Bolshevik would be enough for any man), this item did not seem
to Stalin to honor him. He made no public comment on the
implication that he was in his youth, as all Georgian Social
Democrats were, for a while a follower of the main body of
Georgian Social Democracy, whose outstanding figure was
Noah Zhordania. No attempt has ever been made to refute the
item, to examine or explain it. Nor was it denied. It was simply
never referred to in print again. Whoever had been responsible
for its publication has doubtless long ago gone the way of all
flesh.

Once started in the nineties, Georgian socialism expanded
with amazing rapidity in the political vacuum of Transcaucasia.
Tsarist officials had looked with complacency on its early
growth. Just as they gave a certain legality to Marxism in the
nineties in Central Russia because they saw in it a useful counterweight to the more dangerous Narodnik terrorism, so they
gave even greater legal freedom to Georgian Marxism, because
they hoped it would sow divisions within the nationalist movement. Even after the brief honeymoon of legality was over in

Russia as a whole, it continued in Transcaucasia. By the time the authorities began to doubt the wisdom of their maneuver, it was too late. Georgian socialism had developed into a mighty mass movement and there was no forcing it back into the womb of time. Unlike Marxist organizations elsewhere, it enjoyed a great following among the peasantry as well as among the numerically weaker working class and intelligentsia. It became the first open mass party of Social Democracy anywhere in Russia. During the revolutionary days of 1905-1906, it ruled over whole districts, had mayors and deputies and Georgian princelings in its ranks, enjoyed the support of peasant villages and city Dumas, and of the nascent middle class and intelligentsia. Municipal councils voted funds to arm its Red Guards. The Tsar's Viceroy, Vorontsov-Dashkov, even asked it to intervene to stop the Armenian-Tartar massacres which less enlightened officials had encouraged, and he provided a thousand army rifles for the purpose! (Chavichvili: *Patrie, Prisons, Exil*, p. 132). In 1906, the authorities deliberately postponed the national Duma elections in Transcaucasia until other provinces had voted, lest the expected Social Democratic sweep should set an undesirable example.

The mass character of the movement helps to explain the slower ripening of bolshevism (which slowness Stalinist historiography would now conceal as something shameful), and the comparative freedom from splits and fine-spun theoretical debates such as possessed the narrow underground and émigré circles of Russia. When, during 1905 and 1906, the Social Democratic movement became a mass party in Russia proper, unity was forced upon the factions in Central Russia, too.

Lenin's principal ideological stock-in-trade after the 1903 split—"opportunism in the organization question"—could find no echo in a movement organized so differently. The word "opportunism," moreover, sounded strange in the ears of a party which was unanimous in favoring armed conflict with tsarism.

The real father of Transcaucasian socialism was Noah Zhordania. Of the same age as Lenin, this Georgian intellectual first participated in the Central-Russian underground, then went abroad as Lenin did to work with Plekhanov. Zhordania and his close associates and disciples remained all their lives orthodox Marxists in the sense that Plekhanov was such. And, like him, they sometimes assumed a position between the two factions.

In 1897, Zhordania had returned from his stay abroad to take over the editorship of the progressive journal *Kvali* ("The Furrow"), which he transformed at once into the Georgian-language organ of "legal Marxism." So complacent were the tsarist authorities about Georgia that long after "legal Marxism" had been forgotten in Russia, *Kvali* continued to appear freely. It was not suppressed until 1904! During more than six years it carried on a notable work of polemic, exposition, education, adaptation of Marxism to the regional characteristics of Transcaucasia. In it Zhordania wrote personally all the major programmatic documents of the movement. The paper helped to form many men of such ample caliber that when, following Plekhanov, the Georgian Social Democracy went over to menshevism, it was able to supply leaders of national standing for the Menshevik faction. Thus, the leader of the Social Democratic deputation in the Second Duma was that body's youngest and most able Deputy, the twenty-six-year-old Georgian, Hercules Tseretelli. ("A mad man," wrote the arch-conservative *Novoe Vremya,* "a mad man, but the most brilliant Deputy in the Duma.") When the government jailed Tseretelli and barred his further candidacy, it was another Georgian, Nicholas Chkheidze, who assumed leadership of the entire Social-Democratic fraction in the Third and Fourth Dumas. In 1917, Tseretelli was to become a member of the Provisional Government, and Chkheidze the first Chairman of the Petrograd Soviet and then of the All-Russian Soviet Executive. So much had their influence become national.

It was from the journal edited by Zhordania and his associates that Soso Djugashvili got his first taste of Marxism. For any Georgian Marxist to fail to acknowledge indebtedness to Zhordania would be a mark of ingratitude equivalent to a failure on Lenin's part to acknowledge indebtedness to Plekhanov. Such acknowledgement Lenin gave in full measure. So did Trotsky, despite Plekhanov's openly expressed antagonism toward him. But neither Stalin nor his official biographers are willing to admit that he owes an iota to *Kvali* and Zhordania. Factional differences are extended backward retroactively to make the youthful Soso spring fully armed out of the high, bald forehead of Vladimir Ilyich.

It was the government that sowed the first seeds of the future Bolshevik movement in Transcaucasia by its deportations and administrative exilings. Since the nineties they had been sending "released" Russian politicals to this "safe" and distant march to live "under police observation." Along with them, it sent a number of native Georgians, arrested in Central Russia, back to their homeland. Two of these rusticated Georgians would become leading Bolsheviks, Lado (Vladimir) Ketskhoveli and Abel Enukidze.

Here are four typical Great-Russian newcomers to Georgia for the year 1900. Leonid Krassin, engineer, was brought in to manage the power station in Baku. Michael Kalinin, machinist, and Sergei Alliluev, locksmith, were hired by the Tiflis railway shops. Victor Kurnatovsky, close friend of Lenin, received police permission to work in Tiflis as a chemical engineer. All four were to play important roles in the life of Soso Djugashvili.

Engineer Krassin managed the power company until late in 1904. In his office he met with trustworthy Georgian leaders, arranged the smuggling of literature, forging of passports, raising of funds, carried on his duties as a member of the Central Committee, contrived to expand the local clandestine printing plant into one serving all Russia. Of this printing plant, we shall hear more.

So well did the chief engineer lead his double life that, even to the day when he was promoted to a higher post in Central Russia, neither management nor police nor workers suspected his underground role. Four years of such intense activity without discovery was rare indeed in the annals of the movement. The workingmen under him went so far during one of their strikes as to demand his removal as manager! No wonder Lenin set a high value upon him.

The reader will remember that this man, who during his four years in Tiflis, was the most influential Leninist in the whole of Russia, became a "conciliator" shortly after Lenin contrived his election to the Central Committee. He was unconvinced of the seriousness of the split of 1903, and sceptical concerning the need of devoting one's major energies to internecine rather than anti-tsarist struggle. Thus his influence helps to explain why a split was retarded in Transcaucasia and why the Tiflis printing plant, the largest underground plant in all Russia, kept right on printing the works of both factions until 1905. And in that year, as the reader may remember, it was Krassin who arranged for the printing of the leaflets of the Menshevik, Leon Trotsky. Yet another member of the Lenin-selected Central Committee of 1903, Victor Nogin, who lived for a while in the Caucasus, was also a "conciliator."

If Krassin's influence was a retarding one, what of the other three Great-Russians we have mentioned? Though Michael Kalinin probably met Stalin at this time, he did not stay long in the Caucasus. After a few months he took part in a railway shopmen's strike there and then returned to Central Russia. Twenty-one years later, he would become "President of the Soviet Union," i.e. President of the All-Russian Executive Committee of the Soviets, an honorific but otherwise unimportant job. A man of limited horizon and simple, homely ways, he would remain high in the façade of government as a symbol of the proletarianized peasantry whence he had sprung. And he would remain close enough to the favor of Joseph Stalin to attain to a ripe old age and die a natural death in office in 1946 —of all deaths the most unnatural for members of the Bolshevik Old Guard of his generation.

Kalinin's fellow-shopman, Alliluev, settled down permanently in Transcaucasia and married a Georgian woman. He was not important politically but of personal importance in the life of Soso Djugashvili by reason of a bilingual daughter born of his Georgian marriage. In 1918, when Soso became Commissar for Nationalities of all Russia, he engaged this girl, Nadezhda Allilueva, as his secretary. A year later, she became his second wife, she then being seventeen and he forty. She was the mother of his son Vasili and his daughter Svetlana.

The fourth of the 1900 immigrants from Great-Russia, Victor Kurnatovsky, was a lesser figure than Krassin but a more unconditional follower of Lenin's. It is probable that Kurnatovsky first apprised Djugashvili of *Iskra's* and Lenin's existence, and gave him his first push in the direction of "irreconcilable bolshevism." In Beria's biography of Stalin (1935), the relationship between the two is described in this fashion:

"After Kurnatovsky's arrival at Tiflis, he established close contact with Comrade Stalin and became his intimate friend and co-worker."

This would imply equality, or perhaps the subordination of Kurnatovsky to Stalin. But on the next page, the Tbilisi (Tiflis) Branch of the Marx-Engels-Lenin Institute is quoted as recording: "All the comrades went to Kurnatovsky with their disagreements and disputes. His opinions and conclusions were always accepted without objections."

The spirit of that sentence, so different from the democratic and turbulent spirit of the early Georgian movement, is a result of the retroactive injection of the idea of personal leadership and blind obedience. But it is interesting to note that, in contradistinction to everything said by Beria in the rest of the book, the absolute leader is clearly not Stalin here, but Kurnatovsky as the emanation of the spirit of Lenin.

In the autumn of 1904, the Bolsheviks Vladimir Bobrovsky and his wife were sent to the Caucasus by Lenin, as was Lev Borisovich Kamenev to fill the vacancy left by the arrest of Kurnatovsky and the transfer of Krassin. Kamenev had spent his childhood in Georgia and knew the region. He worked hard to bring about a split in the solidly unified and strong Georgian movement. By ones and twos he gathered them, no doubt Soso Djugashvili among them, but he has since been purged, so no trace of his activity is any more permitted in official historiography. If we limit ourselves to it, we can no longer explain such passages as this in the memoirs of Victor Taratuta (the Victor whom the reader has already met in the chapter on expropriations): "I first met Comrade Kamenev, Lev Borisovich," writes Taratuta, "in his capacity as leader of the Caucasian Bolshevik organizations..."

Strangely, Taratuta, like Krassin, mentions innumerable Caucasian Bolsheviks, but the name of Koba-Djugashvili-Stalin is not among them. Still harder to reconcile with Beria's and all post-Berian biographies, are the simple memoirs of Mrs. Bobrovsky, whose book, written in 1934, was published in Russian, and then by the Comintern in various languages. In the autumn of 1904 she worked in Tiflis and Baku, was coopted into the newly formed Bolshevik Committee for Transcaucasia, became Secretary of the Baku Committee, reorganized the underground printing plant, which she found running "on too large a scale and with too little secrecy," and broke it up into two separate plants for greater safety. She notes the activities of her husband, of Tskhakaya, Japaridze, Tsulukidze and others. Concerning Djugashvili, who, according to Beria, was then running the whole district committee of the Bolsheviks and indeed the whole activity of the entire party in the Caucasus, she has nothing to say with the exception of the single reference to him as "the still quite young Stalin (Soso)" on page 113!

When she describes the great strike of 1904, which, according to official historiography, Stalin is now alleged to have led, she says quite simply and frankly that it was led by the Mensheviks. This she explains by

> ... the exceptionally talented demagogic oratory of their mass leader, Ilya Shendrikov. ... The error of the Baku (Bolshevik) leadership in their approaching the masses not quite correctly, somewhat academically. A special role was played by the fact that we had not one single agitator who could compare with Ilya Shendrikov's fiery talent as a speaker.

She pictures the Bolsheviks as trying to criticize him at a meeting, and being heckled by the workingmen. "We left the meeting not exactly with light hearts." They tried a rival meeting, but Shendrikov prevented its success by the simple device of prolonging his own speech so that the workers did not leave his meeting in time to go to theirs. Except for the half-sentence about Soso's "youth," he does not figure in her memories at all. Having been published in 1934 with the approval of Stalin's apparatus, it undoubtedly represents a true picture of the state of affairs in the autumn of 1904 and the spring of 1905. But that was before Lavrenti Beria got to work on the remaking of the past and the memories of men. Today, Mrs. Bobrovsky's book has been burned in Russia along with countless other pre-purge accounts.

According to Beria, the great movement created by Zhordania was limited to "legal Marxism," and "the minority of the Mesame-Dasi, headed by Comrades Stalin, Ketskhoveli and A. Tsulukidze" began a struggle for an illegal paper with the result that "the minority headed by Comrade Stalin adopted Lenin's position, the position of bolshevism."

But if we turn to Volume XIX of the *Big Soviet Encyclopedia,* which volume was published in 1930 under Stalin's dictatorship, we find a different order of names and a different story:

At the head of the revolutionary Leninist tendency—we find on page 578—stood M. Tskhakaya, F. Makharadze, Soso Djugashvili [Stalin], A. Tsulukidze, and others. . . .

The Social Democratic movement from the beginning of the nineties developed simultaneously on a legal and illegal basis. . . . In the journal *Kvali,* the editor of which from 1898 on was N. Zhordania, were printed the articles of both tendencies. . . . The articles of the advocates of Revolutionary Marxism were also printed in the pages of *Kvali.* These, as far as that was possible in the legal press, advanced a clear class ideology. Such, for example, were the articles of F. Makharadze. At the end of 1898, one of the future leaders of Georgian bolshevism, A. Tsulukidze, came out with a protest against the position of Zhordania in *Kvali.* . . . At that time [in 1903] all Transcaucasia, including the Georgian Social Democratic Organization, stood on the platform of *Iskra.* Economism had no open supporters. In 1904 *Kvali* was closed. There was felt a great need of an illegal organ. . . . The Bolsheviks, with Lado Ketskhoveli at the head, organized in Baku an illegal journal, *Proletarii Brdzola.* . . . The situation changed at the beginning of 1905 when the majority of the Georgian Social Democrats stood on the position of menshevism. . . . During the course of 1905 there developed a bitter struggle between bolshevism and menshevism. . . .

From all this dull and contradictory evidence, a few essentials begin to emerge. First, it is clear that Stalin was not born number-one man in the Caucasus but apprenticed himself to others and learned from others. Second, that a Bolshevik group was formed in the Caucasus in 1904, after Kamenev was sent there to call into being an organization, but it developed under the imposing shadow of a mass organization and large Georgian figures, and did not make a sharp break with the general organization there. It was in this little circle that Stalin got his first training as a faction fighter.

The official biographies assure us that Stalin immediately converted Transcaucasia into "a stronghold of bolshevism," but mountains of evidence testify to the contrary. At the two united congresses of Bolsheviks and Mensheviks (Stockholm, 1906, and London, 1907), the Caucasian Bolsheviks were not able to muster up enough votes to entitle them to a single un-contested delegate. In all four Duma elections, while the Social Democratic Party won many Transcaucasian seats, all the Dep-uties were Mensheviks, no single Bolshevik appearing among them. Whatever tendency to bolshevism may have developed in 1904, once more in 1905, according to the *Big Soviet En-cyclopedia,* "the majority stood on the position of menshe-vism." In 1906, Bolsheviks and Mensheviks continued to form part of a single unified movement. Thus in *Sotsial Demokrat,* published in Petersburg with Lenin as one of its editors, the issue of October 13, 1906, page 7, carries a report from Trans-caucasia, which reads:

> Within the last few days ended the Fourth Congress of the Caucasian Social Democratic organization. Forty-three dele-gates attended with one vote for every three hundred members of the Party. About ten were there with voice but no vote. In the number of the former there were six Bolsheviks, the rest be-ing Mensheviks. . . . The greatest number of delegates were from Tiflis—twenty-two—where at present there are six thousand members. . . . The elections were direct, almost all members took part in them. Baku sent four delegates. All were Menshe-viks. . . . The Bolsheviks did not put through a single Bolshevik resolution. . . .

Thus neither Tiflis nor Baku, where Stalin had worked, was in Bolshevik hands, and the Bolshevik total was less than one in seven.

Skipping to 1910, we once more find a report in *Sotsial Dem-okrat* (now published in Paris), this time signed "K.S.," i.e. Koba Stalin. It is dated Baku and says that there are not more than three hundred members in the Baku organization of Bol-sheviks. They are in a majority there but are trying to unite with the Mensheviks ("about one hundred members") but "uni-fication with the Menshevik comrades has not yet been realized, since mere wishes alone do not liquidate a split."

Skipping again to 1912, we find that the Bolsheviks have still failed to break for good with the Transcaucasian Regional

Committee led and controlled by the Mensheviks! Even Beria involuntarily testifies to the fact of this being the first attempt at a "disrecognition" of the Transcaucasian Committee:

> In April, 1912—he writes on page 150 of his book—the Tiflis Bolshevik organization came out against the Transcaucasian Regional Committee of the R.S.D.L.P. which was led by the Menshevik-Liquidators . . . and called upon the Social Democratic organizations to boycott the Transcaucasian Conference being called by the Regional Committee. . . .

Again I sought the real outlines of the event in contemporary papers. In *Sotsial Demokrat* No. 32, there is a report from the Caucasus signed "Sr.," which reads:

> At the Regional Conference were present delegates from seven localities. Baku was not represented. From the group of Tiflis Bolsheviks also no one was present since it was proposed to the latter to take part only with an advisory vote—and our people completely refused. The chief and most important point was the question of Party work. A report was given which was based on the idea that the legal organization ought to work under the control and leadership of the illegal. The conference approved and accepted the report. . . . There were present Liquidators of the first water, but they hid their character. . . . In the newly elected Organization Committee was elected one Bolshevik and one who strongly vacillates between Caucasian menshevism and our position. . . .

This report is dated December 15, 1913! Still no clean and clear break!

As long as Lenin was alive—and even three years after his death—the leading Communist historian, Philip Makharadze, could write without challenge:

> In the Transcaucasian Social Democratic movement of that time [1897-1904], opportunist and revisionist tendencies were rarely encountered in general. We may even say that they did not exist at all. . . .

In the Revolutions of 1917, the Georgian Mensheviks, unlike their Russian counterparts or associates, had no misgivings about taking power locally and had sufficient following to set up an independent democratic republic with Noah Zhordania as President. In accordance with his doctrine of self-determination and his quest for desperately needed peace on his frontiers, Lenin was in favor of recognizing the Georgian Republic. So too, as it appears from his still unpublished papers, was Trotsky. (Some evidence on this point is to be found in the posthumous *Stalin,* by Leon Trotsky, Harpers, 1946, pp. 266-8, and confirmatory documents were found by the editor, Charles Malamuth, among Trotsky's papers in the Harvard Library.)

But Stalin felt otherwise, as did his bosom friend Orjonikidze. Covertly they arranged an invasion by troops of the Red Army in 1921. Zhordania's government was ousted. Thereupon Lenin sent Orjonikidze the following significant instruction:

> Gigantically important to seek an acceptable compromise for a bloc with Zhordania or Georgian Mensheviks like him, who even before the uprising were not absolutely hostile to the thought of a Soviet structure in Georgia under certain conditions. [*Collected Works,* Third Russian Edition, pp. 187-88, dated March 2, 1921.]

Two things are notable in this message: the recognition of the strength of Zhordania with the Georgian masses ("gigantically important") and the recognition of the exceptional political character of Georgian menshevism. Even in 1924, the Zhordania forces were still strong enough to stage a general uprising. Publicly, Stalin characterized it as a "comic opera uprising" but in the Politburo, he said: "All Georgia must be plowed under." Apparently poor Makharadze was not so wrong after all in the histories against which Lavrenti Beria in 1935 began thundering his anathemas.

Why we say "poor Makharadze" will appear in the next chapter.

CHAPTER TWENTY-FIVE

HOW HISTORY IS MADE

"Paper will put up with anything that is written on it."
—JOSEPH STALIN

othing in the preceding chapter should surprise us were it not for its conflict with the new Russian historiography, for it is only natural that Lenin's break with the other Iskrists at the 1903 Congress should have taken some time to penetrate into the Caucasus. And no less natural, when even Lenin's decorative key figure, Plekhanov, and his loyal Central Committee partisans deserted him, that the rank and file inside Russia should have been puzzled by the split and hesitant to take sides. Then from 1905 to 1912, the whole movement was to some degree reunified, so that in the Caucasus, where there was a powerful, orthodox, Left-Plekhanovist mass movement, not Bolshevist nor yet Menshevist in the same sense as in the rest of Russia, the little Bolshevik faction of which Stalin was a part should have continued within the general organization. All memoirs written while Lenin was alive, all Party documents and reports of pre-revolutionary days, all evidence that can stand the test of ordinary historical investigation, have had to be ignored, explained away, supplanted, suppressed, destroyed, before a new version could be established. The decisive turning points are: the year 1929, the first of Stalin's absolute rule and of that cult which required the bringing of every moment of his past into accord with his present infinite glory; the year 1935, when Lavrenti Beria, then head of the Georgian GPU or Secret Police, went to work on the streamlining of the new history; the years 1936-38, when the purges persuaded innumerable memorialists to lose or revise their memories; the year 1938, when Stalin himself took over the task of writing history in the originally anonymous official *History of the Communist Party of the Soviet Union,* which now forms Volume XV of Stalin's *Collected Works;* and the year 1946, when those *Collected Works* began to appear with biographical and other notes under Stalin's own supervision.

What this has meant in human terms can be seen by following the fate of Stalin's old friend, Abel Enukidze. Enukidze was one of the best of that corps of second-string leaders recruited from the working class, which made up the most dependable strength of Lenin's party. Unlike the intellectuals who followed him, these professional revolutionaries from the working class essayed little independent thinking, vacillated less, more seldom questioned or broke with him. They found the meaning of their lives in carrying out the orders of the machine. A proletarianized son of peasants, two years older than Djugashvili, Enukidze early left Georgia for Central Russia, where he learned a skilled trade and got his first training in Marxism. Deported from Central Russia in 1897, he entered the railway shops in Tiflis. In April and September, 1902, he began an endless round of arrests and escapes interspersed with brief periods of underground work. He escaped from Siberia in 1903, spent a long period living literally underground and working in the sub-cellar printing plant in Baku from 1903 to 1906. His record then continues: arrest 1907, escape; arrest 1908, deportation to Archangel, escape; arrest 1910, escape; arrest 1911, escape; arrest 1914, deportation to Turukhansk whence he was drafted into the Army. In 1917 he appeared at the First Congress of Soviets as a soldier delegate, reached high positions in the Soviet Government and became a member of the Central Committee of the Communist Party. So close was this solid, dependable Georgian to Stalin that in 1929, on the occasion of the latter's fiftieth birthday, he was one of four friends considered intimate enough to contribute to a symposium called *The Life of Stalin.* The other three were Orjonikidze, Voroshilov, and Kaganovich, which last was later to become Stalin's brother-in-law and chief industrial trouble-shooter.

Nineteen twenty-nine was the year of the first great glorification of Stalin and the first attempt to bring every moment of his past into accord with his present glory. Enukidze's contribution was an effort to link Stalin's name with the Baku underground printing plant, with which, as Krassin's and Enukidze's earlier memoirs had amply demonstrated, Stalin had not had the slightest connection. That celebrated printing plant had been discussed in innumerable memoirs in 1923; whole books had been published concerning it and everybody connected with it. Not a single memoir so much as mentioned the name of Stalin! Enukidze was handicapped by too much knowledge of the past and too much respect for facts to do a job such as Beria would attempt a few years later. Enukidze's efforts to enlarge Stalin's past were therefore strangely destined to contribute to his downfall. His fateful contribution began:

> Today Stalin is fifty years old. How quickly time flies! I see quite clearly before me the young Soso Djugashvili at Tiflis, where I had my first business interview with him . . . Vladimir Ketskhoveli was organizing a small illegal printing press at Baku. He wanted two reliable compositors and type for them. The then existing Tiflis Committee of the R.S.D.L.P. was prepared to give all this on condition that all publications and the whole work of the Baku printing press . . . be subjected to the control of the Tiflis Committee. . . . Ketskhoveli sent me for the second time to Tiflis for the type and compositors. "Try and find Soso Djugashvili, he's a good chap, tell him everything and he'll help." After a short conversation with Soso I obtained everything. . . .

This obliging invention contained one fatal implication: either Djugashvili was not a member of the Tiflis Committee, or, being a member, did not control and head it, or else, far from "instructing" Ketskhoveli to set up the Baku plant, opposed him when he learned of the latter's initiative, even withholding support in an effort to get control. All the voluminous literature on the plant published in 1923, while Lenin and most of the veteran participants were still alive, makes clear that Tiflis had no control over Baku at the time, that Ketskhoveli did indeed start the plant on his own initiative, did meet jealousy from Tiflis, and that eventually, with the support of Krassin, the plant came to service not only all of Transcaucasia but all of Russia.

However, Lavrenti Beria, as Stalin's agent and inquisitor, wanted to paint another picture. According to this picture, the Caucasian organizations were born fully centralized: Batum and Baku had no organizations and did nothing except when Tiflis ordered something or sent someone there. Enukidze's standing declined steadily as Beria forced him to explain away his own

earlier memoirs. The process is pitiful but worth following for
the indirect light it throws on Stalin's past, on its revision, and
on the major event in Stalin's subsequent life, the great purge
of the later thirties. Here, then, are the successive versions of the
origin and activity of the celebrated Baku printing plant. The
first version carries us back to the year 1903.

In that year, Lado (Vladimir) Ketskhoveli, the most important of all those arrested in the raids of 1902, was shot dead in
his prison cell on secret police order. In honor of the martyred
leader, the Party issued a pamphlet, containing the following
eulogy:

> Lado was the *first* to create a Georgian revolutionary litera-
> ture. He was the *first* to organize a revolutionary printing plant
> here, the *first* to sow the seeds of revolution among the Baku
> workers. . . .*

This then, is the first reference to the great printing plant. In
1923, when the Bolsheviks were celebrating the twenty-fifth anniversary of the founding of the Social Democratic Party, a
voluminous literature appeared dealing with the most notable of
all underground presses. Here is Leonid Krassin's own account:

> The most important printing plant was our press in Baku. This
> press was planned in 1901 by our Georgian comrade, Lado
> Ketskhoveli, who died prematurely. . . . Comrade Lado solved
> the problem [of a government permit to buy a press] very sim-
> ply. He issued an authorization in his name, forging the gov-
> ernor's signature . . . then got a notarized copy of the false docu-
> ment. . . . The successor to Lado in the direction of our plant was
> Tifon Timurazovich Enukidze [underground name "Semion,"
> not to be confused with Abel Enukidze]. He who at present,

---

* From *The Life and Revolutionary Activity of Lado Ketskhoveli,* Tiflis, 1903. Italics in the original. The
revolutionary paper referred to is the clandestine *Brdzola* ("Struggle"), which Ketskhoveli founded and
edited. *Kvali,* edited by Zhordania, was the legal Marxist paper. The pamphlet from which we quote
was issued by a united party prior to the split in the Caucasus and therefore expressed the opinion of
both future Bolsheviks and Mensheviks. In his "Biographical Chronological Data" to Vol. I of his
Collected Works Stalin now writes: "Sept. 1901. In Baku appears No. 1 of the illegal paper *Brdzola,*
founded on the initiative of I. V. Stalin." Here, however, Stalin makes no claim to having founded the
Baku printing plant in 1901 but merely to having organized a lesser plant in Batum in January, 1902.

1923, is the director of our plant for printing paper money. . . .
Semion installed the press in the Tartar quarter, so well hidden
that even if the entire personnel, with A. S. (Abel) Enukidze at
the head, had been arrested, the printing plant would have been
safe. . . . In 1904 Comrade Semion handed all the affairs of Baku
over to A. S. Enukidze and went to Moscow. . . .

If we turn to Abel Enukidze's memoir on the printing plant,
published the same year as Krassin's, and collate it with the
statements of others who worked in the plant, we learn many
additional details. Ketskhoveli had first run a legal print shop.
When he decided to devote himself fully to underground printing, he got two hundred rubles from his wealthy, conservative
brother, on the pretext that he was going to give up revolutionary activities and needed the money to aid him in establishing
a "respectable" career. From various sources in Tiflis he collected an additional hundred rubles. Krassin got together eight
hundred rubles from wealthy liberals and finally even a loan of
two thousand rubles from the municipality of Baku, at the head
of which was the old Narodnik, A. I. Novikov. Under Krassin's
financial tutelage the plant expanded until it covered a vast area
underground and contained a cutting machine, type in several
languages, presses, binders, even a casting machine for using
stereotype mats. Krassin personally designed a disappearing
trapdoor. In this steadily enlarging plant underneath the houses
of Tartar Baku, first two, then five, then seven selfless printers
worked and lived together like friars in a cloister. They worked
ten hours a day, and in emergencies, hours without limit. The
plant was without heat or ventilation; windows leading to the
street were sealed with brick and mortar. To avoid notice, no
one ever emerged during the day. At night they took turns going
up for air for three-hour periods. All got the same food; each
received twenty-five rubles a month; they read and discussed the
same books. First Ketskhoveli, then Semion, then Abel Enukidze became the contact man with the outside world.

Krassin arranged for Krupskaya to make a mat of each issue
of *Iskra* abroad, and send it to him bound in a scientific book.

From the mat they made castings. Suddenly the police were astonished to find that, despite their skill in stopping *Iskra* from being smuggled over the borders, a flood of copies was issuing northward from the Caucasus. They doubled and trebled their guards on the Persian frontier, but to no avail. The secret plant printed ten thousand copies of *Iskra;* the *Communist Manifesto;* Kautsky's *Erfurt Program* (of which one hundred copies were done on de luxe paper, one being sent to Kautsky and the others sold by the ingenious Krassin to liberal sympathizers for large donations); Parvus's *War and Revolution;* Trotsky's first 1905 pamphlet; Lenin's *What's to Be Done?* and *To the Peasant Poor;* and countless other things—over a million copies in all of leaflets, pamphlets, periodicals. "Among us," wrote Enukidze in 1923 (i.e. while Lenin and Krassin were still alive), "the Bolsheviks were in a majority but there were some Mensheviks in the plant, too. Our differences did not affect our work at all." Not until 1905, after the Bolshevik Third Congress, did it become an exclusive Bolshevik plant. At that time Krassin had ceased to be a "conciliator" and had become once more a 100 percent Bolshevik, while the Third Congress itself had adopted a decision for negotiating unity with the Mensheviks. All the memoirs of 1923 substantiate this general picture in all its circumstantial details.

As late as 1926, Volume IV of the *Big Soviet Encyclopedia* carried the following account of the Baku printing plant:

> The initiator and organizer of the Baku printing plant was Ketskhoveli. . . . In 1903 the director of the plant was T. T. Enukidze (Semion) . . . the general direction and financing was transferred to the Central Committee represented by L. B. Krassin. . . . During the time between the beginning and liquidation of the Baku printing plant, I. Bolkvadze, V. Dumbadze, S. Todria, K. Josha, I. Sturua and A. Enukidze worked in it.

But, at the beginning of 1935, Lavrenti Beria, head of the Transcaucasian GPU, went to work on the printing plant's story. His first step was to force Enukidze to write a "confession" of inaccuracy in *Pravda*. His next was to summon a Conference of Party Functionaries in the Caucasus on July 21 and 22, 1935, and deliver his two-day lecture *On the History of the Bolshevik Organizations in Transcaucasia,* later printed in Georgian, Russian, and all leading languages of the world, in various, frequently revised editions, both under the above title and under the alternative title of *Stalin's Early Writings and Activities.** The two titles are properly interchangeable for the Bolshevik organizations in Transcaucasia are reduced to emanations from the early writings and activities of Joseph Stalin.

According to Beria, the Baku plant was established by Ketskhoveli, but "on the initiative of Comrade Stalin and under the direction of the Tiflis Committee headed by Comrade Stalin." And Stalin had caused the leading group to "supply Comrade Ketskhoveli with the type, equipment and money."

Ketskhoveli, who had cozened the first two hundred rubles from his brother and secured the type and press by forging the governor's signature, was dead. So was Krassin, who had raised the major sums. But not so Abel Enukidze. Therefore the readers of *Pravda* were treated on January 16, 1935, to the public prologue of this drama, the spectacle of Enukidze's self-denunciation, the purpose of which was not to establish the outlines of the "new truth" but to discredit the old truth and himself, and muddy the waters of public memory. The performance was the more startling because he had always been looked up to as one of the most dependable of the veteran fighters, a distinguished Central Committee member, and a bosom friend of Joseph Stalin.

> Unfortunately—Enukidze now found himself obliged to write —until the present these questions have not been sufficiently and not always accurately elucidated. . . . I too must correct the errors I have admitted into the *Encyclopedia Granat* and the *Big*

* The "American" edition is issued under the imprint of the Communist publishing house, International Publishers, from sheets printed in Moscow and bound here. It bears both titles and was translated from the fourth Russian edition, which edition reveals the further workings of the process of revision of history by some significant alterations of the "truths" established in the first.

Soviet Encyclopedia. There the story of my life is told as if I had founded in Baku the Social Democratic organization. This is untrue.... The outstanding role was played by Lado Ketskhoveli, sent to Baku by the Tiflis Central Party Group made up at that time of Jibladze, Tsulukidze, Ketskhoveli, Stalin and others. ... Lenin maintained connections with the Baku Party organization through Comrade Ketskhoveli.... Along with a number of other comrades, I merely helped Ketskhoveli. Therefore, it is completely unjustified to reduce in any way the role of Comrade Ketskhoveli in the creation of the Baku Committee and in giving of a Bolshevist Iskrist face to this organization. I did relatively little work in comparison with Ketskhoveli....

This peculiar breast-beating continued through six columns of *Pravda,* making a half of one of that paper's oversized pages. The reader will note that while Enukidze is made to denounce himself as a liar and a boaster and throw doubt on all his memoirs, the account he gives is still substantially the one just quoted from the *Big Soviet Encyclopedia* and the one he gave in 1923. There is, indeed, a tendency in Enukidze to boast of his long and honorable record and perhaps to enlarge somewhat his services to the printing plant. But those who suddenly began to denounce him as a boaster were not engaged in restoring the exact outlines of that record: rather was their interest that of arrogating to Stalin the credit for initiating and directing everything that had happened in the Caucasus. Not the human weakness of boasting was Enukidze's crime, but the setting down of facts that stood in the way of the credibility of Stalin's claims.

Before Enukidze submitted his article to *Pravda,* he negotiated with Beria concerning every sentence and secured the latter's approval for its publication in the official Party organ. But for Beria that was just the beginning. Once a man is made to discredit himself by a public confession, the drama of his inexorable downfall has begun.

Six months later, when Beria got around to delivering his celebrated lecture *On the History of the Bolshevik Organizations in Transcaucasia,* the fallen leader's comparatively innocent crime of "boasting" had been transformed into:

> A. Enukidze, deliberately and with hostile intent, falsified the history of the Bolshevik organizations of Transcaucasia . . . cynically and brazenly distorted well-known historical facts, crediting himself with alleged services in the establishment of the first illegal printing shop in Baku. . . . In view of the imminent danger that these fallacies and distortions of his would be exposed, A. Enukidze was obliged to admit these "mistakes" in the columns of *Pravda.* . . .

Next Beria had the compositor V. Tsuladze (who, incidentally, is not so much as mentioned in the earlier memoirs as having worked in the plant) make the following declaration:

> During its entire period of existence, no one worked in the printing shop besides Comrade Ketskhoveli, myself, and one other compositor.

Thus Enukidze's very participation, vouched for by Krassin, is officially effaced, although it thereby becomes obvious that Tsuladze's "memory" is false, since it reduces the total number of workers in the great plant to only three (one mysteriously nameless), and eliminates all but one of the names which figure in Krassin's account and that of every other participant.

Less than three years later, when the Fourth Edition of Beria's fateful lecture appeared, the sentence on Enukidze bore a new note. "A. Enukidze," it read, "since exposed as a mortal enemy of the people . . ." "Mortal" indeed, for by that time he lay dead with a GPU bullet in the base of his brain.

The text of this Fourth Edition, the one chosen for translation into all the major tongues of the civilized world, bristles with such ominous sentences. On page 9 is still repeated the warning to Philip Makharadze, which we quoted in Chapter XXII. It is repeated without the awful footnote, which means that at that moment the seventy-year-old Georgian historian

and one-time Communist Chairman of the first Provisional
Council of Commissars of the new-formed Georgian Soviet
Republic, was still alive. But how much more fearful it sounds
now when we read the words, "so far Comrade Makharadze
has not taken the trouble to revise his works and correct the
mistakes and distortions they contain"! For now we must read
them in the context of such footnotes as "A. Enukidze, since exposed as a mortal enemy of the people" (p. 35). So, on page
155 we read:

> In their articles and reminiscences T. Zhgenti, B. Bibi-
> neishvili and others [!] maintained silence about the great his-
> torical significance of the struggle of the Transcaucasian Bol-
> sheviks against the Mensheviks . . . under the leadership of
> Comrades Stalin, Orjonikidze and Spandaryan. . . . Is it not
> clear that Zhgenti and Bibineishvili slandered the Bolsheviks of
> Georgia and unceremoniously falsified and distorted the history
> of our Party?

Once more there is a footnote: "In 1937, B. Bibineishvili was
exposed as an enemy of the people."

On page 168, Makharadze's name is brought in again, this
time not to be charged with "distorting historical fact dishon-
estly," but as one of a group of "national deviationists" who in
1922 thought it preferable for Georgia to enter directly into the
Soviet Union as an autonomous republic, in place of entering indirectly through a Transcaucasian federation which would af-
filiate directly with the Soviet Union.

> The leading group of the Georgian national deviationists
> [says the text] included Ph. Makharadze, B. Mdivani, S. Kav-
> taradze, M. Okujava, M. Toroshelidze, and K. Tsintsadze.

And a footnote writes finis to four of the names thus grouped:

> In 1936, B. Mdivani, S. Kavtaradze, M. Toroshelidze—and
> K. Tsintsadze at an earlier date—were exposed as enemies of
> the people.

In 1907, the Koté Tsintsadze thus disposed of had been immediate director of the great expropriations carried out by Kamo. In Lenin's day he too had written memoirs which "boasted" of his role in starting the terrorist and expropriation groups in the Caucasus ("Our prominent comrades, especially Koba-Stalin, approved of my initiative"). And in Lenin's day he had been entrusted because of that past with the direction of the Tiflis Cheka (future GPU) and then of the All-Caucasian Cheka. In other words, he had been Beria's predecessor in office. But in 1931, after a faction quarrel with Stalin, he had been exiled to Siberia, where he died. Budu Mdivani and Sergei Kavtaradze, like Philip Makharadze, had been successive Chairmen of the Council of People's Commissars of Soviet Georgia. Like Lado Dumbadze, Chairman of the first Bolshevik Soviet in Tiflis, like Misha Okujava and Misha Toroshelidze, members of the Presidium of the Tiflis Soviet Congress of 1922, their memories have been silenced by the successive refutations of prison, exile and death. Only the aged Makharadze, stubbornly "refusing to correct his errors" and effectively silenced, so far as I know is still alive.

This "Georgian national deviation" referred to by Beria in his lecture of 1935 has an interesting past, and was destined to have an interesting future. In 1923, when Lenin lay paralyzed, too ill to participate in political life, he became increasingly alarmed at what Stalin and Orjonikidze, aided by the GPU Chief Dzierszinski, were cooking up against the local Georgian Communist Party, the Georgian Soviet Government and its leaders. On March 5, 1923, Lenin dictated the following note to Leon Trotsky:

Strictly Confidential. Personal.
Esteemed Comrade Trotsky:
I earnestly ask you to undertake the defense of the Georgian matter in the Party Central Committee. It is now being "prosecuted" by Stalin and Dzierszinski, so that I cannot rely on their impartiality. Indeed, quite the contrary! If you would agree to undertake its defense, I would rest easy. If for some reason you

do not agree, please return all the papers. I shall consider that a sign of your disagreement.

> With best comradely greetings,
>
> LENIN.

And the very next day, he wrote to

Comrades Mdivani, Makharadze and Others: (Copies to Comrades Trotsky and Kamenev.)
Esteemed Comrades:
    I am with you in this matter with all my heart. I am outraged by the rudeness of Orjonikidze and the connivance of Stalin and Dzierszinski. On your behalf I am now preparing notes and a speech.

> With esteem,
>
> LENIN.

As in other matters, Lenin has been censored by his "best disciple" and neither of these notes is now reprinted in the *Collected Works,* the *Selected Works,* or the *Letters* of V. I. Lenin. But their genuineness is attested to by each of Lenin's three secretaries of the period, Miss Glyasser, Miss Fotieva, and Miss Volodicheva. To the first of these he said that he "was preparing a bombshell for Stalin at the Twelfth Congress." But two days later, Lenin suffered his third stroke and was unable to attend the Congress, which took place in April. There is reference to these notes in the minutes of the Central Committee meeting of April 16, 1923, in remarks of Stalin made at that meeting, in a note of Trotsky to Stalin dated April 18, and another to the Central Committee dated April 17, and in a speech of Stalin's at the Congress itself on April 23. However, it would now be a form of suicide to so much as refer to these matters in the Soviet Union. Officially, they have no longer happened.*

The death of Tsintsadze in 1931 and of Mdivani, Kavtaradze and Toroshelidze in 1936, did not end this affair. There is

---

* The texts can be found in English in Trotsky's "Letter to the Party History Bureau," October 21, 1927, subsequently republished in *The Stalin School of Falsification,* by Leon Trotsky, Pioneer Publishers, 1937, pp. 69-70, and in Trotsky's *Stalin,* Harpers, 1939, pp. 361-62.

another note on page 178 of the same Fourth Edition of Beria's book which reads: "In 1936, R. Akhundov was exposed as an enemy of the people." Akhundov is not a Georgian but an Azerbaijanian. In 1922, Azerbaijan, too, or at least its Communist leadership, had opposed Stalin's scheme for incorporation in a Transcaucasian federation and had preferred direct entry into the Soviet Union as an Autonomous Republic. It is this crime that Stalin and Dzierszinski were "prosecuting" as alleged Georgian and Azerbaijanian "nationalism"—a prosecution which gives us an indirect insight into Stalin's conception of the famous right of national self-determination.

But the ironical climax to this list of "national deviationists" who had been "exposed as enemies of the people" is that the "crime" alleged against them in the First Edition of Beria's book was actually consummated by Stalin himself in the year after their liquidation. But GPU Chief Beria was nothing if not a flexible prosecutor. The same Fourth Edition which announces their fate comes to a conclusion on page 190 with the news that Stalin now considered "the conditions ripe for the abolition of the Transcaucasian federation and the incorporation of Georgia, Azerbaijan and Armenia into the Union of Soviet Socialist Republics in accordance with the great Stalin Constitution."

"Paper will put up with anything that is written on it," Stalin once wrote (in *Marxism and the National Question*). Need we wonder then that so valuable a historian as Lavrenti Beria should in 1938 have been promoted from Transcaucasian to all-Russian historical activities as the All-Union chief of the GPU or NKVD, now MVD? Or that, in the course of Beria's historical revision, the broken Enukidze, the broken Mdivani, and all the others, including many whose passing was not marked by so much as a footnote, should have perished with bullets in the base of their brains, sure end to all undesirable memories?

CHAPTER TWENTY-SIX

DJUGASHVILI BECOMES A DISCIPLE

And make it his mature ambition
To think no thought but ours,
To hunger, work illegally,
And be anonymous.

—W. H. AUDEN

When Djugashvili fled from Siberia in early 1904, he returned to his native Georgia. This would suggest that he was either not yet marked as a well-known figure, or had peculiar talents for acting secretively. Probably both, for we have already noticed that the Mensheviks held him responsible for the attack on the Batum jail, while the police did not. This talent for discreetly moving other actors while remaining invisible will appear many times in our story.

That he returned implies, too, that the Georgian tongue and scene were most natural for him. He had not yet sufficiently attracted the attention of the national leaders to be invited abroad for conference, training, reassignment elsewhere in Russia. Not for another seven years—a long time in the life of a revolutionist—would he undertake activities in Saint Petersburg which indicated that he had become part of the national leadership. And it would be nine years before Lenin would call him abroad for theoretical training in connection with the national question. It is probable that jealousy of those of his own generation who earlier went abroad—Trotsky, Kamenev, Zinoviev—figured in the subsequent official belittling of all those who "did not stick to the Russian underground." Actually Kamenev, for example, spent quite as much time in the underground as Stalin, a good part of it in Georgia, too. Born in 1883—four years later than Stalin and Trotsky—he graduated from a Tiflis *gymnazia,* was arrested while a student at the Moscow University, served a brief sentence, and then was deported back to Tiflis. There he taught a circle of railway workers and another of shoemakers, until the middle of 1902, when he went abroad to live near Lenin. In Paris he met Olga Bronstein, Trotsky's younger sister, whom he later married. After the Second Congress, Lenin sent him back to Georgia, where he organized the Bolshevik faction. His activities in a strike on the Transcaucasian railway caused a police search for him in January, 1904. He fled to Moscow, where he was arrested and deported once more to Tiflis in July, 1904. After the years of the 1905 revolution he went abroad again only to be sent back to

Russia by Lenin in 1913 to take charge of *Pravda*. Most of the World War, like Stalin, he spent as a deportee to Siberia. Such comings and goings were natural events in the life of all professional revolutionaries.

A more serious target of Stalin's envy was the career of the young man of like age with himself, Leon Trotsky, for in the year 1905 this young revolutionist attained nationwide prominence as the outstanding figure in the famed Petersburg Soviet. In October, 1917, and the years succeeding until Lenin's death, the name of Trotsky was always linked with that of Lenin in inseparable union. It was largely to bury the memory of the duality Lenin-Trotsky, and substitute therefor the duality Lenin-Stalin that the peculiar revision of history was first undertaken.

Shortly after his flight from Siberia, Joseph Djugashvili set up his own home. The date of his marriage, like all aspects of his life, is cloaked in secrecy. His boyhood chum, Iremashvili, gives it as 1903, which would imply that the marriage took place while he was in prison. Others make it 1904, immediately after his escape from Siberia. Trotsky maliciously suggests that the latter date would account for his comparative inactivity in politics during 1904, owing to the counter-attractions of the first year of married life. Iremashvili, certainly not friendly but generally well informed, is most likely right.

Djugashvili's wife was a Georgian girl, Ekaterina Svanidze, sister of a comrade whom Stalin would one day make president of the Soviet Bank for Foreign Trade. But she herself was not a revolutionary. From all accounts, she appears to have been a girl of simple, domestic, peasant mentality, devoted to her husband, deeply religious, submissive, loyal, unquestioning. Trotsky construes this marriage to a religious girl as a sign of Djugashvili's indifference in matters of Marxian theory. There is perhaps some justification for this view, but we must understand the marriage in terms of Djugashvili's Caucasian origins and environment. The Georgian organization did not consist of a small and doctrinaire band of professional intellectual revolutionaries like that in Central Russia. It was already a broad mass movement, influencing great numbers and being influenced in turn by the attitudes of the masses which followed it. Moreover, there was lacking in Georgia that close comradeship between men and women and that sense of equality which was part of the tradition of the Russian parties, inherited from several generations of idealistic terrorist bands, recruited from both sexes. The Caucasus produced no Sophia Perovskaya, no Vera Figner, no Vera Zasulich, or—to select at random from the women that people these pages—no Nadezhda Krupskaya, Angelica Balabanoff, Rosa Luxemburg, or Alexandra Kollontai. Nor was it likely to, for among the mountain tribes, amidst the Mohammedan city dwellers, even among Georgian and Armenian Christians, women were subordinate creatures, kept close in the home. Few indeed were the Caucasian revolutionaries who found their mates in the course of the struggle, in underground meeting, prison or exile; few were the unions in which love and comradeship-in-struggle were inseparable.

Iremashvili has this to say on Djugashvili's relations with his wife:

> His marriage was a happy one. True, it was impossible to discover in his home that equality of the sexes which he advocated. . . . But it was not in his character to share equal rights with any other person. His marriage was a happy one because his wife, who could not measure up to him in intellect, regarded him as a demi-god. . . . Being a Georgian woman, she was brought up in the sacrosanct tradition which obliges a woman to serve . . . With all her heart she served her husband's welfare. She passed her nights in ardent prayer waiting for her Soso, who was busy at his meetings, praying that he might turn away from ideas that were displeasing to God and turn instead to a quiet home life of toil and contentment. . . . This man, so restless in spirit, could find love only in his own impoverished home. Only his wife, his child and his mother were exempt from the scorn he poured out upon all others.

The child was Yasha (Jacob) Djugashvili, born several years after their marriage. When Stalin left the Caucasus in 1911, his wife was already dead and he did not take his child with him. Jacob remained either with Stalin's mother or his mother-in-law. We hear nothing more about the boy until 1919, when Iremashvili became a teacher in a Tiflis secondary school and found Jacob Djugashvili among his pupils—not, according to the teacher, a particularly bright one. That was in Social Democratic Georgia. When it became Soviet Georgia, Stalin sent for his son and installed him in his apartment in the Kremlin. There he began to study railroad engineering. According to the frequently fanciful account of the Czech journalist Kurt Singer, "he proved himself a poor student . . . At last Stalin lost patience and ordered Yasha home from college saying: 'If you can't be an engineer, you can at least be a shoemaker.' But Yasha disobeyed [sic]. He ran away to the Caucasus, where he worked as an electrician."

In 1942, a German communiqué reported that the Wehrmacht had captured one "Jacob Djugashvili, Stalin's son." The Soviet press, usually so attentive to everything concerning the *Vozhd,* said nothing. In 1944, sources close to the Vatican gave further details:

> Jacob was a lieutenant in the Red Army when he was taken prisoner near Lesno by the Germans on July 24, 1941 . . . The Vatican has a report on the conversation between Goering and young Mr. Stalin in September 1941. . . . Goering, in his discussion with the then 24-year-old Communist, tried to impress him with Germany's military and industrial power . . . to convince him also of the superiority of Western civilization as a whole. Jacob was not only not impressed but expressed contempt for all that was non-Russian. Moscow, he tòld the astonished Nazi leader, would become the mightiest political, scientific and economic center of the world. As far as his private career was concerned, Jacob said, he saw his father rarely and had no personal privileges at all because he was the Premier's son . . . [New York *Times,* Oct. 4, 1944.]

The difficulty with this story is the age given to Jacob, 24 in 1941. Actually he was then closer to 34 than 24. On May 1, 1945, the New York *Times* carried a dispatch from Dachau,

Germany, concerning the liberation of 32,000 inmates by American troops. "These were said to have included Premier Stalin's son, Jacob, who was captured in 1941." Again no comment in the Russian press. A possible explanation of the discrepancy in age lies in the existence of yet a third son, illegitimate, by a Siberian peasant woman of Turukhansk, where Stalin spent a term in exile. According to Anton Ciliga, Yugoslav Communist deported to Turukhansk by Stalin, he met such a son there who boasted of his paternity and was 20 in 1935. (A. Ciliga: *Siberie*. Plon, 1950, p. 287.)

On June 30, 1945, Edgar Snow wrote in the *Saturday Evening Post*:

> His one daughter, Svetlana, an attractive girl of 18, is perhaps closer to him than anyone else. . . . Stalin used to call her his "housekeeper," but recently she married and went to live elsewhere. . . . Stalin also had two sons, both in the Red Army. The elder, Jacob, by Stalin's divorced [*sic*] wife, fell into the hands of the Nazis early in the war, and is reported as having committed suicide in a prison camp near Berlin. The other son, Vasili, by Stalin's second wife, is a bomber pilot and has been awarded the Order of the Red Banner and the Order of Suvorov, Second Class.

On Vasili, son of Stalin's second marriage in 1919 to the young Nadya Allilueva (also the mother of Svetlana), the Russian press has not been so reticent. On October 9, 1944, as Colonel Vasili Yosifovich Stalin, he was given honorable mention along with a number of other officers, in his father's Order of the Day. On May 30, 1945, Colonel Stalin was one of seventy-six officers awarded the Order of Suvorov, Second Class. On March 2, 1946, Generalissimo Joseph Stalin signed a decree promoting his son Vasili from colonel to major general. Then it was recorded that he had won the Order of the Red Banner in 1942 and that of Suvorov in 1945 for "skilled and courageous leadership." In May 1948, *Ogonek* released a picture of "Major General Vasili Stalin, son of Premier Stalin, at the controls of his plane in command of the air section of the May Day parade in Moscow." More honors have been heaped on him since.

It is worth noting that Jacob, son of the simple Georgian peasant woman Svanidze, bears the name Djugashvili, while the son of the Party comrade, Allilueva, bears the proud name Vasili Yosifovich Stalin (Basil, Son of Josif Stalin). Jacob, and the son Ciliga found in Siberia, seem less eager to be known as sons of Russia's ruler, while the tight silence of the Soviet press on their very existence suggests that their father has been no more anxious to be known as the sire of these sons. If Vasili has received a big share of publicity, the dictator's daughter, Svetlana, has not. Even when she married, there was no public announcement, and the very name of Svetlana's husband has been preserved a state secret.

During the course of the years 1905 and 1906, the boyhood friends Soso Djugashvili and Soso Iremashvili drifted apart as the Caucasus began belatedly to feel the rift between Bolsheviks and Mensheviks. It is no doubt to this period that the *Little Soviet Encyclopedia's* remark under "Stalin" begins to have application: "For the Mensheviks, Stalin was the most hated of all Caucasian Bolsheviks."

This is confirmed by Iremashvili:

> The brunt of his struggle was henceforth directed against us, his former friends. He attacked us at every meeting and discussed matters in the most savage and unscrupulous manner, trying to sow poison and hatred against us everywhere. He would have liked to root us out with fire and sword. . . . But the overwhelming majority of Georgian Marxists remained with us. That only angered and enraged him the more.

About the time these debates were getting fully under way, Djugashvili lost his beloved wife Ekaterina. The already alienated Iremashvili went to her funeral for old friendship's sake. He gives this account of the occasion:

> He was very downcast, yet he met me in a friendly manner as of old. This hard man's pallid face reflected the heartfelt anguish

caused by the death of his faithful companion. . . . When the modest procession came to the cemetery gate, Koba firmly pressed my hand, pointed to the coffin and said: "Soso, this creature softened my stony heart. She is dead and with her have died my last warm feelings for all human beings." He placed his right hand over his heart: "It is all so desolate here inside, so unutterably desolate!" . . .

From the day he buried his wife, he indeed lost the last vestige of human feeling. His heart filled with the unutterably malicious hatred which his cruel father had already begun to engender in him while he was still a child. . . . Ruthless with himself, he became ruthless with all people. . . .

It was while Djugashvili was in prison awaiting deportation to Siberia that the unexpected split had occurred at the Congress called to form a unified party. Lenin, as we already know, soon proposed a "Third Congress" to settle the crisis arising from the Second. By the time Djugashvili resumed activity in the Caucasus in 1904, Lenin's movement to force a Third Congress was already in full swing. In November, 1904, that is, ten or eleven months after Djugashvili's return from Siberia, the Bolsheviks succeeded for the first time in setting up a faction in Georgia, and held their First Conference at Tiflis. To this conference came fifteen delegates from four local Caucasian organizations in Tiflis, Batum, Baku and Kutais. They met under the chairmanship of Leo Kamenev, whom Lenin had dispatched to Transcaucasia to build his faction. Startling as the fact may seem if we permit ourselves to be persuaded by the official version of Stalin's early and primeval prominence, Djugashvili was not even a delegate. Either he was not yet prominent enough to be one of the first fifteen Caucasian Bolsheviks, or in November, 1904, he had not yet made up his mind between Lenin and the Mensheviks.

Naturally, present-day hagiography can accept neither of the two possible explanations. Hence the Marx-Engels-Lenin Institute biography of Stalin discreetly ignores this conference, though it gave birth to Georgian bolshevism. Beria, however, in his *History of the Bolshevik Organizations in Transcaucasia,* finds it impossible to ignore it. He gives the number of delegates, reports on the election of a leading committee to continue the struggle, but, in a book peppered with names of great and small, carefully avoids giving the names of the delegates or those elected to the committee. Yaroslavsky's *Landmarks in the Life of Stalin,* published yet a few years later, when the purges had enormously furthered the science of rewriting the past and revising one's memories, brazenly states that the First Conference was "presided over by Stalin"!

Actually, a complete list of delegates is available in older Party histories and records and in various memoirs by participants in the Conference, written while Lenin was still alive. In no case is Stalin's name among them. Moreover, all memoirs written in Lenin's day, or indeed until the purges had finished with most of the participants, specifically declare that Kamenev presided. Not only did Djugashvili fail to attend the Conference or to get elected on the leading committee it set up, but he was not chosen, either, as a delegate from the Caucasian region to the national faction leadership which Lenin was then constituting under the name of "Bureau of the Committees of the Majority." The Caucasian Conference chose Kamenev to represent it on this Bureau. There were seventeen in all, constituting Lenin's general staff in 1904. Djugashvili was not among them. Yet, according to the Marx-Engels-Lenin Institute biography, Stalin was already "Lenin's faithful lieutenant in this campaign for the Third Congress, the leader of the Transcaucasian Bolsheviks." And at the same time, according to the same work, he was "the virtual director" of the Caucasian Federal Committee of the Russian Social Democratic Party, which committee was under the control of the Mensheviks whom Lenin was fighting! Obviously, the two claims contradict each other, while there is ample evidence that both are wide of the truth.

Finally, when the Caucasian Bolsheviks came to choose their delegates to the Third Congress itself, they selected Kamenev,

Tskhakaya, Japaridze, and Nevsky. (According to some accounts the fourth man was not Nevsky but Lehmann.) But once more, the name of Djugashvili is missing!

All party histories and memoirs written while Lenin was alive, or indeed throughout the twenties, give the above four names, differing only as to whether the fourth man was Lehmann or Nevsky. All histories written in the first half of the thirties, as weapons in Stalin's faction war on his associates, are purposely evasive on the makeup of the Transcaucasian Delegation to the Third Congress. Thus Popov's *History* (Moscow, 1934) gives a list of leading members of the Third Congress, including among them the Caucasian representatives Tskhakaya, Kamenev, and an unnamed "Baku Worker." Knorin's history (Moscow, 1935), though it gives names of delegates for all other congresses, avoids a list for this one. Stalin's own history (Moscow, 1938) omits any list of delegations. Nor does a single memoir written while Lenin was alive give Stalin the remotest connection with the organization of the Third Congress, with the fight for its convocation, with its actual guidance, or the Central Committee of Bolsheviks elected by it. Even as late as 1935—when Beria was already getting busy with his major operation on men's memories—the faithful Piatnitsky, writing on the occasion of the thirtieth anniversary of the Third Congress, had not one word to say of Stalin. None of these omissions would appear in the least remarkable, were it not for the effort, begun with the purges, to make it appear that from the beginning Stalin was the leading Bolshevik in the Caucasus and one of the two nationwide leaders of bolshevism. To make that legend stick, the mighty Russian state would have to undertake one of the greatest book-burning operations in all history, not only burning, as the Nazis did, the works of opponents but, with no less zeal, all the records of their party published prior to Stalin's own history. Not only the writings of Lenin, but even Stalin's, have been censored wherever they might contradict the present official tale. To give only one example:

On December 31, 1910, Stalin wrote a letter from his then exile in Solvychegodsk to Paris. It has been published many times in Russia, and always, until the purges, it began: "Comrade Semeon! Yesterday I received from a comrade your letter. First of all, warmest greetings to Lenin, Kamenev and the others . . ."

But after the purge of Kamenev, the letter was quoted by Beria, and by Stalin himself in his *History,* without any salutation whatsoever. Semeon's name disappeared along with Lenin's and Kamenev's and the letter began with the second paragraph. Finally, in 1946, the letter was published once more "in full" (in Stalin's *Collected Works,* Russian Edition, Vol. II, p. 209) but it now read: "Comrade Semeon! . . . First of all, warmest greetings to Lenin and the others . . ."

Thus the effort is made to cover the fact that Leo Kamenev was in 1910 Lenin's closest associate in Paris, and, because of his prior leadership of the Bolsheviks in the Caucasus, the most important Bolshevik that Stalin knew intimately.

Before we leave the subject of the Third Congress, we should note that Krupskaya's *Memories of Lenin* throws an ironic sidelight on the state of organization of the Caucasian Bolsheviks at the time it was held:

> Four delegates came from the Caucasus—she writes—but there were but three mandates. Vladimir Ilyich inquired as to which of the four were entitled to the three mandates. "Who received the majority of the votes?"
>
> Mikha [Tskhakaya] replied in consternation: "Why, do you think we put things to a vote in the Caucasus? We decide all matters in a comradely way. They sent four of us, and it's not important how many mandates there are."

During 1946 Stalin began to publish his *Collected Works.* From a source which must remain nameless I learned that Beria directed the preliminary gathering of the material, and put it into his chief's hands as early as 1935. In that year, Beria himself used the early writings which now appear in the first two volumes of Stalin's *Collected Works* for his own *Stalin's Early*

Writings and Activities. Stalin hesitated from 1935 to 1946 before he released the first two volumes of his early writings! Volume III, however, represented no problem since it contains pretty largely only material much published and republished before. The suspicion is inescapable that the long delay between Beria's editing and Stalin's releasing of the early work is due to hesitation on Stalin's part as to which of his early writings should, and which should not, see the light of day in permanent form. When it finally appeared it contained three pieces (originally unsigned) dated 1901 and then nothing until late in 1904. Moreover, the articles dated 1901 present several problems of content and style to the biographer.

The initial piece is an anonymous Editorial Statement of Policy for the first issue of the underground Georgian paper, *Brdzola* ("Struggle"), dated September, 1901. As we have already seen, it was Lado Ketskhoveli, two or three years older than Djugashvili, who founded the underground printing plant and paper for which Stalin's biographers now assign him the credit of "initiator, inspirer and director." There is, of course, nothing inherently impossible in the claim that Djugashvili and not Ketskhoveli wrote the editorial statement for the first issue. The ideas are manifestly drawn from *Iskra* and the style is quite different from that of Stalin's later, signed writings. The style may conceivably be explained by the fact that it was a general editorial statement, and may have been gone over by several people.

But when we come to the second article in the *Collected Works,* the problems of both style and content become more complicated. It is a longish article, written, judging from internal evidence, by a rather soft-spoken, humane person who is much influenced by Western Europe and thinks very highly—too highly—of the Russian student movement and quite disparagingly of strikes in Russia whether as economic or political weapons. None of the easily identifiable characteristics of Stalin's style or thought, as manifested in all his signed articles, is to be found here. There is none of the catechism type of self-answering questions, no mixed figures of speech such as we will find in all Stalin's efforts to attain pathos in print. The style is more conventional, smoother, more lyrical, more bookish, less combative, less energetic, lacking in rudeness toward opponent classes or viewpoints. The phraseology and ideas are rather Plekhanovist than Leninist. In it the student body is assigned an excessively important role and represented as "entering the social movement at the present time almost as the conductor, the vanguard . . . To the students we ought to be grateful for the lesson they have taught us: they have shown what a great significance is possessed by the political street demonstration in the revolutionary struggle." Follows an exaltation of street demonstrations and a disparagement of strikes:

> In the present political conditions an economic struggle [strikes] cannot give anything essential. Strikes even in free countries are two-edged weapons. Even there, despite the fact that the workers have the means of struggle—political freedom, strong unions, rich treasuries—strikes often end in defeat. . . . But with us, where strikes are a crime bringing arrest, suppressed by armed force, where all unions are forbidden—here strikes have only the significance of a *protest*. As a protest, demonstrations are a much stronger weapon. . . . The organization of general strikes is very difficult even in Western Europe but with us it is altogether impossible. But it is in the street demonstration that the workers at once unite their forces. . . . [Stalin: *Collected Works*, First Russian Edition, p. 29.]

This article is supposed to have been written by Stalin at the very moment when he is likewise supposed to have been organizing the Mantashev and Rothschild factory strikes! Its attitude toward strikes is so different from that of Stalin and the Bolsheviks generally that either someone else wrote the article "The Russian Social Democracy and its Immediate Tasks," here printed in his *Collected Works,* or in December, 1901, the youthful Djugashvili was far from being a Leninist and a strike leader. Whichever horn of the dilemma the reader prefers, the fact remains that after 1901 Stalin wrote nothing more or did not choose to reproduce anything written between 1901 and the end of 1904. Significantly, Beria in his *Stalin's Early Writings and Activities* actually quotes from the first of the two articles cited above but does not claim it as having been written by Stalin! In fact, the implication is that it was written by Ketskhoveli (see Beria, English-language edition, pp. 34-37).

During the course of the year 1905 we gradually move onto firmer ground. Now we have definite records showing that Djugashvili has joined the Bolshevik faction and become one of its outstanding propagandists in the Caucasus. By the end of 1905 he rates high enough to be one of the delegates to the Bolshevik Conference at Tammerfors. Whereas all earlier evidence is equivocal and vanishes into thin air as soon as we apply ordinary methods of historical verification, now we can find documents, articles, facts, which are clear in their significance and incontrovertible. In 1906 and 1907 Djugashvili becomes a fairly frequent and consistent expounder of Lenin's Doctrines in Georgian in polemical articles signed at first I. (Iosif) Bibineishvili, and then with such names as Koba, Ko. K., K.Ko, Comrade K., K. Kato, Ivanovich, Koba Ivanovich. In 1908 he begins to experiment with the names K. Stefin, K.S. and K. St., and, after ringing the changes on K. Solin and K. Salin, in 1913 signs the name K. Stalin to his article on "Marxism and the National Question." This represented a combination of the name Koba, under which he became known on a Georgian scale, and the name Stalin ("Man of Steel") which was destined to become world-famous.

During the years 1905-07 there is also manifest a ripening in knowledge, abilities and self-confidence in the still young (twenty-six to twenty-eight) Djugashvili. A number of causes contributed to this. One was the death or departure of those who had been his superiors in experience and capacity: Ketskhoveli was assassinated in 1903; Tsulukidze died of tuberculosis in 1905; Kurnatovsky was exiled to Siberia; Krassin and

Nogin, reconciled with Lenin, worked in 1905 in Central Russia, as did Kamenev and the two Enukidzes; Zhordania returned to Geneva. Djugashvili's path was further cleared by the fact that most prominent Georgian leaders now aligned themselves definitely with menshevism, including all three delegates to the Second Congress (Topuridze, Zurabov and Knunyantz), and such future leaders of the Georgian masses as Tseretelli and Chkheidze. Nascent Transcaucasian bolshevism had to develop a new leadership in the persons of Tskhakaya, Nevsky and Japaridze (the three delegates to the Third or Bolshevik Congress of 1905) and the already well-known Shaumyan and Makharadze. Among these the young Koba Djugashvili was perhaps still not the first, but certainly no longer an obscure figure.

It is from the year 1905 that are to be dated the first articles with a definite Stalinist style. Thenceforward, signed or unsigned, there is no mistaking their authorship, or their Bolshevik intention. Except for occasional leaflets, they are invariably exegetical, taking some proposition of Lenin's and translating and expounding it in Georgian. Their style tends to quasi-religious characteristics: ". . . only the proletariat can lead us to the Promised Land . . ."; "the Government has trampled on and mocked our human dignity, our Holy of Holies . . . ." They make frequent use of the catechetical method: dogmatic questions and answers. They are full of such expressions as: *kak izvestno* ("as is known"); *vsem izvestno* ("it is known to all"); *kak yasno* ("as is clear"), etc., precisely at those critical points where, for all but the already convinced, some solid proof is necessary. Since Stalin has become the undisputed leader of his land, this characteristic has become so widespread in his agents that there is not a diplomat of top rank from England and the United States who has not known moments of speechless fury when Molotov or Gromyko or Vishinsky or Manuilsky trots out a *kak izvestno* ("as is well known") as a surrogate "proof" of the most controversial assertions.

As "style is the man," it might be well to examine this question a little more closely. On January 19, 1905, there was issued in Georgian a leaflet, anonymous save for the words "Union Committee," with the title: *Workers of the Caucasus, It Is Time for Revenge!* The style is undoubtedly Stalin's. Beria, in an effort to make it appear that this January leaflet was Stalin's contribution to the leadership of the 1905 Revolution, a call for an armed insurrection in response to the events of "Bloody Sunday," deliberately left the leaflet undated (Beria, pp. 62-64). Trotsky, in his posthumous *Stalin,* relying on Beria, commits a serious injustice by contrasting Lenin's strong indignation at the massacre of January 22 ("make way for the anger and hatred . . .") with Stalin's bureaucratic cold calculation ("Rally round the Party committees . . . only the Party committees can lead us . . . to the Promised Land"). But an examination of the leaflet reveals that it was written before the events of Bloody Sunday and printed a day before the massacre of the people marching to the Winter Palace. Its main fire is directed not so much against tsarism as against "the liberals." It accuses them of "extending a helping hand to the Tsar . . . soliciting alms from him . . ."

> Yes, gentlemen—his leaflet continues—your efforts are in vain! The Russian revolution is inevitable, and it is just as inevitable as the sunrise! Can you stop the sun from rising? That is the question! The chief force of this revolution is the urban and rural proletariat, whose standard bearer is the Social Democratic Labor Party, and not you, Messrs. Liberals! Why do you forget this obvious "trifle"? . . .

> Russia is a loaded gun at full cock, liable to go off at the slightest concussion. Yes, comrades, the time is not far off when the revolution will hoist sail and drive the vile throne of the despicable Tsar off the face of the earth! . . . Let us join hands and *rally round the Party committees.* We must not forget for a moment that *only the Party committees can lead us as we should be led, only they* will light our way to the "Promised Land" called the socialist world! The Party which has opened our eyes and shown us our enemies, which has organized us into a

formidable army ... which has never deserted us in joy or sorrow and which has always marched in front of us ... And it will continue to lead us, *only it!* A constituent assembly, elected by universal, equal, direct and secret suffrage, is what we must fight for now! ...*

The mixed figures concerning the liberals whose outstretched hand simultaneously sustains the tottering throne and begs for alms, concerning the revolution that is a gun at full cock, hoisting sail and driving the vile throne from the face of the earth, are typical of the ornamentation that bedizens Stalin's writings wherever feeling and eloquence seem called for—as if there were a lack of real depth of feeling, or some barrier denying expression to it. Whenever Stalin attempts to express any other emotion than personal anger, this hollow rhetoric appears. The rhetorical question which reduces the political issue between liberals and socialists to "Can you stop the sun from rising? That is the question!" is typical too.

And the words in italics in the original (*"rally round the Party committees ... only the committees can lead us ... only it ..."*) are no less typical. They give us a key to Djugashvili's career and to the things that attracted him to Lenin. Of the old *Iskra* leadership, Lenin was the organization man *par excellence,* the one who insisted on the Party as leader rather than servant of the labor movement, on organization as the key to victory and the brake against opportunism, on control of the Party by the Central Committee and of the masses by the Party.

Did these ideas mean the same thing to master and disciple? Many fateful issues in our story will turn about that problem. For the moment, it is sufficient for us to note that when Lenin was taken by surprise by the initiative displayed by the masses themselves in 1905, he began to belabor his own followers for trying to force that great initiative into the constricting molds of the old Party committees and the underground, narrow-circle and close-control Party structure.

* Beria: *Stalin's Early Writings and Activities.* English language edition, p. 63; Stalin: *Collected Works,* Vol. I, pp. 74-80; all italics are in the original.

This is wartime—he reminded his committeemen followers in letter after letter from his 1905 exile—Push the usual hierarchical committee follies entirely into the background . . . Else you will perish with the honors of *Komitetchiki* ["committeemen" or "committeeites"], perish with the official seal imprinted upon you. . . .

And again in the stormy year 1917 he would have to war against his routine-incrusted lieutenants with their fetishistic cult of the Party organization. He would remind them of 1905 and of "those 'Old Bolsheviks' who have more than once played a melancholy part in the history of our Party by repeating mechanically a formula which they have learned by heart, instead of studying the special character of the new and living reality . . ."

"Grau, teurer Freund, ist alle Theorie, und gruen des Lebens goldner Baum," he would cite them from Mephistopheles. That was the strength of Lenin as revolutionist that, despite his passionate and dogmatic attachment to centralized organization and its rigid control of the masses, he could thrust both into the background whenever the foaming, tumbling, creative and uncontainable life of the million-headed mass in motion made their doctrinaire application dangerous to the Party's life.

One searches in vain through Stalin's writings of 1905 or 1917, indeed through all his writings of a lifetime, for any analogous flexibility in his attitude toward his master's organization dogmas. In fact, Stalin's main programmatic writings of 1905—their total volume is not large—are nothing more than exegesis of quotations from Lenin's writings of the prerevolution years on the need for the Social Democratic Party to control and lead the masses and "import socialist consciousness into the spontaneous labor movement."

If Stalin was attracted to Lenin as the creator and glorifier of a strong centralized party machine, it was this aspect of "Leninism" which alienated Trotsky for many years. He did not scorn to use the machine dictatorially once he was in the Kremlin at Lenin's side, but his distaste, or incapacity, for building himself a party organization was to cost him dear in the struggle with his great opponent after Lenin's death. Perhaps in some obscure way Trotsky's Jewish heritage as a descendant of "the People of the Book" and, more directly, his Marxist heritage as a disciple of the greatest sociological thinker of modern times; his literary heritage as a lover of the Russian tongue and master of the written word; his revolutionary heritage as the pre-eminent tribune of the people able by flaming eloquence to stir the masses and lift them outside their petty, personal concerns to the level of action in the arena of history—all these combined to make him set the highest possible value upon ideas, originality and clarity in their formulation, exactness in their expression, eloquence in writing and in speech, contagious personal magnetism and attractive force. Deceived by Stalin's inept and awkward writing and lackluster public speech, Trotsky, insofar as he was compelled to notice his rival at all, set him down as "a gray and colorless mediocrity." As writer, as orator, as theoretician, Stalin was and remains a mediocrity. But first as a subordinate part in Lenin's machine, then as an appropriator and transformer and enlarger of that machine, Stalin has few equals. Nineteen five and nineteen seventeen, the heroic years when the machine was unable to contain the flood of overflowing life, would bring Trotsky to the fore as the flaming tribune of the people, would show Lenin's ability to rise above the confining structure of his dogmas, and would relegate Stalin, the machine-man by antonomasy, to the background. But no people can live forever at fever heat and when that day was over and Lenin was dead, the devoted machine-man's day would come.

I do not mean to imply that only Djugashvili thus absorbed the organizational fetishism and Leninist formulae, against which Lenin himself had to fight in 1905 and 1917. Nor to imply that the indignant letters of Lenin's in 1905 were addressed principally, or at all, to Djugashvili, of whose very existence he was as yet scarcely aware. It was this side of Lenin, which Vladimir Ilyich himself could slough off at need, that attracted to him all the "hard" professional revolutionaries who, by natural selection, came to make up the bulk of his permanent officer staff. Had Djugashvili been alone in this regard, it would be impossible to explain how he could one day assume the driver's seat when Death had compelled Lenin to vacate it.

> He was the *komitetchik par excellence*—Trotsky wrote in his posthumous *Stalin*—Lacking the personal qualifications for influencing the masses directly, he clung with redoubled tenacity to the political machine. The axis of his universe was his Committee—the Tiflis, the Baku, the Caucasian, before it became the Central Committee. In time his blind loyalty to the Party machine was to develop with extraordinary strength; the committeeman became the super-machine-man, the General Secretary, the very personification of the bureaucracy, its peerless leader . . .

True enough. And Trotsky might seem to have the right to be critical, since he alone of the Bolshevik leaders who made the October (1917) Revolution had held out for fourteen years against Lenin's machine and been critical of it. Had he not written with Cassandra-like prevision the warning with which we are already familiar:

> The organization of the Party will take the place of the Party; the Central Committee will take the place of the organization; and finally, the dictator will take the place of the Central Committee?

Was ever prophecy more fatefully fulfilled by history? And yet, as we read Trotsky's strictures on the *komitetchik par excellence* based on Stalin's sparse and dreary writings of the memorable year 1905, we are reminded that Trotsky too came to accept Lenin's machine in 1917. Once he had swallowed Lenin's conception of the machine, was it not increasingly inevitable that that machine in turn might swallow him, verifying with himself as object lesson all his earlier forebodings? Yet even to the day when an agent of that machine buried an Alpine pick in the back of his skull, his criticism would never again be of the machine as such, but only of Stalin's use or abuse of it. In the unfinished life of Stalin thus terminated by death, Trotsky would approach perilously close to a new fundamental critique of the Leninist conception of organization, then shy off, squidlike in a flood of his own ink:

> It is rather tempting—he says at one point—to draw the inference that future Stalinism was already rooted in Bolshevik centralism, or more sweepingly, in the underground hierarchy of professional revolutionaries . . .

Rather tempting—but he refuses to be tempted. Throughout that pathetically unfinished last book of his, nowhere does he dare to subject Lenin's machine to genuine reexamination, that machine which, in Trotsky's words, "was not created by Stalin but created him," which lent itself so easily to "the usurpation of the driver's seat" by the absolute, personal dictator. For, once having accepted Lenin's machine and organization doctrine, Trotsky thenceforth reduced himself from the role of a genuine critic of "Stalinism" to that of a pretender denouncing a usurper.

one plot in the book of his skull, his criticism would never again be of the machine example but only of finite size of
some of it. In the unfinished life of Strato they remained by death. Fantasy would approach perilously close to the line
beyond which lies only the rational conception of extinction in the shape of equilibrium a . . . flood of his . . . with his . . .

in rather different . . . the Hungarian meaning. To say the least is that Imre Hermann was already rooted in biology something strange. symptoms in the . . . a . . . somewhat . . . of . . . of protection. Devaluation . . .

Roheim implied that he refuses to be ensnared. Throughout the analytically conceived last work of his, nowhere does he question anyone? I was knowledge. a getting new, unique in little mobility, neither it receives verily as not created by some bay created him? whether it itself creativity as Thus, imputation of the drives which by the absolute personal fictions. For once having wrecked Imre's situation and deprivation of his tribal. Trough, him, too imagined himself into a people of the germinated of casting itself to that of experiences of a nourishing situations.

CHAPTER TWENTY-SEVEN

STALIN AND LENIN

Dressed in Caucasian costume, with rows of white-tipped cartridge cases, he carried some spherical object in a napkin. Every one in the restaurant left off eating . . . 'He has brought a bomb!' . . . But it turned out to be a watermelon. Kamo had brought the melon and some sugared nuts as a present for Ilyich and me. 'My aunt sent them,' he explained rather shyly. This fighting man, with his colossal courage . . . seemed at the same time an extraordinarily unsophisticated and gentle comrade. . . . Kamo often travelled between Finland and Petersburg, always going fully armed. Mother used to tie his revolvers on his back each time with particular care.

—KRUPSKAYA: "MEMORIES OF LENIN."

In December, 1905, Stalin first met Lenin, at the Tammerfors Conference. Koba does not seem to have made much of an impression on Krupskaya if we are to judge from her memoirs, published when Stalin was already ruler of Russia:

> It is hardly likely that any of the delegates to that conference could ever forget it. Among those present were Lozovsky, Baransky, and Yaroslavsky. I remember those comrades because their reports from their localities were so enthralling.

But neither does Djugashvili seem to have been much impressed by the man whose leadership he had accepted:

> I was hoping to see the mountain eagle of our Party—Stalin told the Kremlin cadets a week after Lenin's death.—I was hoping to see a great man, great not only politically but, if you will, physically, for in my imagination I pictured Lenin as a giant, stately and imposing. What, then, was my disappointment to see a most ordinary-looking man, below average in height, in no way, in literally no way, distinguishable from ordinary mortals . . .
>
> It is the accepted thing for a "great man" to come late to meetings so that the assemblage may await his appearance with bated breath; and then, just before the great man enters, the warning goes up: "Hush! Silence! He's coming!" This rite did not seem to me superfluous because it creates an impression, inspires respect. What then was my disappointment to learn that Lenin had arrived at the conference before the delegates, had settled himself somewhere in a corner and was unassumingly carrying on a conversation, a most ordinary conversation with the most ordinary delegate . . . I will not conceal from you that at that time this seemed to me to be rather a violation of certain essential rules.

During sessions of the Comintern and its Executive, and on public holiday occasions, I had many occasions to note that Stalin himself was careful not to neglect this "rite." The words tell us far more of Stalin than of the "great man" he had come to wonder at.

In the Stockholm Unity Congress of 1906, Djugashvili saw Lenin again, this time "in defeat."

I remember the Bolshevik delegates gathering together in a small group gazing at Lenin and asking advice . . . I remember Lenin saying sharply through clenched teeth: "No sniveling, comrades . . ." Hatred for sniveling intellectuals, confidence in one's own strength, confidence in victory—that is what Lenin talked to us about at that time.

Djugashvili may well have joined those who gathered around the defeated leader, but, for some reason, he did not sign the manifesto which Lenin drew up in criticism of the Stockholm Congress. Issued in the name of "Delegates Belonging to the Former Bolshevik Faction" ("former" because all groups had been "dissolved"), it bore twenty-six signatures, including Krassin, Rykov, Bubnov, Taratuta, Voroshilov, Yaroslavsky, Krupskaya, and Lenin. But Stalin's name, for reasons never explained, is missing. (The complete list may be found in the Third Russian Edition of Lenin's *Collected Works,* Vol. IX, p. 521.) Yet, the sharpest of the issues arising at the Stockholm Congress, an issue still more acute a year later in London, would bind Stalin to Lenin with bands of steel and make Vladimir Ilyich appreciate the qualities of his Caucasian adherent. It was the issue of the "exes."

At the Stockholm Congress the Bolsheviks were allowed only three members on the incoming Executive of ten. They named Krassin, Rykov, Desnitsky. At the London Congress, they won a total of fifteen members and alternates. These included Lenin, Bogdanov, Krassin, Zinoviev (a newcomer at this congress), Nogin, Rykov, Taratuta. The Bolsheviks also chose a secret faction center of seventeen. Besides those mentioned above, it included Kamenev, the Marxist historian Pokrovsky, and others of lesser interest to us. But neither on the three, the fifteen, nor the seventeen, do we find Koba-Djugashvili. Once more, the omission is surprising only if we take seriously the Beria, Yaroslavsky and Lenin Institute biographies, which make the still immature Stalin, already then, Lenin's chief adviser and second-in-command.

At Stockholm, Djugashvili differed with Lenin on the peasant question. As the reader may remember, Lenin was for "nationalization" of the land and Plekhanov and the Mensheviks advocated "municipalization." Djugashvili, along with the majority of the Bolsheviks, rejected both Lenin's and Plekhanov's proposals:

> Since we are making a temporary revolutionary union with the fighting peasantry—said Djugashvili—we ought to support their demands, provided they do not by and large contradict the tendency of economic development and the course of the revolution. The peasants demand division. Division does not contradict the above phenomena. That means that we ought to support the full confiscation of the land, and its division. From this point of view, both nationalization and municipalization are alike unacceptable. [Minutes of the Congress, p. 59.]

It was Djugashvili's view that prevailed. And in 1917, the Bolshevik seizure of power was aided, just as Djugashvili had foreseen, by accepting the peasants' demand for partition instead of nationalization. One would think, then, that Stalin biographers would give great space to this example of political originality and prevision. But not a word!

If it was Lenin's theory of party organization that proved most fitted for the seizure of power; if it was Trotsky's theory of immediate "proletarian dictatorship" or "permanent revolution" which provided the formula for the minority, one-party government that emerged; it was Stalin's proposal to "support the real demands of the fighting peasants" by "division of the land" which drew the peasants into benevolent neutrality toward the new Bolshevik power. The impartial biographer must recognize this as Stalin's contribution.

But not a word! And that for two reasons. The first, because Stalin professes that until Lenin's death he was no more than Lenin's "best and most faithful disciple." Originality could and did come later. Between Lenin's death and Stalin's final attainment of uncontested power (i.e. between 1924 and 1929), it was the "best disciple's" proudest boast that all his rivals had at some time opposed or differed with Lenin, but he never. "Of all the Old Bolsheviks," he once declared to admiring Comintern leaders, "my vest is the cleanest."

And the second reason: that, in due course, Stalin himself shifted from "supporting the peasants' desires" to enforcing the state's desires upon the peasants, i.e. he undid the one great achievement of the Revolution so far as the peasants were concerned, substituting, even as Plekhanov had feared, direct state ownership of the land and fixing the once freed peasants once more upon the land as appurtenances thereto. This "collectivization" is really a more total "nationalization" than Lenin advocated or Plekhanov could imagine in his nightmare prevision of total statism. And it was, indeed, as Plekhanov had foreseen, the real economic and political foundation for a "Restoration"—of personal absolutism, labor fixity, purges, forced labor, bureaucratic privilege, police rule—a swelling of the state that would make tsarism seem a limited state by comparison.

Today, Stalin claims credit for the "collectivization" as one of his greatest achievements, a claim incompatible with emphasis on his earlier proposal of a democratic way to win the support of the peasantry. But the biographer not guided by reasons of state can note this speech of Djugashvili's in 1906, and two expository articles of the same year on the same theme, as the first fruits of Stalin's independent thought and social foresight in the field of the seizure of power of November, 1917. It is a contribution no other biographer friendly or hostile has noted!

When Djugashvili returned to the Caucasus in 1907, he wrote in Russian, in the *Bakinskii Proletarii,* a "Report on the London Congress." Two things are worth noting in this report, both of them in the nature of rather clumsy jests.

> Not less interesting—reads the first—is the composition of the Congress from the standpoint of nationalities. Statistics showed that the majority of the Menshevik faction consists of Jews—and this of course without counting the Bundists—after which come Georgians and then Russians. On the other hand,

the overwhelming majority of the Bolshevik faction consists of Russians, after which come Jews—not counting of course the Poles and Letts—and then Georgians, etc. For this reason, one of the Bolsheviks observed in jest (it seems, Comrade Alexinsky) that the Mensheviks are a Jewish faction, the Bolsheviks a genuine Russian faction, whence it wouldn't be a bad idea for us Bolsheviks to arrange a pogrom in the party. [Stalin: *Collected Works,* Vol. II, Russian Edition, pp. 50-51.]

We leave it to the reader to judge the factional purpose of this coarse-grained jest and its possible effect in a Russia that had just gone through three years of pogroms. In passing we might note that this same Alexinsky whom Stalin was citing against the Mensheviks would one day point to Zinoviev, Kamenev, and Trotsky as evidence of the number of Jews in the leadership of the Bolshevik Party!*

The second "jest" dealt with the question of the "exes" or revolutionary holdups. Djugashvili might easily have ignored this question, as he did a number of others. Or he might simply have reported that the "exes" were condemned by the Congress, by a vote of all the Mensheviks and an overwhelming majority of Bolsheviks. Instead he reported:

Of the Menshevik resolutions the only one to pass was the one dealing with guerrilla crimes, and that passed only by accident: the Bolsheviks for this once did not give battle, or rather, they did not want to carry it through to the end, simply out of the desire to give the Mensheviks at least once something to be happy about . . . [Stalin: *Collected Works,* Russian Edition, p. 52.]

This is a strange picture of the Bolshevik faction and its methods of deciding matters of principle! Moreover, it is simply not true. Lenin, as we know, failed to give battle on this issue

* This same Alexinsky invented the story of Lenin's "affair with Elizabeth K.," and produced a poem he claimed Lenin wrote in 1907. Lenin did it to show a comrade that it was not harder to write poetry than prose. Compare this with Gorky's report of Lenin's words: "I couldn't write two lines of poetry if you flayed me alive." The poem bears marks of Alexinsky's style. A French translation is in *L'Arche,* Paris, Feb., 1946. Alexinsky offered to sell Lenin's letters to Elizabeth K. to the Soviet Government, then to the Columbia Library. To prove their authenticity he finally "confessed" that Elizabeth K. was his own wife. No sale!

because he did not think it politic, and still more because he had been defeated on it within his own faction. But Djugashvili chose to report it thus because he was even then intending, with Lenin's approval, to ignore and violate the decision. And he wanted to inspire in his determined partisans, Tsintsadze, Kamo, and their band, contempt for the decision of the Congress, by portraying it as having passed "only by accident" and for a a ridiculous reason, "to give the Mensheviks for once something to be happy about."

Back in the Caucasus from his secret conference with Lenin on the question of the "exes," Djugashvili found that Zhordania had come home after a two-year stay abroad, and was earnestly trying to liquidate the widespread banditry which by then involved members of all factions and parties. The Social Democratic Party set up a committee to disarm the partisan detachments, and threatened with expulsion anyone who should continue to play the role of revolutionary highwayman. The result was an accession, for the first time in Transcaucasia, of some real strength to the Bolsheviks, a natural selection of all those who were already too far outside the law, or too enamored with the life of revolutionary adventure, to lay down their arms. Whenever conditions required it, these would formally resign from the Party (to "preserve discipline" and prevent expulsion), but would maintain contact with a secret center now set up in Baku, whither Djugashvili had gone. This was the first "Caucasian Center" that he really led, as contact man between Lenin's secret Center in Saint Petersburg and the local bands under Tsintsadze and Kamo. Skillful and conspirative, he worked behind the scenes. The exact degree of his participation has to this day remained unclarified.

The London Party Congress decisions were but little more than a month old when the Tiflis "ex" shocked the world. The flurry of investigations which followed led ever closer and closer to the person of Koba Djugashvili. As all the findings had to be veiled in mystery lest the police get wind of them, the full details may never be known. But on March 18, 1918, Martov lifted the veil a little. In his Moscow paper, published legally under the Soviet Government, he wrote:

> That the Caucasian Bolsheviks attached themselves to all sorts of daring enterprises of an expropriatory nature should be well known to that same Citizen Stalin, who was expelled in his time from his Party organization for having had something to do with expropriation.

When this appeared, Citizen Stalin was the powerful Commissar for Nationalities, and Citizen Martov the leader of a barely tolerated Menshevik opposition. The Commissar had Martov and fourteen colleagues indicted for "criminal libel of a Soviet official and slander of the Soviet Government." Stalin's chief lawyer was *Pravda* Editor Sosnovsky, subsequently to perish in Stalin's purges. Martov chose Lapinski (Pavel Lewinson), Polish Left Socialist lawyer, subsequently to be a leader in the Comintern, and then also to perish in the purges. As "lay defender," something permitted then by Soviet judicial procedure, Martov chose Rafael Abramovich. But chiefly in his own hoarse, barely audible voice, he conducted his own defence, as if it were a prosecution of plaintiff Stalin. Martov demanded a jury trial. Stalin, alleging his high office and the implication of the good name of the government, insisted on a Supreme Court hearing, before three Bolshevik judges. This was before the days of bureaucratic privilege, and the Commissar winced as Martov denounced him for refusing to take his chances with a democratic court and jury of his peers. But Stalin had his way.

> Never in my life—Stalin swore—was I placed on trial before my party or expelled. This is a vicious libel . . . One has no right to come out with accusations like Martov's except with documents in one's hand. It is dishonest to throw mud on the basis of mere rumors . . .

The defendant asked for a postponement to produce the documents. He asked that summonses be issued to Isidor Ramishvili, chairman of the Transcaucasian Party court that had tried Stalin; to Shaumyan, Caucasian Bolshevik leader; Soviet Finance Commissar Gukovsky (Bolshevik), under whose chairmanship, according to Martov, there had been an investigation of an attempt on the life of one Comrade Zharinov for exposing Stalin's part in an expropriation; and various other members of the Caucasian District Committee for the years in question. Stalin objected on the ground of "the difficulty and unreliability of communication with the Caucasus." He said nothing about the qualifications of the proposed witnesses, and nothing about the new charge concerning the attempt to assassinate Zharinov. "I was never tried," he repeated doggedly in the first day's summary. "If Martov says so, he is a vicious libeler."

The court granted a postponement and Boris Nikolaevsky, who, though no Bolshevik, was in 1919 made Director of the Historical Archives of the Revolution, was sent down to the Caucasus on Citizen Martov's behalf. There he gathered affidavits from Sylvester Jibladze, Isidor Ramishvili, and others who had taken part in the Tiflis Court of Honor. The second session was to be a consideration of this documentation, and cross-examination on it. But there never was a second session! When the matter came before the court again, all the records of the first session had somehow "disappeared." Martov was dismissed with a mere "social reprimand" for "insulting and damaging the reputation of a member of the government."

As the records are gone, I have reconstructed the trial from interviews with Rafael Abramovich, Boris Nikolaevsky, and Samuel Levitas, all of whom were present in the courtroom. Perhaps I might add as a gloss a conversation which Gorky reports he had with Lenin, precisely during the period in question: "I am sorry, deeply sorry, that Martov is not with us. What a splendid comrade he was, what an absolutely sincere man."

In all his bitter feuds with Martov, feuds in which he aimed, as he had once promised a Party court, to "bring his opponent into public contempt," Lenin could never bring himself to impugn directly Martov's personal honesty. This was the more remarkable because all Martov's attacks upon Taratuta, Djuga-shvili, and other accomplices in the holdups invariably laid the real responsibility at Lenin's feet.

After the Tiflis "ex," the lean years set in, years of stubborn self-delusion for a few, of decay, despair, renegation for many, years for Lenin of returning to the picking of agents by ones and twos where formerly there had been thousands. It was at this moment that Lenin came to put a high value on Joseph Djugashvili. Since Vladimir Ilyich had approved, even directed, the deeds with which his lieutenant was charged, he saw no dishonor in the cloud under which the latter moved. When, amidst the general decay, the rift between Bolsheviks and Mensheviks deepened until they became two separate parties, Lenin placed the expelled or self-dismissed Stalin directly on his Central Committee. Peculiarly, he was not democratically elected by the Bolshevik Prague Congress (1912). Was it because Lenin did not want to stir up old rancors among those of his followers who had opposed expropriations? Or because Stalin was not generally known in the faction? At any rate, Lenin did not propose his name to the Congress, but, as soon as it adjourned, proposed that the newly elected Central Committee should coopt Djugashvili. Since the Congress had already elected Orjonikidze, that made two Georgians to carry the war into the Menshevik stronghold of Transcaucasia. Moreover, as part of that war, Lenin needed some Georgian to become his spokesman on the national question. It was with this promotion in mind, that Lenin applied to him the term in his letter to Gorky of February, 1913: "a wonderful Georgian." It is interesting to note that in all his articles and letters, this is the only time that Vladimir Ilyich ever referred to the nationality of any Party member. Daring and secretive agents, spokesmen from minority peoples who were immune to their compatriots' nationalism, Georgians to carry the war into the fortress of menshevism in Georgian—such disciples were precious few now. He would have need of them in the lean years that had set in.

That the picture we have painted of Stalin's early development is closer to the truth than the official versions of Beria, Yaroslavsky and Company, has received confirmation on at least one occasion from the lips of Joseph Stalin himself. The time was 1926. Lenin was dead. The hero cult was just beginning and its object was not yet used to incense and adulation, nor dreaming of the destruction of almost all his associates and of all contrary evidence. He revisited Tiflis that year and addressed a gathering of its workingmen. After listening for hours to sycophantic speeches from some future priests of his cult, he replied:

> I must in all conscience tell you, comrades, that I have not deserved half the eulogy that various delegates have given me . . . This is mere fantasy, comrades, and a perfectly useless exaggeration. That is the way one speaks at the grave of a revolutionary. But I am not preparing to die. Therefore I must give you a true picture of what I once was and say to whom I owe my present position in the Party . . .
>
> I remember the year 1898, when for the first time the workers in the railway workshops put me in charge of a club . . . In comparison with these comrades (Jibladze and others) I was then a tyro . . . Here, among these comrades, I became an apprentice of the revolution . . . My first teachers were the workers of Tiflis. Allow me to express to them the sincere gratitude of a comrade.
>
> Then I remember the years 1905 to 1907, when at the desire of the Party I was thrown into the work at Baku. Two years of revolutionary work among the oil workers made me a practical fighter and a practical leader . . . I learned for the first time what the leadership of great masses of workmen really meant . . . I became a journeyman of the revolution . . .
>
> I remember 1917, when by the decision of the Party, after prison and deportation, I was thrown into Leningrad. There, among the Russian workers, in close contact with the great educator of the proletariat throughout the world, Comrade Lenin, in the storm of the mighty struggle between the proletariat and the bourgeosie during the World War, I learned for the first time to understand what it meant to be one of the leaders of the great working-class party . . . There, in Russia [as opposed to Transcaucasia], under Lenin's direction, I became a master-workman in revolution . . .

From apprentice at Tiflis, to journeyman at Baku, to master-workman in our revolution at Leningrad—such, comrades, is the course of my apprenticeship to revolution. Such, comrades, is the true picture, honest and without exaggeration, of what I was and what I have become.

These appear to be substantially the outlines of the truth. Many present at that meeting in Tiflis were able to judge of its correctness from their own knowledge. Since then, some have risen to high place by testifying to quite another picture; others have been cowed into silence or acquiescence; yet others, with too stubborn a regard for the facts, or unfortunate enough to have published reminiscences before they knew what to remember, have vanished from the scene. Today, no one any longer dares say that Djugashvili was a mere tyro in 1898, an apprentice until 1905, a journeyman revolutionist on a provincial scale from 1905 to 1907, on a national scale to 1917, and a master-workman only during 1917, as part of the collective leadership of many such "master-workmen," under Lenin's overseership.

CHAPTER TWENTY-EIGHT

NIGHT OF EXILE

"If a tooth could feel after being knocked out, it would probably feel as lonely as I did . . . 'Everything is lost,' people said, 'they have crushed, annihilated, exiled, imprisoned everybody!' . . . I often felt as if a pestilential dust were blowing from Russia."

—MAXIM GORKY

Emigrant life is now a hundred times more difficult than it was before the Revolution of 1905," wrote Lenin to Gorky. In his first emigration he had stayed abroad five years, but they were years of confidence and hope. This second exile was a flight from failure. For most of the decade that followed, Lenin felt sure that he would die abroad.

Revolutionists who but yesterday had stood at the head of millions saw the bonds which linked them to the mass dissolve without a trace. Driven to impotent fury by each day's increment of evil, they fell to quarreling among themselves, meanly, bitterly, denouncing error in each other, apportioning blame for defeat. The isolation which seemed the more silent for the tumult that had just been stilled, they filled with the sound of their own quarrels. No secret admiration sustained them, no generous contributions nor general sympathy nor public expectation followed them as they returned to alien places.

Only now did the self-exiled know the full misery of the émigré's estate: separation from family, friends, country, from all the round of activities that go with belonging to some land's daily life. Exile may be "the home of the virtuous" but too often it is likely to be short of the homelier virtues: tolerance, humor, proportion, charity, love. The very principles which raise the refugee above the ordinary citizen serve also to deprive him of organic relation either with the land of his longing or the land of his exile, contracting him to something less than the ordinary citizen's estate. This lack of a place in the society with which they are at war throws these lonely, high-minded groups utterly in upon themselves, turning their talents to controversy, recrimination, intrigue and schism.

Even Vladimir Ilyich, more rugged, more self-sufficient, more sure than most, was not exempt from the ravages of the émigré's malady. In keeping with the slow, contradictory nature of his spiritual retreat from the certitude of a new uprising, he withdrew by stages. Since the Tsar's Government showed enormously more respect for the autonomy of Finland than would today be conceivable for the "autonomous republics" of the

Soviet Union (or even for the still "independent" Finland of to-day), Lenin was able to work openly there, less than two hours by train from Petersburg. Within the Empire but free from im-perial persecution, he lived with the Leiteisens, Krupskaya, her mother, his younger sister Maria, the Bogdanovs, and Dubro-vinsky, all in the Leiteisen home. By a simple raid, the govern-ment could have captured this entire Bolshevik general staff.

Each morning Krupskaya, known to the police, left by early train for Saint Petersburg, with articles, proofs, instructions, returning each night with news, arrangements for appointments, questions to be resolved. But the government, though it shot batches of men caught in open rebellion, in acts of terror or robbery, gave even the Executive Committee of the Soviets a public trial. For a year the authorities debated the right or ex-pedience of making arrests for plots against the régime on "autonomous" Finnish soil.

> At that time—writes Krupskaya—the Russian police had de-cided not to meddle in Finland and we had considerable free-dom there. The door of the house was never bolted, a jug of milk and loaf of bread were left in the dining room overnight, and bedding spread on the divan so that in the event of anyone's coming on the night train he could enter without waking any-body, have some refreshments and lie down to sleep. In the morning we often found comrades in the dining room who had come in the night.

To grasp this situation fully, we need only try to imagine centers of open plotting against the Stalin régime, functioning, let us say, in Soviet Karelia or in the "independent" Finland of today, sending messengers, instructions, legal literature (if we can imagine such) and illegal, across the frontier from Karelia to Leningrad. Yet, despite the daily contact, Lenin began to feel the demoralizing effect of the declining movement and growing isolation.

> He could not help getting into such a mood sometimes—writes Krupskaya—that he needed some distraction. Thus it was

that the inmates of the great house would sit down to play the game of "dunce." Bogdanov played with calculation, Ilyich both calculated and gambled, Leiteisen became greatly enthralled. If at such moments someone happened to come from the District Committee on an errand, he would generally display annoyance and bewilderment. Fancy Central Committee members playing "dunce" for money!

Though less ruthless and thorough in the suppression of opponents, and enormously less numerous than the GPU to which we have become accustomed, the Okhrana was second to no other secret political police of its day. Where peasant risings and mutinies gave it the pretext, it proclaimed martial law and used gallows and firing squad. In other provinces, it made use of the power of administrative deportation without trial, up to a maximum of five years in Siberia. But a roster of millions of prisoners in concentration camps would have seemed an incredible nightmare to this little band of routine-incrusted police officials. According to the testimony of its chief, Vasiliev, at the height of its power it never had more than one thousand secret agents in all Russia, nor more than one hundred in the capital. He complains that he had "very few" operatives abroad and, every time a congress was held in foreign parts, had to further debilitate his Moscow and Petersburg forces by sending some of his best agents.

But, with its years of political experience, the Okhrana sensed earlier than Lenin the nature of the new political situation, and prepared, too, to "go underground" once more. With forces that seem numerically so modest today, it now developed a system of espionage that eclipsed even the Zubatov and Gapon experiments. If, at every stage of our story so far we have found a police agent in the midst of each fairly numerous gathering, now we shall find them penetrating into the topmost secret hierarchies of the Social Revolutionary Party and the Bolshevik faction of the Social Democratic Party.

Krupskaya got her first taste of the new brew when she set up machinery for smuggling Lenin's newly revived *Proletarii* from

Finland into Russia proper. Lenin had resuscitated it even while there was still a legal, i.e. police-sanctioned, Bolshevik paper in Saint Petersburg. Two members of the Petersburg District, husband and wife, named Komissarov, presented themselves.

> The first moment a strange feeling came over me, a kind of acute mistrust. I could not think where this feeling came from and it soon disappeared. Katya Komissarov proved to be a very business-like assistant, did everything quickly, accurately, and with secrecy . . . After smuggling arms into Petersburg, Katya took them into the Urals . . . Her husband became caretaker for Simonov, owner of a house at 9 Zagorodny Prospekt . . . During the years of reaction, Komissarov put up any number of illegal comrades in that house, supplying them with passports.

The trip of Katya Komissarov to the Urals was followed by the arrest of all concerned, the confiscation of the arms and breakup of the armed bands. The comrades whom Komissarov supplied with shelter and false passports always seemed to come to grief while crossing the European frontier.

Spies entered the military organization of the Bolsheviks so that after the mutinies at Sveaborg and Kronstadt (in 1907) all the secret organizers were arrested (but not executed, one more evidence of the sporadic and often surprising liberality of the tsarist police régime).* They permeated all the local committees, none in the end remaining exempt, so that "every man regarded his comrade with suspicion, was on guard against those nearest to him, did not trust his neighbors." As the movement declined, the shortage of qualified people made it easier for secret agents to rise in the underground hierarchy. They hastened their own promotion by causing the arrest of those whose posts they coveted. By a series of such carefully planned arrests, the provocateur Kukushkin rose to the very summit of the Moscow organization in 1910. The curve of Moscow membership reflects alike the general decay and the success of Kukushkin's

---

* Compare the account of Krupskaya (Vol. I, p. 170) of the arrest of the Bolshevik military organization, including its head, Vyacheslav Rudolfovich Menzhinsky, with the fact that he lived to become Commissar of Finance (1917) and first vice-president (1923), then president (1926) of the GPU.

career: end of 1908—500; middle of 1909—250; end of 1909—150; 1910—all threads fall into the hands of Kukushkin and the Moscow District ceases to exist.

Nor was this, the headship of the second most important district, the highest post which a police spy attained. Abroad, as we have seen, it was Dr. Zhitomirsky who took care of Kamo, arranged for the carrying of explosives and the storing of banknote paper for counterfeiting, took charge of the disposal of the five-hundred-ruble notes from the Tiflis "ex."

In 1912, when the legal Bolshevik daily, *Pravda,* was founded in Saint Petersburg, two police agents, Miron Chernomazov and Roman Malinovsky, were on its editorial staff, the former as a regular editor and chairman of the Board and the latter as contributing editor and treasurer. A legal Moscow paper was founded for the Bolsheviks by a police agent. One of these agents, whose story we shall consider separately in Chapter XXXI, was so admired by Lenin that he was called abroad for the smallest and most confidential meetings and made privy to the most secret and dangerous matters. He became a Central Committee member and, for several years, the leading authoritative spokesman for the Bolsheviks inside Russia.

This fantastic state of affairs found its counterpart in the case of Yevno Azev of the Social Revolutionary Party. The son of a poor Jewish tailor and an informer since his student days, Azev actually became the top leader of the Social Revolutionary Party's dread Terror or Fighting Section. For the last five of his fifteen years of political life (until the middle of 1909, when his dual role was exposed), Azev was the actual director of the entire work of the Fighting Section. In this post he took funds both from police and revolutionaries, deceiving and cheating both. He betrayed the plans for many acts of terror, prevented many intended assassinations, delivered many of his comrades into the hands of the authorities. But other projects he permitted to be carried out, even planned some and saw to their success. His motives? To raise the price of his services to the police, to retain the confidence of his associates, to serve the obscure intrigues of one official against another, to settle grudges, even to satisfy his own strangely ambivalent personal convictions. In the end he scarcely knew himself whether he was a terrorist spying upon the government or a police agent spying upon the terror. In varying degrees he was responsible for the assassination of at least one Minister of the Interior, Plehve (1904); one of the Tsar's own uncles, the Grand Duke Sergei (1905); for the wounding of General Dubassov, after the latter had suppressed the Moscow insurrection (1906); the execution of two of his fellow-agents, including Father Gapon when the latter reentered the service of the police in 1906. Apparently as an act of vengeance for the Jewish pogroms which Minister of the Interior Plehve fomented, Azev actually organized all the details of the latter's assassination in 1904, leaving the throne without a firm and trusted adviser when one was needed most. And it is probably not Azev's fault that a plot against the Tsar himself miscarried at the time when Azev's double role was being exposed. But Yevno Azev's strange life lies outside the scope of the present work, while the story of Lenin's lieutenant belongs to a subsequent chapter.

When Lenin returned from the London Congress in the summer of 1907, mustache clipped, beard shaved off and wearing a huge straw hat by way of disguise, Krupskaya found him extraordinarily fatigued, and unable to eat. She packed him off to the pine forests of Stirsuden, deep in Finland, where "Little Uncle" (Lydia Knippovich) was living.

> The first few days he kept dozing off to sleep. He would sit under a fir-tree and immediately drop off. The children called him "old sleepyhead." Those were wonderful days at Stirsuden: the woods, the sea, the wildest of the wild . . . "Little Uncle" fed Ilyich assiduously on omelettes and reindeer-ham. He got steadily better and became his old self again.

So Krupskaya. But it was evident that he was not his old self. The isolation grew. He retreated from current politics to more theoretical reading and writing, another form of relief for his exhausted spirit. Then he went to Oglbu, Finland, where he could no longer maintain day-to-day contact with his followers. In Petersburg the police had picked up Zinoviev, Kamenev, and Roshkov, three of his most important lieutenants. Rumors reached him that they were beginning to search for him, despite Finnish autonomy. (Actually, they were hunting, on a tip from Azev, for one Karl Trauberg and his "Flying Terrorist Detachment of the Northern Region," responsible for the death of General Pavlov and now plotting to blow up the State Council and execute the Tsar.) Not until December 5, 1907, did they venture to violate Finnish autonomy in order to raid Trauberg's apartment. News that the Okhrana had entered Finland made up Lenin's mind to go abroad once more.

But if the police were indeed looking for him, it would not do to board the little steamer at Åbo which, following a channel cut by icebreakers, made weekly winter trips to Stockholm. Åbo would be the place the police would most likely be watching. He engaged a guide to conduct him over the ice to an island—three versts, about two miles, out over the frozen sea—a port of call for the same steamer. The journey was undertaken at night, without lights. The guide proved to be drunk, the way perilous. Somewhere in the darkness, near the channel, the ice began to crack and move under Lenin's feet. " 'Oh, what a silly way to die,' I thought," he told Krupskaya later. It teases the imagination to contemplate how the history of Russia in the fateful year 1917, indeed, how the history of Europe and the world might have been altered, if Vladimir Ilyich Ulyanov had gone under the shifting ice near the channel over the open sea, that night at the end of 1907.

Krupskaya joined him in Stockholm and then went on to Berlin. It was Christmas Eve but they felt anything but festive. The comrade who met them warned them not to go to the home of any Russian émigré, since the German police were engaged in widespread raids. All day they were led around the cold streets, from café to café. In the evening they went to the home of Rosa Luxemburg, whose future was to be so fatefully linked with theirs. Vladimir Ilyich felt very close to her at that moment, despite their old quarrels over the question of organization. At the London Congress she had taken a position close to Trotsky's on the forces and perspectives of the Russian revolution. Though the Mensheviks had repeatedly challenged Lenin to attack Trotsky's and her theory of "the permanent revolution," he had refused. Rosa and her Polish delegation in turn had supported him, if not on the organization question in principle, yet on the organization question that mattered most to him: the proportion of Bolsheviks on the Party Central Committee. Thereafter, he had met her again at the International Socialist Congress at Stuttgart, and they had joined forces to draft a resolution on war which was very close to both their hearts and deeply significant for their common future. "For that reason," writes Krupskaya, "their talk that evening was particularly friendly."

From Berlin they went to Geneva, home for so much of their happy first emigration. But they arrived there now (January 20, 1908) sick from eating bad fish, then caught a chill. "Geneva looked cheerless . . . dead and empty. While we walked along the empty Geneva streets which had turned so friendless, Ilyich murmured, 'I feel just as if I had come here to be buried.'"

His letters home, hitherto so unfailingly cheerful, were gloomy and complaining. "For several days now," ran his first letter to his sister Anna in 1908, "I have been stuck in this damned Geneva. A sordid hole, but it cannot be helped. We will adapt ourselves."

And planning to leave for Paris a year later, he wrote his mother: "We hope that a large city will cheer us up a little; we are sick of sitting in a provincial backwater."

Yet another year later, at the end of 1909: "Paris is a rotten hole . . . I have still not been able to adapt myself . . . All the same, I feel only special circumstances could drive me back to Geneva."

In the autumn of 1911, when his second exile had run for almost four years, his sister Anna went to visit him in Paris. He could not conceal from her that the second emigration had been excessively painful and remained so. "His state of mind was noticeably less gay . . . One day when we were walking together, he said to me: 'Will we be able to live until the next revolution?'"

But Lenin was not one to waste time in self-pity. In Geneva he found an old Party printing press which had been forgotten in the excitement of the departure for Russia in 1905. He started up *Proletarii* afresh. Of the first issue, only thirteen copies reached Russia, of the second, third and fourth, only sixty-two. But Lenin wrote to Gorky and Lunacharsky in Italy and to Trotsky in Vienna, urging them to contribute. He sent letters to Russia, too ("but we waited for the answers more than we received them"). He drafted leaflets, started work on pamphlets and books, analyzed Stolypin's new agrarian policy and the unexpected development of a conservative constitutional monarchy; studied every word of the Duma proceedings; gathered statistical reports; engaged in polemics on the Duma and on philosophy—the bitterest in his whole life with the people who had been and were closest to him. He still spent his days in the library, though he no longer knew what to do with his nights. He kept up with national and international affairs. He struggled to train new people to replace those who were deserting and those he was breaking with and driving away. In short, all his activities had the same external appearance as before, the old habits serving as a protective armor for his spirit. But everything was emptier, less satisfying, less absorbing. He was irritable, restless, frequently melancholy.

Watching him closely from day to day—writes Krupskaya—I noted that he had become more reserved . . . more reflective, and when interrupted in reveries one seemed to catch a glint of sadness in his eyes . . .

We found it difficult to get accustomed again to life in exile. Vladimir Ilyich spent his days in the library, but in the evenings we did not know what to do with ourselves. We did not feel like sitting in the cold, cheerless room . . . we longed to be among people, and every evening we would go to the cinema or to the theater, although we rarely stayed to the end but left in the middle of the performance and would go wandering off . . .

During those most difficult years of the reaction, years about which Ilyich always spoke with such pain even when we were back in Russia—he sustained himself by dreaming . . .

Such passages testify to the effect of those bleak years upon him who was perhaps the most robust of the émigrés. They supply one key, hitherto neglected, to the character of the new round of polemics into which he now entered. They left permanent scars on Lenin's spirit which we will have to bear in mind when we consider his influence as Russia's leading figure in the years after he came to power.

Among the few inside Russia who remained with him, or indeed with Social Democracy at all, there grew up during these difficult years a tendency to safeguard themselves from all the new quarrels and make light of them and of the "make-work" activities of the second emigration abroad. In 1912 this attitude nearly provoked a break between Lenin and the editors of the legal Bolshevik daily *Pravda,* founded that year in Saint Petersburg. To answer the scoffers, he wrote:

Yes, there is much that is hard to bear in the émigré environment . . . more want and poverty here than elsewhere . . . a high percentage of suicides . . . [Yet] only here and nowhere else have been posed and considered the most important and fundamental questions of the entire Russian democracy during these years of confusion and interregnum.

He himself did not have to endure physical poverty. His sister relates that he lived badly, ate poorly, dressed shabbily, spent parsimoniously, suffered from restlessness, insomnia, recurrence

of his old stomach trouble, headaches, and more frequent spells
of illness than before. But Party wages, small earnings from
writing, occasional help from Krupskaya's mother or his own,
provided all that was needful. Except for the purchase of cheap
tickets to cinema, theater and music hall in the working-class
district, and walking trips, cycling trips, long summer stays by
the seashore in modest housekeeping quarters, his expenditures
were as frugal and ascetic as ever. Even in Paris he drank no
wine, for a time went without meat, not on principle or for
economy, but for health's sake.

> Such poverty as when one has not the wherewithal to buy one's
> bread, we never knew—writes Krupskaya.—Our life, it is true,
> was simple. But does the joy of life consist of eating one's full
> and living in luxury? Vladimir Ilyich knew how to take pleasures
> from life.

Even now he could laugh heartily at times and stir others to
hearty laughter. This is testified by all who came in contact with
him. In this ability to snatch moments of unrestrained joy and
laughter out of a tragic existence, he was a true son of the Russian people.

"As at every new stage of the Revolution," Krupskaya in-
forms us, "he turned to the masters for advice and consolation."
He was especially attentive to the public utterances and private
letters of Marx and Engels to each other during their own
"sleepless night of exile" after the collapse of the Revolution of
1848, a long night which ended only with their death. They,
too, had been dominated for a time by an illusion, bred of revolutionary ardor, that the uprisings of 1848 could not be over
for good. But when the sober examination of key political
events and underlying economic trends had convinced them
that a new revolution was only possible as the result of some
new crisis, they broke with the romantic Left that could not
cure itself of unjustified hope.

You make sheer will instead of real conditions the driving force of the revolution—Lenin read in Marx's debate with his opponents in the Communist League (1850).—While we say to the workers: you have fifteen or twenty or fifty years of bourgeois and national wars to go through, not merely to alter conditions but to alter yourselves and make yourselves fit to take over political power, you tell them on the contrary that they must take over political power at once or abandon all hope. Whilst we point out how undeveloped the German proletariat still is, you flatter the nationalism and craft prejudices of the German artisan in the crudest fashion . . .

Those words Lenin could understand and take to his heart, to fortify himself for the coming struggle with the romantics in his own faction.

But there was another side of Marx's and Engel's reaction to the defeat of 1848 which was alien to Lenin's nature. On Marx's motion, the famous Communist League, progenitor of the *Communist Manifesto,* had declared itself dissolved as "no longer opportune." The two friends, distressed by the madness that seizes defeated émigrés, had breathed a sigh of relief as they separated themselves from the intrigue-ridden foreign colony, its disintegrating organizations and outbreaks of romantic folly. Never again in their lives did they consent to belong to a German or international conspirative organization. They were convinced that such a secret league was appropriate only to the circumstances of imminent revolution, that broad, legal workers' unions and parties had become feasible, that underground conspiracies could serve only as breeding ground for self-deception and police espionage, that they themselves could do more to build the real movements of the future by engaging in theoretical labors than by participating in organizations inappropriate to the emerging times.

Lenin felt, however, that his times were different. The conservative constitutional monarchy of Stolypin seemed to be stabilizing its existence, so that there were moments when he despaired of living to see a second upheaval in Russia. But

Europe did not seem to him, as it had to Marx in 1850, to be on the eve of a long epoch of relatively peaceful expansion. On the contrary, capitalism had reached a stage that smelled of imminent decay: a world war was in the offing which might call forth a crisis greater than that brought on by the Russo-Japanese War of 1904-05. A half-century had elapsed since Marx had spoken those words, a half-century which had brought into existence solid, mighty, permanent-seeming parties. These, in Lenin's estimation, had made the workers "fit to take over political power." The "fifteen or twenty or fifty years of bourgeois and national wars" had been a bit slow in coming or drawing to an end, but the general upheavals might soon begin. From the great international socialist movement and from the Russian socialist movement, thought Lenin, convinced socialists could not now dissociate themselves if their actions squared with their theories and beliefs. Moreover, at heart, he was a man of organization, a man of action; for all his display of theory, a man in whom there was a primacy of will. Of all his writings, there is not one which was not dedicated by some practical need of the immediate struggle. Never could he feel himself, as Marx had felt in 1850, pregnant with a work of such great theoretical import that it might justify his withdrawing from the broken party and its spasmodic struggles. Whether party meant the narrow circle of conspirators, the mighty movement of great masses, or the tortured, inbred, defeated émigré cliques and quarrels, Lenin was always and above all a man of party. Though it might dwindle to the point where the very name would seem a tragic jest, yet to whatever he should call "party," to that he would remain attached. He could never have written as Marx to Engels in 1851:

> I am much pleased with the public and authentic isolation in which we now find ourselves, you and I. It perfectly corresponds to our principles and our position. The system of reciprocal concessions, of half-measures tolerated only in order to keep up appearances, and obligation to share in public with all

these asses in the general absurdity of the party—all that is done with now. [Letter of February 11, 1851.]

Nor as Engels in his answer to Marx:

> We now have a chance again at last . . . to show that we need no popularity, no support from any party whatsoever . . . from now on we are responsible only to ourselves, and when the moment comes that these gentlemen need us, we shall be in a situation to be able to dictate our own terms. Till then we shall at least have peace. To tell the truth, even a certain loneliness . . . How can people like us, who avoid official positions like the plague, ever find ourselves at home in a "party"? . . . The principal thing for the moment is: some way of getting our ideas into print . . . What will all the gossip and scandal mean which the whole émigré pack may circulate against you, once you answer them with your political economy? [Letter of February 13, 1851.]

Lenin was not critical of that withdrawal, for to it he owed such works as Marx's *Critique of Political Economy* and *Capital*. But he could not follow their example. When he learned of the double suicide of Marx's daughter and son-in-law (the Lafargues, in 1909), he said to Krupskaya: "If one cannot work for the Party any longer, one must be able to look truth in the face and die the way the Lafargues did."

In that utterance is the core of Lenin. By 1909 the Party had crumbled away until Krupskaya could write "we have no people at all." In retrospect, Zinoviev, very close to Lenin then, would say, "at this unhappy period the Party as a whole ceased to exist" (*Lectures on Party History, 1922*). In Russia, spies and apathy would combine to decimate and destroy. Abroad, the majority of his collaborators would desert, or be read out of the faction by him, in a succession of tactical and ideological quarrels of incredible bitterness. Yet through it all this man who first came to leadership on the basis of an organization doctrine would remain the man of party, and "party" would continue to mean to him wherever he and even two or three might foregather together to serve as a leading committee for whatsoever adherents might be induced to follow its lead. This selfless egocentrism, held unconsciously, rooted in the inescapable conviction of the rightness of his views, would sustain him even when he was most shut off from Russia and from his fellow-émigrés.

Trotsky's spirit seemed less bruised than that of the others. His previous stay abroad had been too brief to have any effect upon him. Younger than most of the leaders—he was only twenty-eight when this second emigration began—he was happy to have escaped from perpetual exile in Siberia to a Western Europe which possessed for him many attractions. His theories as to the nature of the Russian revolution made him sure that he would live to see its triumph and that that triumph would not be too long delayed. Like Marx and Engels before him, he sought for some correlation between the ebb and flow of economic crises and the rise and fall of the revolutionary spirit, coming to the conclusion that not depression and misery but a rise in all the indices of economics and employment would restore self-confidence and militance to the Russian working class. (The year 1907 was a year of world depression.)

Always of a self-confident temperament, his belief in his own destiny had been enhanced by the events of 1905. On the public stage of the fifty-day Petersburg Soviet he had acquitted himself with distinction, becoming despite his youth its outstanding and most popular leader. During the trial of the members of its Executive Committee for high treason, he had further enlarged his reputation. And the events of the year 1905 had fortified his theoretical self-assurance. At the year's beginning he had published his first sketchy outline of the doctrine of "permanent revolution"; at its end he had witnessed what seemed to him the doctrine's fulfillment and verification in the springing into being of the Soviet and in the powers which that "embryonic workers' parliament" had taken unto itself. In prison he worked serenely on a series of pamphlets, each of which was to form a chapter in his subsequent work, *The Year 1905*—the greatest piece of writing from any hand to come out of that memorable year.

His escape from Siberia brought him to London in time to attend the Unity Congress of 1907. There he found that the over-all unity of the year 1905 was already dissipating and the Party disintegrating into factions once more. He was pleased to note that Rosa Luxemburg, who like him had gained enormously in prestige during the past year, stood close to him in her conceptions as to the nature of the Russian revolution, and that Lenin did not stand sharply against him. To his profound surprise, the great political gulf was that between him and the Mensheviks, despite the fact that he and Parvus had been editors of their journal, *Nachalo,* and that he had risen to leadership in the Council of Workingmen's Deputies with their support. This discovery led him to the conclusion which was to be the principal determinant of his conduct for the next five years. Since Bolsheviks and Mensheviks had fought so bitterly from 1903 to 1905, then united in common action when the opportunity for action presented itself, surely the next wave of revolution would bring them together once more. Then the clear need and demands of the awakened working class would again overwhelm these Byzantine disputations and faction animosities. Again the mighty power of the millions would overcome Lenin's organization narrowness and the Menshevik mistrust of power. Again great general strikes would call into being Soviets or Councils more inclusive, more authoritative, than any faction or party. Again the class would find its voice and drown out the petulant quarrels of groups and sects. From this position, neither argument nor event could dislodge him until "the next wave of revolution" brought him to a different conviction.

Hence the ever angrier and ever more bitter quarrels of those unhappy years from 1907 to 1914 found him at his self-chosen station in the no man's land between the contending bands, exposed to cross fire from both. Much of the official literature of "anti-Trotskyism" published in Russia today consists of quotations from Lenin's indignation at his supra-factional stand during this period. They could be matched by no less indignant denunciation from the pen of Plekhanov, Axelrod and Martov. As he self-confidently berated now one side, now the other, as if he stood far above all their little quarrels, he infuriated both at once. His aloofness from issues looming ever larger in their eyes seemed to them either vanity or unprincipled indifference. His vain attempts to form a faction of his own on the basis of his "non-factional" platform, they deemed ambition. His claim to speak for party while they each spoke for group, was intolerable arrogance. If he sought to give his platform more positive content by stating his organization views, he found himself against Lenin and with the Mensheviks. If he injected his political perspectives, he was forced inevitably in the direction of Lenin. Leaving aside defects of personality and temperament which made it hard for him to form a collective leadership in which he would have been at most *primus inter pares*—and there were such defects in his makeup—how could he possibly form a successful faction on the narrow basis of "unity," where everyone was agitated precisely by the divisive matters of organization and politics which he was forced to ignore? And if he did not ignore them, how could he form a faction either, when his message to others was *peace* while inwardly he was at war with himself? As an orator, a pamphleteer, a tribune of the people, this young man had been splendid during the culminating moments of the year 1905. But as an organizer of a group and as a club to force the contending factions into unity he was to be an ignominious failure.

What has the split done for you?—he challenged both sides at the London Congress.—To do the same thing side by side, to march on common ground, but mutually tread on each other's toes? And what is the result? You are compelled to reunite, first on a federative basis and now here in a unity congress.

There would be further splits, he warned them, if they did not morally disarm, moderate the spirit of faction, dissolve the groups into the single unified party they were supposed to be. Small consolation to see the prophecy of further splits verified beyond the scope of his imagining!

On the whole, his position brought him closer to the Mensheviks during the ensuing five-year period than to the Bolsheviks, for, in the matter of splitting, Lenin was invariably the aggressor. In 1910, when Lenin's spirit of faction was temporarily brought to bay by a combination of Mensheviks of all shades with those Bolsheviks who believed in party unity (the so-called "Party Bolsheviks" or "Conciliators"), the Conference of the United Party declared Trotsky's personal organ, the Vienna *Pravda,* the organ of the Party. And in August, 1912, while Lenin was openly reading his opponents out of the organization and proclaiming his faction the legitimate party, Trotsky became the rallying center once more for "Party Mensheviks," "Menshevik Liquidators," "Party Bolsheviks," "Bolshevik Vperyodists." This so-called "August Bloc" was Trotsky's last effort to unite all the other groups against "the aggressor," to force Lenin to keep the peace, or at least confine the controversies and methods of struggle within the bounds permissible to comrades in a single organization and a common cause.

> In a large Marxist community embracing tens of thousands of workmen—Trotsky proclaimed—it is impossible that divergences and discords should not exist. Every member of the community has not only the right but the duty of defending his point of view on the basis of the common program. But in fulfilling that duty none should forget that he is dealing with differences among a band of brothers . . . Discipline and cohesion in the struggle are inconceivable without an atmosphere of mutual esteem and confidence, and the man who fails to observe these moral principles, whatever may be his intentions, is undermining the very existence of Social Democracy.*

* Cf. Engels to Bebel: "The greatest party in Germany cannot exist without allowing full play to all shades of feeling in it."

If this conception could have been adhered to, how different might have been the fate of the Russian Revolution, of the Soviet Government, of Trotsky himself! But could it? The question would obtrude itself again in 1917. This time, Trotsky would be as insistent as Lenin that they were not "dealing with differences among a band of brothers." He would deny that there could be "an atmosphere of mutual esteem and confidence." Later he would deny too that "every member of the community has not only the right but the duty of defending his point of view" within the Bolshevik Party. Later still, too late indeed, he would take the road back toward the conception of party structure proclaimed above. Then the fateful years between 1907 and 1917, when he had struggled for the unity of the Party and proved unable to build a faction of his own, would cost him dear.

His aloofness from the issues dividing the emigration was emphasized by physical detachment. Instead of going to Paris, Berlin, Geneva or Zurich, where most of the Russians were, he chose Vienna. There, in 1908, he founded an organ of his own, the Vienna *Pravda,* which made itself fairly popular inside Russia by its insistence on unity and its extreme political radicalism ("permanent revolution"). For three and one-half years, he got it out as a bimonthly, almost single-handed. He wrote most of its articles, arranged for its smuggling through the Sailors' Union of the Black Sea, carried on correspondence with adherents of his non-factional faction. But the police had their agents in the Sailors' Union, too, and shortly before the World War—when it would have been most important to have such a smuggling apparatus—they bagged all the leaders and broke up the union.

Trotsky's chief editorial aid was A. A. Joffe. Joffe suffered from a nervous or psychic disorder which caused him to submit to psychoanalysis by Alfred Adler. The Adlers became household friends of the Trotskys, and from this dates his interest in Freud. When Trotsky sent Joffe to Russia as an underground organizer, the police got him immediately; he did not emerge from Siberia until 1917. As Soviet Ambassador to Germany, he was the first to breach the *cordon sanitaire*. In 1927 he committed suicide as a protest against the expulsion of Trotsky by the Party he had helped to victory.

Other friends of Lev Davidovich in Vienna included Riazanov, also a unity advocate and trade union organizer, who by then was by way of becoming the leading Russian Marx scholar; Skobelev, a revolutionary student who would later become Minister of Labor in the Kerensky Government; and Kopp, who, like Joffe, would become a Soviet diplomat. Skobelev, Kopp, Joffe—that was about all there was to the staff of Vienna *Pravda,* aside from the indefatigable editor.

While he lived in Vienna, his second son, Sergei, was born, and his older son, Leon (Lev, Lyovik) got his early schooling.

> When Lyovik entered school—writes Natalia Ivanovna Trotsky—the question of religion came up. According to Austrian law, children had to have religious instruction in the faith of their parents. As none was listed in our documents, we chose the Lutheran for our children, because it seemed easier on the children's shoulders as well as their souls . . .

Trotsky's aging mother and father came to visit him. They brought his daughter (by his first marriage). In Berlin his mother underwent a kidney operation and treatment for actinomycosis, which burdened the last decade of her life. She and her husband seemed reconciled at last with their son's radicalism. ("The final argument," Trotsky writes in his autobiography, "was probably my first book in German.") After their visit in 1910, his mother, aged sixty, went home to Yanovka, where she had borne him, and died the same year.

During his second exile, the young man who had once used the Party name of *Pero*—"Pen"—earned his living by the use of that implement. He became correspondent for *Kievskaya Mysl* ("Kievan Thought"), a legal journal with a socialistic tinge. He wrote on literary subjects, German and Austrian affairs, economics and politics. Later the Soviet Government republished the essays. The writing brought him enough money for his modest needs, except

> . . . when he was too busy with *Pravda.* Then my wife learned the road to the pawnshops, and I had to resell to booksellers books bought in more affluent days. There were times when our modest possessions were confiscated to pay the house-rent. We had two babies and no nurse; our life was a double burden to my wife. But she still found time and energy to help me in revolutionary work.

During all this time Trotsky dedicated some of his vigor to studies of the correlation of economic crises and political upheavals, to national and labor questions as they presented themselves in the Austro-Hungarian Empire (three-quarters of the population of which were Slavs!). Eloquent in any language that he mastered, he was soon addressing meetings of Vienna workingmen.

It is worth noting that of the émigrés from the Tsarist Empire, the four who were able to feel most nearly or completely at home in the parties of other lands—Rosa Luxemburg, Angelica Balabanoff, Parvus and Trotsky—were all of Jewish origin. There seemed to be something in that heritage (something too in their temperaments and views) which made them less concentratedly Russian or Polish, more European, more instinctively and radically international in outlook, than most of the other émigrés. This did not automatically follow from "Jewishness," for Axelrod, Martov, Zinoviev, Kamenev were Jewish too, yet they never entered into the life of the parties and lands of their emigration. Nor did Plekhanov, Zasulich and Lenin ever become part of the movements in the capitals in which they lived, though Lenin spent fifteen years, and the others their entire adult lives, in exile. Parvus was a leader in the German Social Democracy; Rosa Luxemburg in three parties; Angelica Balabanoff became more deeply identified with the Italian working class than with that of her native land. Trotsky was somewhat less "international" than these. Russia always took first place in his thoughts until the day of his death. But he became a brilliant orator in German and French and an intermittent participant in the affairs of the Austrian party. It helped preserve him from the émigré inbreeding and despair.

In the unwonted stillness of Vienna after the turbulence of Saint Petersburg, he turned to Marx and Engels, as Lenin did. He read the Marx-Engels letters, and their effect upon him is worth quoting, not for what it tells of them but of him:

> The correspondence was for me not a theoretical but a psychological revelation. *Toutes proportions gardées,* I found proof on every page that to these two I was bound by a direct psychological affinity . . . Their attitude to men and ideas was mine . . . Marx and Engels were revolutionaries through and through. But they did not have the slightest trace of asceticism or sectarianism. Both of them, and especially Engels, could say of themselves that nothing human was alien to them. But their revolutionary outlook lifted them always above the hazards of fate and the works of men . . . What philistines and vulgarians considered aristocratic in them was really only their revolutionary superiority . . .

Like Lenin, Trotsky turned, too, to the Marx pamphlets of the immediate post-1848 period. But he did not find his wisdom in the call to retreat, but in Marx's last enunciation of a program for a new wave of revolutions. Written early in 1850 while Marx still clung to the delusion that a new uprising was on the way, it said:

> While the democratic petty bourgeoisie would like to bring the revolution to a close as soon as their demands are more or less complied with, it is our interest and task to make the revolution permanent, to keep it going until all the ruling and possessing classes are deprived of power, the governmental machinery occupied by the proletariat . . . the more important forces of production concentrated in the hands of the proletarians . . .

Besides the official government, the workers must set up a revolutionary workers' government, either in the form of local executives and communal councils or workers' clubs or workers' committees, so that the bourgeois democratic governments not only lose immediately all backing among the workers, but from the commencement find themselves under the supervision and threats of authorities behind whom stand the entire mass of the working class . . .

In order that this party, whose betrayal of the workers will begin with the first hour of victory, should be frustrated in its nefarious work, it is necessary to organize and arm the proletariat . . . with their own chiefs and general staff, to put themselves under the order not of the government but of the revolutionary authorities set up by the workers . . . They must not be diverted from their course in proletarian independence by the hypocrisy of the democratic petty bourgeoisie. Their battle cry must be: *The revolution in permanence!*

The reader will perceive in these words the schematic outlines of the program on which both Lenin and Trotsky sought to act in 1917. In this "Address to the Communist League" of March, 1850, we can find, too, Lenin's attitude toward independent parliamentary action of labor, a source of his attitude toward the liberal Kadets in the Duma elections, an outline of the agrarian expropriation program he favored, an injunction "to concentrate as much power as possible in the hands of the central government," and much else that is regarded as characteristically Leninist. There can be no doubt that Lenin no less than Trotsky drank deeply at this source.

Because of Trotsky's seven years in Vienna, because of his aloofness from the émigré struggle and its issues, and because his subsequent wanderings will carry him to the Balkans as a war correspondent, then to Spain and far-off America, we shall lose sight of him for long periods between 1907 and 1917. Before we permit him to vanish thus from our view, it would be well to examine the brilliant portrait done by the sensitive pen of Anatole Lunacharsky, future Commissar of Education of the Soviet Government:

I first met Trotsky in 1905, after the January events . . . Trotsky was then unusually elegant, in distinction to all of us, and very handsome. That elegance of his, and especially a kind of careless, high-and-mighty manner of talking with no matter whom, struck me very unpleasantly. I looked with great disapproval on this dude who swung his leg over his knee and dashed off with a pencil an outline of the impromptu speech he was going to make at the meeting. But Trotsky spoke mighty well . . .

I remember how somebody said in the presence of Lenin: "Khrustalev's star has fallen and the strong man of the Soviet now is Trotsky." Lenin seemed to darken for a moment, then he said: "Well, Trotsky has won that with his tireless fine work . . ."

Trotsky's popularity among the Petersburg proletariat up to the time of his arrest was very great, and it increased as a result of his extraordinarily picturesque and heroic conduct in court . . . Of all the Social Democratic leaders of 1905 and 1906 Trotsky, in spite of his youth, undoubtedly showed himself the best prepared. Least of any did he wear a certain stamp of emigrant narrowness which impeded even Lenin at that time. More than any other did he realize what a broad struggle for power really is. And he came out of the revolution with the greatest gain in popularity. Neither Lenin nor Martov made any essential gain. Plekhanov lost much . . . Trotsky stood from that time on in the front rank . . .

Trotsky succeeded very badly in organizing not only a party but even a little group . . . A tremendous imperiousness and a kind of inability or unwillingness to be at all caressing and attentive to people, an absence of that charm which always surrounded Lenin, condemned Trotsky to a certain loneliness . . .

For work in political groups Trotsky seemed but little fitted, but in the ocean of historic events where such personal features lose their importance, only his favorable side came to the fore . . .

I believe that Lenin never looks at himself, never glances into the mirror of history, never even thinks of what posterity will say of him—simply does his work. He does his work imperiously, not because power is sweet to him but because he is sure that he is right and cannot endure to have anybody spoil his work. His love of power grows out of his tremendous sureness and the correctness of his principles, and out of the inability, if you please—an inability very useful in a political leader—to see from the point of view of his opponent . . .

Unlike him, Trotsky looks at himself often. Trotsky treasures his historic role and would undoubtedly be ready to make any personal sacrifice, not even excluding that of his life, in order to remain in the memory of mankind with the halo of a genuine revolutionary leader . . .

These observant and prophetic words were written while Lenin was still alive and published in the first edition of *Revolutionary Silhouettes,* Moscow, 1923. In that edition there was no silhouette of Stalin, not because Lunacharsky had anything against Stalin, but because in 1923 it still occurred to no one to consider the latter as a figure of the first rank. The sketch of Trotsky was omitted from later editions as part of the general conspiracy to substitute in the public mind another picture of him and remove all traces of his part in the Revolution. But in justice to Lunacharsky it must be said that the omission was made under compulsion and not by any choice of his.

CHAPTER TWENTY-NINE

LENIN
AS
PHILOSOPHER

The belief in an external world independent of the percipient subject is the foundation of all science.

—ENGELS

Politics as the cure for the sickness of Russian society having been tried and found wanting, men withdrew from the political arena or limited their vision to the narrow horizon of constitutional possibilities. As after Spartacus came Christ, after Muenzer and embattled Tabor the sword-rejecting Mennonites and Brethren, so after Gapon, Khrustalev, Trotsky, Lieutenant Schmitt and the Man-with-the-Leather-Belt* came the day of Bulgakov, Berdyaev and Tolstoy. Hope of changing the world dwindled, the minds of men turned inward: to self, to personal cares, searching of the spirit, anodynes, individual salvation.

The period of reaction is generally presented as if all the movements which possessed it arose directly as a result of the defeat of 1905. Actually, Tolstoy's doctrines were formulated in the eighties after the failure of the Narodovoltsi terror. Bulgakov and Berdyaev abandoned Marxism for Christian Socialism around 1900. Symbolism, frantic hedonism, "art for art's sake," all were subordinate but persistent currents at the turn of the century. They had almost been overwhelmed by the rising revolutionary tide. Now that it ebbed, they appeared to dominate the desolate scene.

The exhaustion and follies that characterized the period known as "the decadence" possessed high and low from working class to court. In 1904 the Tsarina Alexandra gave birth at last to a male heir, thanks to the intercession of Saint Seraphim, a thaumaturge who had been irregularly canonized on the insistence of Nicholas II. The child of this miracle was cursed with the hereditary curse of hemophelia, which had been transmitted by so many women of royal households to their male children. A deep sense of personal guilt took possession of Alexandra, and she had need of daily miracles to keep this precarious life in being. She delivered herself into the hands of a

---

* The Man-with-the-Leather-Belt is an almost legendary figure reported by many witnesses to have directed the Moscow uprising; Lieutenant Schmitt was the leader of the Black Sea mutiny; Khrustalev and Trotsky were successive chairmen of the Soviet which called for general strike and armed uprising.

succession of quacks and wonder-workers, then wholly into the keeping of the shrewd and mystical, dissolute and holy "Man of God," the muzhik Rasputin. At first it was only the affairs of the household, then of the Court, then the affairs of state that were entrusted to him. The ascendancy of Rasputin is as truly a phenomenon of the post-1905 decadence as is the wave of drunkenness and gambling among workingmen or the cult of Saninism among students. While the Bolshevik armed bands degenerated into banditry and the underground crumbled and became honeycombed with spies; while students forgot politics and turned to purely academic concerns or the tavern and the brothel, the Court was taken over by the corrupt camarilla around Rasputin. A whole society was moving toward its end.

Among the young, eroticism and suicide became mass phenomena, embraced with the same headlong extremism that had been given to revolution. The brief celebrity of Artsybashev's *Sanin* (published in 1907) was due to the fact that it combined both themes in one. Two suicides, two seductions, a glowing description of nudity, a toying with incest; the glorification of bodily strength, voluptuousness, physical joys; the ridiculing of those who waste their time on politics or knowledge; the admonition to live like animals, follow instinct and impulse, abandon principles, plans, regrets, and to use reason only as devil's advocate and instrument for liberating oneself from all codes, conventions and principles—such is Saninism. It was as symbolic of its moment as the nihilism of *Fathers and Sons* had been for the sixties of the preceding century.

Among the older intelligentsia, many who had been sucked into the radical movement from their student days paused for the first time to examine its premises. Some shrank shuddering from the abyss over the edge of which they had just peered. Even those ardent men of action, the terrorists, found themselves, amidst forced inaction, reflecting over the meaning of their deeds. How did I get to this pass that my ideals and my

life are dedicated to executing sentence of death upon my fel-
lowmen? Boris Savinkov, one of the assassins of Minister of
the Interior Plehve, gave expression to this wonder in two novels: *Pale Horse* (1909) and *The Tale of What Was Not* (1912):

> Why shouldn't one kill?—asks the protagonist of *Pale Horse*.
> —And why is murder justified in one case and not in another?
> People do find reasons, but I don't know why one should *not*
> kill. And I don't understand why to kill in the name of this and
> that is considered right, while to kill in the name of something
> else is wrong . . . I am on the boundary between life and death,
> and there where death rules, there is no law, for law relates to
> life alone.

Terror is a creed to live and die by, a religion in which love,
and sacrifice, and . . . damnation, are inextricably linked together:

> Just remember the words: *Greater love hath no man than this,
> that a man lay down his life for his comrades.* And he must lay
> down more than his life—his soul!

Still expressing the ambiguities of Savinkov's own inner debate, one of the terrorists in *The Tale of What Was Not* cries in
anguish:

> Where shall we find the law? In the Party program? in Marx?
> in Engels? in Kant? . . . Neither Marx, nor Engels, nor Kant
> ever killed anyone. They never killed, do you hear me? They do
> not know, they cannot know what you and I know . . . What-
> ever they may have written, it still remains hidden from them
> whether we may or may not kill . . .

Nor did Russian Marxism's greater certitudes, its denser body
of doctrine and higher degree of extroversion, immunize it
against the epidemic of self-examination. Because of the recent international socialist controversy on "revisionism" versus
"Marxist orthodoxy," the argument largely turned about the
question: is it permissible, is it "orthodoxy" or "revisionism,"

for a Marxist to take any significant ideas from the prevailing fashion of neo-Kantian revival?

This debate, too, had started before the 1905 defeat. In 1900 and 1901, Bulgakov and Berdyaev, two leading Russian "neo-Kantians," had broken completely with Marxism and gone over to religion. Whereas the German and Austrian neo-Kantian Socialists had fought to retain their places inside the movement and had won recognition as a legitimate tendency, the Russian revisionists soon flung themselves passionately into the path of schism. Bulgakov became a leading theologian of the Orthodox Church, spending the last twenty years of his life (1924-44) as the director of its theological seminary in Paris. Berdyaev developed into one of the outstanding religious writers of our time, preaching a synthesis of socialism, personalism and corporate Christianity. In this, as in all things, the intensity of Russian thought made for extremism. German revisionism was a reformist dilution or an apologetic "modernization" of Marxism; Russian revisionism was a heterodoxy, a fanatic schism, a *raskol*. And the impulse of Russian "orthodoxy," particularly as embodied in Lenin, was to resort to excommunication.

The year 1904 had marked the hundredth anniversary of the death of Kant. For several years thereafter there was an intense discussion of Kantian ethics, and of "neo-Kantian" epistemology as it figured in modern scientific thought. In this discussion, the acknowledged leader of the forces of orthodox Marxism was Plekhanov. Lenin longed to support him, but refrained at first because he "did not know enough about philosophy" (Letter from Siberia to Potresov). Later he became silent for another reason: in 1904 he made a bloc with Bogdanov, who was the chief target of Plekhanov's philosophical attack! Lenin had to keep silent thereafter for five years, until he was ready to break that bloc. This enforced and humiliating abstinence explains much of the violent intensity with which he finally expressed himself when the restraint was removed.

It is hard to explain why Plekhanov (and Lenin following in his footsteps), reared as he was in a land where every question tended to be viewed as a question of ethics, should insistently have ignored the ethical aspects of this great controversy on "neo-Kantianism." For it was a two-pronged controversy, dealing as much with ethics as with epistemology. To both Plekhanov and Lenin, however, ethics itself was preconscious, as religion is for most men: something which has been acquired once and for all in one's youth, or at the moment when one made his decisive choice. Thereafter, rules of personal conduct, relations to others, and moral problems of means and end, were assumed to be settled self-evidently by one's cherished total belief. Socialism was the end which determined and sanctified the means by which it was to be arrived at. The central means was the movement to which one had dedicated one's life. Even to discuss that self-dedication seemed to these men a little "philistine" or in bad taste. Hence Plekhanov, and Lenin after him, ignored the ethical aspect of neo-Kantianism and limited their contributions to epistemology.

It was not till the period of reaction that the debate on epistemology and Marxism took full possession of the defeated movement. What was left of the Marxist intelligentsia found a measure of distraction and solace in these theoretical pursuits. Though they might seem disparate phenomena, Krassin's ceasing to make bombs in his laboratory and his gradual withdrawal from socialist activity to devote himself to engineering; Riazanov's abandonment of trade union work and of his struggle for Party unity, in order to become the greatest Marx scholar and textual critic of his generation; Lunacharsky's growing preoccupation with literature and religion and Bogdanov's with proletarian culture; and Lenin's "shameful neglect of my work on *Proletarii*" in order to immerse himself in philosophy—are all related symptoms of the deep crisis that had set in within the Social Democratic Party.

At the home of Maxim Gorky on the idyllic island of Capri, all the Bolshevik tendencies opposed to Lenin foregathered to set up a training school for Russian workers. It was by Lenin's choice, not theirs, that Gorky's home became an "opposition school" for "ultra-Leftist" Bolsheviks. Repeatedly they urged him to become one of its teachers, but he stayed away from Capri for reasons which will appear in the course of this chapter. The school did not limit itself, as Vladimir Ilyich would have liked, to politics and economics. It dealt with philosophy and natural science, the history of art, the theory of proletarian culture and proletarian "ideological organization," the history of Russian literature, of the Russian state and Church, problems of revolutionary ethics, and, of course, the "Leftist tactics" on the Duma boycott and other matters that were being pursued by the bloc built around Bogdanov. Almost insensibly Bogdanov had become a rival to Lenin for the tactical, i.e. the practical political, leadership of the Bolshevik faction. Even if Lenin had not been fighting for his very position as head of his group, still his intense concentration on politics, and on theory only insofar as it had bearing upon immediate problems of practice, would have made him regard this predominantly cultural school with misgiving. To understand the peculiar ambivalence of his attitude toward the goods of culture, we need only ponder this revealing anecdote from Gorky's *Days with Lenin:*

> One evening Lenin was listening to a sonata by Beethoven
> . . . and said: "I know nothing greater than the 'Apassionata'
> . . . I always think with pride: what marvelous things human
> beings can do! But I can't listen to music too often. It affects
> your nerves, makes you want to say stupid, nice things, and
> stroke the heads of people who could create such beauty while
> living in this vile hell. And you mustn't stroke anyone's head—
> you might get your hand bitten off. You have to hit them over
> the head, without any mercy, although our ideal is not to use
> force against anyone. Hm, hm, our duty is infernally hard" . . .

Bogdanov had come to Lenin in 1904 at a time when the latter's political fortunes were at their lowest ebb. As the reader will remember, Lenin had formed his Bolshevik faction only a year earlier (1903), with Plekhanov as its ostensible ideological leader, himself as group organizer, and Krassin as chief lieutenant inside Russia. But by 1904 Vladimir Ilyich had lost Plekhanov to the Mensheviks, had lost control of *Iskra,* and even of the Central Committee, leaving the irreconcilable "Majority" leader of yesterday virtually without a faction. It was at this critical moment that Bogdanov and his friends, most of them just released from Siberia, rallied to Lenin's standard. The newcomers were all men with a penchant for cultural and philosophical speculation, a speculation which in no wise resembled the unquestioning Marxist orthodoxy of Vladimir Ilyich. But it was enough for him that they agreed with him on organization and tactics. Almost the only continuity between the original Bolshevik leadership of 1903 and the new Bolshevik leadership of 1904 was provided by Vladimir Ilyich himself and his tactical-organizational views. This phenomenon would occur again in 1909 (when he broke with Bogdanov) and several times more. Where Lenin and two or three were gathered together, there was bolshevism.

Bogdanov (real name A. A. Malinovsky) was a medical doctor and a writer of considerable reputation on economics, sociology, natural science, and philosophy. He accounted himself a Marxian, but his was an independent and speculative mind which abhorred authoritarian attitudes in the realm of thought and rejected the notion that in the scriptures of Marx and Engels could be found the answers to all problems that might be raised by men who lived after them.

Lenin had known Bogdanov by reputation since 1898, when a copy of the latter's *Short Course in Economic Science* reached him in Siberia. Lenin found the work so good that he himself rejected a proposal from a publisher to write a manual of political economy because "it would be difficult to compete with Bogdanov." (Letters to his mother, February 12 and June 10, 1898.)

When they joined forces in 1904, the two men exchanged presentation copies of their latest works. Lenin's gift was his *One Step Forward, Two Steps Backward,* and Bogdanov's was the first volume of his *Empiriomonism*. (The second volume was published in 1905 and the third and last, written in prison, was published in 1906.) *Empiriomonism*, strongly influenced by the philosophical writings of Ernst Mach, was the work which, in 1909, was to be the chief target of Lenin's philosophical polemic.

Why did he delay for five years before he made his disagreement public? If the work was indeed a service to religion and reaction, as he was later to assert, why did he take its author into leadership in his faction?

One thing is certain: the delay was not because Vladimir Ilyich was slow to read his new associate's book. We have Lenin's own word for it (in a letter to Gorky) that he read it at once, at once disagreed with it, and wrote a long letter of private criticism to its author. When the third and final volume of *Empiriomonism* appeared in 1906, Bogdanov sent him a presentation copy from jail. Lenin immediately wrote a further "declaration of love, a little letter on philosophy which took up three notebooks!" (Lenin to Gorky, February 25, 1908.) But that did not prevent his forming his bloc with the unrepentant and unconvinced philosopher, nor his maintaining that bloc for five years until it broke up, not on philosophical matters but on tactical. This is important to establish beyond a cavil, not merely for the light it throws on Lenin as philosopher, but also for its bearing on the contention of the Leninist epigones that there is a necessary, direct and inescapable correlation between 100 per cent orthodoxy in Marxist philosophy and the very possibility of being a good revolutionist. The whole of Russian philosophical literature under Stalin is based upon this supposed deduction from Lenin's book. And Leon Trotsky has been no less insistent on this matter in the polemic he conducted during the last year of his life against his American followers, James Burnham and Max Shachtman, when they were breaking with him. (See Trotsky: *In Defense of Marxism*, Pioneer Publishers, New York, 1942, pp. 45-48, 52, 54, 79.)

Doubtless the general strength of the moods of "decadence" in 1908 contributed to Lenin's anxiety to reprove his associates publicly for their heterodox philosophy. Yet even then, as he sensed that the Bolshevik tactical bloc might be heading toward a permanent break, he reviewed the whole experiment in a letter to Gorky, and found it right and good. Moreover, he still pleaded for its continuance:

> In the summer and autumn of 1904—he wrote to Gorky in 1908—Bogdanov and I joined each other finally as Bolsheviks, and formed that tacit bloc which tacitly excluded philosophy as neutral ground. The bloc lasted throughout the entire time of the Revolution and gave us the possibility of introducing together into the Revolution those tactics of revolutionary socialism (bolshevism) which, according to my deepest conviction, were the only correct ones . . .
>
> A certain amount of conflict among the Bolsheviks on the philosophical question is, I think, unavoidable. But to split on that account would, in my opinion, be stupid. We have formed a bloc for pursuing a given set of tactics in the Party. These tactics we have pursued and are pursuing so far without differences (the only differences of opinion were on the boycott of the Third Duma elections . . .). To hamper the cause of carrying out the tactics of revolutionary Social Democracy in the Party because of arguments as to materialism or Machism would, in my opinion, be an unpardonable folly. We must carry on our scrap with each other about philosophy in such a way as not to affect *Proletarii* at all, or the Bolshevik fraction either . . . You can help . . . [Letter of Feb. 25, 1908.]

"In 1903, when I worked with him on *Iskra*," Lenin wrote to Gorky, "Plekhanov analyzed for me the error in Bogdanov's views." Hence it was after the *caveat* of his teacher that Lenin entered into the "tacit bloc" with Bogdanov.

Nor was Plekhanov slow to taunt his philosophical disciple. Your tactics, he wrote of Lenin in *Iskra,* are a revision of Marxism in politics; Bogdanov's theories are a revision of Marxism in philosophy. Since each theory gets the practice it deserves,

Machism is the proper philosophy for bolshevism. You are welcome to your Bogdanov and his Machist philosophy, "and may
all possible Machs and Avenariuses be with you!" The embar-
rassed disciple could only pretend not to understand the taunt:

> Plekhanov drags in Mach and Avenarius by the hair—he told
> his followers at the Third (All-Bolshevik) Congress of 1905.—
> It is absolutely incomprehensible to me what these men, for
> whom I haven't the slightest sympathy, have to do with the so-
> cial revolution. They write on individual and social organiza-
> tion of experience, or something of the sort, but really they have
> no ideas on the democratic dictatorship.

It would carry us too far afield to discuss Mach and his school
in the present work. But that last sentence of Lenin's is worth
holding on to. If not altogether adequate as a characterization
of Mach, it is of Bogdanov's "Machism."

*"They write on individual and social organization of experi-
ence."* Those nine words contain a clearer, fairer, more exact
account of what Bogdanov had borrowed from Mach's views
and assimilated to his own thinking, than Lenin would subsequently give anywhere in all his four hundred pages of philosophical polemics, when the bloc with Bogdanov had been
broken. In 1905, disagreeing with Bogdanov's views, he had
known how to characterize them briefly, honestly, exactly. In
1909, he distorted those views the better to discredit them. Thus
was Lenin's clear intellect ever subject to the torsion of his
powerful factional passions.

The year 1908 marked the turning point in his relations with
Bogdanov. Until that time, Lenin still hoped for a fresh armed
uprising, in which case such matters as the boycott of the Duma
would be of secondary significance. But the growing reaction
now convinced him that these tactical differences were central
instead of marginal. Philosophical differences, too, seemed more
important in the midst of the general ideological reaction. Le-

nin became increasingly restless concerning the tactical bloc "neutral on philosophy."

Bogdanov, Bazarov and Lunacharsky chose that particular moment to join hands with the Mensheviks Yushkevich and Valentinov and other writers, in the publication of a symposium on philosophy. The last straw was the title: *Outlines of the Philosophy of Marxism*! If at least they had not invoked the name of Marx to cover—as he complained to Gorky—"their smuggling of the contraband of neo-Kantianism or Machism." The articles made him "simply mad with indignation. . . . Today I read one Empiriocriticist and scold like a fishwife; tomorrow another and curse like a trooper."

Alarmed for the unity of the faction, Gorky urged him to restrain himself.

> Once a Party man has become convinced that a certain theory is decidedly wrong and harmful—Lenin answered—then he is in duty bound to oppose it . . .
> Plekhanov is entirely in the right against them . . . only he doesn't know how, or doesn't want to, or is too lazy to say it concretely, completely and simply, without frightening the public with philosophical subtleties. And I shall say this in my own fashion, cost what it may . . .

"Cost what it may!" Yet still he hoped, or so he assured Gorky, that they could continue to maintain the tactical bloc while they had it out in philosophy. But in truth the bloc itself was in a bad way, and Lenin was slowly coming to the conclusion that a split was necessary. In December, 1905, he had let "the Siberians and Caucasians" override him on the Duma question, because it seemed unimportant in the face of imminent armed uprising. In 1907, at the July Conference of Bolsheviks and Mensheviks to consider elections to the Third Duma, fourteen out of fifteen Bolshevik delegates (all but Lenin!) had been for boycott and they had named Bogdanov instead of him as spokesman for the faction. All through 1908 this nagging

conflict smoldered and flared up again: now as "boycottism," now as *otzovism* or "recallism," now as "ultimatism." Not till the middle of 1908 did Lenin win a slender majority on tactical questions in Moscow, and not until 1909 in Petersburg.

The group which thwarted him on tactical reconversion from the period of storm to the period of calm were men who had originally been attracted to him by his call for armed uprising and seizure of power. Those formerly big issues had become remote and marginal for Lenin now, while the questions of Duma elections, and practical trade union work, had become urgent and central. His associates were poets like Lunacharsky, philosophers and scientists like Bogdanov and Bazarov, historians like Pokrovsky, novelists like Gorky, romantic revolutionists in politics for whom Lenin's extremism was attractive, "softs" for whom a "hard line" possessed irresistible fascination. When they came to Lenin, he appeared to occupy the extreme red end of the Social Democratic spectrum. Now that from more somber circumstances he deduced soberer slogans and devices, shifting his place in the tactical spectrum to match the blue realities of the period, he lost much of his attractiveness and seemed to them unfaithful to "true bolshevism or Leninism." But Lenin knew that to repeat the same slogans of armed uprising and seizure of power now would be to lose contact with the masses and with reality. Their "true bolshevism" was to him but a caricature. In this Lenin was wiser than any philosopher, more attuned to social moods than any novelist, poet, or historian in his faction. The time had come, he concluded, to bring his old associates to their senses, or to sweep them aside, lest his group perish from neglect of the real possibilities and the actual tasks before it. Since the independent and self-confident Bogdanov was the leader of the heterogeneous bloc that stood in his way, Bogdanov must be discredited. Perhaps the faction would listen to him on tactics after he had discredited his opponents on the ground of philosophy. He could get off his chest the long-suppressed disagreements on philosophical matters; he could strike a blow, albeit a trifle late, for orthodox Marxism against this heterodoxy, and contribute to the counter-offensive against ideological decay and reaction.

While he was turning this over in his mind, new aberrations, not of the professional philosophers, Bogdanov and Bazarov, but of the poetic amateurs, Lunacharsky and Gorky, suddenly put into his hand an excellent stick with which to beat the lot of them and arouse the indignation of the rank and file against them all . . .

Lunacharsky and Gorky were prone to talk in the language of metaphor. Return to religion was in the air. Sensitive, as creative writers are apt to be, to all the currents charging the surrounding atmosphere, they now turned their attention to religion, about which the whole intelligentsia had been talking. Not that they proposed to serve religion, as Lenin was to charge against them. Quite the opposite: they sought to fight the recrudescence of religious orthodoxy by borrowing from its arsenal metaphorical weapons to use against it.

In 1908, Lunacharsky published *Religion and Socialism* (the first volume had appeared in 1907). It was a mixture of the history of religion, sociological analysis, and poetic enthusiasm. The second volume culminated in an apotheosis of Marxism as a "natural, earthy, anti-metaphysical, scientific and human religion" which was to put an end to all supernatural, unscientific, fetishistic, authoritarian, hierarchical faiths and substitute the "faith" of man in his socialized self, in his own powers, unity, solidarity. Hitherto God had been a reflection of man's dreams and aspirations projected into an external object of worship. God's omnipotence had been but the reflection of man's potentially unlimited power over nature, once he had socialized his own nature. "Religion is enthusiasm, and without enthusiasm nothing great can be accomplished by man." But Marxism would turn that enthusiasm and faith into their proper channels, from belief in external gods, a belief which humiliates man, into an enthusiasm for, and faith in, man's own creative powers. The future socialized humanity was the only "god" worthy of man's worship.

Gorky, doubtless influenced by Lunacharsky, next wrote a novel, *The Confession,* which reached its climax in such passages as this:

> The people, they are the creators . . . In them dwells God . . . I saw the earth, my mother, in space between the stars . . . And I saw her master, the omnipotent, immortal people . . . and I prayed: *Thou art my God, the creator of all the gods . . .*

Lenin's first impulse was to pronounce anathema against the two of them:

> A Catholic priest who violates young girls—he wrote to Gorky —is much less dangerous to democracy than are priests who do not wear surplices, priests without vulgar religion, ideological and democratic priests, who preach the creating and construction of little gods . . .

Yet at bottom he was tolerant of the vagaries of artists and had a deep and abiding affection for the two "little-god creators." Moreover, the real opponent was Bogdanov, free, to be sure, for all "god-creating" and all metaphorical talk of "faith" and "worship," but the leading contender in the realm of tactics for the command of his faction.

> I am completely and unconditionally of the opinion—he hastened to reassure Gorky—that you possess the most unerring judgment in artistic creation and that, when you create such views, both out of your artistic experience and out of philosophy, even if this philosophy is an idealistic one, you may come to conclusions which may be of enormous value to the workers' party . . .

This respect for the creative freedom of artists and their "unerring judgment in artistic creation" was one of the nobler aspects of Lenin which he never succeeded in handing down to his disciples.

Significantly, when Lenin's book on philosophy appeared, it did not contain one reference to Maxim Gorky. Lunacharsky, however, had some pretensions as philosopher and sociologist. More important, his metaphorical avowals of "religion" and "faith" were a most useful stick with which to beat Bogdanov. Lunacharsky, therefore, appears on the very first page as if he were going to be the central target in the book:

> Leaning upon all these supposedly most recent doctrines, our annihilators of dialectic materialism go so far as to speak openly in favor of fideism (in the case of Lunacharsky this is most outspoken, but in this he does not stand alone by any means!).

Since Lenin defines fideism as "putting faith in place of knowledge," the charge is not even true of Lunacharsky, still less of Bogdanov, who deplored the latter's coquetry with religious terminology. Moreover, if Lunacharsky is indeed "the most outspoken advocate of fideism" and fideism is the objective of Lenin's attack, one would expect that somewhere in the three-hundred-odd pages there would be an analysis and refutation of Lunacharsky's views. But nothing of the sort. He is mentioned a dozen times, but always glancingly and ironically in a series of three names in order to tie up his "outspoken fideism" with Bogdanov and Bazarov.

Bogdanov pointed out in answer (in *Faith and Science,* 1910) that Lunacharsky had already repented of his religious metaphors by the time Lenin's book appeared. Those metaphors of Lunacharsky's, said Bogdanov, could "only hinder the exact scientific analysis of historic religions, which have always been in the first place *authoritarian* . . . and might preserve in the minds of readers remnants of an unconscious respect for notions which ought to be abandoned." It was all right to criticize such terminology before Lunacharsky had abandoned it, just as

Engels had criticized the similar religious terminology of Feuerbach. But Engels had been careful to expound the real content
of Feuerbach's views, and "had not dreamed of confounding
those views with actual historical religions, or 'fideism' . . .
Lenin uses a diametrically opposite method with Lunacharsky,
obscuring and hiding from the reader the true content of the
views of his opponent, to give the reader the idea that Lunacharsky speaks of religion in the usual traditional sense . . ."

Lenin's authoritarian attitude toward the founders of scientific
socialism, Bogdanov continues, caused him to treat similar
aberrations in Dietzgen, and profounder ones in Feuerbach,
with gentle respect, for had not "the masters themselves" pronounced Dietzgen a "proletarian philosopher" and had not
"they themselves" acknowledged Feuerbach as a precursor and
teacher?

> Rudeness and high-handedness toward people whom one
> holds lower than oneself in position; respectfulness toward
> those whom one acknowledges as higher than oneself—is a
> common feature of *authoritarian* psychology in present-day
> society—concluded Bogdanov (italics in the original).

Lenin might be thus rude with Lunacharsky in public, but
privately he confided to Krupskaya concerning the target of
this attack:

> He will return to the Party. He is less of an individualist than
> the other two. He has a highly gifted nature such as is rarely
> met with. I have a weakness for him. What stupid words—*to
> have a weakness!* I am really very fond of him, you know, he
> is a splendid comrade! There is something of French brilliance
> about him. His levity is the result of his estheticism.

At the end of 1908, Vladimir Ilyich's sister, Anna, found a
publisher for *Materialism and Empiriocriticism* by "Vladimir
Ilyin," a pen-name already known to us—and to the police.

> From what you tell me—he wrote to Anna—everything is arranged. Splendid! I am agreed to the tone of my remarks being softened so far as Bazarov and Bogdanov are concerned. As to Yushkevich and Valentinov, it is not worth altering what I have said...

Strange notion, this, that he could keep a comradely tone toward Bolshevik "Machists" and a less comradely one toward Menshevik "Machists."

But on March 19, 1909, as the show-down in the faction nears, he writes:

> Please do not tone down the passages against Bogdanov and Lunacharsky. Our relations with them are completely ruptured. It is not worth while to modify the passages...

Such statements give us the intimate psychobiography of Lenin's work on philosophy and open a window into the innermost recesses of his temperament and methods of polemics, philosophical as well as political. Indeed, for him philosophy and politics are so closely connected that on April 8, 1909, he writes:

> It is *hellishly* important for me that the book should come out at the earliest possible date, not only for literary but also for political reasons.

This "hellish importance" derived from the fact that he had called an enlarged conference of the Editorial Board of *Proletarii* for the end of June. Only an "editorial conference," but he was secretly planning to place political and organizational matters before it. Some time earlier he had already written to Vorovsky that a split would probably occur "at the next conference." He urged Vorovsky to come personally, see to the proper election of delegates from the Russian underground, for whose expenses "we will send money." Now he wrote Vorovsky again: "If the line of the 'Left' prevails, I will leave the faction immediately." Thus the threat to resign, the big book on philosophy, the use of the funds which Victor Taratuta's maneuvers had gotten from the Schmitt estate, and the careful selection of delegates, whose addresses, as always, were in the hands of faction secretary Krupskaya, were so many careful chess moves for the checkmate of the unsuspecting co-editor, Bogdanov, at the forthcoming editorial conference. He even had replacements ready, for he was training two younger men, Zinoviev and Kamenev, to make up the second and third on the new *troika* with him, after Bogdanov had been ousted. If the new co-leaders did not possess the spirit of independence, the unshakable sense of man-to-man equality, the speculative originality, which had made Bogdanov such a troublesome collaborator, so much the better.

At the beginning of May, 1909, the book appeared in Moscow, and from July 4 to 13, the enlarged Editorial Board of *Proletarii* met in Lenin's apartment. Lenin had prepared all the resolutions and motions. On his proposal, the editorial conference set aside the old Bolshevik Center, elected at the London Congress of 1907, and assumed the power to appoint, remove and legislate. It decided that "boycottism, recallism, ultimatism, God-construction and Machism" were all of them "incompatible with membership in the Bolshevik faction." In vain did Bogdanov question the right of a mere editorial conference to remove people appointed by the Bolshevik Center, or to repeal the resolution on "neutrality in philosophy" on which the Bolshevik bloc had been based. In vain did he protest the attempt to split the faction, and the methods of "coup d'état." The moves had been prepared and thought out to the last detail, and Lenin had the votes to carry his motions. There is no way of knowing how much the big book, which nobody had yet had the time to read but which seemed to tie all the "Leftists" up with religion and "God-creation," helped to weigh in the scale. By a small but safe majority, Bogdanov and his associates were declared to have "placed themselves outside the faction."

> Not outside the Party—Lenin explained precisely.—A party can include a wide range of opinions, the extremes of which may even be diametrically opposed to each other . . .

But in 1912, Lenin's faction was to declare itself the Party! And after 1917 it was to make the state a mere instrument of the Party. What then would happen to the "wide range of opinions"?

The dissidents, a sizable minority despite the fact that Lenin had pretty largely in advance determined who should come to the enlarged editorial conference, withdrew at last and proclaimed themselves the only "true Bolsheviks": legally, because they regarded the acts of the conference as a usurpation; ideologically, because in their own minds they were true to the "original tactics of bolshevism" which had so often in recent years commanded a majority against Lenin. In token of the continuity of their bolshevism, they revived for their new journal the name borne by the first Bolshevik paper, founded by Lenin and Bogdanov at the end of 1904: *Vpered* (pronounced *Vperyod*), whence they were called for the next few years the Vperyodist Bolsheviks.

> Go your way, friends—Lenin admonished them in the columns of *Proletarii*.— We did our best to teach you Marxism and Social Democratic methods of work. We now declare decisive and irreconcilable war on the Liquidators of the Right [a subtendency among the Mensheviks, of which more later], and the Liquidators from the Left, who are corrupting the workers' party by theoretical revisionism and philistine political and tactical methods.

Materialism and Empiriocriticism, then, is first of all a document in an intra-Party struggle. This should not surprise us, for the same can be said of every line Lenin ever wrote for publication. Its primary concerns are to defend orthodox Marxism against every species of modification, revision, criticism or attack, and to convict Bogdanov and his associates of deviations from Marxist orthodoxy. But over and above this, the work has a more ambitious aim: to expound afresh the basic philosophical position of Marx and Engels, and to evaluate from its standpoint the main philosophical currents and scientific discoveries of Lenin's day.

Engels had insisted, and now Lenin insisted after him, that the recognition of a world independent of the percipient subject, and the recognition of man's ability through analysis and action to form an ever more exact notion of the nature of that world, are the prerequisites of modern science. To those who assert that there is no such "objective" world, or that it is forever unknowable, Engels answers that science and industry, man's knowledge-in-action, teach us how the unknown becomes known, how out of ignorance arises knowledge. It is this knowledge-in-action which enables us to test the correctness of our conceptions of a given phenomenon, by producing it out of its elements or determinants, by devising critical tests, by predicting and foreseeing, by revising and refining our hypotheses in terms of crucial experiments and observable errors. Many of the best pages in Lenin's book are quotations from Engels, followed by explanations and illustrations of this view. Passionately he asserts that, though the *known* be little and the *unknown* vast, the area of man's knowing and power to predict and plan and control is capable of indefinite enlargement. To postulate an *unknowable,* however, is to set arbitrary, self-degrading limits upon man's efforts to understand and master his world. In the midst of all the anti-rationalism that surrounded him in the post-1905 reaction, and that surrounds us in our own day, Lenin's plea for a rational, experimental approach to nature and society—however much he may have deviated from it himself in his own dogmatic authoritarianism in the sphere of "Marxist orthodoxy"—represents an important contribution.

Man's intelligence—he cries—may be only a feeble rushlight
in the darkness of night, but I am not going to let that flickering
flame be blown out by mystics and metaphysicians . . .

The one chapter of Lenin's book that has meaning beyond
the limits of the immediate philosophical-factional controversy
is Chapter V, entitled: "The Latest Revolution in Natural
Science." Here Lenin handles the "crisis in science" that had
just been proclaimed by Poincaré; the notion that "matter is
disappearing," or being swallowed up by energy or dissolved
into pure mathematical formulae; or that the material universe
was dissolving, merely because science was stumbling from the
one-sidedness of inert matter-without-motion into the contrary
one-sidedness of motion-without-anything-which-moves. The
approach here employed by Lenin, and more skillfully and
subtly by Engels before him, is helpful, too, in considering
fresh muddles which have arisen since their day: the supposed
entrance of "spirit" into every phenomenon by virtue of the
alleged inseparability of the thing-observed from the observer;
the emergence of "free will" inside the atom via the principle
of indeterminacy; along with other bewilderments of certain
recent scientists turned amateur philosophers and philosophers
turned amateur scientists, without sufficient mastery of the ac-
cumulated heritage of philosophic and scientific thought.

The weakness of Lenin's work, as Bogdanov hastened to
point out, was its authoritarian character. Its proofs are all
proofs by authority—the authority of Marx and Engels. The
final touchstone is always a quotation from one of their works.
The authority, on closer examination, almost always proves to
be Engels. Curiously, though Lenin mentions the name of Marx
scores of times, there is only one three-sentence quotation from
the philosophical writings of Marx in the entire book. To be
sure, Engels's more specialized *Anti-Duehring* and *Feuerbach,*
if less seminal, are more systematized, more apposite to Lenin's immediate purposes. Still, the neglect of Marx by this

orthodox Marxist suggests something concerning the limitations in his orthodoxy, like the Christianity of a theologian who forever quotes Paul but finds no use for the words of Christ.

When Lenin has succeeded in confronting some quotation from Bogdanov (or from anyone whom he can, by whatever literary stratagem, link up with Bogdanov) with some quotation from Engels, and has shown some divergence between them, his task is finished. Lenin is not only "authoritarian" himself, but he insists that all his opponents must be authoritarian, too:

> Your clamor against argument from authority—he writes—is only a screen to conceal the fact that you substitute for the socialist authorities—Marx, Engels, Lafargue, Mehring, Kautsky—the bourgeois authorities—Mach, Petzold, Avenarius and the immanentists.

In pursuance of this idea that every man must have his authorities, Lenin matches a maze of quotations from Engels with a counter-maze of quotations from the "other camp," lumping together the most diverse names, on the philosophical theory, as Bogdanov wryly observed, that "who is not with us, is against us." By this device Lenin blames Bogdanov for things he has not said, and even for things he specifically rejects. It is sufficient that Mach has said them and that Bogdanov is a "Machist" and therefore "responsible" for all of his "authority's" views. And for all other Machists! And for all the utterances of any who has praised Mach or been praised by him! This "philosophical chain-reaction method," and "quotational shock treatment," as Bogdanov dubbed them, were calculated as much to impress the reader as to overwhelm the opponent. It was the method of all authoritarian organizations, Bogdanov observed shrewdly, to "hold the chief responsible for the activities of his subordinates" and oblige them to "reflect exactly his conceptions." Bogdanov's reply did not do a very good job of defending his own philosophical speculations, but he had probed the weakest spot in Lenin's intellectual armor.

The most notable difference between Engels and Lenin is the angry moral tone of Lenin's attacks, the opprobrious moral epithets that pepper his pages. Engels had spoken of three philosophical "camps": materialism, idealism and agnosticism. Insensibly, Lenin converts "camps" into "parties" and proclaims that "philosophy is a *partisan* struggle." Where Engels finds "philosophical agnosticism" to be a "shame-faced way of accepting materialism by the back door," Lenin enlarges the "shame" until it becomes a monstrous thing, a plot to drag in not materialism but "religion by the back door." Those in the "idealist camp" are at least to be respected as "open agents of reaction and religion," but those in the "agnostic camp" are to be exposed as covert agents, whose agnosticism is "only a despicable cloak of servility to idealism and fideism."

Marx and Engels could be scornful and ironic in theoretical controversy, and devastating and reckless in their private letters to each other. But even in the *Anti-Duehring,* which so largely served Lenin as source and model, all that Engels aims at is to convict Professor Duehring of inconsistency and "higher nonsense." Nowhere do we find the imputations of evil intention that abound in Lenin's pages, or the passionately held belief that defects in a man's epistemological theories are defects in his character, willful immoralities of the spirit leading to inevitable political sin. ("Genuinely scientific works," Engels had admonished Duehring, "avoid such dogmatic-moral expressions as truth and error.")

If Lenin's philosophical targets disavow a view he has imputed to them, it is sinister trickery. If they have modified a view under criticism (his criticism or another's), it is but the better to deceive. If their views seem very close to his, or to his masters' —still worse: they are "surreptitiously and illegally borrowing" from materialism to hide their true intentions and confuse the right-thinking. As a whole, "professors of philosophy are scientific salesmen of theology." Mach and his school are "graduated flunkies of theism." They are all conspirators, plotting against science and the further progress of mankind. "The philosophy of Mach, the scientist, is to science what the kiss of Judas is to Christ."

This method of polemics, and the very epithets employed in it, derive from the intense ethical bias and passionate fanaticism of Russian thought. For reasons suggested in the first chapter, Russian nineteenth-century thought reduced politics to ethics, without so much as a residue of mere practical concern or experimental interest. Art and literature and criticism were no less questions of morality. Even science was a moral creed to live by. "Science," cried the gentle Herzen, "there is no reason why I should hide words in the depth of my soul—Science is Love!" And the problems of epistemology, the most difficult, subtle, and general problems that can engage the thought of mankind, were made into moral issues, too. The reader will find Lenin at enormous pains, by the "chain-reaction and quotational shock-treatment" methods, to reduce every opponent's views to "solipsism." When he has driven his opponent into that corner, his indignation knows no bounds. As we read, we are reminded of the men of the Russian enlightenment, who, like Belinski and Herzen, regarded solipsism (extreme subjectivism) as a kind of logical-moral defect of character, arrogant, egotistical, vile. Consistent solipsism, they thought, makes the petty ego of its disciple into the measure of truth and error, right and wrong, good and evil, permitting him to betray all ideals, logically leading him to commit any crime from murder to suicide. When dealing with such issues, there is more to Lenin's scorn than worked-up indignation and the desire to discredit his factional opponents (more than his "I shall always act thus whenever a split is involved"). The overtones of anathema and excommunication are part of that Russian polemical heritage which caused the Slavophiles to brand Chaadaiev an "apostate," Granovsky a "corrupter of the youth," Herzen a "lackey in Western livery." And we can hear no less the Westernizers retorting with the epithet "Slav gendarmes in the name of Jesus Christ" or Merezhkowsky accusing Gogol of "betraying Pushkin" by his "all-devouring sickly mysticism."

Belinski, atheist though he was, had proclaimed the need of a "faith" for "without faith I cannot live." Herzen had rejected "the heavy cross of disillusioned knowledge." Odoevski had cried that "to be happy, man must have a luminous axiom, one that is all-embracing, one that brings deliverance from the torment of doubt." This spirit, unexpressed, goes far to explain the fury with which Lenin attacked any slightest "deviation" which might sow in the solid granite of his own faith the fissuring seed-corn of a doubt:

> You cannot eliminate even one basic assumption, one substantial part of this philosophy——it is as if it were a solid block of steel——without abandoning objective truth, without falling into the arms of bourgeois-reactionary falsehood.

Materialism and Empiriocriticism appeared too late to have much influence upon the conference proceedings which expelled Bogdanov and his friends. It was little noticed, little sold, little read. Bogdanov as philosopher was not of large enough caliber to have attracted much general attention. Moreover, by 1909, the entire controversy, epistemological and ethical, was already on the wane. Insofar as the book represented a determined counter-thrust against the religious, mystical, soul-searching, anti-rational moods of post-1905 Russia, it had been delayed too long because of Lenin's "tacit bloc" with the "empiriomonist." It turned out to be a deployment of heavy artillery to a part of the battlefield that had largely been vacated. It is significant that Lenin failed to follow it up, as he had his other large works, with a series of special articles in the press. When Bogdanov answered it in a brief defense (the eighty-page pamphlet *Vera i nauka*—"Faith and Science"—Moscow, 1910), Lenin did not even trouble to make a rejoinder.

As Lenin had shrewdly suspected, Lunacharsky did, but Bogdanov did not, return to his camp after the tactical and philosophical controversies had blown over. During the war, Bogdanov was an internationalist, which prompted Lenin, despite his previous anathemas, excommunications and thunders concerning the "kiss of Judas," to write Shlyapnikov in October, 1916, suggesting the possibility of a "new bloc with the Machists." (Lenin, Vol. XXXV, p. 185.)

After the Bolshevik seizure of power in 1917, in which he took no part, Bogdanov sought to serve the new society by founding and guiding the Prolecult movement. Driven out of this field by Lenin, he returned to his first love, the medical laboratory. He became founder and Director of the Moscow Institute for Blood Transfusion, a new field in which blood types and their importance had not yet been established. In 1928, because of his uncertainty as to the outcome, Bogdanov performed a blood transfusion on himself, and died in its course.

Bazarov served the new Lenin regime for many years in economic construction and planning, only to be framed up in one of the earliest show trials, the "Menshevik Trial" of 1931, whereafter he disappeared, no doubt dying in the purges. Valentinov, who scored third in condemnatory passages in Lenin's book, also served the Soviet Government in the realm of economic planning. Sent abroad with Piatakov in 1928, he is still alive in Paris, well up in his eighties, enfeebled in body, but young and vigorous in spirit. He has contributed a steady stream of essays, memoirs, pamphlets, dealing with Russian philosophical, political and economic thought in—rare virtue in these fields—a beautiful Russian prose. His "Vstrechi s Leninym" ("Meetings with Lenin") is the best close-up of Lenin's spirit that has been done by any one.

Lenin's book against Mach and these "Machists" created no stir when published. But after he came to power, and still more in the hands of his successors, it has acquired considerable influence in the history of contemporary thought. Published in enormous editions, translated into many tongues, it has been studied and cited by zealous disciples all over the world. In Russia it is now a basic text for the "training" of intellectuals and Party theoreticians. As Lenin used Engels, so the Leninists use Lenin: as a sword to slay the lurking dragon of "fideism";

as a "quotational shock treatment and chain reaction" to link up and overwhelm all opposition, dissent, or independent thought; as a thread to guide the faithful through the labyrinth of modern science and philosophy. It has been used as a reagent to test new doctrines in such diverse fields as relativity, atomic theory, psychoanalysis, genetics, cybernetics, and theoretical mathematics. Its exegesis of the philosophical insights of Engels and Marx stands today as a coarsening screen between official Russian Marxist thought and the more flexible, receptive, penetrating thinking of the founders of Marxism. On this exegesis by Lenin has been superimposed an exegesis of the exegesis by Stalin.* Thus do commentaries upon commentaries upon texts which have become scriptures continue to grow into a body of official state philosophy. Inevitably, where there is orthodoxy there must be heresy. And where the state enforces the orthodoxy, inevitably there must be the burning of heretical writings and autos-da-fé of the heretics. Not for nothing does purge suggest purification.

Lenin's angry moral tone, dim echo of anathema and excommunication, has become the model for the official polemical style employed in the most subtle fields of abstract thinking and scientific and philosophical discussion. Lacking Lenin's strong intellect and originality, lacking his "weakness" for a Gorky or a Lunacharsky, and possessing infinitely more power and zeal to enforce their anathemas and edicts of excommunication, innumerable disciples hurl their fragments of text and torrents of epithet. If we are to accept the aphorism—a little unjust to philosophy—which holds that "philosophy consists in asking questions, sophistry in answering them, and fanaticism in enforcing the answers," then Lenin's work, though intended as a blow against anti-rationalism and religious obscurantism, has been fated to serve a quasi-religious fanaticism of its own: developing into a state philosophy or a state faith, the faith of a state relentless, irreconcilable and omnipotent in "enforcing the answers."

* Stalin: *Dialectical and Historical Materialism*. First published as Chapter IV of Stalin's *Short History of the Communist Party of the Soviet Union*, and then reprinted as a separate work.

CHAPTER THIRTY

THE
SPLIT
BECOMES
PERMANENT

When the Central Organ was being discussed, I attacked its editors sharply because they forgot at times that *The Social Democrat* was not only written for the comrades abroad who knew all about the inner party fights . . . but mainly for the comrades in Russia. I quoted some unsigned passages from *The Social Democrat,* which made rude personal attacks on the representative from the Social-Democratic Party of Poland-Lithuania on the Editorial Board of *The Social Democrat.* I demanded to know who had brought such methods into our Central Organ . . . But just as I finished the quotation, I was called to order by the Chairman because of 'the uncomradely tone of my attacks.' He had not noticed that it was not my words but those of the quotation which I was reading. At this point Comrade Lenin rose to declare that the words in question were his. The Chairman became confused and the Party Congress broke into loud laughter.

—FROM OSSIP PIATNITSKI'S
MEMORIES OF THE PRAGUE CONGRESS (1912).

he five years preceding World War I are largely a tale of splits and spies. Lenin's enemies blame all the splits on his lust for power or his "splitting mania," while his admirers attribute them to his prophetic foresight. Since he was crowned by the Goddess Success in 1917, runs their argument, everything he did before must have been wise and right.

As we shall see, we cannot completely ignore Lenin's role as "aggressor" in these splits—nor discount the secret intervention of the police either. Yet the fact that the divisions affected all movements alike, even those with which Lenin had little or no connection, suggests that there must have been some wider social and political meaning as well.

If the Bolsheviks split into three factions, so did the Mensheviks. So did the Social Revolutionary Party. The Social Democratic Party of Poland and Lithuania (Rosa Luxemburg's party) split into two bitterly hostile parts, as did the Polish Socialist Party (Pilsudski's party). Clearly, the defeat of 1905 had served to engender a split atmosphere and bring out differences of political approach in a previously undifferentiated revolutionary movement.

But if we examine the Polish splits, we arrive at unexpected results. Both factions in the Social Democratic Party, as well as the Left Wing faction of Pilsudski's Polish Socialist Party, all joined Lenin and the Communist International after 1917! Yet, during the bitter years we are examining, they denounce one another with the fury of schismatics, schismatics who must have been very close to each other though each of whom fancied that his minuscule fragment of difference was truth's infallible touchstone. The Leading Committee of the Polish Social Democracy (Luxemburg, Tyszka, Dzierzinski, Warski, Marchlewski), located in Berlin, expels the "Warsaw Opposition" (Radek, Hanecki, Unschlicht, and others), charging them with being "Lenin's splitters," and "agents of the police." The aggressor is not Lenin but Tyszka, who ran his Leading Committee even more dictatorially than did Lenin his Bolshevik faction.

What must be our astonishment then to find Jan Tyszka (Lev Grozowski), under the name of Leo Jogiches, Rosa Luxemburg and Marchlewski among the founders of the Spartacus movement, which became the nucleus of the German Communist Party. Marchlewski in turn becomes a Soviet official and a founder of the Polish Communist Party, while Dzierzinski becomes the head of Lenin's secret political police, the Cheka or GPU! In short, those who voted to expel the "Leninist splitters" and "police spies" were so close to Lenin in spirit that when it came to the test of war and revolution they and he found themselves fighting side by side.

And "the Leninist splitters" whom they expelled also became their co-workers and Lenin's, Radek as chief journalistic spokesman for the Soviet Government and the Comintern, Unschlicht as Assistant Chief of the GPU of which his old opponent Dzierzinski was the Chief. This last fact provides another curious problem for us to consider: why so many Poles became high officials of the Soviet Secret Police. Besides the two top officials, Dzierzinski and Unschlicht, there was the Russified Pole of the Vperyodist Bolsheviks, Menzhinski, acting GPU Chief after Dzierzinski's death. Similarly, three members of the NKVD figure today as rulers of the new Poland: President Beirut, Commissar of Security Radkiewicz, and that silent figure who manipulates things behind the scenes, Henrykowski (real name Saul Amsterdam). We cannot pursue any further here the curious story of Poles in the Soviet Secret Police. What interests us for the moment is that all three Polish factions, the two wings of the Social Democracy, and the Left Wing of the Polish Socialist Party, are found fighting shoulder to shoulder with Lenin after 1917, from which we are forced to conclude that there must have been a good deal that was personal, artificial and atmospheric in their horrendous battles with Lenin and each other in the pre-war years. Actually, the generation of Luxemburg, Tyszka-Jogiches, Dzierzinski, Radek, Warski, Unschlicht, etc., provided the only group of political revolutionaries in Europe comparable to Lenin's group and spiritually close to it.

Leaving on one side the Polish quarrels and those that tore apart the Social Revolutionary Party, let us see if we can extract some political meaning from the splits in which Lenin was more directly concerned.

If we begin with the Bolsheviks, our point of departure is Lenin's expulsion of the Vperyodist Bolsheviks (Duma boycotters, recallists, ultimatists, "Machists" and "God-creators") in 1909: Bogdanov, Lunacharsky, Polyansky, Alexinsky, Manuilsky, Pokrovsky, Menzhinsky, and others less important to our story. Clearly this is a heterogeneous group, some of whom differed with Lenin mainly on theoretical matters, but all of whom differed with him on the tactical matter of the Duma. In the next few years, the Vperyodists split into two groups: a "Proletarian Culture" group (Bogdanov, future founder of the Proletcult; Lunacharsky, future Soviet Commissar for Education; Polyansky, leading Soviet literary critic)—and an "Orthodox Marxist" group (Alexinsky, Manuilsky, Pokrovsky and Menzhinsky). Since we have here not only the future Soviet cultural leaders but also a future Comintern leader (Manuilsky, now "Ukrainian" delegate to the United Nations), and a future GPU leader (Menzhinsky), once more we are confronted with the fact that all these excommunicated heretics—with the exception of Bogdanov, who served the Soviet Government, and Alexinsky, who opposed it—find their way back to Lenin during the World War.

Still it is not as difficult as with the Polish factions to find some meaning in the split between Lenin and the Vperyodists. All of the latter differed with Lenin on a key tactical matter: their attitude toward the Duma. Hence we can reduce their various shadings to a common denominator: all are revolutionary romanticists reluctant to abandon the "pure revolutionary tactics" of 1905 and to utilize the narrow legal opportunities

offered by the Stolypin constitution during the years of reaction. They are, therefore, but the one-sided extension of a major aspect of Lenin's more complex and flexible approach to
armed uprising. This would explain why they came back to
him in the years of direct revolutionary storm.

The question arises: why did Lenin choose to expel such sub-
jectively loyal revolutionists, in place of taking his chances on
persuading them, or persuading his faction against them, while
permitting them to remain within it? The answer to this we
find in Lenin's temperament, in the "orthodoxy-heresy" atmosphere of Russian political thought, in the bitterness of the
years of reaction, in Lenin's conception of the nature of a faction, and, above all, in his fear that they might capture the
group machinery or get in the way of its proper functioning.
They were the more dangerous to him because the type of instinctively rebellious Russian workers to whom bolshevism appealed was easily influenced by this one-sided, romantic extension of a major aspect of that in Lenin which appealed to them
most.

If we turn to the Mensheviks, we find them in the same year
1909 developing a tendency that is the symmetrically opposite
pole to the Vperyodist Bolsheviks: namely, the Menshevik Liquidators. If the Vperyodists made a fetish of illegality and abhorred every effort at legal work in trade union or Duma, their
Menshevik antipode was an analogous one-sided extension of
the Menshevik zeal to seek opportunities for legal, open, public activity.

The new constitution permitted such activity: Duma elections
and campaigns; parliamentary activity inside the Duma; the
legal chartering of trade unions; and, after 1910, legal newspapers. To be sure, all this was circumscribed within rather narrow limits and often the new legalism was arbitrarily violated.
Yet the opportunities were genuine and their scope slowly expanded.

Many advanced Menshevik workers became so engrossed in
these union and electoral activities—particularly the former—

that they began to feel that the underground party had outlived its usefulness. Its conspirative methods seemed to them now a handicap; it was honeycombed with spies; its illegal papers with their large phrases and negligible circulations provided pretexts for police raids and withdrawal of union charters. (The Bolsheviks were particular offenders in their carelessness about union legality and their zeal to distribute their illegal press directly through the unions.) The efforts of the underground to control from secret places and even from abroad the activities of the legal organizations were so many violations of autonomy and democracy. "Abroad" was a breeding ground of bitter faction controversies that reached Russia muted, dim, divisive and unintelligible. It was time to "crawl out of the cellar hole" into the light of public life. "Liquidationism" was thus as natural and one-sided an extension of an important Menshevik aspiration as the Vperyodist trend was of Leninism.

Lenin was more ruthless than the other Russian leaders in his zeal to excommunicate heresies—in his own camp no less than in the opposing one. He seized upon this antipodal symmetry to proclaim his famous "war on two fronts": against boycottism and against liquidationism. Both movements led "objectively" to the "liquidation" of the kind of movement he thought necessary. He would expel both "the liquidators of the right and the liquidators of the left," and out of the remainder build a revolutionary socialist party which would know how to combine both legal and illegal work—but of course, under the control of the underground. Since Lenin was ready to expel those closest to him, he was in a particularly strong position for his struggle with Martov, who did not believe in expulsions, for Martov was, in Lenin's language, temperamentally a "conciliator." By his fight on two fronts, Lenin was aiming a blow not merely at the two opposed "deviations," but no less at the very core of menshevism, since the Menshevik faction as a whole was striving for a displacement of the main center of gravity from the illegal to a legal party.

On the surface, Martov and Lenin were close to each other. Each was for continuing the underground party, and each was for taking advantage of the legal opportunities afforded by Duma elections and the law of March 4/17, 1906, permitting the forming of legal trade unions. But as Martov conceived the underground, it was to be a mere skeleton apparatus held in reserve in the event of a forced relapse into complete illegality. To Lenin, on the other hand, the legal activities were always a skeletal affair, utilized to broaden the sphere of operations of the underground party.

As we know from his *What's to Be Done?*, Lenin distrusted legal trade unions under any circumstances, fearing the independence they might develop and the "bourgeois ideology" they might generate. Hence, his conception of trade union work was largely limited to

> ... utilizing the trade unions and other organizations, legal and semi-legal, in order to guarantee in them the predominant influence of Social Democracy and to transform them, as far as possible, into points of support of the Social Democratic Party.

He would have the underground build tightly disciplined secret "cells" or "fractions" within them to secure control and "the recognition by the unions of the ideological direction of the Social Democratic Party . . . the leadership of all activities of the unions by the Party."*

Martov, on the contrary, regarded the trade unions and the party as two equally justified autonomous forms of the general socialist labor movement.

This distrust of the trade unions and limitation of trade union work largely to organizational and political control was to cost the Leninists dear in 1917. "We did not win the trade unions until after the October Revolution of 1917," Zinoviev was

---

* *Collected Works* of Lenin, Third Russian Edition, Vol. XII, pp. 441, 447-48. For a complete study of Lenin's views on the trade unions, see S. Schwarz: *Lénine et le mouvement syndical*, Ed. Nouveau Prométhée, Paris, 1935.

to record in his Party History of 1922. "Up till then the Mensheviks had the majority there." The "dictatorship of the proletariat" had to be set up in 1917 against the will of the majority of the organized proletariat!

An analogous difference of approach is observable in the attitudes of the two men toward the Duma. Martov was inclined to give considerable independent value to parliamentary activity. The Menshevik Deputies were generally men of high leadership caliber; the Bolshevik, with one exception to be noted later, were all simple workmen lacking in self-confidence on the floor of the Duma. The Mensheviks saw in the Duma faction democratically elected spokesmen of broad masses of workers, capable of forming a legal leadership for a broad, legal labor party. The socialist Deputies, they thought, should operate as a largely autonomous fraction, guided, to be sure, by the program and major aims of the Party, but empowered to decide matters of policy and technique in their day-to-day activities without continuous dictation and instruction by the émigré underground executive committee. Lenin, however (who, except for the single year 1906-07, always managed to control that underground committee), felt that it should instruct the Social Democratic Deputies on all matters large and small, review and pass on all their speeches, motions, interpellations, projects of "law." Lenin and Zinoviev and Kamenev even wrote entire speeches to be delivered as their own by individual Deputies.

The Mensheviks held that their representatives in parliament should introduce actual legislative proposals in the interest of labor and of democracy generally. They should work, besides, for the independence of the Duma as a whole from the Tsar, for the creation of a cabinet responsible to the Duma, for an opposition bloc of liberals and laborites against reaction and absolutism. The Tauride Palace (where the Duma met) might even serve someday as a symbol and rallying center for the entire nation against the Tsar, much as the Estates General had served in the French Revolution. (It actually served so in March, 1917.)

But to Lenin, the Tauride Palace was only a vast sounding-board from which revolutionists, clothed with Deputies' mandates and parliamentary immunities, might expose this whole game of parliamentarism; expose too the liberals and Constitutional Democrats (Kadets) as "the main enemy of the revolution." The aim of their speeches and proposals inside the Duma was neither to secure parliamentary legislation nor to strengthen the Duma's powers, but to summon the masses to street demonstrations, strikes, and other forms of extra-parliamentary struggle. To parliamentary activities as such, Lenin always assigned an auxiliary, never an independent, value.

No sooner had Lenin expelled the Vperyodist Bolsheviks than a new opposition arose within his ranks: the "Conciliators" or, as they called themselves, the "Party Bolsheviks." They were opposed to his ruthless policy of split and expulsion. They were "conciliatory" not only toward the expelled Bolsheviks, but toward the Mensheviks, too. It was all very well, said they, to form factions and tendencies, argue for one set of tactics rather than another, and seek to get a majority for one's trend. But it was not all right to split the Party into two separate parties or sliver it into fragments. Repeatedly they restrained Lenin, got into the way of his driving energies, forced him into new unity gestures, temporary organizational compromises or retreats.

In January, 1910, shocked by the revelation that Lenin had been the secret guiding hand behind the Tiflis holdup, the "expropriation" of the heirs of the manufacturer Schmitt, and other exploits, they joined with Vperyodists, Mensheviks, Liquidators, and with Trotsky's "non-factional" group, against Lenin. The combination, expressive of the longing for all-in unity among ordinary Russian workers, forced him for a time to the wall. At the "united" plenary session of the Party Central Committee held in January, 1910, Vladimir Ilyich was on the defensive for three rage-filled weeks. He had to agree to burn the remaining five-hundred-ruble banknotes of the Tiflis holdup; he had to turn over the Schmitt money. He had to liquidate his faction paper, *Proletarii*, and agree to a new general Party paper, *Sotsial Demokrat*, with an equal number of Bolshevik and Menshevik editors: Lenin and Zinoviev, Martov and Dan, with a representative of the Polish Social Democracy, Warski, to break any deadlock that his parity editorship might get into. Trotsky's non-factional Vienna *Pravda* was declared an official Party organ: Kamenev was dispatched to assist him in editing it; and the Central Committee was instructed to provide it with funds. Lenin tried to turn the new bloc unity into a narrower "Leninist" political unity "against Liquidators and Boycotters" but in this, too, he was checked. He succeeded in getting the two "heretical" tendencies condemned in a resolution (Plekhanov deserting the Mensheviks for this purpose), but the Plenum voted to invite the Liquidators to participate in the life of the underground party and to name three of their number to the underground Central Committee.

How this "unity" looked to the temporarily cornered Lenin we know from a letter to Gorky of April 11, 1910—the first Lenin had written to him since the quarrels over the Otzovist-Machist-God Creators in 1908:

> In the plenum of the Central Committee ("the long plenum" —three weeks long the torture continued, all nerves went to pieces, a hundred thousand devils!) to the serious and deep-going forces making for unity . . . were added trivial and petty ones. There was a mood of "reconciliation in general" (without clear thoughts as to with whom? for what? how?). There was hate for the Bolshevik Center for its merciless ideological war. There was squabbling and, among the Mensheviks, the desire to make a scandal. And out of all this was born a child suffering from an abscess . . . Either we will lance the abscess, drain it, cure the child and bring it up. Or the child will die. Then we will remain childless for a while (that is: we will rebuild the Bolshevik faction) and then we will give birth to a healthier child . . .
>
> The Plenum wanted to unite *everybody*. Now the Golosites (Martovites) are backing out. This abscess *must* be removed. Without squabble, scandal, torture, filth, and scum, this cannot

be accomplished. Here we are sitting now right in the midst of the thickest of the mess. Either the Russian Central Committee will clip the wings of the Golosites by removing them from the important posts (for example, from the Central Organ, etc.) or we will have to restore the faction . . . To sit in the midst of this squabble and scandal, torture and scum is nauseating. But it is unpardonable to yield to one's mood. Émigré life is now a hundred times more oppressive than it was before the revolution. Émigré life and squabbling are inseparable.

But the squabbling will die away . . . The development of the Party on the other hand strides on and on through all the devilish difficulties of the present situation. The cleansing of the Social Democratic Party of its dangerous "deviations," of Liquidationism and Otzovism, strides undeviatingly forward; within the framework of unification it has *advanced significantly farther than before.* With Otzovism we finished, essentially, at the Plenum. With Liquidationism we didn't; the Mensheviks managed to *hide the snake,* but now it is dragged out into God's light, now we will wipe it out and are wiping it out! . . .

Clearly, the Mensheviks did not yet know their Lenin after all the quarrels they had had with him. They had backed him into a corner at the Plenum. He was morally under a cloud. They had rallied a majority against him and for unity. But they did not use their majority as he would have used it. They did not remove him from the strategical posts. Not only did they misjudge him; they misjudged the Liquidators whom they were trying to protect against him. On Martov's motion and against Lenin's opposition, the Plenum had voted to invite the Liquidators to delegate three of their number to join the underground Central Committee in Russia. But to the Liquidators as to Lenin, the question of an underground party had become a question of principle—from opposite viewpoints. The three invited men flatly refused to have anything to do with this underground committee. ("We will not fall into that trap!") That was all Lenin needed! "The snake has been dragged out into God's light . . . The Plenum decision has been violated," he cried, and reopened his "merciless war."

When the Bolshevik "Conciliators," who had a majority in

Russia, proposed further negotiations with yet other Liquidator-leaders, Lenin ignored them. When Martov and Dan tried to write of their viewpoint in the *Sotsial Demokrat* (which they supposedly edited jointly with Lenin and Zinoviev), he barred its columns to them. (The Polish "arbitrator," Warski, voted with him, giving him a majority of three to two on the Editorial Board, so that the paper no longer represented a united party but only his tendency once more.)

At the same time, Lenin sought to make unity with the Plekhanov wing of the Mensheviks, against the Martov majority and against the Liquidators. Plekhanov had been forming a separate grouping since 1909 because he, too, thought Martov too conciliatory toward the Liquidators. "My dear and much respected Comrade," Lenin now wrote to him in San Remo, Italy:

> I fully share your thoughts expressed in Number 11 of *Dnevnik* [*Dnevnik Sotsialdemokrata*—"Diary of a Social Democrat," Plekhanov's own paper], on the need for a close and sincere union between all true Social Democratic elements in the struggle against the Liquidators and Otzovism. I should like very much to talk to you about the new situation arising in the Party. If you think it necessary, too, and if your health permits, write or wire a few words to me saying when you can arrange a meeting with me in San Remo. I am ready to go to you for that purpose. [Letter of March 29, 1910.]

The rapprochement with Plekhanov was brief and unhappy. Plekhanov wrote dithyrambs to the underground. He abhorred the Liquidators. He wanted to defeat them, convince them, convert them—anything but expel them. To him they were, after all, advanced socialist workingmen who had "gone astray." Lenin, however, wanted to expel them at once. And not only them! He wanted to expel at the same time Martov and all the Menshevik majority, who were guilty of "hiding and protecting" the Liquidators. And of course, he wanted to confirm the expulsion of his own private heretics, the Otzovist Bolsheviks. That would have left the Plekhanovites alone in the Party with the Leninists, a situation similar to the one Lenin had tried to bring about after the first split of 1903. Plekhanov had shrunk from it then. He shrank from it now. To cap the climax, Lenin and his supporters lost no time in using their contacts with the Plekhanovites to try to win them away from Plekhanov and his "party-loyal menshevism" over to complete bolshevism—the first example of a method of "uniting" which in later days was to become known under the name of the "united front from below."

All through 1911, a crucial year, Lenin drove steadily ahead toward his own kind of "unity"—unity of those who accepted his political line, which, as always, he was convinced was the only right one; under the leadership of the Central Committee he controlled, which he was convinced was the best possible leadership for the Party. Two events of the year 1911 assured the triumph of his solution of the Party crisis.

When Alexei Rykov, future Premier of the Soviet Union and at that time the outstanding leader of the "Party Bolsheviks" or "Conciliators," left for Russia to line up the Bolshevik faction against Lenin's splitting and expulsion activities, the police intervened. For reasons which will appear in the course of the next chapter, they had detailed reports on where everyone in Lenin's group stood politically, and they knew everybody's whereabouts. When Rykov left for Russia with good prospects of getting a majority for his position in the Bolshevik underground, the police picked him up immediately and prevented him from reaching Lenin's adherents. At the time it seemed a mere accident, one arrest like any other. But it left the "Conciliator" Bolsheviks under such inept, second-string leaders as Lozovsky (real name Solomon Abramovich Dridzo), whom we shall meet later as head of the Communist trade union international. He soon became sick of the squabbling and weary of the effort of opposing the implacably tireless Lenin. He gave up the struggle, concerning himself entirely with activity in the French trade union movement. The police helped to discredit the Conciliators by circulating a report to the effect that Rykov had been picked up with a number of addresses of members of the Russian underground carelessly carried on his person. Writes Krupskaya:

> Later this matter was cleared up . . . In Leipzig, where Piatnitsky was working on the shipping of literature to Russia, there lived a certain Brendinsky, who transported the literature . . . Later it was discovered that this Brendinsky . . . was an *agent provocateur*. He coded the addresses for Rykov. This explains why the police were in possession of all the addresses although nothing was taken from Rykov when he was searched.

The other decisive event of 1911 was an act of desperation on the part of Martov. Only a year ago, he had had a majority against Lenin at the January 1910 Plenum. That majority had voted for re-enlisting the Liquidators, for Party unity, for an equal co-editorship of the Party official organ by Lenin and Zinoviev, Martov and Dan. But they had forborne to remove Lenin from his posts so as "not to provoke a split." Now Lenin ignored the decisions of the Plenum; denied Martov space, even for an individual, signed article in the paper they were supposed to be editing jointly; drove ahead, under more favorable circumstances, toward a split in which he should remain in control of the official apparatus. In desperation, Martov tried to restore the favorable situation of 1910 by exposing once more, in more public fashion, Lenin's complicity in the revolutionary holdups, in the passing of stolen funds, preparations for counterfeiting, extortion from the Schmitt heirs. He published in Paris, in the Russian tongue, his detailed account of all he had been able to learn, insofar as it was already known to the police. The pamphlet, *Saviors or Destroyers,* with which the reader is already familiar, was intended to back Lenin into a corner once more and compel him to moderate his "implacable war." It served only to steel his will and widen the breach. The things Martov exposed seemed to Lenin good and right, if not in themselves, then in their origins (out of the armed bands) and in their sanctifying end, which for him justified all such means.

But he was not likely to forgive their exposure, or find it possible to work together with the man who had made it. Kautsky, who in the International Socialist Bureau was working for the reunification of the splintered Russian Party, appraised the pamphlet as a provocation to the widening of the breach.

> We do not see, as you do—he wrote to the Vperyodist Bolshevik Lunacharsky—we do not see in Lenin and his supporters the cause of the split. In the actions of Lenin we see only an answer to the offensive pamphlet of Martov against him, which appears entirely senseless if it doesn't aim to force a split.

Plekhanov made the same appraisal. At the very least, Martov had made a blunder in trying to use the same weapon twice. Its positive effect was bound to be weaker the second time, and its more public use could but embitter further the strained relations in the émigré world and in the underground. Only if he were prepared to seek the expulsion of Lenin and his supporters from the movement did it have practical sense. But such an expulsion was alien to Martov's thought. Moreover, it would have been only the obverse side of what Lenin was seeking at the moment.

Lenin's answer to this unintended declaration of war was the calling of an "All-Russian Party Conference." He ignored the protests of the Bolshevik Conciliators, and the very existence of the joint Central Committee of which he and Martov were members. As in 1904, he set up a new, rump "Organization Committee" of his own followers, and dispatched invitations to all the units of the Russian underground. As usual, his connections with that underground were superior to those of the other side, since his wife was Party Secretary, and since he had been in possession of the funds necessary to dispatch organizers and agents to the localities.

The Conference was held secretly in Prague, in the People's House of the Czechoslovak Social Democratic Party. But when the delegates arrived from the Russian underground, though they heard only Lenin's version of the splits and schisms, they were deeply upset. Before the Conference began, the first seven to arrive voted over his protest to send invitations to Plekhanov and his group of Party Mensheviks, to Trotsky and his non-factional faction in Vienna, and to others whom Lenin had quietly excluded. The invitations came too late, and were not accepted, which was all right with Lenin. Plekhanov wrote: "The makeup of your conference is so one-sided that it would be better, i.e. more in the interests of Party unity, if I stayed away." Trotsky wrote a long letter (which came too late for the Conference) in which he recognized the nonfactional character of some of the delegations from the Russian underground, but urged that the makeup of the Conference was too one-sided, its manner of convocation too arbitrary, and that the way to Party unity lay through an agreement of all tendencies to join in a call for a common convention. Two Plekhanovites showed up, one to protest in Plekhanov's name, the other ripe for winning over by Lenin. The Poles and Latvians and other national border parties stayed away; the Martovites and Liquidators were not invited; the Conciliators were leaderless and in eclipse. Lenin was left alone with some unconditional followers, some waverers, and some uninformed delegates from the Russian underground whose desire for unity was no match for his driving desire for split.

With characteristic boldness, he persuaded the Prague Conference of 1912 to consider itself a "Congress of the Russian Social Democratic Labor Party" and to assume all the rights and functions of a Party congress. The old Central Committee was declared to have broken down and to have ceased its organized existence. The "Congress" elected a new one of Lenin, Zinoviev, Orjonikidze, Goloshekin, Spandaryan, Malinovsky and Schwartzman. The last named was a Plekhanovite who had been won over. The others were 100 per cent Leninists. Neither Rykov, who was in prison, nor any other Conciliator was included. No place was left for Martov or Dan, for Plekhanov or

Trotsky or any of their adherents. This was to be a pure, "irreconcilable" Bolshevik Central Committee to speak in the name of the entire Party. The other factions, including even the Conciliator Bolsheviks, would have to submit or be read out. The alternates, too, who were to function in case of arrest of the regular members, were all Lenin's men: Bubnov (later to be Stalin's Commissar for Education); Kalinin (future President of the Supreme Soviet); Stassova (who would take Krupskaya's place as Secretary in 1917 when the affairs of the Bolsheviks became too big to remain in Mrs. Lenin's hands); and A. P. Smirnov.

As in the case of earlier central committees, or leading committees of the Bolshevik faction, Stalin's name does not appear. He had written to Paris a few months earlier, hinting at his desire to be a member and by now Vladimir Ilyich had a high enough estimate of this daring and secretive agent to favor his candidacy. Moreover, Lenin was soon to assign a new and important task to him, that of presenting a non-Russian voice on the national question in Russia. But, he did not venture to propose Stalin's name to the Prague convention. Instead, he introduced a motion to return to the system of coopting additional members whenever the Central Committee should see fit—a system which had fallen into disrepute in the more democratic mass party days of 1905-07. Shortly after the Prague Congress adjourned, Lenin had the new committee coopt Djugashvili and Belostotsky as members. Stalin's name never thereafter disappears from the lists of successive Bolshevik leading bodies. But neither then, nor at any subsequent time in his career, was his name to emerge victorious from any general election in which there was a real choice of candidates.

A curious example of the malleability of the past is exhibited in connection with the above. All Party documents published in Russia from 1917 to 1937 confirm the facts as just stated. Even as late as 1937, Volume XV of Lenin's *Collected Works* appeared under the editorship of Adoratsky, Molotov and

Savelyev, with exactly the same story. A note on page 653 of the Third Russian Edition reads:

> At the (Prague) conference a C.C. was elected with the following composition: Lenin, Zinoviev, Orjonikidze, Schwartzman, Goloshekin, Spandaryan, Malinovsky. As candidates [alternates] in case of arrest of the members of the C.C. were chosen: Bubnov, Smirnov, Kalinin, Stassova. Shortly after the conference were coopted into the C.C.: Stalin and Belostotsky.

But shortly after Volume XV appeared with the above note, came the great blood purges. Then Stalin himself wrote a history of the Bolshevik Party in which he coolly set down an entirely new version of his and the Party's past.

> The Prague Conference—he wrote—elected a Bolshevik Central Committee of the Party, consisting of Lenin, Stalin, Orjonikidze, Sverdlov, Spandaryan, Goloshekin and others.

Gone was the name of Malinovsky, the *agent provocateur*. Gone the name of Zinoviev, who had appeared second in all Party documents because he was at that time Lenin's closest associate. Wherever, in Stalin's *History,* the words "and others" appear, there the reader may know that Stalin is simply suppressing retroactively the honors and historical services of the men he has since executed. Gone, too, is the information that Stalin was coopted only after the conference adjourned: in fact, retroactively, he is moved up to second place, immediately after Lenin. And gone are the names of the alternates, Bubnov, Smirnov, and Stassova. One (Stassova) has since been demoted to nonentity and two have disappeared in the holocaust of the purges. Therefore, Stalin's *History* reduces the list even as his fury did the survivors.

Before the Prague Conference adjourned, on Lenin's motion it read all the other factions out of the Party. Henceforward, to use the words Lenin employed in answering a query of the International Socialist Bureau, there would only be:

. . . a number of groups abroad which are more or less socialist, but which in any case are completely isolated from the Russian proletariat as well as from socialist work in general, and consequently are completely irresponsible . . . These groups can under no circumstances speak for or pass themselves off as the Russian Social Democratic Labor Party, nor does the Party take any responsibility for these groups. . . . All relations with the Party are to be undertaken only through the agency of the Central Committee elected at Prague . . .

That was Lenin's method of disposing of the Menshevik faction which that same year would be able to elect seven deputies to the Fourth Duma to Lenin's six. That was his method of disposing of Plekhanov, Axelrod, Martov, Trotsky, Chkheidze, Zhordania, or indeed anyone else who was unwilling to accept the rule of the self-proclaimed Central Committee. Thus was consummated a coup d'état, a seizure of power within the Party. As we shall see, it gave Lenin a decided advantage inside Russia, where the labor movement was beginning to bestir itself once more after five years of despair and depression.

Too late, all the other groups raged and stormed and called counter-conferences. Already they were in the ridiculous position of having to assert to the bewildered masses in. Russia that "we too are part of the Party." Their chief effort, under the personal leadership of the professional non-factionalist, Leon Trotsky, was a conference of all other groups, called in August of that same year. To it were invited Bolshevik Conciliators, Bolshevik Vperyodists, Martovites, Plekhanovites, Liquidators, Trotskyites. But the "August Bloc," as it came to be known after the month of its assembling, began to fall apart as soon as it came together. Lenin knew what he wanted: he wanted to exclude them and run his own organization according to his own ideas. But they, what did they want? What did they have in common besides the desire not to be excluded from the Party which they had helped to build? Nor did they want Lenin to be excluded either!

Plekhanov refused to attend because he disliked Trotsky, who was the rallying center, because the Liquidators were invited, and because he thought it unseemly to have to demonstrate that he was a part of the party he had founded and whose very program he had written. The Poles refused to attend because they did not know which group to recognize and did not care to unite with a split Russian organization. The Petersburg Liquidators came in reluctantly because they wanted no ties with the old underground. The "Party Bolsheviks" or Conciliators were too close to Lenin tactically to be willing to attend. The Vperyodist Bolsheviks sent two representatives. One of them, Polyakov, who came from the police-ridden Moscow Bolshevik organization, seemed to have attended only with the intention of blowing up the Conference. He bided his time, then raised a rumpus, denounced the whole business for its "antibolshevism" and "factional character," and staged a demonstrative walkout. After the revolution it was revealed that he had been acting on the orders of the police to add to the splits and oppose Party unity. He was shot as a spy. The representatives of the Georgian Mensheviks, always a radical group, denounced the Liquidators present, Trotsky joining in the denunciation. The babel of voices and jangle of creeds were a poor counterweight to Lenin's resolute, close-knit organization.

The August Conference set up a provisional committee to unify the Party, but it served only as a battle ground for continuing the quarrels of all against each. There were quarrels between Trotsky and the Party Mensheviks and between both and the "Liquidators." In 1914, Trotsky finally broke away to form a new "non-factional" faction of his own and set up a new "non-factional journal for workers," the legal Petersburg paper *Borba* ("struggle"). To list the contributors is to mirror the uncertainty and confusion of the moment: Lunacharsky, Radek, Kollontai, Pokrovsky, Polyansky, Trotsky, all of whom were to become Bolsheviks in 1917, along with men like Noah Zhordania, outstanding leader of the Transcaucasian Mensheviks, who was to become President of the non-Bolshevik Georgian Republic. Trotsky's *Borba,* during its brief life from February, 1914, until war broke out in July, attacked Lenin for his factionalism, the Liquidators for their liquidationism, the Martov Mensheviks for "doctrinaire legalism . . . opportunistic overestimation of the liberals . . . clique mentality . . . factional fanaticism." Verily, in the Russian movement the lot of the peacemaker was hard!

Late in 1913, the International Socialist Bureau took a hand to see if it could unify the faction-torn Party. In the Communist International that Lenin was to form later, the authority of such a bureau or executive committee would be so great that no party or faction could resist its orders on unification or anything else. The Communist International would dictate to its "sections" final decisions on tactics, on the rightness and wrongness of each faction, on the very personnel and composition of a given party's leading committee. What would have happened to Lenin and his methods if the Socialist International of that day had been able to exercise upon its Russian section the authority which the International he founded claimed over its affiliates?

Be that as it may, Lenin found it necessary in 1913 and 1914 to resist very circumspectly, albeit stubbornly, for the moral authority of the Socialist International was high among Russian socialists, and the longing of the Russian underground for unity was strong. He was determined that the split should continue, until the other factions accepted his tactics and the authority of the Central Committee he had set up in the Party's name at Prague. But he knew that in the end he would have to yield, unless he could make his opponents appear to have the responsibility for the prolongation of the split.

The International Socialist Bureau, for its part, tried persuasion rather than command. It sent delegates to the Russian foreign colonies scattered through Europe, to investigate, to take testimony, to ask proposals from all sides. Its chairman, Vandervelde, came to Saint Petersburg for three days in June,

1914. Then it called for an all-Russian conference in Brussels on July 17, 1914, and prepared to force unity at its next International Socialist Congress set for August in Vienna. In the last days of July of that fateful year, however, war broke out in Europe; the Congress was never held. Instead, differences on the war appeared in every section of the International. It was torn to pieces by them, Lenin becoming the chief driving force for promoting a split in all its parties and for the foundation of a rival body: the Communist International.

CHAPTER THIRTY-ONE

THE CASE OF ROMAN MALINOVSKY

"At that time there was not a single local organization into which some provocateur had not crept. Every man regarded his comrade with suspicion, was on his guard against those nearest to him, did not trust his neighbor."
—G. ZINOVIEV: *History of the Communist Party of Russia.*

Lenin had called his congress in the unaccustomed city of Prague to get away from the spies that seemed to be privy to every activity. To Anton Nemec, Czech socialist leader, he made the plea: "Everything must be kept *ultra-conspirative.*" Krupskaya personally examined each delegate, sending Brendinsky, whom she already suspected, on a wild goose chase to Brittany instead of Prague. The police took the hint, paying off their agent with a villa in a Paris suburb, costing forty thousand francs. But they were not too upset, for of the fourteen delegates coming from the Russian underground, two more, Romanov from Tula and Malinovsky from Moscow, were their men. Agent Malinovsky so captivated Lenin that he emerged a member of the new Central Committee and returned to his superiors with the exciting news that Lenin wanted him to run for the Duma.

If we were to list only the more important spies that had so far entered intimately into the life of Vladimir Ilyich, that list would include Gurovich, who financed the first legal Marxist organ, *Nachalo,* with police funds; the surgeon dentist N. N. Mikhailov, who turned in Ulyanov, Martov and the other organizers of the underground League for Struggle at the end of 1895; Dr. Jacob Zhitomirsky, who, as Lenin's confidential agent in Berlin, made the arrangements for Kamo and his case of dynamite, for Krassin's counterfeit banknote paper, and for Litvinov's and other arrests in connection with the disposal of the five-hundred-ruble notes of the Tiflis holdup. So well did he work that Lenin continued to consider him as a "man of confidence," to be used for the most delicate tasks. After the Berlin arrests, Zhitomirsky moved "for safety" to France, whence he visited Geneva in 1909 to urge Vladimir Ilyich to move to Paris, "a large city where there will be less spying." Writes Krupskaya: "The argument was convincing to Ilyich." Thus the shadowed moved in order to be closer to his shadow.

In 1911, Zhitomirsky finally fell under suspicion, but it was not his chief who suspected him. Lenin received a warning from Vladimir Burtsev. Now warnings from Burtsev were no small

matter, for he was a self-constituted, one-man, counter-espionage agency. As some collect coins or stamps or feminine con-
quests, he collected spies. He it was who had shortly before
exposed the incomparable Azev, director of the Fighting Section of the Social Revolutionary Party. Yet so sure was Lenin of
his most trusted agent that he ignored the warning.

A revolutionary bloodhound by vocation, Burtsev, once he
had scented a spy, was not to be put off the trail. By 1913 he had
gathered so much evidence that he sent Lenin an ultimatum.
He would create a public scandal if trust were not withdrawn
from this man. "If my charges are false, let him haul me before
a revolutionary tribunal. There he will prove his innocence or
I my charges."

Alarmed at last, Lenin sent another "man of confidence" to
take up the Zhitomirsky matter with Burtsev, and, at the same
time, to discuss the whole problem of combatting the spies with
which the Bolshevik movement was now obviously infested.
The man whom Lenin sent was Roman Malinovsky!

Malinovsky questioned Burtsev with strained interest. Who
in the police or the government was giving him his secret tips?
what reasons had he for suspecting Dr. Zhitomirsky? how could
the Bolsheviks judge the reliability of such grave charges unless
they were given the sources? what other Bolsheviks did he suspect? Insistently, Malinovsky pleaded that Burtsev communicate "in strict confidence" his sources in the government. For his
part, Burtsev had not the slightest reason to suspect his inter-
locutor, whom he knew as a prominent trade unionist, as a
member of the Central Committee which the Bolsheviks had
just set up allegedly as the Central Committee of the entire
Party, and as the newly chosen chairman of the Bolshevik fraction in the Fourth Imperial Duma. Yet an old habit of caution
and a respect for confidences caused him to withhold the names
of the officials.

I will give you two or three names of agents in your midst—he
told the Duma Deputy with a pardonable flourish.—Check

them. Check the names of people arrested and their last contacts with men I name. If you are successful, I shall speak further . . .

In 1917, when the Tsar fell and the Provisional Government opened up the police archives, they found proof that Zhitomirsky had been a spy during all the years he enjoyed Lenin's confidence. This, of course, was no surprise to Burtsev. But what did startle him was the realization that Malinovsky (whom he did not even begin to suspect until the end of 1916) had come to him that day on a double mission, charged simultaneously by Vladimir Ilyich and by the director of the Russian Police, S. P. Beletsky, with the task of finding out which spies Burtsev knew of in the Bolshevik faction, and from what governmental personages he derived his tips concerning these most jealously guarded secrets of the police. How deep must Malinovsky's personal interest have been in learning Burtsev's secret, and knowing what revelations or whose turn was coming next!

Before we go on with our story, we must note a version, less flattering to Burtsev, of his interview with Malinovsky. The account we have just given is Burtsev's own, but from the well-informed Boris Nikolaevsky, biographer of Azev, who had many interviews with Burtsev, I got an account less favorable to the famous counter-espionage specialist. According to Nikolaevsky, Burtsev did not come to suspect Zhitomirsky as a result of his own investigations, but merely received a tip, couched in general terms, that someone very close to Lenin was a police agent. The tip came from Syrkin, a liberal official high in the Moscow Okhrana, who offered to give details to someone whom he could trust. Thereupon, Burtsev wrote to Lenin asking him to come himself or send a man of absolute confidence, to whom he would divulge an important secret. When Lenin sent Roman Malinovsky, Burtsev confided to him that Syrkin of the Moscow Okhrana would give him the name of a police spy close to Lenin. Malinovsky took no chances. Instead of going to Syrkin,

he reported the latter's offer to the chief of the Moscow Okhrana. Syrkin was dismissed from his post and exiled to Siberia.

What follows has been reconstructed by me from the police
archives as published by the Provisional Government of 1917
and by the subsequent Soviet Government, and from the testimony of Roman Malinovsky's Party and police superiors before
the Extraordinary Commission of the Provisional Government
which investigated the Ministry of the Interior and its police in
1917.

Among those who testified before the Extraordinary Investigating Commission were former Minister of the Interior Makarov; Assistant Minister Zolotarev; the latter's successor,
Assistant Minister Junkovsky; Police Director Beletsky; Assistant Director Vissarionov; Chief of the Moscow Okhrana
Martynov; and other lesser officials. Citizens Burtsev, Ulyanov
(Lenin) and Radomyslsky (Zinoviev) were summoned to testify
before a special subcommission on the Malinovsky case. All
the testimony before the main investigating commission was
stenogrammed and subsequently published by the Soviet Government in a seven-volume work called *The Fall of the Tsarist
Régime*. The testimony of Citizens Ulyanov and Radomyslsky
before the subcommission were not so published, but I have
been able to reconstruct the text from contemporary accounts
in the daily press: *Pravda* (Bolshevik), *Rabochaya Gazeta*
(Menshevik), *Den* (Liberal), and *Vestnik Vremennago Pravitelstva* (Official News Bulletin of the Provisional Government).
Fortunately, this last contains a fair amount of direct quotation in its issue of June 16, 1917, the accuracy of which is confirmed by the reports in the other dailies, including Lenin's
Pravda. Other sources are the writings of Burtsev, personal
reminiscences of men who knew Malinovsky, and documents
summarized from memory by Boris Nikolaevsky, who was director of the Historical Archives of the Russian Revolution in
Moscow during the years 1919-21, that is, under the Soviet

Government at a time when Lenin was alive and active in the leadership of its affairs. Except where otherwise noted, the source is always the seven-volume publication by the Soviet Government of the stenogram of testimony before the Extraordinary Commission of the Provisional Government.*

From these sources we can reconstruct the amazing life and deeds of Roman Malinovsky, as well as the political line pursued by the Police Department in the Bolshevik Faction, the Duma and the Social Democratic Party. For, as is characteristic of Russian officials, the Department had a definite political line.

Roman Vatslavovich Malinovsky was a Russified Polish workingman of peasant stock, born in the Plotsk Province of Russian Poland in the year 1878. When he met Lenin at the Prague Conference of 1912, he was thirty-four, robust, ruddy complexioned, vigorous, excitable, a heavy drinker, a rude and eloquent orator, a gifted leader of men. In the closing years of the preceding century he had been convicted several times of common crimes, the third offense being that of burglary ("robbery with breaking and entry"), for which he had served a prison term from 1899 to 1902. The police noted that he was a heavy spender. Though he earned a living first as tailor and then as metal turner, his wages were never sufficient for his expensive tastes. In his youth he had worked for a while in Germany, then returned to Saint Petersburg. Here he entered the labor movement, probably in 1902, with a perfect background for the role of police informer.

How early he became a regular agent is unclear. For years his chief source of income was his wages as a metal worker, while he used his police connections only to pick up a bit of extra cash. When he thought he had something which would interest them, he would telephone, or send in a written report signed *Portnoi* ("Tailor"), for which he would be paid a sum like

* *Padenie Tsarskogo Rezhima, po materialam Chrezvychainoi Komissii Vremennago Pravitelstva. Stenograficheskie otchety doprosov i pokazanii dannykh v 1917 g. v Chrezvychainoi Sledstvennoi Komissii Vremennago Pravitelstva. Gos. Izdat.* Leningrad, 1924-27.

twenty-five or fifty rubles. Even after he became a professional agent with a regular salary, he did not become a "professional revolutionist"—his usefulness consisted in his continuing to be a worker at the bench. He himself was to confess to the Bolsheviks, and the police confirm it, that one of his motives was always the ambition to rise to a place of prominence in the revolutionary movement. This ambition felt a double spur: the higher his advancement, the more he meant to the police and the higher the sum they set on the value of his services.

In 1906 he was one of the founders of the Petersburg Metal Workers Union. In 1907 he became its secretary, serving till the end of 1909. Here he steered a careful course between Bolsheviks and Mensheviks. The former were more interested in control and political leadership of the union, the latter in the preservation of its autonomy. Therefore, as an active unionist, he inclined to the Mensheviks. In 1908 he successfully resisted an attempt of the Bolsheviks to capture his union, but, after he went over to them completely, he helped them to win control. Zinoviev, who met him while he was its secretary, testified to the Extraordinary Commission that he thought him to be "rather a Menshevik," and the Mensheviks had the same opinion.

Five times he was arrested for his activities, either by police who had no inkling of his role, or because he was at a meeting which he himself had betrayed, where everybody had to be taken in. His early reappearance on the scene after each arrest was so managed as not to excite suspicion. A typical arrest was that of late November, 1909. He had tipped off a secret caucus of the labor delegates to an impending anti-alcoholic congress and was present when it was raided. Released in January, 1910, he was exiled from Saint Petersburg to avert suspicion from him. This ended his secretaryship of the Petersburg union, but he immediately turned up in Moscow in the spring of 1910, where he was welcomed by the entire labor movement and was able to report to the police on every phase of it. On the rolls of the Moscow Okhrana he appears as of March, 1910, no longer as a "piece worker," but with the regular salary of fifty rubles a month, plus expenses. In addition, of course, to his wages as a metal turner.

The police had come to the conclusion that the chief danger to the régime was the possible unification of all opposition forces against it:

> Malinovsky was given the order to do as much as possible to deepen the split in the Party. [Testimony of Police Director Beletsky, Stenogram Vol. III, p. 281.]
> I admit that the whole purpose of my direction is summed up in this: to give no possibility of the Party's uniting. I worked on the principle of *divide et impera*. [Ibid., p. 286.]

Since this political aim coincided in an essential respect with that of Lenin, Malinovsky was now instructed to take the earliest possible opportunity to come out as a Bolshevik and to attach himself as closely as possible to the Bolshevik leader. Police Director Beletsky testified that, in view of this important mission, he freed his agent at this time from the further necessity of betraying individuals or meetings (though not from reporting on them), as arrests traceable to Malinovsky might endanger his position for the more highly political task. It was the easier for the police to make this exemption since they had by now advanced their men to a number of key posts in the Bolshevik underground, including the headship of the Moscow organization itself, which had just been taken over by agent Kukushkin, aided by the spies Romanov, Poskrebuchin and Marakushev. The agents ascended quickly in the Party hierarchy by the simple expedient of arranging the arrest of incumbents, persons who suspected them, and others who stood in their way.

But Malinovsky seemed to enjoy denunciatory work, and, despite the exemption, continued it. Indeed, he could not resist one more grand coup before he went to the Bolsheviks. As a leading official of a legal trade union, he was highly esteemed by the "Liquidators" who set their hopes on legal unions and the legalization of other mass activities, and found Lenin's underground a hindrance. Malinovsky helped with the conference which was to plan the fight for legality, then tipped off Police Chief Beletsky to raid the planning committee. Most of the "Liquidators" were bagged and their hopes ended for some time to come. Thus the police aided Lenin against the "Liquidators," while agent Brendinsky was clearing another obstacle from Lenin's path by arranging for the arrest of the Conciliator Bolshevik Rykov. In the retrospective light of the 1917 police testimony, all of Lenin's and Malinovsky's subsequent polemics against the Liquidators as "police agents," "police unionists," and "advocates of a police labor party" make strange reading indeed. Beletsky's testimony on the raid on the Liquidators is confirmed by a note in the official edition of Vol. XVII of Lenin's *Collected Works:*

> Malinovsky clearly did not break with the Liquidators completely. He took part in a conference of their supporters, and played his hand in such fashion that the conference, called by them for the fall of 1911, was raided by the police. At that time a suspicion arose in a narrow circle of Moscow workers and Social Democrats who were in contact with Malinovsky . . . but the rumors concerning him soon died down.

About the same time, Malinovsky learned that Lenin was summoning a Party conference too, at which he was to "remove" the Central Committee regularly elected by the last united party congress, and set up in its place a Bolshevik-dominated central committee. The conference, as we know, was held in Prague in January, 1912. Malinovsky appeared as the representative of the Moscow trade unions and of the Bolshevik underground political organization, of which his fellow-agent Kukushkin was the head. Lenin had of course heard of this well-known trade unionist, newly won from menshevism. As we know, he was so taken with the convert that Malinovsky was elected to the new Central Committee, and was urged to become the Party's standard-bearer in the contest for the Moscow deputyship.

A police spy with a record of convictions for common crimes as a Duma Deputy—the idea was so audacious that the highest authorities had to be consulted. Now Beletsky met with his agent only in private rooms of fashionable restaurants. He claims that he took his agent in person to see the Minister of the Interior, consulted with the Assistant Police Chief, the Assistant Interior Minister, the head of the Moscow Okhrana, the Governor of Moscow, Junkovsky. The testimony of these persons before the Investigating Committee of the Provisional Government is often contradictory. It is probable that Junkovsky, when he claims not to have known, was telling the truth, for it was he who finally caused the dismissal of Malinovsky. In any case, many in high places knew the secret.

Interdepartmental communications on the subject were now so cautious that they no longer referred to their agent by his old pseudonym of *Portnoi,* but each used such circumlocutions as "the personage of whom I spoke to Your Excellency on such and such occasion."

Both police and Bolsheviks set to work with great energy to secure their candidate's nomination and election. The newly founded daily *Pravda,* the Bolshevik apparatus, and—what proved more important—the whole machinery of the Department of the Interior and its police were mobilized to further Malinovsky's fortunes. The first hurdle was his criminal record. The Ministry saw to it that he got the necessary "certificate of good repute" from local authorities in his native province. Next, all the more popular of his possible rivals were eliminated by the simple expedient of throwing them into jail. This included the most likely candidate of the Moscow workers, Krivov.

As election day approached, Malinovsky reported that a hostile foreman was planning to fire him from his factory. The electoral system provided for workingmen to vote by secret ballot in their factories, where they chose delegates to the next higher nominating body, which in turn chose electors for the Workers' Curiae of the Provincial Electoral College, where actual selection of Deputies was made. (Thus neither voting in the factories nor indirect elections are Soviet inventions, as is so widely believed, but were inherited from tsarism.) But no workingman was eligible to vote or to be chosen as delegate, elector, or Deputy unless he had worked in the given factory for the six months preceding the election. The Police Department came to their candidate's rescue once more by throwing the astonished foreman into jail, releasing him after the elections with the explanation that the arrest had been "an unfortunate mistake." (Neither in Tsarist nor in Soviet Russia has there ever been any recourse against officials for false arrest.) Aided by such campaign methods, the Bolshevik and police joint candidate swept all before him. The Department showed its appreciation of his advancement in the secular world by raising his salary from fifty rubles a month to five hundred. It was the first time that any police spy ever got such princely salary. And this was now supplemented not by a metal worker's wage but by a Duma Deputy's.

> *For the first time* among ours in the Duma—wrote Lenin in a letter full of the underscorings with which he showed his excitement—there is an *outstanding* worker-*leader*. He will read the Declaration [the political declaration of the Social Democratic fraction on the address of the Prime Minister]. This time it's not another Alexinsky. And the results—perhaps not immediately—will be *great*. . . .

The Fourth Imperial Duma, to which Malinovsky was elected, began its term in late November, 1912. It was to be a long Duma, destined to continue in being until the Revolution of 1917 thrust power into its reluctant hands. Its thirteen Social Democratic Deputies (seven Mensheviks and six Bolsheviks) formed a single Fraction, for the split which Lenin had started abroad at the Prague Conference at the beginning of that year had not yet taken effect inside Russia. The Fraction chose Chkheidze, Georgian Menshevik and leader of the Georgian revolutionary armed forces in 1905, as chairman, and Malinovsky as vice-chairman, and commissioned the latter to read the first political declaration.

Lenin was highly displeased with this unity in the Duma Fraction, for, as long as it endured, here was an authoritative and conspicuously public leading body around which the longing for unity inside Russia might crystallize, as against the Prague (Bolshevik) Central Committee. So strong was "conciliationism," i.e. the mood for unity, that the six Bolsheviks had gotten elected only by pledging themselves to work for a united party. Thus the entire bloc of Deputies lent their names as contributing editors both to the Bolshevik legal daily, *Pravda*, and the Menshevik daily, *Luch*, and four of the six Bolsheviks even signed a call for the fusion of the two papers. Indeed, from reading them, one could not then deduce any very good reason for their remaining separate, for Lenin was having great trouble with his editors. *Pravda* had been founded on the eve of the election campaign to take advantage of the increasing liberality of the government with reference to the press. The better to direct it, Lenin had moved from Paris to Cracow in Austrian (Polish) Galicia, only a day and a night by express from Saint Petersburg.

Despite the closer contact, *Pravda* continued to assume a "Conciliator" attitude in response to the popular mood inside Russia. It went so far as to censor, mutilate, or suppress Lenin's articles where they sought to sharpen the fight against Mensheviks, Liquidators, Bundists and Vperyodists.

> Vladimir Ilyich was so upset when from the outset *Pravda* deliberately struck out from his articles all polemics with the Liquidators . . . Ilyich became nervous, wrote irate letters to *Pravda*, but they did not do much good . . . [writes Krupskaya].

Here are excerpts from some of his "irate letters":

> We received a stupid and impudent letter from the Editorial Board. We will not reply. They must be kicked out . . . We are exceedingly upset by the absence of plans for reorganizing the Board . . . Better yet, complete expulsion of all the veterans . . . They praise the Bund and *Zeit*, which is simply despicable. They don't know how to proceed against *Luch*, and their atti-

tude toward my articles is monstrous ... [Letter of Jan. 12, 1913.]
   We must kick out the present editorial staff . . . . Would you call such people editors? They aren't men but pitiful dishrags, who are ruining the cause. . . . [Letter of Jan. 20.]

And to Gorky:

And how did *you* happen to get mixed up with *Luch???* Is it possible that you are following in the footsteps of the Deputies? But they have simply fallen into a trap!

At the time these angry letters were written, Stalin was in Saint Petersburg and Molotov was secretary of the Editorial Board. The fact that they were on the receiving end of these bursts of anger probably explains why Stalin's recent *History of the Communist Party of the Soviet Union* eliminates all traces of the quarrel.

As early as December 18, 1912, that is to say a few days after the Duma Fraction was organized, the astute Malinovsky was able to report to his superiors the news that he would be able to split the Fraction and would have Lenin's support for this purpose. On that date Assistant Police Director Vissarionov wrote to the Minister of the Interior:

The situation of the Fraction is now such that it may be possible for the six Bolsheviks to be induced to act in such a way as to split the Fraction into Bolsheviks and Mensheviks. Lenin supports this. See his letter.

The letter referred to, a copy of which Malinovsky supplied to Vissarionov, was one Lenin had written a few days earlier to "Vassiliev" (the name then being used by Stalin). It had been written in invisible ink between the lines of a commercial letter to an official of the Russian Bank for Foreign Trade.

If all of our six are from the Workers' Curiae—said the secret writing—they cannot silently submit to a lot of Siberians. The six must come out with the sharpest protest if they are being majorityized (*mayoriziruyut*, i.e. being overridden by the seven), they should publish a protest in *Pravda* and announce that they are appealing to the ranks, to the workers' organizations.

This was to be the gist of Lenin's argument and of Malinovsky's strategy for disrupting the united Fraction. Malinovsky of Moscow, Badaev of Saint Petersburg, and the other Bolsheviks from Tula and lesser centers, all six in short, had been chosen by the Workers' Curiae, ran Lenin's argument. Not one of the Menshevik Deputies had come from a Workers' Curia; thus the Georgian Mensheviks, for example, had been elected by the entire Georgian population. Therefore the Bolshevik six must be regarded as representing a majority of the working class and the Menshevik seven a minority. They were not representatives of the industrial working class, but "a lot of Siberians." It was a curious foreshadowing of the argument of 1918 concerning the superior representative character of the Soviets as against the Constituent Assembly.

Finding Malinovsky able and willing ("the other Bolshevik Deputies," writes Krupskaya, "were shy, but it was quite obvious that they were good, reliable proletarians"), Lenin left to him the task of finding pretexts for leading the Bolshevik Duma group toward an open break with the Mensheviks, while he himself turned his attention to *Pravda*. He called Stalin to Cracow to instruct him on the matter, and sent Jacob Sverdlov, his best organizer, to Saint Petersburg to whip the editors into line. Soon he was able to write gratefully to Sverdlov:

> Today we learned about the beginning of reforms on *Pravda*. A thousand greetings, congratulations and good wishes for success . . . You cannot imagine how tired we are of working with a completely hostile editorial staff. [Letter of Feb. 8, 1913.]

Malinovsky dutifully reported the arrival of Sverdlov. He hid in Duma Deputy Petrovsky's home, but was arrested when he left there to "move to a safer place" (Feb. 10, 1913). Thereupon Lenin dispatched Stalin to Saint Petersburg, now fully prepared to carry out the splitting or "irreconcilable" line. On March 13, after confiding his plans for that night to Malinovsky, Stalin went to a concert for the benefit of *Pravda,* where he too was arrested. Both Sverdlov and Stalin were sent to Siberia. This time they stayed, all through the war, until released by the Revolution of February, 1917.

Next Kamenev was sent to take charge. The mood of Lenin's household when Kamenev left is reflected in this passage from Krupskaya's memoirs:

> We all—Inessa Armand, the Zinovievs, Krupskaya and Lenin —went to the station to see them off . . . We spoke very little. Every one was wrapped up in his own thoughts. We all asked ourselves how long Kamenev would hold out, how soon we should meet again? When would we be able to go to Russia? Each of us secretly thought about Russia; each of us had a strong desire to go. Night after night I would dream of the Nevsky Gate [a suburb of Saint Petersburg]. We avoided speaking on the subject but all of us secretly thought about it . . .

Unexpectedly, Kamenev's stay was made legal by an act of the government: an amnesty for all "literary political" offenders, decreed to celebrate the three-hundredth anniversary of the founding of the Romanov dynasty. So, instead of turning Kamenev in, Malinovsky provided him with excellent copy by fiery denunciation of his Menshevik fellow-Deputies. The new line found a willing supporter in the new editor-in-chief of *Pravda,* Miron Chernomazov, another police agent. In October, 1913, Lenin expressed his satisfaction to Kamenev on *Pravda's* line:

> Here everybody is satisfied with the newspaper and its editor [doubtless, Kamenev is meant, for he was the real behind-the-scenes editor]. In all this time I haven't heard a single word of criticism.

And Lenin had every reason to be satisfied. The Duma Fraction had split at last. The mellow mood of conciliationism had vanished. *Pravda* was engaged in daily "merciless and irreconcilable war" with both Menshevik tendencies (now all lumped together as "Liquidators"), the Bundists, and the Trotskyite "non-factionalists." Most of the Vperyodists had abandoned their independent standard and either gone over to Trotsky's league of party-unity advocates or had returned, repentant, to the Leninist fold.

The police, too, were satisfied. Yet this business of having the Bolshevik leader of the Duma on their payroll was bringing its complications. First, there were his speeches. He was undeniably eloquent and forceful. Sometimes Malinovsky wrote them himself and sent them to his two chiefs, Lenin and Beletsky, for approval. At other times Lenin or Zinoviev or Kamenev drafted them, or even wrote out whole speeches in detail. These, too, were sent to Police Chief Beletsky for his opinion. In the police files were found drafts in Malinovsky's hand, with amendments in the handwriting of both Lenin and Beletsky, as well as drafts by Lenin, Zinoviev and Kamenev. Realizing how popular their Deputy was, the police tried to cut out some of the most "subversive" passages. But Malinovsky had difficulty following instructions. In reading the first declaration of the Fraction, he managed to eliminate an offending passage on "sovereignty of the people" by pretending to get rattled and skipping an entire page of his manuscript. But *Pravda* and *Luch* next day followed his original script. When his speeches were attacks on the Liberals, Constitutional Democrats (Kadets), or Mensheviks, the police were glad to give him full rein. Sometimes he tried to substitute a belligerent "revolutionary" fight with Duma Chairman Rodzyanko for the delivery of the speech itself, thus managing to get himself interrupted and denied the right to continue. Yet, on the whole, the Leninist régime so closely limited the autonomy of a Deputy and of the Duma Fraction that the police had little success in modifying his speeches. Without doubt he enjoyed both roles and there must have been moments when he thought of himself as a Bolshevik doublecrossing the police rather than a police agent spying on the Bolsheviks. So Azev had become confused as to his double role, and Father Gapon, and the Bundist police agent Kaplinsky, who as the "Azev" of the Bund plotted many acts of terror and denounced many terrorists to the police, but conscientiously refused to inform on a single member of the Bund! And so Dmitri Bagrov, who murdered Stolypin under such circumstances that it could never be disentangled whether it was on the order of revolutionaries, on the behest of some other official, or to avenge the pogroms against Jews for which Bagrov, wrongfully, held Stolypin responsible. There was something in the Russian temperament and scene that engendered these men of ambivalent spirit and double role, these Gapons, Azevs, Kaplinskys, Bagrovs, and Malinovskys—figures without parallel in the police and revolutionary movements of other lands.

Another complication was the danger of exposure. Some official high in the Ministry of the Interior or the Police was privy to the arrangement and did not like it. From the outset, this still today unknown personage tried to communicate with the socialist "underworld" without revealing his identity. When Malinovsky was elected, *Luch* received an anonymous warning on his role. A year later the wife of Theodor Dan received a letter telling her that a high police official wanted to see her in confidence, and that she could signify acceptance of the appointment by a code advertisement in a stipulated newspaper. Both warnings were ignored.

When Bukharin, living in Vienna, learned of Malinovsky's election, he wrote to Lenin that he had escaped from exile in 1910 only to be seized again in Moscow, suspiciously, right after a meeting with Malinovsky. He was puzzled by the angry tone of Lenin's answer: there was a dark campaign of slander being waged against this wonderful Bolshevik; if Bukharin joined it, Lenin would brand him publicly as a traitor. He desisted.

Then there were the February and March, 1913, arrests of Elena Rozmirovich (Mrs. Troyanovsky), Sverdlov and Stalin. Acting on a hunch, Troyanovsky wrote from abroad in a "shot-in-the-dark" letter to his wife's relatives in which he said that he knew who had caused her arrest: "a man playing a double role." If she were not freed, he would make an exposure which would "stagger society." As Troyanovsky had calculated, the police opened the letter. Director Beletsky testified in 1917 that when he had shown the letter to Malinovsky the latter had "become hysterical" and demanded her release as a condition for serving the Department further. She was released.

To ward off suspicion, Malinovsky declared at a meeting of the Central Committee that "someone close to the Duma Six was a person who had police connections." The axe fell on agent Miron Chernomazov, already under investigation, in February, 1914; he was quietly removed from the editorial board of *Pravda*. He had been its editor-in-chief while Malinovsky was its treasurer. The latter position enabled the Duma Deputy to turn in copies of the paper's balance sheet, and a complete list of the names and addresses of all who contributed money. On the other hand, he held meetings, raised funds for the paper, contributed himself from time to time—amounts which he always added to his Police Department expense accounts. These sums the police more than recouped when they levied fines on the paper, in one case a fine of five hundred rubles for an article written by none other than Duma Deputy Malinovsky.

During all this time he was practically a commuter between Cracow and Petersburg. Aided both by police and Bolshevik underground, it was easy for him to cross the frontier. Lenin summoned him at every important juncture, giving him entry into the most highly confidential meetings, when the only other persons present were Lenin and Krupskaya, Zinoviev, and Kamenev. The Police Department received full transcripts of the decisions taken, all Lenin's most secret acts and plans. Every biographer and historian owes a debt to these complete and competent police reports for the period. Malinovsky went on joint lecture tours with Lenin to all the Russian colonies in emigration. Together they attended a secret congress of the Lettish Social Democrats and another of the Finns. He was entrusted with setting up a secret printing plant inside Russia, which naturally did not remain secret for long. Together with Yakovlev he "helped" start a Bolshevik paper in Moscow. It, too, ended promptly with the arrest of the editor. Inside Russia, the popular Duma Deputy traveled to all centers. Arrests took place sufficiently later to avert suspicion from him. Thus a Bolshevik "Conciliator" group headed by Miliutin disappeared, as did the regular Bolshevik organization in Tula and other local bodies. The police raised his wage from five hundred to six hundred, and then to seven hundred rubles a month.

On the 8th of May, 1914, Roman Malinovsky handed in his resignation to the Chairman of the Duma, Rodzyanko, "for reasons of health," and the same day left the country. He had notified neither Central Committee nor Duma Fraction nor constituents. The amazement at this inexplicable action was enormous. At each session of the Duma, whenever a Bolshevik arose to speak, the reactionary Deputy Markov would cry out with intentioned malice: *"But where is Malinovsky?"*

The leaderless Fraction—for the others were smallish figures who had let him guide the day-to-day struggle with the Mensheviks—reviewed the events leading up to his disappearance in an effort to find a key to the mystery. Recently he had been quick-tempered, more so even than usual. He had complained of his health, and of wearying with "mere parliamentary means of struggle." On April 22, the new Chairman of the Council of Ministers, the reactionary Goremykin, aroused a storm in the Duma by warning the Socialist spokesman, Chkheidze, against using the Duma for radical attacks on the government. Deputies pounded their desks; Chkheidze and Chkhenkeli had to be dragged out by guards; both Social Democrats and Trudoviks were suspended by Chairman of the Duma, Rodzyanko, for fifteen days. Malinovsky tried to persuade the ousted deputies that it would be "shameful to return to the Duma." But on May 7, he returned with the rest of the Deputies. One by one they attempted to read into the minutes a statement of protest, and one by one they were silenced and declared out of order by Chairman Rodzyanko. When Malinovsky got the floor, he seemed to be beside himself. He refused to be silenced, continuing to shout until the sergeant-at-arms was called to remove him from his seat. Again he urged all Left deputies to resign and "appeal to the people." Next day he went to the astonished Rodzyanko and handed him his resignation.

That same day, Chairman Rodzyanko received a visit from Assistant Minister of the Interior Junkovsky, who informed him, "in strict confidence," that the departed Deputy had been a police agent and had been ordered to resign to avoid a possible scandal. Rodzyanko was told that he might inform the Presidium of the Duma, but that the secret should go no farther, or the good name of the Duma itself would be compromised. The last police entry on Malinovsky was a dismissal bonus of six thousand rubles to start life anew abroad.

Now *Luch* remembered its old anonymous letter. Rumors swirled around the corridors of the Tauride Palace and soon the entire press was speaking of "dark police complications." But when Lenin's friend Bonch-Bruevich, as correspondent of the Kharkov daily *Utro,* sent a dispatch of the same tenor to his paper, he received a sharp telegram from Lenin categorically denying the allegation. For the ever reckless Malinovsky, despite the peril of his situation, had gone straight to Lenin in Cracow!

There he had given several contradictory "political" and "personal" versions of his flight. Then, on closer questioning, he had "confessed" that in his youth he had been sentenced for an attempt at rape, which fact the police now threatened to expose if the most useful of the Bolshevik Deputies did not resign from the Duma. While Lenin was pondering this, the Menshevik and Liquidator press arrived with their reports of rumors that the Bolshevik leader had been a police spy. Martov and Dan raised the question: was it not factionalism itself that enabled unreliable elements to rise so high in the Party? They demanded a non-factional or multi-factional Party tribunal to investigate the case, political and personal, of Roman Malinovsky. For Lenin, and for his faction now representing itself as the Social Democratic Party, the situation was fraught with potential disaster. To accept the proposal of Martov and Dan was to recognize that the "expelled" Mensheviks were still part of the Social Democratic Party. And what a weapon against bolshevism would be provided by the thought that its outstanding spokesman, its leader inside Russia, the driving force of its campaign to split the Duma Fraction, was a police agent! What universal demoralization if this man who knew everybody, had traveled everywhere, had had in his hands all connections, all secret lists of members, sympathizers and contributors of funds to *Pravda,* should turn out to be a spy!

In the name of the Party (i.e. the Bolshevik) Central Committee, an investigating commission was immediately set up. It consisted of Lenin, Zinoviev, and Hanecki, a Polish Social Democrat of the Warsaw Opposition and a close supporter of Lenin's. No Mensheviks were included. This commission heard testimony from Malinovsky, from Bukharin, who reiterated his old charges, from Mrs. Troyanovsky, who told the circumstances of her arrest and release, and testified that her interlocutors had shown knowledge of matters which, in her judgment, only Malinovsky could have told them. Burtsev was asked his opinion. He answered that he thought the Duma Deputy a "dirty fellow but not a police agent."

Bukharin's reminiscences of that difficult moment were published in *Pravda* on January 21, 1925, one year after Lenin's death:

> I distinctly hear Ilyich walking downstairs. He does not sleep. He goes out on the terrace, prepares tea, and up and back he strides on the terrace. He strides and strides, stops and again strides up and down. Thus the night passes. . . .
> Morning. I go out. Ilyich is neatly dressed. Under his eyes are yellow circles. His face is that of an ill man. But he laughs gaily, the accustomed gestures, the accustomed sureness:
> "Well, what do you say, did you sleep well? Ha, ha, ha! Good. Want tea? Want bread? Let's go for a walk?" Just as if nothing

had happened. Just as if there had not been a night of torture, suffering, doubt, cogitation, tense mental effort. No, Ilyich had donned the mail of his steel will. Was there anything that could break it?

That night, sentimentally remembered by Bukharin, Lenin decided to exonerate Malinovsky of the main charge against him, and to pronounce Martov and Dan "malicious slanderers." When Bukharin's reminiscence appeared in 1925, Martov's paper took it to mean that Lenin, during that tortured night, had knowingly decided to defend a police spy and attack his accusers out of cold factional calculation. But the passage we have quoted is capable of another interpretation: that Lenin had succeeded in convincing himself of the truth of the rape story and the falsity of the police agent charge. Which interpretation is correct? Let us examine the available evidence.

Vladimir Ilyich thought it utterly impossible for Malinovsky to have been an *agent provocateur*—records Krupskaya—These rumors came from Menshevik circles . . . The commission investigated all the rumors but could not obtain any definite proof of the charge . . . Only once did a doubt flash across his mind. I remember one day in Poronino [the summer residence of the Ulyanovs where the trial took place], we were returning from the Zinovievs and talking about these rumors. All of a sudden Ilyich stopped on the little bridge we were crossing and said: "It may be true!"— and his face expressed anxiety. "What are you talking about, it's nonsense," I answered deprecatingly. Ilyich calmed down and began to abuse the Mensheviks, saying that they were unscrupulous as to the means they employed in the struggle against the Bolsheviks. He had no further doubts on the question.

"*These rumors came from Menshevik circles . . .*" Here was the key to Lenin's reaction. The Bolshevik press adopted a resolution condemning Malinovsky for "indiscipline . . . desertion of his post . . . disorganizing departure . . . a crime which placed him outside the ranks of the Social Democratic Party." And condemning "the Liquidators" (Martov was now always treated as a Liquidator too) for "hurling dirty and malicious slanders at the former Deputy, like the Rightist press which spreads slanderous rumors in order to bring confusion into the ranks of the workers."

In the Bolshevik theoretical organ, *Prosveshchenie* ("Enlightenment"), Lenin published a long article directed not against Malinovsky but against Martov and Dan, under the title: "The Methods of Struggle of Bourgeois Intellectuals Against the Workers."

In it Dan and Martov are denounced as incurably gossipy old women who live for scandal ("like insects that defend themselves by secreting an evil-smelling fluid"). They are worse than "the other Liquidators." Martov's famous pamphlet against Lenin, *Saviors or Destroyers,* is retroactively denounced as another example of this "impermissible, dirty, slanderous method." To the proposal for an impartial court of investigation, Lenin answered:

> *We do not believe one single* word of Dan and Martov. We *will never* enter into any "investigation" of dark rumors in which the Liquidators and the grouplets which support them may take part ... If Martov and Dan, plus their concealers, the Bundists, Chkheidze and Co., the "August Bloc People," etc., directly or indirectly invite us to a common "investigation," we answer them: we don't trust Martov and Dan. We do not regard them as honest citizens. We will deal with them only as common criminals—only so, and not otherwise ... If a man says, make political concessions to me, recognize me as an equal comrade of the Marxist community or I will set up a howl about rumors of the provocateur activity of Malinovsky, that is political blackmail. Against blackmail we are always and unconditionally for the bourgeois legality of the bourgeois court ... Either you make a public accusation signed with your signature so that the bourgeois court can expose and punish you (there are no other means of fighting blackmail), or you remain as people branded ... as slanderers by the workers ...

So far had the atmosphere been embittered since the Unity Congresses of 1906 and 1907! The main steps toward this impasse had been the exposure of Lenin's responsibility for the revolutionary robberies (Martov's *Saviors or Destroyers,* 1911),

Lenin's seizure of the Party apparatus at the Prague Conference (January, 1912), the maneuvers of Lenin and Malinovsky to smash the unified Duma Fraction (December, 1912, to October, 1913), and now the rumors that the Bolshevik Duma leader was a police agent. Lenin did not have enough faith in Martov and Dan as fellow Social Democrats to sit on a common committee with them. He refused to recognize either of them "as an equal comrade of the Marxist community." This embitterment, this factional momentum, was one of the incalculable component forces entering into the final split of 1917. Even the fact that Martov became a Menshevik Internationalist and Lenin a Bolshevik Internationalist could not bring them together during the World War, which both opposed.

A sifting of the evidence still leaves doubt in our minds. Did Lenin believe Malinovsky's story of an early conviction for attempted rape, and the resignation of his mandate under threat of exposure? Or did he decide "on balance" that a spy could still be useful?

> One feels ashamed for mankind—wrote Lenin on June 4, 1914 —when one sees how a man's personal misfortune is utilized for a struggle against an opposing political tendency.

That was a little over a month before the war began. Lenin's treatment of Malinovsky during the war, when the latter was an obscure prisoner in a German prison camp, demonstrates his conviction of the ex-Deputy's innocence of the spy charge. Lenin sent him reading matter and material for agitation among the other Russian prisoners. Krupskaya sent him food parcels, took care of his laundry and clothes and performed other services that had no political meaning beyond that of personal comradeship. Late in 1916 (two or three months before his exposure) the Bolshevik paper *Sotsial Demokrat* publicly stated that Malinovsky had been "fully rehabilitated" by his subsequent conduct, for his past crime of "desertion of his post."

I did not believe—testified Citizen Ulyanov before the Extraordinary Investigating Commission of the Provisional Government—in provocateurship here, and for the following reason: If Malinovsky were a provocateur, the Okhrana would not gain from that as much as our Party did from *Pravda* and the whole legal apparatus. It is clear that by bringing a provocateur into the Duma and eliminating for that purpose all the competitors of bolshevism, etc., the Okhrana was guided by a gross conception of bolshevism, I should say rather a crude, homemade *(lubochnii)* caricature. They imagined that the Bolsheviks would arrange an armed insurrection. In order to keep all the threads of this coming insurrection in their hands, they thought it worth while to have recourse to all sorts of things to bring Malinovsky into the Duma and the Central Committee. But when the Okhrana succeeded in both these matters, what happened? It happened that Malinovsky was transformed into one of the links of the long and solid chain connecting our illegal base with the two chief legal organs by which our Party influenced the masses: *Pravda* and the Duma Fraction. The *agent provocateur* had to serve both these organs in order to justify his vocation.

Both these organs were under our immediate guidance. Zinoviev and I wrote daily to *Pravda* and its policy was entirely determined by the resolutions of the Party. Our influence over forty to sixty thousand workers was thus secured . . . [*Vestnik Vremmenago Pravitelstva*—News Bulletin of the Provisional Government, June 16, 1917, p. 3.]

As always, to Lenin a gain for the faction was equivalent to a gain for "our Party" and for "the revolution." Whether he was right in calculating that the split in the Duma was a gain, or whether the police were right in thinking it a loss to the revolutionary movement, we must leave to the reader to decide as he considers the events of the year 1917. At any rate, the police were so convinced of the desirability of a split that the loss of Malinovsky's services and the simultaneous alarming news that the International Socialist Bureau was calling a new unity conference of all Russian factions caused the police chief to issue a general circular of instructions to all his subordinates and secret agents. Beletsky was no longer police head, and Assistant

Minister Junkovsky was now the deciding force, yet the political line of the police remained the same. The circular read:

> Information received from political agents points to a tendency recently exhibited within the ranks of the Russian Social Democratic Party toward the unification of the different factions . . . In view of the exceptional gravity of this intention and the undesirability of its taking place, the Police Department considers it necessary to . . . impress upon their secret agents the necessity for participating in the various Party conferences, there to insist, firmly and convincingly, upon the utter impossibility of any such fusion, particularly the fusion of the Bolsheviki and the Mensheviki. [Russian text in *Rabochaya Gazeta*, April, 1917; English text in Kerensky: *The Crucifixion of Liberty*, John Day, 1934, p. 246; also in Gankin and Fisher: *The Bolsheviks and the World War*, Stanford University Press, 1940, p. 106.]

The last act in this strange drama of Roman Malinovsky occurred in November, 1918, when Lenin had been in power for a full year. On November 2, reckless adventurer to the end, Malinovsky crossed the Russian border and turned up in Petrograd. For three successive days he visited the Smolny Institute (Bolshevik headquarters), demanding either to be arrested or taken to see Lenin. On the third day, Zinoviev saw him and ordered his arrest. He was taken to Moscow for trial. The Bolshevik Krylenko, who was later to conduct so many prosecutions until he himself disappeared in a purge, was appointed as prosecutor. He knew the defendant well since he too had reason to believe that one of his arrests by the tsarist police was Malinovsky's work. The trial was swift and secret. But the workers' organizations of Moscow sent deputations to attend, for they feared that Lenin might exonerate their ex-Deputy once more.

Accounts of the trial are confused and sometimes deliberately confusing. But from Bolshevik memoirs, and the writings of Burtsev, we are able to reconstruct some scenes of this last act of the drama. A trick of fate put Burtsev in jail in the same cell as ex-Police Chief Beletsky, when the latter was testifying at Malinovsky's trial. Another important source was Malinovsky's old colleague, the Bolshevik Duma Deputy, Badaev. Where Badaev and Burtsev (in *Struggling Russia*, I, No. 9-10) agree, we are likely to be on firm ground.

Malinovsky's bearing at the trial was proud and challenging. He demanded that Lenin be summoned as a witness. According to some accounts, this was refused. But the Bolshevik Olga Anikst, in a memoir in Vol. IV of the series "About Lenin" *(O Lenine)*, published by the official Gosizdat (Moscow, 1925, p. 93), tells how she watched Lenin closely during the trial. All through it his head remained bowed, and he took notes. But when the defense counsel in his summary said that if Malinovsky had had friends to guide him properly, he would never have become a spy, Lenin looked up at Malinovsky and emphatically nodded his head. If so, it was his only testimony.

Malinovsky asserted that Lenin must have known of his role after his resignation from the Duma. He had further tried to tell Lenin that his past was "filled with abominations," but Lenin had refused to listen, saying that for Bolsheviks these personal misdeeds of his youth had no meaning. Did not Lenin know that the police had a hold on him? Still Lenin had permitted him to rehabilitate himself in a German prison camp, and the Bolshevik organ, *Sotsial Demokrat*, in December, 1916, declared that he had been "fully rehabilitated."

> The best period of my life was the two and one-half years which I devoted to propaganda among the Russian prisoners in Germany. I did a great deal during that time for the spread of the ideas of Bolshevism. [From Burtsev's article.]

And Badaev writes:

> He alleged that he was forced to become an *agent provocateur* because he was already completely in the hands of the police. He represented his career as a long martyrdom, accompanied by suffering and remorse from which he could not escape . . . He

tried to prove that he left the Duma of his own free will because
of personal unhappiness, and that he obtained permission from
the police to quit politics . . . He adopted a pose of sincere repentance while admitting the gravity of his crimes.

A notable procession of witnesses testified in the trial:
ex-Police Chief Beletsky; ex-Assistant Chief Vissarionov; ex-
Minister of the Interior Makarov; ex-Deputy Minister Junkovsky; former Duma Deputies Badaev and Petrovsky; and many
of the Bolshevik men and women whom he had betrayed to the
police. Both Junkovsky and Beletsky were asked leading questions tending to elicit "proof" that his activities had benefited
the Bolsheviks and "the Revolution" more than the police.
Beletsky agreed to this, but Junkovsky answered with dignity
that he was "an honest monarchist and that he could not enter
into a discussion of that question." (Account of Burtsev.)

How much did Lenin know of Malinovsky's past? How well
did he understand what manner of man he was using in the
German prison camps, in disregard of the accusations of the
Mensheviks, of Bukharin and Rozmirovich, and the scandal of
his resignation from the Duma? According to Gorky, Lenin
said that he had been able to see through Alexinsky, but not
through Malinovsky. At the first meeting with Alexinsky, Lenin said:

'I had a feeling of physical repulsion to him. I couldn't con-
quer it . . . I had to use every method to keep myself in check
. . . I simply couldn't stand this degenerate.' Then, shrugging
his shoulders in amazement, he said: 'But I never saw through
that scoundrel Malinovsky. That was a very mysterious affair,
Malinovsky.' (M. Gorky, *Lenin* Centrizdat, Moscow, 1931, pp.
45-46.)

It was indeed. And so, for all the memoirs and analyses, it
remains. Why did Lenin exonerate Malinovsky in 1914, against
the evidence and against the world? Why did he rehabilitate
him in 1916? Why did Malinovsky return to Russia when Lenin

was in power? Did he count on Lenin? Why did Lenin then not lift a finger to save him?

Malinovsky's closing words at the trial, according to Badaev, were a profession of sincere repentance and devotion to the Revolution, a reminder that he had returned voluntarily to Bolshevik Russia.

And according to Burtsev:

> When the Revolution triumphed in Germany and Russia and the possibility of participating prominently in political activities was lost to him forever, he decided to go back and die, rather than to flee into the obscurity of an Argentina or a similar place of refuge. Of course, he could have committed suicide, but he preferred to die in the view of everybody, and had no fear of death.

The verdict was "death." Malinovsky was shot that same night, shortly after the trial ended, at 2 o'clock in the morning. Was there a special reason for the speed?

Until the archives of that period are opened, if they still exist, the only certain verdict in the Malinovsky case is the single sentence of Lenin to Gorky: "That was a very mysterious affair, Malinovsky..."

Even that sentence, in the course of Stalin's great *operation palimpsest,* vanished from subsequent editions of Gorky's memoirs. And the new writings on the palimpsest by Nikita Sergeevich have not restored it.

CHAPTER THIRTY-TWO

WAR CLOUDS

"Only war can again open up the question before the people in its entire scope . . . and draw the land into a period of revolutionary events earlier than seems now conceivable."

—MARTOV IN 1909

"A war between Austria and Russia would be a very useful thing for the revolution, but it is not likely that Franz Joseph and Nikolasha will give us that pleasure."

—LENIN IN 1913

On New Year's Day, 1912, Vladimir Ilyich told his sister Anna: "I do not know whether I shall live to see the next rising of the tide." Yet, even as he spoke, the ebb had ceased. Once more Russia's amazing capacity for industrialization was making itself felt: rails laid down; factories springing up; workingmen gaining confidence to make new demands. As in the past, five years had been enough to produce a new generation. The students and workers who had been children in 1907, the peasants fresh from the villages to man the new factories—what did they know of old defeats, old disputes, old hatreds and allegiances? The Mensheviks, resting secure in their predominance among the older, more experienced, organized workers, suddenly learned that a new working class had to be won all over again. It is a lesson that established institutions and ideologies are forever forgetting.

> Now, when a new historical situation offered the masses the possibility of advancing again—wrote the Menshevik party-historian Dan—they appeared on the political arena not only with the same revolutionary mood . . . but with the same revolutionary naïveté.

That spring, in April, some fourteen hundred miles from the nearest railway in the northern wilderness of Siberia, the miners in an English-owned gold mine on the Lena River, protesting concerning the rotten food, were fired on by troops. As the shocking news filtered through to the capitals, intellectuals found their voice again; university halls rang with speeches; the dispersed working class reformed its ranks.

Lenin's luck was with him. He had just finished the job of ousting ultra-Leftists, suppressing Conciliator Bolsheviks, seizing the Party label at the Prague Congress. Now he could speak in its name to innumerable workers who had never heard of bolshevism and menshevism, while his surprised opponents were in the ridiculous position of pleading: "we too are of the Party."

> The "Liquidators"—wrote Dan—who till then had believed that their purposeful labor in the years of stagnation would

secure for them a position of advantage in the reviving movement, saw to their astonishment that their monopoly position was shattered by these same illegal Bolshevik circles which they had regarded as "living corpses." Now they strove with all their might to accomplish their political consolidation and catch up in all haste with the tasks neglected during the preceding years.

And the underground Mensheviks, weakened by the defection to legal work of these same Liquidators, found that they had no machine to match the single-minded, power-concentrated machine of Lenin.

At that crucial moment, manna fell from heaven into the hands of Vladimir Ilyich. The millionaire Kazan merchant, Tikhomirnov, had recently died, leaving four sons. The oldest continued his business, the second became an actor, the third and fourth joined the little group of Bolshevik intellectuals who were secretly meeting for study and propaganda in the sleepy university town of Kazan. The group's leading figure, Adoratsky, would one day under Stalin become director of the Marx-Engels-Lenin Institute, and would take in the youngest Tikhomirnov as assistant. But our concern is with the third son, Victor (born 1889), who, having received his inheritance, one fine day dropped in on Vladimir Ilyich to offer him one hundred thousand rubles for the purpose of founding a legal Bolshevik daily.

For some time it had been clear that not the rigor of censorship but lack of funds was the chief obstacle to a legal daily paper. The Stolypin Government had entered upon a phase of moderate reforms. Duma elections continued to be held. All opposition parties were permitted to put up candidates (the "higher democracy" of the single ticket had not yet occurred to anyone) and to put out printed matter concerning the electoral issues. The countryside was being rapidly transformed into a system of small farm peasants. Liberty of movement within the country and the right to leave the country were granted more freely than they had ever been before or—after 1917—would ever be again. The number of schools was growing rapidly and the campaign against illiteracy was taking on serious proportions. The year 1912 saw the enactment of an insurance law against sickness and accident, providing two-thirds to three-quarters pay, covering virtually all industrial workers. The workingmen themselves elected their delegates to the insurance councils.

The year 1913 saw a general amnesty for political offenders in connection with the three-hundredth anniversary of the founding of the Romanov dynasty. Martov, Dan, Kamenev returned to Russia to live there openly and legally. If Lenin did not, it is because he did not choose to. Trotsky and Stalin were ineligible because they had escaped from Siberia and had unfilled terms to serve.

In short, the Stolypin constitution, as Lenin assured his romantic ultra-Leftist followers, was a moderate but "by no means a cardboard or comic opera constitution," and Stolypin was really bent on reforming and transforming Russia in accordance with his vision of a modern state. It has become a conventional legend since to pronounce this time a period of unalloyed reaction, but all signs pointed to a peaceful, if leaden-footed, progress.

All signs, that is, except the war clouds over the Balkans and the creeping degeneration at the summit of society: the Court. There, after Stolypin's assassination, ever more doddering and incompetent advisers were brought in, under the influence of the camarilla around the strong-willed, narrow-visioned Tsarina and her Man of God, Rasputin. But Lenin could not count on war, though he fearfully hoped he might, nor was he aware of the progressive paresis in the palace.

> We are fighting better than our fathers fought—he wrote frankly in an article on abortion.—Our children will fight better still than we, and *they will win.*

This article he published in the new paper he had just founded with "angel" Tikhomirnov's money. His weekly, *Zvezda,* had been appearing since December, 1910, and his monthly, *Pros-*

veshchenie, since the fall of 1911. Now he set up a daily in Saint Petersburg, which he called *Pravda* ("Truth"). The name would become world renowned.

Victor Tikhomirnov became the behind-the-scenes business manager (see Lenin's citation of his reports on finance and circulation in Vol. XVII of the *Collected Works,* pp. 417 ff. and 510 ff.). From Kazan, the "angel" brought with him another local youth, a year younger than himself, the student Vyacheslav Mikhailovich Scriabin, to become secretary of the Editorial Board. Young Scriabin wrote a number of articles experimenting with such unimaginatively close pseudonyms as Riabin, then the more poetically proletarian *Prostota* ("Simplicity") and *Molotov* (from *molot,* "hammer"). The aptness of these two names has since received universal recognition.

The Board of Editors and the mass of Party members and readers were overwhelmingly in favor of socialist unity. Lenin stood almost alone in his determination to sharpen the polemical line of the paper, compel it to fight with the other factions, force a split in the Duma Fraction and everywhere in Russia. To oblige the paper to follow his line, Lenin personally wrote controversial articles, which the editors discreetly censored, blue-penciled or suppressed. Lenin was infuriated. He wrote threatening letters. He called conferences of Duma members and Central Committee members in Cracow. Finally he kept Djugashvili, the Central Committee member then in charge of *Pravda,* abroad for several months, while he sent Sverdlov, his best organizer, to Saint Petersburg "for the purpose of reorganizing the Editorial Board and correcting the line of *Pravda"* (*Collected Works,* Third Russian Edition, p. 696).

As secretary, it was young Scriabin-Molotov who had to receive all the furious rebukes. Yet all the editors were responsible. And no less so the Central Committee member, Djugashvili-Stalin. "During that period," read the memoirs of Duma Deputy Badaev, "Stalin ran *Pravda.*" Savelyev says the same, as do all the Stalinist Party histories. When Lenin summoned him to work in Cracow and Vienna on the national question, and sent Sverdlov to reorganize the Board, he showed, as always, his ability to "correct" a useful Party worker without humiliating him or destroying him. Vladimir Ilyich knew how difficult it was to gather capable people and train them. So soon as one who had opposed him yielded, his anger vanished and he had care to save the man's pride and reputation. If his future "best disciple" had but learned this primary skill of the art of leadership, the purges of the thirties might have been avoided.

Once more, because Stalin's relations to Lenin are involved, literary detective work is necessary to uncover the real outlines of the controversy with the Editorial Board. Volume II of Krupskaya's memoirs, already heavily censored, still contains some traces:

> It was necessary to wage a determined struggle against the Liquidators. That is why Vladimir Ilyich was so upset when *Pravda* at first deliberately struck out from his articles all his arguments in opposition to the Liquidators. He wrote angry letters . . . [p. 91.]
>
> Sometimes his articles would be held up . . . This irritated Ilyich and he wrote angry letters to *Pravda* but this did not improve matters . . . [p. 115.]

Many of these letters have been suppressed, nor are they likely to appear while the present historiography continues. But enough were issued before the retroactive revision of the past had begun, so that we can reconstruct the outlines of Ilyich's unremitting struggle to force his paper to adopt an irreconcilable split line.

Late November, 1912, Lenin wrote to Stalin urging that the "Bolshevik Six" in the Duma "come out with a very sharp protest" against their seven colleagues in the Social Democratic Fraction. Apparently Stalin did not answer, or the answer has been suppressed. But the real answer came shortly thereafter in the pages of *Pravda* itself, in the startling shape of a resolution signed by all thirteen Deputies, urging the fusion of the

Bolshevik *Pravda* with the Menshevik *Luch,* because "the unity of the Social Democracy is an urgent need!" And, on December 18, four of the six Bolshevik Deputies put their names on the masthead of *Luch* as contributing editors, while *Pravda* displayed the names of all seven Menshevik Deputies as contributing editors! "As on all other occasions," comments Deputy Badaev cautiously, "our decision was made in agreement with those Party circles with whom we had occasion to discuss our activities . . ." If we are to believe Stalin's own claims that he was directing *Pravda* at that time, "those Party circles" meant in the first instance Central Committee member Djugashvili. It was at this point that Lenin called a Central Committee conference in Cracow and insisted that Stalin should make the journey.

No sooner had he left Saint Petersburg than Lenin trained his heaviest artillery on Editorial Secretary Molotov-Scriabin, and what was left of the Board. Apparently Molotov must have tried to answer back, for on January 12, 1913, Lenin wrote the furious letter already quoted (see page 264) in which he called the answer "stupid and impudent" and proposed the firing of all the "old-timers." A week later (on January 20) he wrote:

> . . . we must plant our own editorial staff in *Pravda* and kick the present one out . . . Can you call such people editors? They are not men but miserable dishrags and they are ruining the cause.

The text of these letters can be found in various places, among them Trotsky's *Stalin,* pp. 146-7. In the third Russian edition of Lenin's works, Volume XVI (published in 1937 under the editorship of Molotov, Savelyev and Bukharin), one can still find them paraphrased in the notes (pp. 695 ff.). But in Volume XXIX published the same year by Adoratsky, Molotov and Savelyev, which contains the letters of 1912-13, they are missing without a trace. In the fourth Russian edition of Lenin's works it is as if they had never been. The poet's dream "that we might catch ere closed the Book of Fate, and make the Writer on a fairer leaf inscribe our names," has become the principle of present-day historiography.

It was the young secretary of the Editorial Board, Molotov-Scriabin from Kazan, who silently took the abuse and the blame, though Stalin in his *History* takes the credit, for "initiating" and guiding the paper during this period. Between the Central Committee director and the Editorial Board secretary a bond was thus forged that has never since been broken. Molotov then and there attached himself to Stalin, the most important Party functionary he knew, as others might attach themselves to Lenin. As long as Vladimir Ilyich was alive, Molotov was never highly valued, receiving only second-string posts. In the unanticipated first revolution of 1917, Molotov again happened to be the only one available in Petrograd to edit *Pravda*. Again the line he took infuriated Lenin. An "incurable dumbbell," Vladimir Ilyich pronounced him. Others, who had to work more closely with Molotov, taking note of his dogged stubbornness and intellectual immobility, dubbed him *Zheleznii Zad* ("Iron Backside"). But when Lenin was dead and all his closest comrades had been hurried to their graves, the pseudonym of Stalin's first faithful lieutenant, along with the man's immobile obstinacy, would become known to diplomats throughout the world.

Other editors of *Pravda*, besides Stalin, Sverdlov and Kamenev, who were the successive Central Committee overseers, and Molotov, who acted as secretary, were Olminsky, Baturin, Savelyev, Samoilova, Soltz, Yurev, Gladnev, Raskolnikov, Vasilevsky, Malyshev, Poletaev, Bubnov, Danilov, Eremeev, Skrypnik, Malinovsky and Chernomazov. The last two, as we already know, were police agents. Of Skrypnik, the leading Old Bolshevik of Ukrainian origin, and Bubnov, who became Stalin's Commissar of Education, we shall hear more. The one committed suicide and the other finally disappeared in the course of the great purges, as did many of the others. Only the tight-mouthed Molotov survives with his closely locked memories.

For the most part, not the real editors but professional "sitting editors" (dummy editors we would call them) were punished, with fines or short prison terms, for offending articles. This was a device made possible by the fact that the government—although, through its spies, it knew better—contented itself with holding responsible the "responsible editor" whose name was given on the masthead, always some loyal, humble and inoffensive person hired especially to "sit" in jail so that the regular editors might continue their work uninterrupted.

It is hard to realize now, since we have become accustomed to think of censorship as total suppression of all opposition literature and extermination of all known and suspected opponents, that the tsarist censorship was in those years little more than a restraining and molesting mechanism. The editors had to keep their real names out of the paper (unless they enjoyed parliamentary immunity—today another vanished institution!). They had to learn a rather humiliating circumspection, an "Aesop" or "slave" language, in which the Central Committee was called "the leading group of Marxists," the Bolsheviks were referred to as "the Pravdists" and the Mensheviks as "the Luchists," and the program of a democratic republic, eight-hour day and land nationalization was advanced under the transparent disguise of "the full and uncurtailed demands of the year 1905." Everything had to be expressed thus in muted and blunted form. But the police knew what was meant and the readers knew also. When, in the eyes of the censor or some zealous official, an expression or an article went too far, an issue might be arbitrarily confiscated, a fine levied, or a "sitting editor" sentenced. In extreme cases, the paper was "suppressed." Yet, even in this, the government respected with surprising literalness and loyalty its own laws and regulations. The paper having been suppressed, it "ceased" to appear. But, the very next day, in the same plant, with the same staff, the same political line, and virtually the same name, a "new" paper was issued. It had to offend afresh before it could in turn be punished. Nine times was *Pravda* thus prohibited. But *Pravda* ("Truth") was succeeded by *Workers' Truth, Northern Truth, Truth of Labor, For Truth, Proletarian Truth, Labor Truth, The Way of Truth.* Always the name *Pravda* reappeared in the title. Always it appeared in the same format. Always the police and the readers knew that it was the self-same paper. Its circulation fluctuated between twenty and forty thousand, running much higher with oversized special numbers. Readers subscribed openly and openly collected money for it. The police, through Malinovsky and Chernomazov, had a complete list of subscribers and contributors of funds, but it never occurred to them to make a wholesale raid throughout the country. Who in those days could think of forty thousand arrests for reading and supporting an opposition paper? In this protean form *Pravda* continued to appear, go through the mails and be sold on the streets, until the eve of the World War. Then, on July 21, 1914, in a general pre-war shutdown of all labor papers, the government suppressed "for good" its eighth reincarnation. But it was destined to have nine lives. The ninth it began to live when the Tsar fell in March, 1917.

> Ilyich became another person—remembers Krupskaya.—When the first number of *Pravda* came out, we prepared to move to Cracow, in many ways more convenient than Paris . . . Whereas the French police assisted the Russian police in every possible way, the Polish police was hostile to the Russian police as it was to the whole Russian Government. In Cracow we could be sure that our letters would not be intercepted and that no one would spy on the newcomers.

So many changes have occurred in the map of the world since the Ulyanovs moved to Cracow, that we must remind ourselves that the "Polish" police she referred to were really Austrian, Cracow then being a leading city in Galicia, or Austrian Poland. So great was the autonomy granted to their Poles by the Danubian monarchy, that it was natural for her to think of the local police and other administrative officials as "Poles" without qualification.

By moving to Cracow, Lenin was breaking with the long tradition of Russian exile in Switzerland, England, Germany and France. Many reasons, subtle and explicit, caused the choice. Deepest, and least conscious, was homesickness, that nostalgia which sooner or later affects all Russian political émigrés.

> All our people in Paris at that time longed terribly to go to Russia . . . We were moving a little nearer . . . Exile in Cracow was only semi-exile . . . Ilyich liked Cracow so much, it reminded him of Russia . . . Vladimir Ilyich became quite jolly . . . how joyfully my mother packed her things . . . Each of us secretly thought about Russia; each had a strong desire to go . . . We avoided speaking about this but all of us secretly thought about it . . .

Many such tell-tale phrases can be culled from Krupskaya's memoirs. To Lenin's mother she wrote from their new Cracow home that Volodya (Vladimir) was "starved" for Russian novels, had nearly "learned by heart" the works of Nadson and Nekrasov, and had read and re-read "a hundred times," until it was in pieces, *Anna Karenina,* the only novel they had with them. "Greedily" they pored over the book ads in the Russian journals.

> Volodya is a terrible nationalist. He wouldn't go to see the works of Polish painters for anything, but one day he got hold of a catalogue of the Tretyakov Galleries . . . and he frequently becomes absorbed in it . . .

Nostalgia found reinforcement in practical and political considerations. Cracow was only an hour and a half by train from the border, overnight by fast express from Saint Petersburg. Equally important, on both sides of the border lived Poles. On the Russian side Polish revolutionaries plotted secretly, on the Austrian openly, against the Tsar. They were sustained by the passive and active sympathy of their fellow-countrymen, while the Hapsburg monarchy looked complacently on because it might sooner or later find itself at war with the Romanovs. An explosive dream, this, of a reunited and autonomous Poland—of course as an Austrian protectorate. But then, all war is a playing with explosives.

When Lenin moved to Cracow in the summer of 1912, it was with the knowledge and consent of the Austrian Ministry of the Interior. Hanecki had taken the matter up with local officials and with certain Social Democratic parliamentary deputies. One of these, Marek from Galicia, had secured assurances from the Austrian Government that Citizen Ulyanov would be welcome. That very autumn was to begin the first of two "little wars" in the Balkans, involving Serbia, Bulgaria, Greece, Montenegro and Turkey. In the background, Russia and Austria-Hungary, two great multi-national empires that had somehow survived into the modern world of nation-states, were maneuvering for position to thrust rival feelers of influence into the Balkan peninsula, each seeking the lion's share of the pieces to be torn out of the third multi-national empire, Turkey, that seemed about to die. If Austria's Polish border officials now became almost as friendly to Russian revolutionaries as they had long been to Polish, the Tsar's Government in turn was secretly encouraging Irredentist Montenegrins and Serbs to sow disruption in the great Danubian monarchy that ruled over more Slavs than it did Germans, or even Germans and Hungarians put together. And the French republican police were becoming friendly to the secret service of the tsarist autocracy in the same proportion as Hapsburg and Romanov agents grew cold toward each other. Nobody had yet invented the terms "Fifth Column" or "ideological" or "psychological warfare," but more than one great power was beginning to play the hazardous game of encouraging its rival's internal and external foes.

Thus it was that Lenin got permission to settle in Cracow, encountered friendly blindness on the part of local officials, and

found more than four thousand self-exiled Russian-Polish conspirators, who taught him some tricks of his own chosen trade.
The local Polish officials found that their governmental duties,
their patriotic feelings, and the sums of money that crossed their
palms, all combined delightfully to make them benevolent on-
lookers while letters, literature and conspirators crossed and re-
crossed the artificial frontier that Russia, Prussia and Austria
had drawn over a century earlier across the living body of their
land. It was here that Lenin learned to intermeddle actively in
Polish faction disputes, had his awareness of the national question intensified by Polish plots and controversies, and could almost see the war clouds that were rolling up from the Balkans,
soon to involve all Europe and the globe in universal war.

> That autumn—writes Krupskaya—the Great Powers inter-
> vened in the Balkan affair, and things began to smell of war. The
> International Socialist Bureau organized protests everywhere . . .
> but here in Cracow they . . . were more like meetings called to
> rouse the hatred of the masses towards Russia than protest meet-
> ings against war . . . The Polish masses were filled with burning
> hatred toward tsarism . . . One remembered what his father had
> experienced during the Polish rebellion . . . another how the tsar-
> ist authorities had desecrated the graves of his nearest and dear-
> est, etc. etc.

It was hard for orthodox Marxists (harder for Rosa Luxemburg as a Pole than for Lenin as a Russian) to take account of
this long national memory and steadily rising national passion.
Was not nationalism a "bourgeois idea"? Was it not supposed
to die away as class consciousness and class hatred grew? The
Communist Manifesto (1847), favorite text of revolutionists
(Stalin with his flare for religious terminology would one day
call it "The Song of Songs of Marxism"), was a seed-bed of
diverse and sometimes contradictory ideas. "The workers have
no country," it had said. But it had been said in answer to the
charge that "the communists have been accused of wanting to
do away with country, with nationality . . . No one can take
away from them what they have not got." And the very next

sentence had proclaimed that the proletariat was aiming to "establish itself as the nation."

In the *Manifesto* was embedded the assumption that nationalism had nearly completed its progressive work, and was on the way out. The bourgeoisie was credited with having constructed the modern unified economies, unified national markets, and nation states, eliminating local customs barriers, dialects, laws, petty local rulers, bringing nationalism into being. But the same class was further credited with having undermined the very foundations of the nation-states by establishing a world market, a world interchange of products "spiritual no less than material," and a world literature. The proletariat in its struggle within each nation to "establish itself as the nation" would find necessary "united action, at least among civilized countries." Hence its revolutions would "efface national distinctions and antagonisms even more" than the bourgeoisie had already done, and, by ending exploitation within each nation, would end the exploitation of one nation by another.

Actually, nationalism, democracy and socialism had grown up together as "triplet" sister-ideologies, all engendered simultaneously in the common matrix of modern industrialism. Two of these sisters, however, nationalism and socialism, were potential rivals for a common heritage, since the struggle for national freedom or national existence implies considerable unity of all classes in an oppressed nation, while the socialistic class struggle implies an inner antagonism more powerful than the outer. In a complex society there is a great variety of overlapping loyalties, whence the question becomes: which shall be the overriding loyalty—loyalty to nation or to class?

Economically, and this was the aspect that Marx tended to emphasize, the ideas and institutions of nationalism had arisen as a movement to overcome medieval particularism by creating a nationwide division of labor, a nationwide market, languages viable over wide areas, a uniform system of laws, unified nation-states, self-governing national economic, political and cultural units: in its "pure" form, theoretically, "one people, one language, one state," in which the people, not the sovereign, was the acknowledged repository of a sovereignty henceforward to be called "national." In the first modern states thus created, the sense of nationality soon lost its passionate charge of energy. People born in a great nation take the right to use their own language, to choose their own officials, to follow their own creeds and pursue and determine their own way of life, quite for granted, like the air they breathe, no longer realizing how precious these rights may be to Catalonians, Lithuanians, or Poles. Nationalism thus loses much of its pathos where successful, or that pathos may perhaps be diverted into new channels of chauvinist, imperialist nationalism. Liberals and progressives, in opposing the latter hateful growth, often develop an abstract "internationalism" that denies the importance of national self-determination to peoples who have not yet attained it. This abstract variety of internationalism expects subject peoples to "outgrow" nationalism without ever having known national freedom or tasted its precious fruits. While in its extreme form triumphant nationalism easily turns into its repressive opposite for peoples awakening a little more tardily to consciousness, in the nationalities still denied their rights, nationalism continues to represent a fundamental democratic demand: the demand for the right of self-determination. All these complexities the *Communist Manifesto* slighted, or telescoped together as, in aphoristic and stirring utterances, one page pronounced nationalism itself on the way out, and the next unconditionally espoused the right of the Poles, for instance, to independent national existence.

The young revolutionaries, Marx and Engels, had written simultaneously as German democrats seeking to create by revolutionary struggle a united German nation, and as long-range social prophets striving to foresee a remoter future in which nationalism itself, having achieved its progressive objects and spent its force, would be absorbed into a higher supra-nationalism or internationalism. But the first order of business for them was the creation of a united Germany in the name of a sovereign German people, by a general revolution calculated to drive out

Hohenzollerns, Hapsburgs, and scores of pettier rulers, and unite all Germans, including those of Austria, into a single, unified German republic. Moreover, their striving lacked some of the pathos of other national movements since the German people had already achieved cultural unity and cultural self-determination, and only the politico-economic superstructure —or "foundation"—was lacking.

In both Prussia and Austria the young socialistic democrats found imbedded large portions of Poland, while the Austrian Hapsburgs, the oldest of medieval houses, ruled over Italians in Lombardy and Venetia in the Italian peninsula, and in what was later (when the peninsula was unified) to be known as the "Italia Irredenta" in portions of Venezia Giulia and the Tyrol; over Hungarians; and, above all, over a variegated assortment of Slavs. Actually, the ruling Germans were in a minority in the Danubian Empire. The total of Germans, Hungarians and Irredentist Italians added together was less than the Slavs, who, after World War I, were destined to constitute Czechoslovakia, Yugoslavia and parts of Poland, and, after World War II, the Galician and Carpathian parts of the Ukraine. By Lenin's day, the Austrian Germans had taken the Magyars of Hungary and the Austrian Poles of Galicia into partnership as ruling layers of the nation. They were in the process of struggle-and-concession that would eventually have given the same rights to the Slavs of Moravia and Bohemia (Czechoslovakia). It was the tensions thus arising between the various nationalities with differing degrees of development and attainment of self-rule that continually threatened to tear the Austrian Social Democracy to pieces and made the national question its central political problem. If one wanted to study the complexities and tensions of the triplet complex, nationalism, democracy, socialism, there was no better laboratory in all the world than the one Vladimir Ilyich had just moved into in the year 1912, as the clouds were gathering for the storms of 1914. In Russia, at least, the Great-Russians had something close to a majority, and, with the exception of Ukrainians, Poles and Finns and Balts, most of the peoples were so backward that they scarcely stirred in their medieval sleep, until the violent earthquakes of 1905 and 1917 shook them from slumber.

Marx and Engels, as Germans and democrats, were quite ready to advocate the right of Italians to unification and independence, of Hungarians to form a separate nation, and of the Poles of Austria, Germany and Russia to break away from all three, to reconstitute an independent Poland. But, as for Czechs, Slovaks, Slovenes, Croatians, Serbs, Montenegrins, Ruthenians (Ukrainians), indeed, all the other assorted Slavic peoples except the Poles, the two young German revolutionaries repeatedly and dogmatically asserted that they were and would forever be unfit for self-rule and independence. These Slav peoples, Marx and Engels declared, were too variegated to unite, too weak to live as separate splinter nations, culturally too backward to aspire to national self-determination, politically too reactionary to be tolerated by progressive democrats. Their nationalist movements were mere powerless fantasies of utopian intellectuals. If they were given independence they would become inevitable puppets or prey of the steadily expanding Russian state, a state which menaced all democratic movements in Western Europe and which therefore must not be permitted to expand.

These conclusions Marx and Engels arrived at partly as a result of their traumatic experiences with Russia and with the Austrian Slavs in the abortive revolutions of 1848, and partly because they assumed that nationalism had already done most of its progressive historical work.

With the unification of Italy and of Germany, the reconstitution of Poland and the independence of Hungary, they thought that the permanent frontiers of the great "historical" nation-states would be pretty largely fixed. The remaining Slavs were *geschichtslose* ("historyless") peoples destined to be civilized and assimilated by their "more progressive and advanced" neighbors, the Germans, the Hungarians, and the Poles. They failed to recognize that the same processes of industrialization, spread of universal education and literacy, universal military training and general suffrage, would continue to shake up the masses of the more backward nationalities and bring them too as actors onto the political stage. This would give the still weak nationalist intellectual movements the mass support they required, and would arouse the same longing for self-determination in Austria and the Balkans and Russia which, in the past, had produced the national idea and national movements in the West, and which, for a hundred years and more, had maintained the idea of nationality as a subterranean flame among the Poles.

The animus of Marx and Engels toward Russia and the Slav peoples of Austria and the Balkans, as I have already suggested, came from the experiences of the year 1848. They refined and modified, but never fully re-examined, those conclusions during the rest of their lives. In that memorable year 1848, Paris had risen, Berlin had risen, Vienna had risen, Budapest had risen, battered Warsaw had strained once more at the leash, and Italian cities had been up in arms. But Russian troops, and the still Hapsburg-loyal, backward Austrian Slavs, had provided the armies to restore Hapsburgs and Hohenzollerns to their capitals and thrones. Marx and Engels then and there became convinced that no revolution could triumph in Western Europe until the power of Russia had been broken or drastically curbed, and that the Slavic peoples of the Danubian monarchy—except for the Poles—would always be instruments of reaction.

Modeling themselves in thought upon the revolutionary wars of the Great French Revolution of 1789, they began, in season and out, to advocate war with Russia.

> Only a war with Russia—Marx wrote in the *Neue Rheinische Zeitung*—is a war for revolutionary Germany, a war in which it can wash away its sins of the past, can become virile, defeat its own autocrats, and, as beseems a people shaking off the chains of a long passive slavery, can purchase the propaganda of civili-

zation with the sacrifice of its own sons, making itself free within while freeing itself externally . . . (July 8, 1848).

Though the situation had soon changed in Germany and in Europe generally, this was the tangent Marx and Engels continued to follow for most of the rest of their lives, as they went into lifelong exile after 1848. For many years they continued to urge war with Russia, urge it on Germany, on Austria, on France, and even on England! In the middle fifties they supported the Concert of Powers in the Crimean War, denouncing them only for not making it a real, all-out effort. Repeatedly they supported Turkey and Austria-Hungary against all the Danubian and Balkan independence movements, because they thought of Turkey and Austria as needed barriers to Russian expansion and they held any possible independent Slavic and Moldavian nations to be inevitable Russian puppets or prey. (Today the Russia calling itself "Marxist" seems determined to show its orthodox zeal by justifying their forebodings.)

Interesting, in view of Marx's conviction that nationalism was a superstructure of ideas and institutions arising on the economic foundation of a wide-area market and wide-area division of labor, is his steady and ardent support of Polish freedom. For here the considerations of economic unity were completely set aside! In the case of the Poles, it was recognized that their economic integration into three other nations (part into the German economy, part the Russian, part the Austrian) was somehow not decisive or final or determinant of ideology. Here Marx was giving recognition to nationalism as a powerful impulsive idea which continued to persist in despite of economic foundations, and which must be given support though Polish liberation should break up, as it must, considerable portions of the Russian, Austrian and German national markets and political outlines. In 1833, in 1846-48, in 1863, the Polish independence movement flared up afresh. And, more than a century after partition, again in 1905. As Krupskaya testified in the passage quoted above, it was a fierce-burning flame still when they moved to Cracow in 1912. At present, no reader needs any longer to be reminded of the pathetic indestructibility of the Polish national spirit.

This recognition of Polish aspirations in despite of the prevailing economic foundation suggests that nationalism is first of all not an economic phenomenon, though certain economic prerequisites must be there before it arises. Rather is it a moving idea, a phenomenon of consciousness, a feeling nourished in the matrix of a common culture and sense of shared historical fate. Perhaps the most fantastic test of this would come in the middle twentieth century in the case of the Jews. All nineteenth-century progressive thought was assimilationist, and all Marxist writers from Marx himself to Kautsky and Lenin, would assert that the Jews were not only not a nationality but that their lack of common territory and common economy and even common language and culture made it impossible for them to become such. Yet, the fearful historical fate thrust upon so many of them in Europe in our time has awakened an unmistakable national consciousness among millions of Jews. After all, was it not the young Hegelian "materialist" Marx who wrote: "The idea, once it takes possession of the masses, becomes itself a material force."

Actually, Marx's deep and abiding interest in the idea which so clearly held possession of the Polish masses arose primarily from his conviction that Germany itself could not be democratic and internally free as long as it helped to enslave a portion of the Poles:

> As long as we help to oppress the Poles—he wrote in the *Neue Rheinische Zeitung*—and as long as we bind a part of Poland to Germany, so long are we bound to Russia and Russian policy, and will be unable to break fundamentally with patriarchal feudal absolutism here at home . . .
> The creation of a democratic Poland is the first condition for the establishment of a democratic Germany . . . And it is not

merely a matter of building a Poland that is independent only on paper, but of building a state on a lasting foundation capable of genuine existence. Poland must regain at least the territory that was hers in 1772.

From the reference to the boundaries of 1772 it is once more clear that Marx had no patience with the argument that the Ukrainians of Austrian Galicia should be given to Russia because Russia already ruled over other Ukrainians, nor did he have any inkling that a Ukrainian national movement might one day arise to demand separation from both Austria (or Poland) and Russia, in an independent Ukraine.

Three events went far to change Marx's and Engels's picture of Europe, though only piecemeal and incompletely. The first was the rise of a revolutionary movement (the Narodnaya Volya) in Russia; the second, the unification of Germany from above, without Austria, by Bismarck and the Hohenzollerns; the third the Franco-Prussian War with its sequel of the Paris Commune and the annexation by Germany of Alsace-Lorraine. In 1891, after Marx's death, Engels predicted that the annexation of Alsace-Lorraine would throw republican France into monarchist Russia's arms in a coming war against Germany and Austria. He foresaw the situation as a race between rapidly growing German socialism, which in "a decade or so of peace" would win control of Germany, and that future war. His utterance on this subject was a mixture of prevision of the future with incompletely examined, vestigial remnants of the earlier conceptions we have been tracing. At the rate German socialism was growing, he expected it soon to have a majority. It was not to iits interest to resort to force, but if the German ruling class resisted that majority, then universal military training, which already provided one socialist recruit in every five members of the armed forces, would guarantee victory to the Social Democracy. However, if war intervened first "with France and Russia on one side, against Germany, Austria, perhaps Italy on the other," then:

If Russia should win, and the victory of Russia over Germany should signify the suppression of German socialism, what will then be the duty of the German socialists? . . . In the interests of the European Revolution they are obliged to keep every position they win, not to capitulate, neither to the inner nor to the outer foe. And that they can only do if they fight Russia and all its allies to the utmost, whoever those allies may be. If the French Republic should put itself at the service of his Majesty the Tsar and Autocrat of all the Russias, the German socialists will fight them—with regret, but fight them it would. As against the German kaiserdom, the French Republic can possibly represent the bourgeois revolution. But as against the republic of a Constans, a Rouvier, and even a Clemenceau, especially as against the republic in the service of the Russian Tsar, German socialism represents unconditionally the proletarian revolution.

A war in which Russians and Frenchmen were to break into Germany would be for the latter a life-and-death fight, wherein it could only insure its national existence by the most revolutionary measures. The present régime, if it is not forced, will surely not unleash the revolution. But we have a strong party which can force it to do so, or, in case of need, can replace it: the Social Democratic Party. And we have not forgotten the splendid example which France gave us in 1793 . . .

In short, peace assures the triumph of the German Social Democratic Party in another ten years or so. War will bring with it either victory for the social democracy in two or three years, or complete ruin at least for fifteen or twenty . . . No socialist, of any nation whatsoever, can wish for the military victory of either the present German régime or of the French bourgeois republic, least of all of the régime of the Tsar that would be synonymous with the subjection of all Europe. And therefore the Socialists of all lands are for peace. But if war comes just the same, then only one thing is sure: this war in which fifteen or twenty million armed men will kill each other off and lay all Europe waste—this war must either bring the immediate victory of socialism, or so upset the old order of things from top to bottom and leave behind such a mass of ruins that the old capitalist society would be more impossible than ever, and that the socialist revolution might, to be sure, be delayed for ten or fifteen years, but would have to triumph then on a still more rapid and fundamental basis . . .

And now Marx and Engels had died (in 1883 and 1895 respectively). The German Social Democracy had grown still greater so that one in every three army recruits was a socialist voter. In Russia, too, a Social Democratic Party (or two or more skeleton parties) had been founded, and in 1905 there had been a revolutionary movement of wider scope than that of Europe in 1848. Nationalism, far from disappearing, was taking possession of greater masses of men than in the nineteenth century. In the Balkans a little war had begun which gave signs of growing into a big war, the outlines of which Engels had foreseen, albeit imperfectly (he had left out England and America from the lineup). But who was there to interpret, to systematize, to select among the many utterances of Marx and Engels the guide-lines for an attitude toward the new nationalisms arising among the nationalities of Russia, and toward the war itself which was at once different from and the same as the one Engels had foretold?

That war, the parties of the International sensed, must at all costs be prevented. At regular congresses and emergency conferences they were planning, threatening, issuing appeals and pledging themselves to struggle to maintain peace. Rosa Luxemburg, backed by both Lenin and Martov, was building up a "Left Wing" in the International, to define more sharply the attitude toward this question. In Poland, including the Austrian Poland which Lenin had now moved into, Luxemburg and her followers were opposing Polish nationalism in their internationalist zeal. Living now in one multi-national empire and dreaming of revolution in another, Lenin felt that he must come to terms with this problem of nationalism. He must "consult" once more with the masters. But clearly he must solve, albeit in their spirit, questions they had judged wrongly, or situations that had arisen since their death. With the national excitement in the Balkans and in Austria and the fringe lands of Russia he must somehow reckon, above all with the nationalism of the Polish Socialist Party and the anti-nationalism of the Polish Social Democratic Party. And with the little war clouds that were spreading so rapidly over the sky from the southeastern Balkan storm center.

He set Zinoviev, writes Krupskaya, to "collecting interesting material on foreign affairs for *Pravda*." He selected one of the sons of an oppressed nationality, the Georgian Djugashvili, to write on the national question. He himself wrote much, pondered much, toured all the Russian émigré colonies in Europe to lecture on the national question, and drew up a set of theses on the subject. To Gorky, sensitive as always to rising tides of emotion, he gave an assurance that he and his faction or party were really undertaking to clarify the matter:

> As to nationalism, I am fully in agreement with you that it is necessary to pay more serious attention to it. We have here a wonderful Georgian who is writing a long article for *Prosveshchenie*, for which he has gathered all the Austrian and other material. We are working on it. But that our resolution is "mere copybook maxims, bureaucratic phrases,"—in that you are permitting yourself to scold without justification. No, it is not mere verbiage. In the Caucasus among us Social Democrats, Georgians + Armenians + Tartars + Russians have worked *together* in a *single* Social Democratic organization *more than ten years*. That is not a mere phrase, but a proletarian solution of the national question. The only solution. So it was in Riga, too: Russians + Letts + Lithuanians; *only the separatists* split away: the Bund. The same in Vilna . . . *No, such vileness as in Austria will not appear among us*. We won't permit it. Besides, our brothers, the Great-Russians, are numerically larger. We will not permit the "Austrian spirit" to develop among our workers . . . [Letter to Gorky, written in the second half of February, 1913.]

And, a few days earlier, he had also written to Gorky:

> The Polish Socialist Party is undoubtedly for Austria and will fight for her. A war between Austria and Russia would be a very useful thing for the revolution—in all of Eastern Europe —but it is not likely that Franz Joseph and Nikolasha will give us that pleasure. . . .

CHAPTER THIRTY-THREE

THE NATIONAL QUESTION

"Nationality . . . like the processes of life, digestion and breathing . . . has no right to be concerned with itself until that right is denied. That is why the Poles, Italians, Hungarians, and all the oppressed Slav peoples, naturally and rightly stress the principle of nationality; and that is perhaps why we Russians concern ourselves so little with our nationality."

—BAKUNIN

"There is a degree of culture where national hatred vanishes, and where one stands to a certain extent above nations and feels the weal and woe of a neighboring people as if it happened to one's own."

—GOETHE

In Stalin's *History of the Communist Party,* written originally under the cover of anonymity, he puts his own name before Lenin's, but concedes to his teacher a share of the credit for evolving "the national policy of Lenin and Stalin." Says his *History:*

> Only the Bolsheviks had a Marxist program on the national question, as set forth in Comrade Stalin's article, *Marxism and the National Question,* and in Lenin's articles, *The Right of Nations to Self-Determination* and *Critical Notes on the National Question.*

There is no hint here that Stalin's solitary systematic article on this question was written directly under Lenin's guidance, or that it looks impressive only by comparison with Stalin's other works (whether written before or since) and not at all impressive if compared with the sweep, insight and many-sidedness of the theses, resolutions, letters, polemical and programmatic articles that Lenin wrote on the same subject before and during the World War.

As we have already noted, in all the writings of Lenin there is only one reference to the *nationality* of a Bolshevik—namely, the remark to Gorky that a "splendid Georgian was gathering all the Austrian and other material . . . and writing a big article for *Prosveshchenie."* That he referred to the writer's nationality was not accidental, for at that moment, as we shall see, he especially needed a Transcaucasian to advance some of his views on the subject.

Until Lenin moved to Austrian Poland in 1912, his polemics on nationalism had been almost exclusively with the Jewish Bund. Despite Jewish dispersion and lack of a distinct territory, the Bund insisted on considering the Jews as a nationality, and on speaking for all Jews anywhere in Russia. For their scattered peoples, they did not dream of demanding the "right of secession" to form an independent state. Instead of "territorial autonomy" and the "right of secession," they limited self-determination to the more modest demand for "cultural autonomy" or "national-cultural autonomy." By this they meant that the Jewish communities should control their own schools, theaters, press and religious life, free from interference or handicap on the part of the state, should elect their own school and community administrators, and speak for and defend the "national-cultural" interests of people anywhere in Russia who chose to regard themselves as Jews. Still worse, in Lenin's opinion, they wanted the same autonomy to prevail in the Party, for themselves and for other national groups. Lenin was willing to concede nationality to Ukrainians, White Russians, Poles, etc., because they had a distinct territory and language and a strong will to secede from the Russian Empire, and therefore constituted a movement which would weaken tsarism. But Jews, he maintained, were not a nationality but a caste; they spoke not one language but various, lived not in a definite territory but scattered throughout the Empire, and, insofar as they were not "bourgeois-minded" were internationalists. The only "progressive solution" of the Jewish question was emancipation and assimilation. Above all in the Social Democratic Party there was no room for nationalism. The "best and most class-conscious" Jews had set an example by rejecting the Jewish Bund in favor of membership in the local mixed units of the Russian Social Democratic Party. If the Bund were to have its way, it would lead to the recognition of national divisions in the labor movement, and to a federated party in which Jews, Ukrainians, Georgians, Armenians, Great-Russians, White-Russians, Poles, etc., would each be organized separately. Then the Party and the Party Central Committee, instead of being centralized would be a mere federated body. And the new Russia to issue out of the revolution would be a federated, not a centralized, republic.

Obviously, Lenin was not altogether consistent on this. He had never quarreled with the Poles for having a separate organization only loosely federated with the Russian party. Perhaps this might be explained by the fact that Marx and Engels had always envisaged the right of Poland to independence, and the further fact that the Poles cut across three empires, Russian, German and Austrian. Nor had he quarreled with Latvians and Esthonians, though he had tried sporadically to draw them into closer federal (!) union with the Bolsheviks. Unceasingly he maintained the absolute right of the Ukrainian people to separate from Russia, though he regarded the Ukrainian nationalistic socialist party with hostility and sought to include all Ukrainian workers in the same organizations with the Russians. Above all, Transcaucasia had long been for him a model region in regard to nationalism. Alongside such national socialistic parties as the Armenian Dashnaks and the Georgian Federalists, and quite overshadowing them, was a general, multi-national, social-democratic party, containing Georgians, Armenians, Tartars, Russians and members of other Transcaucasian vest-pocket nationalities, in a single organization. Until 1912, both Georgian Bolsheviks and the far more powerful Georgian Mensheviks had taken this "internationalist," i.e. multi-national, structure for granted.

But in 1912, as we have seen, many things coincided to sharpen Lenin's sensitivity on the national question, drew him into new and extensive polemics, and compelled him to clarify all the hazy aspects of his views. Foremost of these was the Balkan War and the general intensification of national feeling that presaged a coming world war. Then his move to Cracow in Austrian Poland made him aware of the struggle being waged between the Polish Socialist Party (of Pilsudski) and the Polish Social Democratic Party (of Rosa Luxemburg) on the national question. The latter was so ardently internationalist that it zealously combatted all Polish nationalism and the Polish independence movement as "economically and politically retrogressive and out of date." Before long Lenin found it necessary to start a polemic against this, to him, one-sided and abstract internationalism. It might be all right for Polish socialists to fight Polish nationalism as inexpedient, but Russian socialists could do so only at peril to their principles of democracy and self-determination.

Moving to Austria also shocked him into a realization of the difference between the attitude of the Austrian Marxists on the national question and his own. The Austrians were faced with a congeries of more developed nationalities than those of Russia. The Germans of Austria were a leading minority in a majority sea of Hungarians, Poles, Czechs, and other Slavic peoples, some nationally awake and others just beginning to stir. Distinguished Austrian Marxists like Renner and Bauer did not chart their course on the expectation of the immediate disruption of the Danubian state as Lenin did his on the disruption of tsarist Russia. Instead, they anticipated Austria-Hungary's rapid democratization and federalization with equal national-cultural and administrative rights for all the nationalities within it. Hence, as Lenin found to his dismay, they did not stress, as he did, territorial autonomy and the right of secession, but national-cultural autonomy and federalism. Since this tended to reinforce the federalist and cultural-autonomy views of the Bund and other socialistic national parties in Russia, he began to prepare a trenchant criticism of the Austrian views. That is why he sent Djugashvili, who knew only the Georgian set-up, to Vienna, "to gather all the Austrian materials."

But his main reason for wanting a Transcaucasian to write such an article, and not a Great-Russian or a member of some other nationality, was the fact that the Georgian Social Democracy, the stronghold and fortress of menshevism, had just begun a slight but perceptible shift on the national question, and Lenin needed a Georgian to carry his "national" war into Menshevik-dominated Transcaucasia.

This shift of views had arisen directly out of the faction struggle.

As the reader will remember, the year 1912 began with Lenin's seizure of power in the Social Democratic Party by his Prague Congress.

In August of that year, all the outlawed and excluded had

tried to unite against Lenin in their "August Bloc." In order to
present a common front against Lenin, they had sought to
blur their differences on all matters other than Party unity. In
order to include parties like the Jewish Bund, they found it expedient to adopt a resolution which said that the Bund's "demand for national-cultural autonomy is not incompatible with
the point in the Party program concerning the right of nations
to self-determination." (In other words, national-cultural
autonomy is one of the conceivable forms of national self-
determination, and it is up to each people to determine for
itself whether it wants national-cultural autonomy or separation.) When the Georgian Social Democracy adopted the
same resolution at its own Transcaucasian Conference, Lenin
saw the opportunity to carry the war into the most powerful stronghold of menshevism. That is the chief reason why
he sent for Stalin early in 1913, initiated him into the basic
differences between the Austrian and Russian Marxist views,
and sent him on from Cracow to Vienna "to gather all the Austrian materials."

Writing the second volume of her *Memories of Lenin* in the
early thirties, under an increasingly rigid Stalinist censorship,
Krupskaya cautiously hints at the relationship between Lenin's
many-sided consideration of the national question and Stalin's
article. She uses the devices long known to Russian revolu-
tinaries as the "Aesop" or "slave language" which seeks to
evade an obtuse or hesitant censorship and yet suggest its point
to the perspicacious reader.

> In the middle of February 1913—she writes on page 115-16
> (of the English translation)—a conference of the members of
> the Central Committee was held in Cracow . . . Stalin also came.
> Ilyich had long discussions with Stalin on the national question.
> He was glad to meet a man who was seriously interested in
> this question and who was well informed on it. Prior to his
> arrival in Cracow [to write his article], Stalin spent two months

in Vienna where he studied the national question. There he became closely connected with our people, Bukharin and Troyanovsky.

When she wrote this, Bukharin was already out of favor and within a few years was to be executed. Yet, as Stalin knew no German, it is clear that either Troyanovsky or Bukharin must have helped him "study the national question" in Vienna. From other sources we know that Bukharin was his mentor on Austrian theory, and that Troyanovsky was only mentioned here to cover up.

Three pages later, ostensibly in another connection, Krupskaya launches into a detailed account of how Ilyich helped "inexperienced authors":

> In discussing their work with them, he would get right down to the heart of the subject, to fundamentals, and make suggestions for improvement. But he did all this very discreetly so that these authors hardly noticed that they were being corrected. And Ilyich was very good at helping people in their work. If for example he wanted someone to write an article and was not sure whether he would be able to do it properly, he would start a discussion with him, expound his ideas and get the prospective writer interested. After he had sounded him out on the subject sufficiently, he would say to him: "Would you like to write an article on this subject?" And the author would not even have noticed that his preliminary discussion with Ilyich had helped him and that, in writing his article, he had actually used Ilyich's expressions and turns of phrase.

This was one of the qualities that made Lenin a team-leader and made even his personal leadership assume the guise of a collective leadership. Far from claiming credit for everything others wrote in an effort to build himself up into an all-knowing and infallible *vozhd,* he sought every opportunity to push credit from his person and build up the reputations of those around him.

On page 122, Krupskaya casually returns to the national question long enough to say:

> The other important resolution which was passed [at the "Summer Conference" of 1913] was that on the national question, which expressed the views of Vladimir Ilyich Lenin.

Doubtless she would have liked to put the last eight words in italics if she had dared! In any case, Ilyich could get no "help" from Koba at the "Summer Conference," for the latter was in jail. Therefore, the Bolshevik leader was already looking for another Transcaucasian to carry on in Transcaucasia the war which had been opened by Stalin's article on *Marxism and the National Question*.

That this is so is proved by Lenin's correspondence with other Transcaucasians, particularly with Stepan Grigorevich Shaumyan. There are a number of such letters, from which we select a few typical passages.

> Do not fail to send me as much material as possible on the national question in the Caucasus . . . and the *statistics of nationalities* in the Caucasus, in Persia, Turkey and Russia . . . everything you can get. If a misfortune should befall you [Lenin means the same misfortune as had befallen Stalin, i.e. arrest], so that you cannot write, I hope you will find someone else to hand over the task to. Do not forget either, to *seek out* Caucasian comrades who may be able to write articles on the national question in the Caucasus . . .

The above is from a letter of August 11, 1913, shortly after Stalin had been removed from the scene by arrest and deportation to Siberia. Shaumyan answered, sending both material and a full statement of his views, which deviated from Lenin's in the direction of what Lenin thought a too abstract internationalism and an un-Leninist belief in the superior democracy of a federated state, with regional autonomy and local self-government. In the case of Stalin he had doubtless corrected these common "Transcaucasian errors" by long and tactful personal conversation. But in Shaumyan's case, he had to accomplish the same pedagogical work by mail. He wrote:

Dear Friend,
   Your letter of November 15 has given me great joy. You must know that in my situation the opinions of comrades in Russia, especially those who think deeply and occupy themselves with current problems, are most highly appreciated. Your swift answer was therefore particularly pleasant to me. One feels less cut off when one gets such letters. But enough of lyricism. To business. . . .

Follows a gentle but firm correction of those opinions of Shaumyan on the national question which Lenin considers erroneous:

1. An inclination to promote Russian as the general national speech, because it contains the highest culture and the greatest possibilities of unity. ("The Russian tongue," Lenin answered, "would be for a number of unfortunate and backward peoples of progressive significance—no doubt of it. But do you not see that it would be of still greater progressive significance if there were no *compulsion* to use it?")

2. An inclination to prefer local self-government and autonomy, and to give each nationality a choice between the "right of separation" and the "right of federation." ("We are in principle against federation," answered Lenin, "it weakens the economic connection and is inappropriate for a unified state. Do you want to separate? we say. Then go to the devil and cut yourself off altogether if you can break the economic connection or, rather, if the yoke and friction of 'living together' are such that they *spoil* the economic relationship. You don't want to separate? Then, please, don't decide *for me,* don't believe you have the 'right' to federation . . . The right of self-determination is an *exception* from our general premise of centralism. This exception is absolutely necessary

in view of Great-Russian arch-reactionary nationalism and
the slightest renunciation of this exception is opportunism, it
is a simple-minded playing into the hands of Great-Russian
arch-reactionary nationalism.")

The letter concludes with the news that Lenin is writing an
article on the subject for three issues of *Prosveshchenie,* begs
Shaumyan to give his opinion after he has read it, and tactfully
suggests that it would be a fine thing if the latter would write
a "popular pamphlet on the National Question." Lenin closed
"with a tight, tight handclasp."

Several things are notable in this letter. The warm tone—
warmer than in any letter Lenin ever wrote to Stalin. The tact
and generosity with which Lenin rebutted the views of a man
who was "thinking deeply and fundamentally on current problems." The fact that Lenin did not ask any opinion on the supposedly epoch-making article of Djugashvili, but was writing
another, actually two more lengthy articles in six issues of *Prosveshchenie,* to clarify the whole question. The fact that he
urged Shaumyan to write a popular pamphlet on the subject
to follow up on the one he had urged on Stalin. This was in
December, 1913. Our next letter brings us to May 19, 1914:

> I hope you will answer me after reading my article on self-
> determination of nations in *Prosveshchenie* (I am writing it
> now). You *must* give some self-advertisement *(Selbstanzeige)*
> or an outline of your own pamphlet against *An* [pseudonym
> of an Armenian Socialist and cultural autonomist] in *Prosvesh-
> chenie* [Shaumyan had by now written a pamphlet entitled *On
> National Cultural Autonomy*]. I also propose to you the fol-
> lowing plan:
> In order to struggle against the stupidity of the cultural-na-
> tional autonomists, the fraction must introduce into the Duma
> a draft law on the equality of nations and the definition of the
> rights of national minorities. I propose that we draw up such
> a project:
> The general situation of equal rights—the division of the
> country into autonomous and self-governing territorial units
> according—among other things—to nationality (the local pop-
> ulation determines the boundaries, the general parliament con-

firms them)—the limits of the administration of the autonomous districts and regions, as well as the self-governing local units;—the illegalization of any departure from equality of nations in the decisions of autonomous districts, zemstvos, etc.; general school councils democratically elected, etc., freedom and equality of languages—the choice of languages by the municipal institutions, etc. The protection of minorities: the right to a proportional share of the expenditures for school buildings (gratis) for students of "alien" (non-Russian) nationalities, for "alien" teachers, for "alien" departments in museums and libraries, theaters and the like; the right of each citizen to seek redress (before a court) for any departure from the corresponding equality of rights, for any "trampling upon" the rights of national minorities; a census of population every five years in the multinational districts, a ten-year census in the country as a whole, etc. . . .

The draft might be worked out by the Marxists of *all,* or of very many, of the nations of Russia. Write at once whether you agree to help. In general, write *oftener,* and not less often than once a week . . .

These letters are a model of the tact with which Lenin knew how to suggest ideas and draw others into writing articles and pamphlets embodying them. Moreover, the last letter is striking evidence of how far Lenin had already worked out in his own mind in 1914 the general outlines of the policy which Stalin himself now modestly calls "the nationalities policy of Lenin and Stalin." By an accident of history he confided this detailed plan first not to Djugashvili but to Shaumyan. Then by another accident of history, Shaumyan was removed from the scene by death in 1918. If the curious reader picks up Volume XVII of the Third Edition of Lenin's *Collected Works,* published just before Beria and Stalin got busy on their wholesale revision of the past, he will find the following biographical note on S. G. Shaumyan (1878-1918):

Old Bolshevik Party official . . . Expelled in 1900 from Polytechnic Institute for participation in student unrest . . . Went to Berlin, studied philosophy and Marxism, became acquainted with Kautsky, Martov . . . Lenin and Plekhanov . . . Took part in the Second Party Congress and immediately joined the Bolshevik faction (1903). In 1904 returned to Tiflis and stood at the head of the Bolshevik faction in the Social Democratic organization there. In 1906 and 1907 . . . delegate to the Stockholm and London Congresses. From this year on he led the entire Party work in Baku, editing the legal and illegal Party organs . . . In the February (1917) Revolution, he was chosen by the workers as Chairman of the workers' Soviet of Baku. Elected to the Central Committee at the Sixth Congress (summer of 1917). After the October Revolution he was Extraordinary Commissar for the Caucasus and in May, 1918, Chairman of the Council of People's Commissars in Baku and People's Commissar for Foreign Affairs. On September 20, 1918, he was one of the 26 People's Commissars of Baku shot by the English.

At the head of the Tiflis organization in 1904 . . . from 1907 on *"led the entire Party work* in Baku . . ."! The more we ponder this biographical note, the clearer it becomes that here is another Transcaucasian leader whom death so timely removed so that Beria might "expropriate" his activities and reputation in favor of Joseph Stalin, even as he had done with Ketskhoveli (died 1903) and Tsulukidze (died 1905), who had also been Stalin's teachers and superiors in the early history of Transcaucasia. On the basis of Lenin's letters to Shaumyan, particularly that of May 19, 1914, it is not too much to conjecture that, had Shaumyan not been executed in 1918, he and not Stalin might have been the chief executor of Lenin's nationalities policy in Transcaucasia, perhaps even in all Russia. Thus, more than once, and, even in greater instances than these, as we shall see, death was kind to Joseph Stalin and removed from his path men who might have been obstacles to his climb to singular greatness and singular power.

If Lenin had written nothing more than his articles on the national question and the right of self-determination, his place in the history of Russian socialist thought would have been ambiguous. In them we seem to see Lenin as a complicated strategist and political thinker, and a would-be democrat. On the one hand there is the Lenin of the mocking formula of "democratic centralism," the undemocratic splits, contempt for majorities whether of the people, or the working class, or the unions, or the party, or even of his own committees and *troikas*. On the other hand, both for tactical reasons and because of unexamined inherited formulae, there is the Lenin who, in such matters as the national question, appears to remain a democrat. Both in his polemics with "Great-Russian chauvinists" and with those "abstract internationalists" whose zeal for the unity of the human race found no place for the right of subject peoples to self-determination, Lenin seemed to speak with conviction in favor of democracy. So embarrassing are these utterances for latter-day anti-democratic disciples and practices that when the Lenin Institute was preparing a twelve-volume edition of his *Selected Works* for wide distribution, it found room for only one of his articles on the national question. And then it censored Lenin by omitting two whole sections because they culminated in this categorical affirmation:

> Not a single Social Democrat, unless he is ready to declare that questions of political freedom and democracy are indifferent to him, and in that case it is clear that he has ceased to be a Social Democrat . . .

No socialism without democracy! No one is a socialist who is indifferent to questions of political freedom and political democracy! To lose your attachment to freedom and democracy is to lose your socialist soul! So Lenin urged in 1905 when his polemic against Trotsky and Parvus concluded with his "whoever attempts to achieve socialism by any other route than that of political democracy will inevitably arrive at the most absurd and reactionary results, both political and economic." So Lenin urged in 1913-14 when he began his polemics on the national question. So he appeared to think until 1917. How he came to abandon democracy and reveal the anti-democratic essence of his creed and temperament provides the tragic climax of his life . . .

There is a peculiar ambivalence in the attitude of Lenin toward nationalism. On the one hand he regarded it with aversion as a product of the bourgeois (bourgeois-democratic) era. Nationalism was not to be preserved, strengthened, or "purified," but surmounted, outlived and overcome by internationalism. ("Marxism is incapable of being united with nationalism, be it ever so 'just,' 'purified,' refined . . . Marxism puts in place of any and every nationalism its internationalism, the fusion of all nations into a higher unity.") On the other hand he recognized that it would not be internationalism but nationalistic or imperialistic chauvinism if a victorious revolution in a dominant nation should deny to peoples incorporated into it by conquest the right to determine their own fate themselves, and to separate if they desired. ("The awakening of the masses from their feudal sleep, their fight against national oppression, for popular sovereignty, for the sovereignty of the nation—that is progressive. From this it follows that Marxists have the *unconditional* obligation to fight for the most determined and consistent democracy in every aspect of the national question. . . . To demolish every kind of national oppression, every privilege of one nation over another or of one language over another is the unconditional duty of the proletariat as a democratic force.")

But for Lenin there is a boundary line, hard to determine but all-important, which must not be overreached. Beyond that, democracy and progress in the national question would turn into their opposites, into the strengthening of nationalism and the "betrayal" of proletarian internationalism. ("Struggle *against* every national oppression—yes indeed. But struggle *for* any national development, for 'national culture' as such—never!") The slogan of "national-cultural autonomy" of the Bundists, Ukrainians, Austrian Marxists, was an attempt to reserve something of national culture and national values and carry these into the future internationalist world. That was where the boundary line was overstepped, where the "negative" task of assuring democratic rights "degenerated" into the positively dangerous one of trying to preserve national values. For Lenin there were no such positive national values. ("The proletariat is not only not willing to defend or further the national development of any nation, but on the contrary it warns the masses against such illusions . . . and welcomes any and every assimilation of nationalities—with the exception of those carried out by force or on the basis of privilege.")

In the West, Lenin continued, the national question had already been "settled," the general pattern being *one-nation, one-state:* the national state. But in the East, in Austria and much more in Russia, there still existed the "backward" multi-national state, sign of feudal backwardness, of need for a bourgeois-democratic revolution. The very fact of national oppression was a sign that these were "states whose internal constitution had remained abnormal and underdeveloped." Above all it was Russia, "more Asiatic than Asia, more backward than Austria-Hungary or China," that required a national self-determination program:

> . . . for those non-Russian peoples, which on the whole form the majority of the entire population—57%; which inhabit precisely the borderlands; in which the oppression of these alien races is much worse than in the neighboring states; . . . in which a number of oppressed nationalities in the borderlands have compatriots across the border . . . suffice it to recall Finns, Swedes, Poles, Ukrainians, Rumanians . . . and in which the development of capitalism and the general level of culture is not infrequently higher than in the center of the Great-Russian state.
>
> Can a nation be free if it oppresses other nations? It cannot. The interests of the freedom of the Great-Russian population demand a struggle against such oppression. . . .

But, inside the Empire, the proletariat of all nationalities must be united—regardless of national origin—into a single, centralized, all-Russian party. And all proletarians, regardless of national origin, must be taught to eschew, outgrow and despise all feelings of nationality as "bourgeois or petty bourgeois." If Russia were more advanced, and were facing like the West a socialist-proletarian instead of a bourgeois-democratic revolution, then, thought Lenin, there would be no problem of self-determination:

> It is precisely and solely because Russia and her neighbors are now passing through this epoch of bourgeois-democratic revolution that we require an item in our program on the right of nations to self-determination . . . The question of the *right* of nations to self-determination, i.e. the guarantee by the constitution of the state of an absolutely free and absolutely democratic method of deciding the question of secession, must not be confused with the question of the *expediency* of this or that nation's seceding. The Social Democratic Party must decide the latter question *in each separate case from the point of view of the interests of social development as a whole, and the interests of the proletarian class struggle for socialism.*

What then would happen to the right of self-determination if Lenin should change his mind about Russia's being ripe only for a bourgeois-democratic revolution? And what would happen if the many-nationed, centralized, proletarian party (the duty of whose members is to agitate systematically against their respective nationalisms) should take power simultaneously throughout most of the lands and borderlands of the Russian Empire? What would happen then, not on paper, not in written constitutions, but in practice, to the right of secession? What if all other parties, including all national parties, should be outlawed? What then would be the worth, what the method of implementation, of "the guarantee of an absolutely free and absolutely democratic method of deciding the question of secession?" Would anything then be left, beyond a shadow of that very national-cultural autonomy which Lenin in all his articles (and Stalin in his article on the national question) considered as tantamount to treason to socialism?

By a turn of the screw of fate, the Austrian Marxists would ere long have to grant the "right of secession" which was not in the Austro-Marxist program, while Stalin would one day make "national separatism" a capital charge in the purges, and would adopt the "Austrian" or "Bundist" conception of "national-cultural autonomy" as one of the proudest achievements of the Soviet Union! And then, with a centralized economy, a centralized police control, a single centralized party to determine everything from Moscow, the Soviet "Union" would become a federal state in name only, but in real content the most rigidly centralized state in all history. "National-cultural autonomy" itself would be reduced to little more than the right to propagate in many tongues the same centrally issued directives and slogans and the same centrally organized cult of the Leader. The national autonomy policy, to use Stalin's own phrase, would be "national in form, but socialist in content," by which he means, centralized and total-statist.

Yet, at least until the Second World War, Lenin's ardent fight during the First for the equality and democratic right of self-determination of nationalities would continue to leave some impress upon the "national cultural" life of the Soviet Union.

CHAPTER THIRTY-FOUR

THE INTERNATIONAL PREPARES

The political impotence of the German Social Democracy, that is what fills all the peoples of Europe with fear. You are a great, impressive, wonderful party, but you do not have any direct influence on the policy of your government.
—JEAN JAURÈS AT THE AMSTERDAM CONGRESS, 1905

Lenin's interest in the national question came late in his career and the views we analyzed in the last chapter ripened only slowly. As a young Social Democrat he had been quite satisfied with the resolution adopted by the International Socialist Congress of 1896:

> The Congress upholds the full right of self-determination of all nations and expresses its sympathy for the workers of every country now suffering under the yoke of military, national or other despotism . . . and calls upon the workers of these countries to join the ranks of the class-conscious workers of the entire world in order to fight . . . for the aims of international Social Democracy.

Significantly, when the *Iskra* Editorial Board was working in 1902 on a draft program for the Russian movement, Lenin had left to Martov the task of preparing the section on national self-determination. Lenin's interests lay elsewhere: in organization and the land question. "It was Martov," Lenin observed ten years later, "who drafted the national program and got it carried in 1903." And as late as 1914, the first public address of Vladimir Ilyich after the war began, once more congratulated Martov—without any reproaches or reservations—for his internationalist stand. Martov's paper, he said, is today "the best Socialist paper in Europe." As the war developed, his differences were not with Martov's own stand and views, but with the latter's willingness to associate with people who thought differently.

It was in 1907 that Lenin first glimpsed for a moment a thin crack in the apparently solid structure of the Socialist International. The occasion was the Stuttgart Congress, a splendid dress parade of the mighty-seeming forces of the world labor movement. There were 884 delegates from 25 nations and every continent. The Russian delegation, this being 1907, was unprecedentedly huge: sixty-three representatives from all factions and parties: Bolsheviks, Mensheviks, Social Revolutionaries, Bundists, Poles, Latvians, Armenians, Finns . . . Lenin, Martov,

Plekhanov, Deutsch, Potresov, Trotsky, Khrustalev, Lunachar-sky, Knuniyants, Litvinov, Meshkovsky, Evgenia Bosh, and many more whose names need not detain us. And of course, Rosa Luxemburg, looked upon as a leader of the Left Wing of the German party, the outstanding leader of the Polish Social Democracy, and the most active spokesman of the Russian delegation on the questions of war and militarism.

The best International Congress that has ever been held, said Lenin. In a popular calendar for workers he wrote:

> It marked the final consolidation of the Second International and the transformation of International congresses into businesslike meetings . . .

It had made "big strides forward" in the condemnation of "ministerialism" (the entrance of Socialists into coalition cabinets with bourgeois parties).*

The Stuttgart Congress was also notable, Lenin continued, for having adopted admirable resolutions on imperialism, militarism, the colonial question, and the slowly enlarging shadow of impending war.

---

* In the pre-war socialist movement, "ministerialism" was the chief chemical test for distinguishing Left from Right. Whoever opposed the entrance of socialists into bourgeois cabinets was a true revolutionist: whoever favored such action was a personal careerist, or, at best, a class-collaborationist, reformist, gradualist and opportunist. Lenin took this for granted, as did the Mensheviks, although, unlike them, he was "unorthodox" enough to make an exception of a provisional revolutionary government in time of actual revolution. In the war years, he would become the chief denouncer of all socialist Ministers entering wartime emergency coalition governments. Their ministerialism was to him no longer mere misguided opportunism but deliberate and calculated treason. In 1917, the roles of Lenin and the Mensheviks, as we shall see, got somehow reversed. They became advocates of socialists' entering the Provisional Revolutionary Government and he opposed it. In the Communist International he made anti-ministerialism one of the tests of eligibility. But today we have becom so used to the spectacle of Communist Ministers entering into coalition governments that Lenin's remark cited above now needs explanation. Of course, "the situation has changed," as has the function of the Communist Ministers, who now enter into coalition governments to get hold of key power posts such as Police, Justice, the Army, in order to eliminate the other parties by purge and set up a Communist police state. They also seek negotiation posts such as Foreign Affairs and Trade so that they may function as agents of the Russian Government within the delegations sent by their own government to negotiate with the Russians. In countries where Russian influence is strongest there are no more zealous collaborationists and ministerialists than the Communist parties. Whether they collaborate or go into opposition, or do both simultaneously, depends primarily on changing Russian interests. Thus Lenin's remark on "the big strides forward of the Stuttgart Congress in condemning ministerialism" sounds today like the echo from another world of primal innocence. Yet, all through the next few chapters we shall have to bear in mind the fact that "ministerialism" was then the chief opportunist sin or treachery, alike to the pre-war Left, to Leninist wartime socialism, and, as long as Lenin lived, to the Communist International.

And let us note this welcome feature—he added proudly—
that *all* the socialists of Russia [Bolsheviks, Mensheviks, Social
Revolutionaries, Poles, Finns, Bundists, etc.] unanimously and
on *all* questions, voted in a revolutionary spirit.

Never had Vladimir Ilyich been so inclusive in his use of
the term "socialist" or so generous in his approbation of the
friendly-enemy parties of the common front against tsarism!

Only one smudge did he find on the shining page written by
the Congress: the "remarkable and sad feature" that the German Social Democracy, revered leader of the International
"which has always hitherto upheld the revolutionary standpoint
in Marxism," had wavered on the questions of colonialism and
war. And the great August Bebel was among the cautiously
equivocal, if not among the waverers or outright opportunists.
But Kautsky and Clara Zetkin and others on the German delegation had joined with the Poles and Russians under the lead of
Rosa Luxemburg, Lenin and Martov, in stiffening the hesitant
Bebel, and repulsing the opportunists.

On the colonial question—continued Lenin in his Almanac
report—an opportunist majority was formed in the Commission, and the following monstrous sentence appeared in the
draft resolution reported out by the Commission:
*"The Congress does not on principle and for all time reject all
colonial policy, which, under a socialist régime, may exercize a
civilizing influence."*

The German, Eduard David, had led the fight for the adop-
tion of this "monstrous sentence." His argument: "You cannot
fight something with nothing. As against capitalist colonial
policy, the socialists must propose a positive program of protection of the rights of the natives." But Karl Kautsky, the other
German leader whom Lenin admired equally with Bebel, had
led the attack on this proposed new departure in colonial policy:

I contend—he said—that democracy and socialist policy have
nothing in common with conquest and foreign rule . . . If we

want to exert a civilizing influence upon primitive peoples, the
first prerequisite is to gain their confidence by granting them
freedom . . . The sentence [proposed by David and the Com-
mission] is at variance with all our socialist and democratic
thinking . . .

When it came to a vote, the "monstrous sentence" was defeated. But it was by a bare majority of 127 to 108. And then
only because the delegations from colonial lands and from
countries having no colonies of their own joined hands with
the solid Russian delegation and the Left Wing minorities from
Germany, England and France. Lenin was satisfied with the
victory, but saddened by the fact that his favorite party, the
honored leader of the International, had wavered for a moment before his eyes. It was not until seven years later that he
came to realize that the momentary divergence had marked a
fork in the road whence would diverge two irreconcilable paths.

More important than the Colonial Question was the related
resolution on Militarism and War. All over Europe arms were
piling up and arms taxation was becoming an increasingly intolerable burden. Since the turn of the century there had been
an unending succession of incidents and alarms: the Fashoda
crisis, the Tangier incident, the Algeciras crisis, the Agadir incident. The leaders of the European socialist parties, particularly
the German and French, had followed these events with mount-
ing tension. The International Socialist Bureau and Congresses
had considered the questions of war and militarism repeatedly,
but always their pledges, adjurations, threats and resolves had
been shrouded in ambiguity, because they were inclined to dis-
tinguish between the duties of socialist parties in defensive wars
and in aggressive wars, and because they staked all on prevent-
ing war.

But what if both sides plotted war? What if the complicated
maneuvers of behind-the-scenes diplomacy should permit all
governments to give their participation the appearance of defense against aggression? And what should the socialist parties

do if, despite all their efforts to prevent war, it should never-theless break out? To these questions, up to the Stuttgart Con-gress of 1907, the International had never given clear and une-quivocal answers.

As early as the International Congress held in Brussels in 1890, the general outlines of the coming war of 1914-18 had been foreseen, and the German leader Wilhelm Liebknecht (father of that Karl Liebknecht who will soon figure promi-nently in our story) had joined with the French leader Eduard Vaillant in a pledge to avert war by joint protests, joint pledges, and the joint cooperation of French and German labor. But a Dutch delegate, Domela Nieuwenhuis, had ventured to ask them: "And what will happen if all our pledges, protests, dem-onstrations and threats fail to prevent war?" If you are pledged to defend your country when it is attacked, he told the delegates, then all is lost, for the distinction between defensive and offen-sive wars is really meaningless and diplomats will always know how to convince their own people that the opponent nation was the aggressor. There was only one pledge that would have meaning and be worth while, and that was for the socialist parties of all countries to pledge themselves to refuse to support any war but their own war for socialism. Hence, if war came between their respective nations they must call upon the work-ers to refuse to render military service and to answer the war by a general strike. His motion was voted down as "impractical" to carry out under the conditions of martial law such as would undoubtedly prevail once war was declared.

In 1893, at the Zurich Congress of the International, he re-peated his proposal. Again it was voted down. One of the strongest arguments against it came from Plekhanov, who said that a call for a general strike would be most effective precisely in the freest and most advanced lands with the best organized labor movements, thereby yielding up progressive Western Europe to the mercies of the "Cossacks of Russia," a land which in 1893 had virtually no labor organization or labor press at all. Engels received the news of the vote with satisfaction and wrote a letter to Lafargue in which he praised the Congress for having rejected "high-sounding and empty phrases."

> People must realize—Engels had written in 1890, in an Almanac of the French Party—that if France, in alliance with Russia, should declare war on Germany, she would be fighting against the strongest Social Democracy in Europe; and that we would have no choice but to oppose with all our strength any aggressor who was on the side of Russia. For, if we are defeated, the Social Democratic movement in Europe is smashed for twenty years. But if not, we shall come to power ourselves. The present system in Germany cannot possibly survive a war.

Engels went on to assure the French workers that he thought the French Republic superior to the German monarchy—as a representative of the bourgeois revolution. But not as an ally of tsarist Russia against a Germany that was on the eve of socialist victory. In Germany socialism would soon triumph (within a decade), and then a socialist Germany would of course undo the injustice of the annexation of Alsace-Lorraine, and would liberate Poland. But if France in her impatience should subordinate herself to the Tsar and attack the Rhine while Russia attacked from the East, "then Germany would be fighting for her very existence." If she won, there was nothing to gain. But if she lost, she would be crushed, reduced in size to proportions that would make it impossible for socialism to develop.

At this article, a storm broke out in France. In due course, Engels had replied to his critics:

> If the French socialists do not expressly state that in a defensive war they would be willing to repulse an attack by Kaiser Wilhelm, it is because this is so glaringly obvious, so self-evident, that it is not worth saying. There is not a single socialist in Germany who does not think that in such an event the French socialists would simply be doing their duty in defending their national independence.

And the following year, 1891, he had even written to Bebel:

> If we are convinced that the thing will start next spring, we could hardly be opposed to the credits [of the military budget] on principle, and then we would be in a pretty desperate position. The lick-spittle parties would boast that they had always been right, and that we had had to eat our own words. Also, such an unexpected change of front would cause appalling friction within the Party—and internationally as well.

Rather fantastically, Engels advised that the Party Deputies in the Reichstag should refuse to approve any credits aiming at transforming the existing equipment or at forming new military cadres, since these "would not be ready in time for war in the spring." But they should vote all military credits for those measures

> . . . which will bring our present army nearer to a people's militia, which will simply strengthen our defenses, which will train and arm all men from 17 to 60 who have not yet enlisted . . . We cannot demand that the existing military organization should be completely altered while the danger of war persists. But if there is an attempt to take the great mass of men who are fit for service but have not been trained, and to train them as well as possible and organize them in cadres—for real fighting, not for parading and all that nonsense—then that is an approach to our idea of a people's militia which we can accept. If the danger of war increases, we can tell the government that we would be ready, if they made it possible by decent treatment, to give our support against the foreign enemy—on condition that they (the government) will fight relentlessly and use every means, even revolutionary ones. If Germany is attacked from east and west, then all means of defense are good. The existence of the nation is then at stake, and we, too, have a position to maintain, and a future which we have won by hard fighting.

Bebel rejected this suggestion of conditional voting of war credits. He and his colleagues in the Reichstag voted against the war credits, and, by the next year, 1892, Engels spoke no more of such concessions. In 1893, Engels wrote a series in *Vorwaerts* called *Can Europe Disarm?* His answer to this question, verging on what Lenin would, in anyone but Marx or Engels, regard as "utopian pacifism," said:

> Such changes are possible at this moment. They can be made by the existing governments and in the existing political situation . . . I limit myself to such proposals as any existing government can accept without endangering the security of its country. I am endeavoring to show that, from a purely military viewpoint, there is nothing to prevent the gradual abolition of the regular army; and that, if a regular army *is* still maintained, it is maintained not for military but political reasons—in a word, that the army is meant for defense not against a foreign enemy but against a domestic one.

Engels's specific proposals included: the gradual scaling down of the length of military service by international agreement and the ultimate substitution of a system of short-term training of the entire male youth of each country in a locally based militia, easily usable for defense but "useless" for wars of conquest, with every citizen keeping his gun in his home. Since Prussia had begun the arms race, Prussia should take the initiative in calling such an international conference to shorten the term of service in all branches. If France accepted, the war danger would disappear. If she rejected it, she would be worse off, since Russia was not yet in a position to be of real help, while England would doubtless have been won by this appeal to a position of benevolent neutrality toward a Germany that had offered to disarm. In case of war, the final decision would lie with England:

> When she puts her fleet at the disposal of one side, the other will simply be starved out and its imports of grain cut off . . . The blockaded side will have to capitulate as sure as two and two make four.

Again Bebel quietly ignored Engels's proposals as utopian. There the matter had rested after Engels's death (1895), with the armies and navies growing, war incidents multiplying, tension accumulating, and the socialists still uncertain about "defensive" and "aggressive" wars, and with no program on what to do if war came despite their efforts to prevent it. In 1900, without mentioning his name, the Paris International Congress finally rejected Engels's idea of voting war credits under certain conditions. It resolved that:

> The socialist parliamentary deputies in all parliaments pledge themselves unconditionally to vote against every military expenditure and all expenditure for the navy and for colonial military expeditions.

Now it was 1907 and all the socialist parties of the world were at Stuttgart to consider the situation created by back-breaking arms budgets, by the open Franco-Russian alliance, by Kaiser Wilhelm's sword-rattling and the repeated crises and alarms. Marx and Engels were dead. Old Wilhelm Liebknecht, who had voted against war credits in the Franco-Prussian War and gone to jail for it, had died in 1900. Marx and Engels had been deceived by Bismarck's forged Ems telegram, and their own general attitude, into believing that the war of 1870 was for Germany a purely defensive war, but Liebknecht had opposed it from the first day. They had not changed their minds until the fall of Napoleon III at Sedan, when they began attacking Bismarck's aggression and defending the new French Republic. Bebel, too, had opposed that war from the first day.

Now, as the grand old man of the German Social Democracy, he prepared the *Resolution on Militarism and War*. Though he was loved and admired more than any other living man in the International, there were in those days no unanimous resolutions or infallible leader cults in this assemblage of men devoted to the cause of freedom and socialism. He was attacked sharply from many points of view. Gustav Hervé of France demanded that the German socialists repudiate "defense of the Fatherland" and that the International repudiate patriotism in every land and pledge itself to "answer" any war by general strike and rebellion. Rosa Luxemburg found his formula "too rigid . . . Hervé is an *enfant,* an *enfant terrible."* But not for that did she exempt Bebel's draft resolution from criticism. Nor reject Hervé's idea of a general strike, if and when a sharpening wartime crisis might make it possible:

> I have asked for the floor—she said—on behalf of the Russian and the Polish Delegations, to remind you that we should think of the Great Russian Revolution in connection with this point (of general strike and war). . . . The Russian Revolution sprang up not merely as a result of the war; it also served to put an end to the war. Otherwise tsarism would surely have continued the war . . . After Vollmar's speech, and partly after Bebel's, we consider it necessary to sharpen Bebel's resolution, and we have worked out an amendment which we shall later submit. In our amendment we go somewhat beyond Comrades Jaurés and Vaillant in that we contend that, in case of war, the agitation should be directed not merely toward its termination, but also toward utilizing the war to hasten the overthrow of class rule in general.

Bebel answered his critics by contending that a merely inflammatory resolution not backed up by the strength to carry it out, would serve only to give the police pretexts for outlawing parties and union.

Lenin said nothing, for Rosa Luxemburg was expressing his view and Martov's and that of the whole group of delegations from Russia. But here is how he summarized the debate in his Almanac article from which we have been quoting:

> Hervé's scheme to "reply" to any war by a strike and an uprising, revealed an utter lack of understanding of the fact that the application of one or other means of struggle depends not on any decision revolutionaries may have made previously but on the objective conditions of the particular crisis, both economic and political, caused by the war. But even though Hervé did show that he was lightminded, superficial, easily carried away by resonant phrases, it would be extreme shortsightedness to reply to him by a mere dogmatic exposition of the general truths of socialism. Vollmar (German Right Wing) particularly

dropped into this error, and Bebel and Guesde were not entirely free of it. With the extraordinary conceit of a man infatuated with stereotyped parliamentarism, Vollmar attacked Hervé without noticing that his own narrowmindedness and hardened opportunism *compel* one to recognize the living stream in Hervéism *in spite* of the theoretical absurdity and folly of the manner in which Hervé himself presents the question. It sometimes happens that at a new turning point of a movement, theoretical absurdities cover up some practical truth. And this aspect of the question, the appeal that not only parliamentary methods of struggle should be valued, the appeal to act in accordance with the new conditions of the future war and the future crisis, was stressed by the revolutionary Social Democrats, especially by Rosa Luxemburg in her speech. Together with the Russian Social Democratic delegates—Lenin and Martov both stood together in agreement on this—Rosa Luxemburg proposed amendments to Bebel's resolution and these amendments emphasized the need for agitation among the youth, the necessity of taking advantage of the crisis created by war for the purpose of hastening the downfall of the bourgeoisie, the necessity of bearing in mind the inevitable change of methods and means of struggle in accordance with the intensification of the class struggle and the changes in the political situation. Thus Bebel's resolution, dogmatically one-sided, lifeless and open to a Vollmarian interpretation, was finally transformed into an altogether different resolution.

The most important amendment offered by Rosa Luxemburg in the name of the delegation proposed to add two final paragraphs to the resolution. They read:

> If a war threatens to break out, it is the duty of the working class and of its parliamentary representatives in the countries involved, supported by the consolidating activity of the International Bureau, to exert every effort to prevent the outbreak of war by means they consider most effective, which naturally vary according to the sharpening of the class struggle and of the general political situation.
>
> Should war break out nonetheless, it is their duty to intervene in favor of its speedy termination and to do all in their power to utilize the economic and political crisis caused by the war to rouse the peoples and thereby to hasten the abolition of capitalist class rules.

After dickering with Luxemburg, Lenin and Martov to tone down the wording of their amendments in the interests of party legality (e.g. the substitution of "agitation among the youth" for "agitation among military recruits")* Bebel accepted the above crucial amendment, and three others unanimously by acclamation.

"Should war break out nonetheless," reads the last sentence we have just quoted, *"it is their duty to intervene in favor of its speedy termination."* This Lenin would later play down as "miserable, utopian pacifism." But the rest of the sentence—*"and to do all in their power to utilize the economic and political crisis caused by the war to rouse the peoples and thereby to hasten the abolition of capitalist class rule,"* i.e. attempt to end the war by revolution—this was to be the core of Lenin's and Luxemburg's activities when war did come. And it was to be the cornerstone of the foundation of the Third or Communist International. Thus, in retrospect, the Stuttgart International Socialist Congress of 1907 proves to have been a decisive turning point in the history of the Second International.

So important an event could not go without the usual touch of Stalinist "editing" of history in the course of the nineteen thirties. As late as 1936, a note in Volume XII of Lenin's *Collected Works* still says modestly that "Lenin took an active part in the work of the Stuttgart Congress" (Third Russian Edition, p. 456). But, despite Lenin's own statement to the contrary, Martov's name is omitted from the note, which speaks of "the amendments of Lenin and Rosa Luxemburg to the resolution" (p. 457). And a similar note to the International Publishers' edition of Lenin's *Selected Works,* Volume IV (the notes were prepared by the Marx-Engels-Lenin Institute) further shifts the picture: "The Left Wing of the Congress (Rosa Luxemburg and others), headed by Lenin, moved an amendment . . ." This peculiar use of parentheses and a comma, and this apparently

---

* Despite Bebel's precautions, the German Government understood the circumlocution and in April, 1908, passed a law forbidding all persons under twenty years of age to attend political or union meetings. All youth organizations, including the Social Democratic Young, were dissolved, and all youth agitation remained illegal until the revolution of 1918.

trivial and "innocent" emendation of history, will yet prove of tremendous importance to our story. As for Lenin himself, he never concealed, nor dreamt of concealing, the fact that Martov had joined with him and Rosa Luxemburg in elaborating the amendments, and that Rosa, and not he, had "headed," i.e. been the spokesman for the Left Wing of the Congress and for the Russian and Polish delegations, and the outstanding leader of the fight, both in the commission and on the floor.

On October 17, 1912, tiny Montenegro (population 230,000 —"together with the Russians we number 170,000,000!") declared war on Turkey. The Great Powers, still shaken by their glance over the precipice at Agadir (Morocco) in 1911, were in no mood to permit another international crisis. But Montenegro had acted on the basis of a secret alliance with Greece, Bulgaria and Serbia, and in a few days the entire Balkans were ablaze.

Turkey was like a wounded animal, followed by beasts of prey large and small. Like China and Persia, she had begun a desperate effort to modernize and westernize herself as a safeguard against extinction. All three of them had been deeply stirred by Japan's defeat of the "Western" power, Russia, and by the Russian Revolution of 1905, and all three were in the throes of civil war, which, until it should be completed, would leave them helpless. Few spectacles of the first half of our "enlightened twentieth century" were uglier than the attempt of powers large and small—England, France, Germany, Austria-Hungary, Italy, Japan, Tsarist and Stalinist Russia—to partition these countries before they should succeed in their own regeneration.

The Young Turk Revolution had begun in 1908. By the introduction of Western ideas, Western technique, Western nationalism, centralism, parliamentarism and democracy, it sought to save Turkey from disintegration. But the beginning of Turkish civil war was taken as a signal by the Bulgarian prince to end the nominal suzerainty of Turkey and declare its independence and by Crete to revolt and join Greece (1908). Then Austria violated the Treaty of Berlin by annexing the Turkish, Slav-inhabited provinces of Bosnia and Herzegovina, over whose Christians she exercised a "protectorate." Since these provinces were largely inhabited by Serbs, Serbian nationalists were outraged and began to look to Russia for support against Austria, whereupon Austria naturally snuggled closer to Germany. In 1911, Italy too declared war on Turkey long enough to seize Tripoli, Cyrenaica, and some of the islands of the Aegean. And now, in 1912, the allied Balkan powers fell upon Macedonia, Thrace, and the Adriatic provinces (Albania).

The uneasy Great Powers tried to localize the war and bring it to a speedy conclusion. But in 1913 it broke out afresh, then spilled over into a second war between Bulgaria on the one hand and Greece, Rumania, Serbia and Montenegro on the other, over the division of the spoils (Macedonia, Thrace, Albania). Peace was patched up a second time (September 29, 1913), but it left all questions unsettled and all nerves on edge. Bulgaria still coveted all of Macedonia and Thrace and the port of Salonika. Macedonia, divided between Greece, Serbia and Bulgaria, began to develop an independence movement of its own. Serbia and Montenegro were prevented from dividing Albania between them, because the latter was regarded as potential booty both by Italy and Austria, which rivals united to make it into an independent state. To her grievance about Bosnia and Herzegovina, Serbia thus added a fresh grievance concerning the Adriatic. The Russian press increased its talk about "protecting our Slav brothers." Germany increased its support of Austria. The situation was becoming so combustible that the tiniest spark might set off a general conflagration. In less than a year, that spark flew at Sarajevo and the fire spread over Europe, then over all the other continents of the globe.

Lenin seems to have underestimated the significance of the Balkan Wars of 1912 and 1913. His occasional brief articles on the subject denounced Russian chauvinism for seeking to "rob a piece of Turkey"; ridiculed the talk of "Slav brotherhood" as a cover for Russian protectorates and annexations; asserted that Slav peasants and Turk peasants were brothers, and that what was needed was a federation of the Balkan peoples, independent alike of Russian and Austrian "protection." But he thought of the whole conflict as a localized one.

Leon Trotsky, living in Vienna, closer to the boiling Balkan cauldron, hastened to the scene of the "little wars" as correspondent for the *Kievskaya Mysl,* liberal Russian daily. He was glad to escape from the failure of his "August Bloc." And he wanted to see war at first hand. The future War Commissar was shocked by the face of war:

> You in Russia—read his first dispatch—know it and believe in it. My mind does not accept this combination of the things of everyday life, of chicken, cigarettes, bare-footed and smut-nosed boys, with the incredibly tragic fact of war. I know that war has been declared, and that it has already begun, but I have not yet learned to believe in it.

In the Balkans he learned something of the politics of Serbia, Bulgaria and Rumania, became convinced of the need of a United Balkan Federation and a United States of Europe, met Balkan socialists whom he was later to bring into the Communist International. Chief of these was Christian Rakovsky, influential in all Balkan socialist parties, a Bulgarian by birth, a Rumanian by virtue of the accidents of map-drawing when frontiers were shuffled, a French physician by education, a master of French, German, Russian, English, Turkish and all the Balkan tongues, and a future leading figure in the Soviet Union, the Communist International and Soviet diplomacy. For a time he would serve as President of the Ukrainian Soviet Republic, which Russia has constantly been supplying with non-Ukrainian leaders from Rakovsky to Khrushchev. He would end up by being purged as a Trotskyist.

The news story of "Antid Oto" (Trotsky's pen-name) which attracted most attention was one concerning Bulgarian atrocities on wounded and captured Turkish prisoners. It was a common matter for the Russian press to dwell on Turkish atrocities against Armenians. Indeed, in a letter of Viceroy Vorontsov-Dashkov of Transcaucasia to Tsar Nicholas, dated October 10, 1912, we find:

> It is necessary to take open action in defense of the Armenians in Turkey, especially at the present time, so as to prepare in advance a sympathetic population in those localities which, as matters stand, might willy-nilly prove to be in the sphere of our military operations.

But what was unique about "Antid Oto" was his venturing to write on atrocities committed by "our Slav brothers" against the Turks. The dispatch attracted national attention, and was met with the suggestion that the pen-name of "Antid Oto" disguised an émigré revolutionary who had entered into the pay of Austria-Hungary. This was an old device: to answer unwelcome criticism by branding the critic an enemy agent. We shall meet with it again!

The leaders of the Socialist International, already frightened by the Agadir incident of 1911, now called a special Emergency International Congress in Basel for November 24, 1912. It met for two days with no other order of business but the war danger and measures for peace. Every prior demonstration against war in the history of the International was eclipsed by the solemn Emergency Congress at Basel. But Lenin, who could have gone as representative of his Central Committee, attached more importance to the problem of completing the split in the Russian party, and especially in the Duma Fraction. He contented himself with sending a Bolshevik delegation of five, headed by Leo Kamenev. The others were Shklovsky, Troyanovsky and his wife, Elena Rozmirovich, and Vladimirsky. The total Russian delegation from all parties and factions was thirty-six. Lenin's chief interest at the moment was in the attempt of his people backed by Plekhanov, to have one of the thirty-six,

Gorbunov, representative of the Petersburg "Initiative Group" or Liquidators, barred from the meetings of the Russian delegation at the Basel Congress. Gorbunov was not excluded, whereupon the Plekhanovists and Leninists walked out of the Russian delegation meeting, one more success of Lenin's effort to spread the Prague split throughout every institution of the Party. But the Congress, intent on the war danger, paid no attention to the "quarrelsome" Russians and their "private" controversy. When delegate Shklovsky finally got around to writing Lenin a suggestion that he should print a pamphlet report on the Basel Congress, Lenin answered testily:

> Rather late in the day! Evidently something was lacking (or was there a surplus of something?) in Basel. Kamenev of course was over his ears in work, but what about the other four? Surely it was obvious that one ought to have written *daily* for *Pravda*. Surely it was not hard to distribute the work. Not a single letter went to *Pravda* from the place, whereas the Liquidators sent several to *Luch* . . . None of the delegates except Kamenev wrote here about Basel . . . I am *enormously* pleased with the Basel results, for those idiots, the Liquidators, allowed themselves to be caught on the Initiative Group!! Those swine [*svoloch,* "riff-raff," "scum," but with overtones that make it about as harsh an epithet as our "those bastards"] couldn't possibly have been trapped any better. But the inactivity of our delegates, and some inexplicable inability to open their mouths, has outraged me. (After all, four or five *knew how to speak* German.) Who spoke? With whom? How? About what? Not a word from anyone except Kamenev. Yet agitation [on the split] among the Germans is *very* important . . . [Letter of early December, 1912, *Collected Works,* Vol. XXIX, p. 55.]

And that is all! Not a word on the war danger, on possible differences in the International, on the solemn purpose and decisions of the Congress! Yet in retrospect, Lenin would come to realize that the Basel decisions were more important even than those taken at Stuttgart. They would provide him in 1914 with his chief wartime platform and talking point against all those who supported their governments in the war.

The manifesto "On the International Situation" adopted unanimously by the Basel Extraordinary Congress began by quoting once more the pledge of the Stuttgart Congress. ("Should war break out nonetheless, it is their duty to intervene in favor of its speedy termination and to do all in their power to utilize the economic and political crisis, caused by the war, to rouse the peoples and thereby to hasten the abolition of capitalist class rule.") Next it noted "with satisfaction the complete unanimity of the socialist parties and trade unions in all countries in the war against war." Upon the Balkan socialists it enjoined opposition to any renewal of hostilities between Serbs, Bulgarians, Rumanians and Greeks, and also the defense of "the rights of the Balkan peoples, Turks and Albanians, who are now in the opposite camp."

> It is the duty of the Social Democratic parties of Austria, Hungary, Croatia, Slavonia, Bosnia, and Herzegovina to work for the prevention of an attack of the Danubian monarchy upon Serbia. [Prophetic words!] . . . The Congress expects that the Russian, Finnish, and Polish proletariat . . . will combat every design of tsarism, whether upon Armenia or upon Constantinople, and concentrate all its force upon the revolutionary struggle for liberation from tsarism . . .
>
> But the most important task in the International's activities devolves upon the working class of Germany, France and England . . . to demand that their respective governments withhold all support from both Austria-Hungary and Russia. . . .
>
> Let the governments be mindful of the fact that they cannot let loose a war without danger to themselves. Let them recall that the Franco-German War was followed by the revolutionary uprising of the Commune, that the Russo-Japanese War set in motion the revolutionary forces of the peoples in the Russian Empire . . . It would be sheer madness for the governments to fail to realize that the very thought of the monstrosity of a world war would inevitably call forth the indignation and the revolt of the working class . . .

Thus we have a constant progression: 1900, the Paris International Congress adopts a pledge for all parties "to vote unconditionally against all military expenditures"; 1907, the

Stuttgart Congress pledges itself "to utilize the crisis caused by war to hasten the abolition of capitalist rule"; 1912, the Basel Emergency Congress warns that a war "would call forth the revolt of the working class." And there is a similar progression in the definition of the war itself, its Balkan causes, its Anglo-French-German and Russian-Austrian-Serbian components, so that it is no longer talk about war in general but about a specific war, the outlines and salient features of which are precisely foreseen—in short, about a war exactly described in September, 1912, which would even break out as foreseen, with an Austro-Hungarian ultimatum to Serbia in July of 1914.

CHAPTER THIRTY-FIVE

A WORLD ENDS

Our one agreed aim in World War I was to break up German militarism. It was no part of our original intention to break up the Habsburg and Ottoman Empires, to create Czechoslovakia or resurrect Poland, to make a Russian revolution, to treble the size of Serbia and double that of Rumania, to create Iraq and Estonia and Lithuania and a Jewish National Home, or to give the keys of the Brenner and the Adriatic to Italy. Yet, in the outcome, all these—and much else—sprang from the war . . . while the one thing which we promised ourselves, the destruction of German militarism, we failed to achieve.

—H. N. FIELDHOUSE

Month by month through the years 1912, 1913 and 1914 international tension mounted. War talk in the air, national feelings rising, the nations spending fantastic sums on "preparations for defense," presidents, kings, ministers, generals, exchanging visits and reviewing each other's armies. Like every acute political observer, Lenin was aware of all this, sensed its meaning; yet he could not quite believe it. To his sister Anna he wrote of his move to Cracow:

> I hope it will be easier for us to see each other, that is, if war does not break out, and I do not believe it will. [Autumn, 1912.]

To his sister Maria:

> There is much talk about war here as you can see by the papers. If war does break out, I shall probably have to go to Vienna or perhaps to the town where we last met [Stockholm], but I do not believe there will be a war. [November, 1912.]

To Gorky in December, 1912:

> There will probably not be a war and we shall stay here for the time being, taking advantage of the Poles' desperate hatred of tsarism.

And yet again, early in 1913, the remark already quoted:

> A war between Austria and Russia would be a very useful thing for the revolution in all of Eastern Europe, but it is not likely that Franz Joseph and Nikolasha will give us that pleasure . . .

The leaders of the Socialist International, closer to the secrets of their governments because of the powerful parliamentary delegations of socialists in Germany, France and Austria, were more alarmed. They arranged frequent emergency conferences of all sorts, but, as we have seen, Lenin did not even attend the Emergency International Socialist Congress at Basel, called in November, 1912, specifically to meet the war danger.

When the International Socialist Bureau gathered in London in December, 1913, again Lenin did not attend, nor did he send Kamenev, but the less known and less important Litvinov, as the representative of the Bolsheviks. All his energies were absorbed at that time in completing the split in the Duma Fraction and making absolute the split in the Russian Social Democratic Party. The leaders of the International, on the motion of Rosa Luxemburg and Karl Kautsky, were attempting to heal splits in the Russian party as well as in the English movement.*

In order that the working class may put forth all its strength in the struggle against capitalism, it is necessary that in every country there should exist only *one* socialist party as there is only *one* proletariat—read Kautsky's motion. Plekhanov, who had till now been supporting Lenin against the Liquidators, joined in the movement for unity, even urging that the time was ripe for uniting the Social Democracy with the Social Revolutionary Party. All Russian factions, including the Social Revolutionaries, agreed, as did both Rosa Luxemburg's faction of the Polish Party and the anti-Luxemburg Warsaw Opposition, and the Left Wing of the Polish Socialist Party, as well. But Lenin would have none of it. Through the Prague Congress he had captured the Party trademark or firm name. With the aid of police agent Malinovsky, he had just split the Duma Fraction and won control of the metal workers' union. *Pravda* was gaining in circulation over the Menshevik *Luch.* The Bolsheviks were beginning to win the upper hand in trade union and social security elections. He had just won a majority in the Lettish Central Committee and had tied up with the Polish Warsaw Opposition against Rosa Luxemburg in the Polish Social Democratic Party. He would press his opponents to the wall. They would accept "unity" on his terms, or he would destroy them. True, the International was the supreme body, the embodiment of internationalism, but what did its leader know of him and his fight or of Russian conditions? He felt confident

* In England they were trying to unite the Labor Party, the Independent Labor Party, the Fabian Society, and the Socialist Party of Great Britain. Unity was effected on a federated basis.

that they would remain true to internationalism without his personal presence. He held them at arm's length, sent Litvinov to "their" Bureau meeting with a prepared statement, then sent Inessa Armand, still less important, to the special all-Russian unity conference called by the International at Brussels, for July 16, 1914, a fateful month in a fateful year! Inessa was selected, according to Krupskaya, because Ilyich wanted a "firm" person who could resist a "storm of indignation" from the other Russian factions and from all the leaders of the International, and who could stubbornly repeat his prepared statement in French and German as well as Russian. War was far from his mind now in that fatal summer of 1914. It had yielded first place in his thoughts to the faction war.

The Russian police became alarmed. What if the International, with its great prestige, did force unity, and all the energies that the various factions and parties had been using against each other should suddenly be turned against the government? What if the news of unity should end the bewilderment and sullen rancor of the working class and arouse a new confidence and determination? The Okhrana instructed all its secret agents in the various factions and parties:

> ... steadfastly and persistently to defend the idea of the complete impossibility of any organizational fusion whatsoever of these tendencies and particularly the union of the Bolsheviks with the Mensheviks.*

The police might be worried, but Lenin was not worried. He did not know of their instructions, but even if he had, it would not have stopped him in his determination "steadfastly and persistently to defend the idea of the complete impossibility of any organizational fusion whatsoever . . . and particularly of the union of the Bolsheviks with the Mensheviks." And he was so sure that he was right, on every difference large and small, of organization, of strategy, of tactics, of principle, of personnel,

---

* *Bolshevik: Dokumenty po istorii bolshevizma s 1903 po 1916 god byvsh. Moskovsk. Okhrannogo Otdeleniya.* Edited by M. A. Tsyavlovsky, Moscow, 1918, pp. 146-48.

that neither a police instruction nor an instruction from the honored leadership of the entire international working class could swerve him from his path. Surely unity was good, but only the right sort of unity, unity on his terms and under his leadership. Certainly, he was a loyal and zealous international-ist and cherished the International as the embodiment of in-ternational solidarity and the means of international action. Of course, he admired the great German Social Democratic Party above all other parties, and Kautsky above all living Marxists. But in Russia he was right and his methods were right. What did the opposition of all the other Russian factions matter? And the pressure of all the other parties of the International? What did they all know about Russia? Why didn't they let him fight his own fight in his own way? He was winning, and he was not going to let any one stop him. He had his "bull-dog grip" (as Vera Zasulich had phrased it), and he would not let go.

> The Mensheviks only want to scold me before the International.
> I shall not give them that pleasure. Besides, it would be a waste
> of time. It is better to serve the cause than to chatter...

The Subcommission on Russian Unity of the Socialist In-ternational met on July 16-17, 1914. Along with Inessa Ar-mand, Lenin sent Vladimirsky, Popov, and also Hanecki of the anti-Luxemburg faction of the Polish Social Democracy. Al-together there were eleven Russian groups, factions and parties represented. Everybody spoke in favor of unity except his delegation. Everybody was ready to reopen all questions for fresh decision, or regard the past as past and start anew. But his delegation stubbornly refused to vote on anything. Inessa read her statement, and that was that. It accused all of Lenin's opponents of not being socialists, of refusing to accept disci-pline, of wanting to liquidate the underground organization, of wanting to form a "bourgeois labor party," of desiring blocs with the bourgeoisie, of wanting to wreck the Party program by substituting "cultural autonomy" for "national self-determina-tion." It culminated in a series of ultimatums which may fairly be summed up in the words: *"Let those who want unity with us unconditionally accept the decisions of the Prague Congress and unconditionally submit to the institutions created by it."*

Inessa was answered with reasoning, pleas, argument, persuasion. A resolution was drawn up to satisfy and dispose of all of Lenin's charges and demands:

1. All groups accept the program of the Russian Social Democracy...

2. All groups recognize as absolutely necessary that the minority within the unified party should always accept the decisions of the majority as binding for party activity.

3. The organization of the party must be secret at present; it is compelled to be. The activity of all party members in legal institutions should be under the leadership and control of the leading party institutions.

4. All groups renounce any blocs with bourgeois parties.

5. All groups declare that they agree to participate in a general congress which must solve all questions now under dispute concerning the interpretation of the program and the question of national cultural autonomy, and which must determine the details of the general party organization....

The international Bureau refuses to investigate accusations relating to the past history of the various groups . . . as unproductive and even harmful, because they are means by which elements who should be united by their viewpoints on the present and aims for the future, are kept divided . . . No greater crime can be committed against the proletariat of Russia than to interfere with and hinder the rallying of its various groups into a single organism.

Proletarians of Russia, unite!

All the leaders of the International voted for the resolution. Out of the eleven Russian groups present, ten voted for it. Inessa Armand got up for the eleventh group and repeated doggedly: "We abstain. In place of the resolution we offer our statement."

"Lenin desires unity as a man desires unity with a piece of bread: he swallows it," Plekhanov commented.

"Where is Lenin?"—demanded Kautsky and Huysmans—
"You are irresponsible underlings who don't understand what
you are doing. Where is he? Why didn't he come? In the long
run, he must obey the crying need for unity of the Russian
masses and the insistent urging of the International."

No answer. Lenin couldn't come. He was too busy. We have
our instructions. Here is our statement. We're not voting on
anything. Unanimously—with the abstention of one faction—
they voted to report the scandalous state of affairs to the forthcoming congress of the Socialist International, to arrange for
a unifying congress of the Russian movement to be called over
Lenin's head, and to prepare a denunciation of the Bolsheviks
before the Russian workers if they continued to stand in the
way of unity. All the leaders of the International would sign
it. It would be solemnly endorsed by the International Socialist
congress to be held in Vienna in August. That would be August
23—not far off. Already it was July 17.

July 17, 1914! But on June 28 a pistol shot had been fired at
Sarajevo. *July 17!* Secret mobilization orders were being drafted. Ultimatums were being prepared. Notes were scurrying from
chancellory to chancellory and staff to staff. *July 17!* The whole
world was ringing with alarms and rumors of war, but Lenin
did not seem to hear them. He was not planning to attend the
coming congress of the International either. For him it would
be just another move in the faction war. It was never held. War
of another sort interceded.

Some weight—the reader will have to judge how much—
must be given to a more personal concern that kept Lenin from
turning the full power of his concentrated mind on the mount-
ing international tension, and kept him away from all the conferences of the two fateful years, 1913 and 1914, where he might
have been joining with the leaders of other parties in plans to
meet the war danger.

Nadezhda, his loyal wife and unquestioning follower, his

ever-dependable secretary, was ill, deeply, seriously, puzzlingly
ill. Her bulging eyes ached so that they could no longer de-
cipher the secret, invisible writing. Her hands trembled and
her knees were weak as water. Her robust health, so robust
that she had never thought of it, was failing. Her capacity
for work dwindled. Weakness, lassitude, dizziness, endless unremitting headaches. One doctor said "nerves" and advised
"rest and a change of air." "A proletarian woman doesn't have
nerves," she jested. But during the prescribed mountain walking tour, she fainted. To his sister Maria, Vladimir wrote:

> We moved here [Poronino, in the Tatra Mountains] the other
> day partly because of Nadya's illness, which greatly worries me.
> We shall spend the summer here . . . I may have to take Nadya
> to Berne to be cured . . . [May 13, 1913.]

And in July he wrote from Berne to his mother:

> At last they operated on Nadya on Wednesday in the Clinic.
> The operation evidently went off successfully for yesterday (Fri-
> day) she already looked fairly well and began to drink with
> pleasure. The operation was apparently rather difficult, for
> about three hours they tortured her without an anesthetic, but
> she bore it heroically. On Thursday she was very ill—high tem-
> perature and delirium—and I was thoroughly frightened. Yes-
> terday, however, things were obviously better . . . Kocher is a
> remarkable surgeon and people suffering from goiter ought to
> go to him . . .

And, as a by-product of his experience with "comrade-phy-
sicians" who had treated her earlier and failed to diagnose her
goiter trouble, he wrote to Gorky in November:

> The news that a Bolshevik is treating you by a new method,
> even if he is only a former Bolshevik, verily, verily upsets me.
> God save you from doctor-comrades in general, and doctor-
> Bolsheviks in particular! But really, in 99 cases out of 100, doc-
> tor-comrades are asses . . . I assure you that except in trivial

cases, one should be treated *only* by men of first-class reputation. To try on yourself the discoveries of a Bolshevik—that's terrifying!!

At the end of April, 1914, he wrote his sister Maria:

> In about a fortnight we shall go again to Poronino . . . I hope Nadya's goiter trouble will soon disappear. Mountain air cures this disease . . . Autumn is magnificent in the Tatras . . . If it is fine this autumn, we shall probably stay in the country . . .

The summer and autumn of 1914 were particularly fine. In the midst of those idyllic scenes, those breath-taking vistas, that gentle golden sunshine, those bemusing tranquil hours, who could believe in war? Vladimir clambered over the Tatra range like a mountain goat, stopping to take in the distant view, then to make notes on the national question, or some other question, in his ever-present notebook. That habit of taking a book with him, and stopping on a height to make notes, nearly cost him his life a few weeks later!

A golden summer! "If it is fine this autumn, we shall probably stay in the country."

That golden summer, on June 28, the Archduke Francis Ferdinand, heir to the Hapsburg throne, went riding with his wife in an open carriage through the old Slavic town of Sarajevo, capital of recently annexed Bosnia. Two shots rang out, and the heir apparent and his wife were dead. The murderers, two young Bosnian (Yugoslavian) nationalists, were tried *in camera*—a procedure the world has grown more accustomed to since. The Austrian Government let it be known that the findings "implicated" the Serbian Government and Serbian nationalist agitators. That was ominous—like the chain-reaction trials that Stalin has been using recently in Hungary, Bulgaria, Rumania, Yugoslavia, Czechoslovakia. But who could believe then that a pistol shot in remote, sleepy Sarajevo would involve England, France, Germany, Japan, China, America? that a pistol shot in

Sarajevo was sounding the death-knell of the Austro-Hungarian, the German and the Russian Empires, and, indeed, of the entire bourgeois world of the nineteenth century? that a pistol shot in Sarajevo was opening a period of global wars and revolutions that would fill with death and transformation all of the century that had just begun?

Officials, diplomats, labor leaders went on their vacations that summer more or less as usual. American tourists swarmed over Europe.

> Peace-loving Russia—wrote General Gurko, who was soon to head the Imperial General Staff—was in the midst of the summer holiday when the storm clouds hanging over Europe for a month finally burst. Petrograd and Moscow were practically deserted . . . Dark though the horizon was after the assassination of the Austrian heir, few imagined that the differences between Austria on the one hand and Serbia and Russia on the other were so grave that they could not be settled by ordinary diplomatic procedure . . .

On July 23, after secret incitement from Kaiser Wilhelm of Germany, Austrian Foreign Minister Berchtold dispatched an ultimatum to Serbia. It demanded an official condemnation of all anti-Austrian propaganda, the establishment of a friendly government, the suppression of "unfriendly" publications and organizations that incited to contempt toward the Danubian monarchy; the dismissal of a number of Serbian officials; the arrest of others; the right of the Austrian police and secret service to enter Serbia to collaborate with the latter's police in the investigation of the crime. The demands are curiously like those which in the last few years Stalin has made upon all his Balkan and other neighbors. Acceptance was demanded within forty-eight hours. Little Serbia's reply was anxiously conciliatory. It accepted all demands except those which would have permitted the Austrian police to enter its territory. It offered to submit disputed matters to the Hague Tribunal or a conference of the Great Powers. Backed by Germany, Austria rejected the reply. Backed by Russia, and impelled by the knowledge that her very independence was at stake, Serbia refused to go further in her concessions.

On July 24th—returning to General Gurko's memoirs—it became generally known that a conflict was inevitable. The troops had already left for their summer training camps. Two days later they were directed to return to their winter quarters; orders had been received for preparatory mobilization . . .

On that same July 24, Philip Scheidemann, one day to become Prime Minister of the German Weimar Republic, was climbing Mount Karwendel, over 7,300 feet high in the Austrian Tyrol. Saddle-maker Ebert, who would become President of the Republic, was dreaming away the hours on a beach on the Island of Ruegen. Vladimir Ilyich Ulyanov, future Chairman of the Council of People's Commissars of the Soviet Government, was one hundred miles from Cracow, where the Carpathian Mountains reach their greatest height, in the wild granite peaks of the Tatras.

On July 26, Sir Edward Grey, British Foreign Secretary, suggested a great-power conference of England, France, Germany, and Italy to settle the Austro-Serb conflict. Germany refused on the ground that only Austria and Russia, the most vitally interested, could call such a conference. On July 28, Austria declared war on Serbia. Next day, Russia issued a mobilization order on the Austrian frontier, and Germany a mobilization order on the Russian and French frontiers.

On July 29, the International Socialist Bureau went into emergency session in Brussels. Austria-Hungary had already declared war on Serbia, but none of the other Great Powers had yet declared war. Among those present from Germany were Kautsky, Haase and Rosa Luxemburg; from France, Jaurès, Vaillant, Guesde, Sembat, Longuet; from England, Keir Hardie; from Austria, Victor Adler and his son Friedrich, and the Czech, Nemec; from Holland, Troelstra; from Switzerland, Grimm; from Poland, Valecki; from Belgium, Vandervelde; from Italy, Morgari and Angelica Balabanoff, the Russian girl who had become an Italian socialist leader. There were a number from Russia, Axelrod, Rubanovich (Social Revolutionary) and several lesser figures. Lenin did not come, nor send a man of the caliber of Zinoviev or Kamenev, or even of Litvinov. He contented himself with being "represented" by Inessa Armand and the Lettish Bolshevik, Berzin. He was still thinking in terms of the faction war. He had won control of the apparatus; he had conquered power in the Party, and was not going to yield it, no, not even to the pressure of the entire international movement.

But, at the Emergency Conference, nothing was said about Russia, except Russia as a Great Power. They talked about nothing but war, turning it around and around helplessly in their minds. They voted a manifesto, a huge·mass meeting, a universal series of mass meetings, their resolve to maintain the peace, to localize the Austro-Serbian War, to demand its settlement by arbitration, to keep Germany, Russia, France, England out. If only they could hold war off until the great congress of the International already scheduled to be held in Vienna on August 23! They switched the congress to Paris, since Vienna was at war, and moved the date closer, from August 23 to August 9, since the situation was too dangerous for a month's delay.

But on July 31, Germany dispatched an ultimatum to Russia demanding the immediate revocation of Russian mobilization orders. No reply within the brief time limit. On August 1, Germany declared war on Russia. On August 3, Germany declared war on France; on August 4, German troops thrust through Belgium simultaneously with another declaration of war. All powers had been preparing for this moment, but Germany felt that she had the edge in preparations, that time was not on her side, that it was now or never.

Not until August 6 did Austria-Hungary declare war on Russia. Thus, on August 6, Vladimir Ilyich and his wife, Zinoviev and his wife, and various other Bolsheviks in Galicia became

Russian enemy aliens on the soil of a country with which Russia was at war. The news surprised Lenin in the Tatra range of the Carpathians, far even from his Cracow home.

War, general universal war, total, all-embracing war, was so new. Nothing like it since the days of Napoleon. Everywhere exaltation and confusion. Everywhere patriotic demonstrations, rumors, alarms, caution about strangers, spies, poisoned water supply. The mighty Russian Army was poised in Russian Poland on the borders of Galicia, ready to drive into Cracow, Przemysl, Poronino, Zakopane, Nowy Targ, one's own fields and doorstep. Peasants hastened to report to the police concerning the stocky, bald-headed Russian who was forever clambering up the heights, "surveying the roads," and making notes in a little notebook. On August 7, one day after Austria declared war, a village policeman visited the lodgings of the strange enemy alien. He paid no attention to the secret addresses of Party members and the Party documents, but pounced upon three notebooks filled with statistical tables and columns of figures—clearly a codebook! Poor Ilyich, would he ever see again his patiently gathered notes on the agrarian question? And the searcher found a pistol, symbol of Lenin's romantic belief in armed uprising, for which the enemy alien had not troubled to take out a permit. Still the village gendarme was a little troubled by the supposed spy's bearing and declarations, and gave him till next morning to report without escort to the police chief at the nearest provincial center, Nowy Targ (Neumarkt).

Would he be arrested? Court-martialed? Interned for the duration? (What duration?) Would he perish, as many did, in the first panicky actions of a universal spy scare? ("During the first days of the war," wrote Krupskaya, "they might easily have put him out of the way.") In this wild corner of the Carpathians, who would know of his fate? Already the Russian Army was advancing on Przemysl and Cracow and Nowy Targ and Poronino. If he fell into *their* hands, what would happen to him then in time of war?

Lenin used the few remaining hours of freedom to map a campaign for his rescue. He wired to the police director of Cracow, who knew his status and his anti-tsarist political activities, requesting a telegram to the local police to clear him of suspicion of espionage. Hanecki telegraphed to the Social Democratic Deputy Marek, who had arranged with the Austrian Government the permission for Ulyanov to settle in Austria. Both police director and Reformist Social Democrat (both class enemies according to the Leninist schema) responded with telegrams urging his release.

> Zinoviev—writes Krupskaya—despite the pouring rain, cycled ten miles to see the old member of the Narodnaya Volya, the Pole, Dr. Dlussky. Dlussky [whom Lenin also classified as a class enemy] immediately hired a carriage and went to Zakopane, where he did considerable telegraphing and letter writing and then went somewhere to conduct negotiations.

But the notebooks, the columns of figures, the pistol, the mountain climbs in which he had surveyed the horizon and made notes, the enemy alien citizenship and documents, the marching Russian armies, the spirit of alarm, were too much. He was jailed as a spy suspect, and his case handed over to a military tribunal. Leaving his cell after she had brought him food, clothes and, of course, books, Krupskaya heard two patriotic peasant women discussing the "Russian spy" and declaring that if "the authorities released him, the peasants would put out his eyes themselves, cut out his tongue, etc." In many a land many a stranger speaking an alien language was lynched during those first turbulent days.

Lenin wired Victor Adler, an outstanding leader of the Austrian Social Democracy and of the International (another whom he would soon be attacking unceasingly as a class enemy), asking his help. Krupskaya sent a separate plea. Adler went immediately in person to the Minister of the Interior, taking with

him another Social Democratic Deputy, Diamant. And yet another, the Right Wing leader of the Austrian Section of the
Polish Socialist Party, Daszinski, who had come to Galicia to
recruit Poles for Pilsudski's Polish Legion to fight against Russia, sent a message on his own to the Minister of the Interior.
Lenin had been attacking both Daszinski and his party for
years. But to none of these did it occur for an instant not to
help out a fellow-socialist in trouble. Such comradeship was
taken for granted in the days of innocence that preceded the
great split in the International.

According to the memoirs of Felix Kon, Hanecki, Karpinsky,
and other Bolsheviks, all published by the Soviet Government,
approximately the following conversation took place in the
Ministry of the Interior:

> *Adler:* Ulyanov is no ordinary Russian citizen and no spy.
> He is a determined opponent of Russian tsarism who has de-
> voted his life to the struggle against the Russian Government.
> If he were to appear in Russia they would arrest him, possibly
> execute him. He enjoys a European reputation as a leader of
> the Russian Social Democratic Party. He is a member with me
> of the International Bureau of the Socialist International. We
> both [Adler and Diamant] guarantee personally that he is no
> spy . . .
>
> *Minister:* Is that really the case? Is he still an opponent of his
> government?
>
> *Adler:* Ulyanov was an enemy of Russian tsarism when Your
> Excellency was its friend. He is its enemy now. And he will be its
> enemy when Your Excellency may again have become its friend.

The Minister was impressed. In his report, dated August 23,
he wrote:

> In the opinion of Dr. Adler, Ulyanov may render great serv-
> ices under present conditions.

On the suggestion of the Minister of the Interior, the com-
mandant in Cracow ordered his release. This was the Central Powers' first tentative approach to the idea that Russian

revolutionists like Ulyanov might possibly "render great services" to their cause. He was not interned as an enemy alien at all, but given a military pass to travel from Cracow to Vienna. But already he had decided that he could serve his own movement better in some neutral country. With Adler's help once more, military permission being needed to use the railroad or leave the country, he and Krupskaya journeyed unmolested to Switzerland. Zinoviev and his wife, Lilina, saved from internment by the same good offices, joined them two weeks later. On September 5, two days less than a month after his arrest as a spy, Lenin was able to write to Adler from his new home:

> Esteemed Comrade!
> I have arrived safely in Zurich with my whole family. They asked to see my pass only at Innsbruck and Feldskirche: your help therefore was very useful to me. For entry into Switzerland they demanded a passport, but they admitted me without one when I gave the name of Greulich. My best wishes and utmost gratitude to you.
>
> With Party Greetings,
—LENIN (V.I. Ulyanov)

Though these were the last friendly words that Lenin ever addressed to Victor Adler, they made clear that the feeling of gratitude was not alien to him. The memoirs published in Lenin's day and shortly after his death all acknowledge this debt. Karpinsky lists this as one of two celebrated "cases in which our enemies helped to protect Lenin."

"Just try to imagine," he adds as an afterthought, "what turn the fate of the Russian Revolution would have taken if Lenin had been interned and had returned to Russia not on April 3, 1917, but only in the autumn of 1918, when revolution overthrew the Austro-Hungarian monarchy!" Try to imagine, indeed! For April 3, 1917, the day when Lenin arrived at the Finland Station in Petrograd, was one of those fateful days that altered the whole course of history. Without April 3 there would have been no November 7!

It remains only to add that by 1943, the Marx-Engels-Lenin

Institute official biography of Lenin had stricken out all gratitude and all traces of indebtedness to Victor Adler. It merely says:

> On August 8, 1914, he was arrested by the Austrian police on a false accusation and taken to the prison at Nowy Targ, but was released on August 19, in view of the utter absurdity of the charge.

The documents I have used were secured by Hanecki in 1922, and subsequently, as a representative of the Soviet Government, and of Lenin personally, to the Polish Government, which opened the old Austrian police archives to him. It even aided Hanecki to recover Lenin's and Zinoviev's papers, left in Austrian Poland, including the three notebooks on the agrarian question, the statistics of which had been the most damning evidence against him. Hanecki secured from the Polish Government over 60 signed documents of Lenin's, over 50 letters addressed to him, 125 books and part of the archives of the Bolshevik Duma Fraction and of *Pravda*. (Ya. Ganetskii: *O Lenine*. Institut Marksa-Engelsa-Lenina, Moscow, 1933, pp. 16-52.)

CHAPTER THIRTY-SIX

SEVEN THESES AGAINST WAR

The experience of the war, like the experience of every crisis in history, of every great disaster and every sudden turn in human life, stuns and shatters some, but it enlightens and hardens others.

—V. I. LENIN, JUNE 1915

Trotsky was in Vienna when the storm broke. With unbelieving eyes he stared at the festive processions of shouting, cheering workingmen. What had they to cheer about? Where was their vaunted internationalism? What had war to offer them? What drew them, rejoicing, to the great square in front of the War Ministry?

What sort of an idea?—he wrote in his *Autobiography*, more than a decade later, still grappling with this mystery.—The national idea? But Austria-Hungary was the very negation of any national idea. No, the moving force was something different. The people, whose lives, day in and day out, pass in a monotony of hopelessness . . . the alarm of mobilization breaks into their lives like a promise; the familiar and long-hated is overthrown, and the new and unusual reigns in its place. Changes still more incredible are in store for them in the future. For better or for worse? For the better, of course—what can seem worse to Pospischil (the Viennese-Czech shoemaker's apprentice) than "normal" conditions? I strode along the main streets of the familiar Vienna and watched a most amazing crowd fill the fashionable Ring, a crowd in which hopes had been awakened. But wasn't a small part of these hopes already being realized? Would it have been possible at any other time for porters, laundresses, shoemakers' apprentices and youngsters from the suburbs to feel themselves masters of the situation in the Ring? War affects everybody, and those who are oppressed and deceived by life consequently feel that they are on an equal footing with the rich and the powerful. It may seem a paradox, but in the moods of the Viennese crowd that was demonstrating the glory of the Hapsburg arms I detected something familiar to me from the October days of 1905 in Saint Petersburg . . . Like revolution, war forces life, from top to bottom, away from the beaten path. But revolution directs its blows against the established power. War, on the contrary, at first strengthens the state power, which, in the chaos engendered by war seems to be the only firm support . . . Hopes of strong social and national movements, whether in Prague or in Trieste, in Warsaw or in Tiflis, are utterly groundless at the outset of a war. In September, 1914, I wrote to Russia: "The mobilization and declaration of war have veritably swept off the earth all the national and social contradictions in the country. But this is only a political postponement, a sort of political moratorium.

The notes have been extended to a new date, but they will have to be paid . . ."

If the internationalism of the masses had been sloughed off like last year's skin, how was it with their leaders? Some, like Hans Deutsch, he found quite obviously pleased and excited, abusive of all Serbs and Russians with little distinction between governments and people, happy that war would rid Austria of the "Serbian nightmare." Others, like Victor Adler, regarded the whole thing as an external cataclysm, not sprung from their activities, beyond their strength to cope with, something to be passively endured until it was over.

Adler intervened for Trotsky, as a few days later he was to do for Lenin. On their way to the chief of the political police, the Russian internationalist drew the attention of the Austrian to the festal mood. "It is those who do not have to go to war who show their joy," Adler sought to reassure himself and his companion. "Besides, all the unbalanced, all the madmen now come out into the streets; it is their day. The murder of Jaurès is only the beginning. War opens the door for all instincts, all forms of madness." Victor Adler was a psychiatrist besides being the outstanding leader of his party. Before the war was over, his own son, Fritz Adler, would commit an act of political desperation which party leaders would attribute to this same "war madness."

Police Chief Geyer hinted to Trotsky that all Russians might be under arrest by morning:

"Good. I will leave with my family for Switzerland tomorrow."

"Hm . . . I should prefer that you do it today."

That was at three. At six-ten that same afternoon, Lev Davidovich and his family were on the train bound for Zurich. Again Adler had helped a comrade who would brand him thereafter as a "class enemy."

The outbreak of war found Joseph Stalin in police exile in the remote Turukhansk Region of Yenisseisk Province on the edge of the Arctic Circle. There he joined Sverdlov, who had preceded him. Their arrest, in 1913, had been the result of association with their fellow Central Committee member, the Duma Deputy and police agent Malinovsky. Together, Sverdlov and Stalin made plans for escape, but the latter's request to Duma Deputy Badaev for a large sum "for food, kerosene and other things before the approach of the harsh Arctic winter" was turned over by Malinovsky to the police. Warnings against their plans went to Yenisseisk in August and December, 1913, and again in early 1914.

> Joseph Djugashvili and I—Sverdlov wrote his sister in February of that year—are being transferred a hundred versts farther north—eighty versts above the Arctic Circle. The surveillance is stronger . . . We have no more than eight or nine mail deliveries a year . . . Because he received money, Djugashvili has been deprived of his [government] allowance for four months. Both he and I need money, but you cannot send it in our names . . .
>
> My arrangements in the new place [the lonely Arctic village of Kureika] are considerably worse. For one thing, I no longer live alone. There are two of us in the room. With me is the Georgian Djugashvili . . . He is a good chap, but too much of an individualist in everyday life, while I believe at least in a semblance of order. That's why I am irritable at times . . . Much worse is the fact that there is no seclusion from the landlord's family . . . children . . . grownups from the village . . . They come, as if for spite, at the very best time for study, in the evening . . . We have had to plan our day differently, to give up the habit of poring over a book until long after midnight. There is absolutely no kerosene. We use candles. Since that provides too little light for my eyes, I do all my studying in the daytime now. As a matter of fact, I don't study much. We have virtually no books . . .

Thus Jacob Sverdlov, future President of the Executive Committee of the Soviets and future Secretary and leading organizer of the Party until his death, and Joseph Stalin, who was to succeed him as Party Secretary, lived in the Arctic wastes through three dreary war years. Sverdlov wrote a number of letters in addition to the one quoted. In 1924, when many reminiscences from this period were being published, a book of Sverdlov's correspondence was announced. But it was never published! Why, we can deduce from a few passages from letters which did see the light before publication was stopped:

> The moral atmosphere—he wrote of his worsening relations with his "too individualistic," i.e. inconsiderate, roommate—is not especially favorable . . . A number of clashes, possible only under the conditions of prison and exile, despite their pettiness, have had a pretty strong effect upon my nerves . . . in exile and prison conditions the naked man appears in all his meanness . . .

Sverdlov finally secured transfer to another settlement in the district. Thereafter, Stalin lived pretty much alone. In a letter to his future mother-in-law, Olga Evgenievna Allilueva, dated November 25, 1913, he thanked her for gifts (food packages), urging her to save her money for her own large family, and hinted of his loneliness and homesickness:

> You need the money yourself. I shall be satisfied if from time to time you send me a picture postcard with scenes of nature and the like. In this accursed region nature is bare to the point of ugliness—in summer, a river, in winter, snow, that's all that nature offers here, and I am stupidly homesick for scenes of nature even if only on paper. My greetings to the boys and girls. I wish you everything, everything good. . . .

This letter, showing the gentler, more sentimental side of his nature, Stalin has excluded from his *Collected Works*. His nearest friend now lived in the "nearby"—125 miles by horse or sleigh—village of Monastyr, the Armenian Central Committee member Suren Spandaryan. He was the leading spirit in a small group of Bolshevik exiles, which included three, his wife (Vera Shveitser), Gaven and Shumyatsky, who have contributed memoirs from which, with the usual "archaeological sifting," we can reconstruct some aspects of Stalin's life in wartime.

Even here, among the Bolshevik prisoner-exiles in the far
Arctic northland, there was the same wavering in attitude toward the war and toward the very government that had deported them, that Trotsky had noted among the workingmen
of Vienna!

"Defensist tendencies," writes Gaven, "were strong among
the exiles. Everybody was disoriented." And the Stalin-sup-
porter Shumyatsky, writing in 1924 when Stalin's star was already rising rapidly, ascribes the leading role in the struggle
with the defensist Bolsheviks to Spandaryan:

> He saw the matter clearly and distinctly . . . was one of the
> the first to assume an unyielding position of defeatism, and, at
> the rare gatherings of the comrades, sarcastically chided the
> social-patriots.

The second place he assigns to Sverdlov, but seeking to find
a little opening for an important role for Stalin—a role which
becomes enlarged in each subsequent edition of the memoirs—
he writes:

> Stalin, being completely isolated in his cave [in later editions
> the cave becomes a "scientist's laboratory"], without any
> vacillation assumed a defeatist line . . . by letter supporting
> Suren against his opponents . . . Only toward the end of 1914
> and the beginning of 1915 [actually it was in February, 1915]
> after Stalin had managed to visit Monastyr and back up Span-
> daryan, did the latter cease to be subject to attacks . . .

Revealing of Djugashvili's real mood and manner at the time
is the following passage from the same work:

> Stalin withdrew inside himself. Preoccupied with hunting and
> fishing, he lived in almost complete solitude . . . had practically
> no need for intercourse with people, only once in a while would
> go to visit his friend Suren Spandaryan at the village of Monas-
> tyr, returning several days later to his anchorite's cave. He was
> sparing in his disjointed remarks whenever he happened to be
> at gatherings arranged by exiles.

Spandaryan died in the Arctic in 1916, and a flood of memoirs in the later thirties and forties progressively expropriate his
role in favor of Joseph Stalin. By 1937, Spandaryan's own wife,
writing under the "editorial" direction of Beria, declares:

> Stalin's authority among the Bolsheviks was so great that his
> very first letter to the exiles put an end to all doubts . . .

Yet even here, another passage suggests the underlying truth
that it was a letter from Lenin, containing his "Theses on the
War," which strengthened Spandaryan's hand. When Stalin
went to Monastyr to visit the Spandaryans in late February,
1915, she writes, she showed him Lenin's letter:

> Lenin's seven theses on the war showed that Comrade Stalin
> had taken an unerringly correct Leninist position in his ap-
> praisal of the complex historical situation. It is difficult to con-
> vey the joy, conviction and triumph with which Comrade Stalin
> read Lenin's theses, which confirmed his ideas and served as a
> pledge of victory for the revolution in Russia.

Through nearly three years of war, Stalin made no further
attempt to escape. ("This time," she writes, "Stalin decided to
remain in exile.") And for the entire period, perhaps the most
decisive in the history of the Bolshevik Party, besides the letter
asking for postcard views of nature (pre-war), there are only
three or perhaps four unimportant pieces of writing which come
directly or indirectly from Djugashvili's hand. The first is a letter which his biographer Yaroslavsky says was composed jointly by Spandaryan and Stalin to Lenin, "scoffing at national
defensists, Plekhanov, Kropotkin, and the French socialist
Sembat." In the biographical chronicle accompanying Stalin's
Collected Works, the author claims this letter exclusively as his
own, and, from the wording, this would appear to be so. But
it is noteworthy that he did not choose to include the text itself in his *Collected Works.* Since it may be of interest to
the reader both as an insight into Stalin's temperament and

style of expression, and as a touchstone to compare with Lenin's theses quoted at the end of the present chapter, we give it in full. Dated February 27, 1915, i.e. during his visit with Spandaryan and after he had seen Lenin's theses, it reads:

> My greetings to you, dear Ilyich, warm, warm greetings. Greetings to Zinoviev, greetings to Nadezhda Konstantinovna. How are you? How is your health? I live as before, chew my bread, completing half of my term. It is rather dull, but it can't be helped. But how are things with you? It must be much livelier where you are. I recently read Kropotkin's articles—the old fool must have completely lost his mind. I also read a short article by Plekhanov in *Rech*—an incorrigible old gossip. Ekh-mah! And the Liquidators with their deputy agents of the Free Economic Society? There's no one to beat them, the devil take me! Is it possible that they will get away with it and go unpunished? Make us happy and let us know that in the near future a newspaper will appear that will lash them across their mugs, and do it regularly, and without getting tired. If it should occur to you to write, do so to the address: Turukhansk Territory, Yenisseisk Province, Monastyrskoe Village, for Suren Spandaryan. Your Koba. Timofei [Spandaryan] asks that his sour greetings be conveyed to Guesde, Sembat and Vandervelde on their glorious— ha, ha!—posts as ministers.

The modest tone of the "if it should occur to you to write" hardly suggests the "chief lieutenant" and "close associate" who for many years had supposedly been assisting Lenin in working out all his views. Nor does the letter which Lenin wrote Karpinsky in the autumn of the same year, inquiring:

"I have a big favor to ask you: find out the surname of Koba (Joseph Dj . . .?? we forgot). Very important!!"

Lenin thought it important to keep up correspondence with this lieutenant, but the need to inquire the surname, which has to be used in all letters to police exiles, suggests that there was no constant interchange of communications.

The other documents with which Stalin is connected during the war period up to the Revolution of March, 1917, are, according to the Biographical Chronology, a second letter to Lenin, dated November 10, 1915; an article on the national question, which either went astray or which Lenin did not find good enough to publish; another letter, to Inessa Armand, asking what had happened to the article; and a round-robin greeting, signed by various Bolshevik exiles, to the newspaper *Voprosy Strakhovanya* ("Problems of Insurance"), enclosing the sum of six rubles, eighty-five kopeks, collected among the Turukhansk convicts. Significantly, Joseph Stalin has not considered any of these worthy of inclusion in his *Collected Works*. Thus there is a complete blank space of four years between Volume II, which ends with a manifesto written for May 1, 1913, and Volume III, which begins after the Revolution of March, 1917, had freed Stalin and the other exiles. And, with the greatest zeal and the highest will in the world, his biographers have not been able to make much more than a blank out of his other activities during the same period.

To be sure, one inventive English writer, David M. Cole, professes to have "perused" articles from Turukhansk directed against Leon Trotsky's war position, and speaks of "a series of short letters expressing, in a simple but direct manner, those ideas which Lenin later [!] set out in his book *Against the Current*,"* which letters from Stalin "kept the small focal centers of bolshevism going in the factories from 1914 to late 1916" (David M. Cole: *Joseph Stalin,* Rich and Cowan, London, 1942, p. 36). But we will be closer to the published record if we accept Yaroslavsky's summary, which limits itself to the following modest claims:

> Thus, even in this remote Siberian village, Comrade Stalin displayed profound attention to, and keen interest in, Party life, read a great deal, kept himself informed of the Party's work in Russia, reacted as far as he was able to every event in Party life, and occupied his leisure with fishing and hunting.

---

* The book *Against the Current* was the joint work of Lenin and Zinoviev and published under both their names. But Mr. Cole, with "scruples" more understandable in a historian writing under censorship inside Russia, avoids mentioning the purged Zinoviev as Lenin's closest wartime collaborator.

He did not, like Sverdlov, manage to get articles through to Lenin which Lenin would deem worthy of publication in the straitened pages of wartime journals. Nor could he win for himself the spontaneous tributes which the Stalinist Shumyatsky and other memorialists gave to Spandaryan in the memoirs of 1924. ("Clearer than many others in the memory of the Turukhanites is the monumental figure of Suren Spandaryan . . . the intransigent revolutionary Marxist and magnificent orator . . . the most active of the revolutionists and their leader," said the first edition of Shumyatsky's work.) For it takes time and persistence to edit one's memories. But we can safely assume that Yaroslavsky's summary is not too wide of the mark; and with that favorable if modest verdict, we can leave Stalin out of our further story until 1917. His turn will come later, and will be large indeed.

There is only one more detail to clear up, the question of Stalin's summons to the army. Of this, too, there are several differing versions. His own Biographical Chronology reads:

> December 14, 1916. I. V. Stalin goes by stages to Krasnoyarsk in connection with the calling up of administrative exiles to the army.

To this Yaroslavsky adds his usual romantic touch:

> Comrade Stalin was sent to Krasnoyarsk but he was not taken into the army because the tsarist government knew how dangerous he would be there. From Krasnoyarsk, he was sent to Achinsk to complete his term of exile. This was almost on the eve of the revolution, which broke out while Stalin was in Achinsk.

If Stalin does not explain why he was not inducted, Yaroslavsky's explanation makes it hard to understand why he was ever moved to Krasnoyarsk or Achinsk at all. But Shumyatsky's memoirs, already quoted, state that Stalin was indeed called up, but then rejected for service because of a "stiffness" in his left arm.

The epidemic of war fever which Trotsky had contemplated so incredulously as it set the masses to dancing in the Vienna streets, the war fever which, even among the Bolshevik exiles of Arctic Turukhansk, had "disoriented everybody" and made "defensist tendencies strong" in relation to the very government that held them in exile—that same war fever took possession of the masses in every warring land. I do not speak merely of the unorganized masses, but of the "class-conscious" workers organized into trade unions and socialist parties (and, no less, of the adherents of the "Prince of Peace" organized into the Christian churches).

Not only the Right Wing but the Center and the Left Wing of the socialist parties were affected. Jules Guesde, who had been the leader of the French Left in its fight against reformism and ministerialism and who had joined with Lenin, Rosa Luxemburg and a handful more to form the Left Wing at the Copenhagen International Socialist Congress of 1910, immediately became a Minister without Portfolio in the French War Cabinet. Gustav Hervé, fire-eating leader of the anti-war and anti-imperialist section of the French Socialist Party who had wanted the International to "answer" a declaration of war by a general strike, changed the name of his paper from *La Guerre Sociale* to *La Victoire*. Paul Lensch and Parvus (Alexander Helfand) who, like Rosa Luxemburg, had been editors of the Left Wing *Leipziger Volkszeitung*, became ardent war propagandists. Lensch eventually accepted editorship of the *Deutsche Allgemeine Zeitung*, while Parvus founded *Die Glocke* to preach the "socialist meaning" of Germany's war aims. Vladimir Burtsev, whom we have so far known as the chief exposer of the Russian secret police and its agents in the revolutionary movement, published a declaration in the French, English and Russian exile press, calling on all socialists to support the

Russian Government in the war. Then, without waiting for permission or promise of amnesty, he set out for Russia to volunteer his services. At the border the police arrested the arch-enemy who had exposed so many of their spies. Only after a year in Siberia, and after intervention by the French Ambassador, was he quietly amnestied. Free in Saint Petersburg, he continued to write pro-war articles. The Social Revolutionary leaders Avksentiev, Bunakov (Fundaminsky), Argunov, Savinkov, Lazarev, Moiseenko, Voronov, all of them men who had been in the Tsar's prisons and Siberia and had fled abroad the better to fight the Russian Government, now formed a group called "Beyond the Frontier" with an ardent defensive program. The veteran leader Breshkovskaya (the *babushka* or "grandmother" of the Social Revolutionary movement) was with them, as was Rubanovich, their representative on the International Socialist Bureau. "At the present time," wrote this group in *Novosti,* "we consider revolutionary action against tsarism inexpedient, as it would only weaken the military strength of the country." Kropotkin, the anarchist leader, became an ardent defender of French culture and liberty against Prussian militarism. Plekhanov, the "father" of Russian Social Democracy, author of its program, advocate of proletarian dictatorship, and, after Kautsky, the leading European defender of "orthodox Marxism," became a passionate patriot, defending the Allied cause and actually recruiting volunteers among the Russian émigrés for the French Army.

What must have been most startling to Lenin was the fact that the division did not come on the familiar lines of "opportunism" versus "revolutionary Marxism," or "revisionism" versus "orthodoxy" at all. In the German party, Parvus, Lensch, Cunow, Haenisch, orthodox Marxists all, became ardent war advocates, while the Left revisionist Karl Liebknecht became the outstanding anti-militarist, and the arch-revisionist of the Right, Eduard Bernstein, was one of the first publicly to condemn the abandonment of the old Marxist tactic of refusing to vote war credits (in the *Archiv fuer Sozialwissenschaft,* reprinted as a separate pamphlet, *Die Internationale der Arbeiterklasse und der europaeische Krieg*, in February, 1915). Similarly, Christian socialist, pacifistic and semi-liberal British laborite leaders like Snowden and Macdonald voted against war credits in England while Hyndman, leader of the orthodox Marxist Social Democratic Federation, became a war supporter. The soft-minded humanitarians inclined to pacifism while many a tough-minded "historical materialist" flung himself heart and soul into the war.

Nor was the Bolshevik contingent in Paris exempt from the ravages of war fever. Lenin was far away, in the Carpathian Mountains. *Pravda* had just been suppressed so that there was no guidance from Russia. The Leading Committee of Organizations Abroad, which served in Paris as the connecting center for Bolshevik sections outside Russia, disintegrated. Two of its five members enlisted as volunteers in the French Army. One resigned from the leading committee and the Party. A minority of two, confused and unsure, remained to carry on. At a general meeting of the Bolsheviks in Paris, out of ninety-four present, eleven favored active support for the war and a number of others, how many we do not know, could not make up their minds one way or the other. Antonov-Britman, member of the leading committee of five, volunteered and soon died at the front. N. V. Kuznetzov (Saposhkov) likewise enlisted and fell in battle. Ilya (Japaridze) joined the volunteers, but sobered up later and became anti-war. "A number of others" volunteered, too. A Bolshevik, *Ekk* (Mukhin), drafted a patriotic manifesto in favor of enlistment, which was adopted by a commission of two Bolsheviks, two Mensheviks, and one Social Revolutionary and was responded to by eighty of these self-exiled opponents of the Russian Government. At the farewell party before they joined the French Army, Plekhanov delivered the valedictory address.*

* Lenin's *Collected Works*, Vol. XVIII, English Edition, p. 413; M. Kharitonov: *Iz vospominanii*, Zapiski Instituta Lenina, II, 119; V. Karpinsky: *Vladimir Ilyich za granitsei v. 1914-1917 g.g. po pismam i vospominanyam*, Zapiski Instituta Lenina, II, 72-82; I. P. Khonyakov: *V podpolie i v emigratsii*, Proletarskaya Revolyutsii, No. 4 (16), 1923, p. 168.

Writes Khonyavko in his memoirs of that time of storm and disorientation:

> Putting it bluntly, the task before everyone—how to be: for or against the war?—was extremely hard for all socialist tendencies. . . . Unexpectedly, in our section too there arose differences on the question. . . . And strangely enough in the bitter two-day meeting of August 2 and 3, 1914, out of ninety-four members of our section eleven were openly on the side of the patriots. We decided to appeal to Comrade Lenin with a letter asking whether our position was right, and he, to our joy, not only approved our position but even praised it as well expressed from the point of view of Marxism . . .

This naive statement, published in *Proletarskaya Revoliutsiya* in 1923 speaks volumes concerning the orphaned condition of the Paris Bolsheviks, with their firm-minded *starik* so far away, their legal Russian paper, *Pravda,* suppressed by the Tsar's Government, and with two of their leading committee volunteering and one dropping out. Lenin and Zinoviev, fleeing from Austria to Switzerland, carried in their pockets or under the domes of their foreheads virtually all that was left of the Bolshevik Central Organization abroad. Once more, there was needed unwavering certitude and iron will for the Sisyphus labor of beginning from the bottom of the slope.

The last days of July, 1914, and the first days of August were full of shocks and surprises. Many convinced pacifists were startled to find their throats open, crying for war. The leaders of the socialist parties were swept off their feet by the advent of what they had so long predicted, prepared for, even exactly described. They were surprised alike by their own actions, and by the reactions of the masses they had been preaching to. On July 25, two days after Austria's ultimatum to Serbia, the mighty German Social Democracy issued an anti-war manifesto condemning the Austrian ultimatum as "precisely calculated to provoke war . . . Not a drop of blood of a German soldier shall be sacrificed to the power itch of the Austrian rulers . . ."

On July 29-30, the International Socialist Bureau came together at their hastily summoned Emergency Conference in Brussels. Only twenty or so could be assembled in mid-summer on such short notice. Lenin was not there. Missing, too, sorely missing, was the beloved leader of the German movement, the veteran of the anti-war campaign of 1870, August Bebel, whom death had claimed in the Summer of 1913.

Fright, incredulity, improvisation, hope for a miracle, defiance, despair, vied with each other for the possession of the delegates. The war between Austria and Serbia would be localized. The rumors of Russian and German ultimatums were inventions of the jingo press. General war was impossible in the enlightened twentieth century. The masses would not permit it. An International Socialist Congress would unite the peoples, frighten the war makers, stay their hand. "It is remarkable," Kautsky was to write six years later, "that to none of us present did it occur to ask what to do if the war should break out before the Congress convened. What attitude were the socialist parties to take in such a war?"

But this is only a half-truth. With a weary and deadly composure, Victor Adler, whose country was already at war, predicted that the masses would remain passive and the parties likewise:

> Expect no more action from us. We are under martial law. Our papers are suppressed. I am not here to make a speech in a mass meeting, but to tell you the truth, that any action now, when hundreds of thousands are on their way to the frontier and martial law prevails at home, is impossible.

Rosa Luxemburg was too sick at heart to speak. Hugo Haase talked directly at Jean Jaurès as if he must convince that brilliant tribune of the French people that he and his party did not want war and expected the same from the French. Keir Hardie pledged English labor to a general strike before it would permit England to be drawn in, but others signified that they doubted his optimism. Angelica Balabanoff returned to the subject: we have so often pledged ourselves to avert war, now a general strike is the only means left us. Adler and Guesde looked at her with the scornful pity one reserves for a fool. "A general strike," retorted Guesde icily, "would be effective only in countries where socialism is strongest, facilitating the military victory of the backward nations over the progressive ones." What socialist could desire the invasion of his own land, or its defeat by a more backward one? (The only man who might conceivably have cried out: "I" was far off in the Carpathian Mountains, staying away out of confidence that the International would never deliver its soul to the war makers, out of disbelief in the immediacy of war, or out of factional stubbornness.)

The delegates drew up one more stirring, unanimous appeal to the workers of all lands. Beyond a new note of anxiety, there was nothing new in it. Then they hastened to set an earlier date for the coming International Congress, transferring it from war-possessed Vienna to "peaceful" Paris, and changing it from August 25 to August 9. Surely this great International, which was about to celebrate the fiftieth anniversary of its existence, would be the mighty world power able to stop the other world powers from madness. But a whole age was to elapse between August 1 and August 9. The two dates were separated from each other by an abyss. Into the abyss tumbled the fragments of the once great structure of the International, and all the kings' ministers and all the Soviets' commissars would not be able to put it together again in the next half-century.

The two days of feverish, fruitless improvisation ended in a gigantic mass meeting in which the magnificent eloquence of Jean Jaurès stirred the multitudes for the last time. Never had he spoken with greater fervor than now, when he pledged himself to continue to his dying breath to wage "war against war." To the heart of Jaurès, a "revisionist" and "ministerialist" for whom Lenin had always had a species of contempt, humanitarianism and pacifism and pity for the victims of poverty and war were ever closer than were class war and revolution. (But, after his death, Lenin's paper would claim his heritage as "pacifism on a revolutionary foundation.") His burning words caught up his hearers jamming the Cirque Royale, overflowed into the streets, where thousands waited who could not get in, took possession of the boulevards and avenues of old Brussels, which rang for hours with the reiterated cries: *"A bas la guerre!" "Guerre à la guerre!" "Vive l'Internationale Socialiste!"*

Two days later, on his return to Paris, Jean Jaurès was shot dead by an inflamed nationalist assassin. He at least had kept his pledge to his "dying breath." Another two days, and the streets of Brussels, like the streets of Paris, Berlin, Saint Petersburg, London, were ringing with other cries: crowds, often the same crowds, possessed by another fervor, were shouting themselves hoarse for war.

From July 31 to August 4, the German Social Democratic Executive Committee and the mighty Reichstag Fraction of 110 socialist Deputies were in almost continuous session.

Where now were Marx and Engels, who had always known what stand to take on each war in the nineteenth century? (They were never pacifists.) Where were Liebknecht and Bebel, veterans of the opposition to war in 1870?

Habits, formulae, pledges, feelings whirled in a maelstrom. On July 31 they could come to no conclusion except to send Hermann Mueller to Paris to consult with the French socialists . . . But they had just consulted two days before! The French leaders were cautious. Jaurès lay dead. Most of the others felt that if France were attacked by Germany, it would have to defend itself. Since Germany would be the aggressor, perhaps the German comrades could vote "no" on war credits, but they would have to vote "yes." Mueller answered that his comrades would surely not vote in the affirmative, but wanted to come to an agreement with the French on voting in the negative or abstaining from voting. The German socialists, he said, felt that Russia was the chief danger, and would invade the Fatherland. Perhaps France could stop the war by pressure on Russia, which was the real aggressor and guilty party. The negotiations stalled; their voices faltered; their thoughts trailed off unexpressed; they did not trust each other chiefly because they no longer trusted themselves. . . .

Perhaps, if Bebel and Jaurès had still been there, they might have understood each other and found a common platform, at least for the first crucial days of the war. Perhaps, perhaps not. Idle to speculate now, but let no one object: what difference could one or two men make? For this was a time of hesitation. For a moment, everything was in suspense, like a tiny spring on the ridge of a watershed which even a twig or a pebble might deflect down one slope or the other. We shall soon see what a difference one or two men could make. . . . The next day or two, and the hesitation was over: the new course had worn itself a deepening channel: another two days later, it was a roaring flood.

On August 3, when Mueller returned to Berlin, the Reichstag Fraction was still in session. But it now knew that the next day the Reichstag would meet and be presented with a bill for war credits. War had been declared on Russia two days earlier, and now (August 3) on France.

Still the maze! *For the war credits,* to show their patriotism and to equip the millions of socialist and trade union members called up to the colors? *Against the war credits,* so as to disclaim responsibility for—but not obstruct—the war? *Against the war credits and the war,* as a preliminary to going underground and carrying on a struggle against their government? As if in a trance, they simultaneously acted on all three premises. By a vote of seventy-eight to fourteen they decided to vote "yes" on the war credits, with a statement disclaiming responsibility for the war. And, incredible as it sounds, they had already secretly sent the Party treasurer, Otto Braun, and the Chairman of the Executive, Friedrich Ebert, to Zurich, to prepare for possible underground existence. (A few days later they came sheepishly back to Berlin.)

The arguments, the statements and counter-statements, the desperate improvisations, the anger and the tears, the searching of souls and the drafting and tearing up of declarations, continued all night. But on August 4, Haase, who was one of these fourteen who had voted "no" inside the Fraction, consented as its chairman to read the declaration of the Social Democratic Reichstag Fraction in the solemn public meeting. Out of a sense of "democratic discipline" the fourteen submitted to the majority will of the seventy-eight. Thus, though one member (Kunert of Halle), unnoticed, walked out while the vote was being taken, so far as the Party, Germany or the world knew, the entire Social Democratic Reichstag Fraction of 110 members had voted solidly to support the war. The French Deputies did the same on the same day, but somehow this was less of a surprise and a shock. For though all the Great Powers had been preparing for war and reaching out for or holding tight to their "spoils," yet the Austrian ultimatum and the Kaiser's support made it clear that Germany and Austria had chosen the time and the way to precipitate the conflict. Moreover, the German party was the party of Marx and Engels, the leading and inspiring, the model party of the Socialist International. With its 110 Reichstag Deputies, its over a million members, its million and a half readers of the socialist press, its almost two and one-half million trade union followers, its specific gravity so great that one soldier out of three who answered the call to arms was a voter for the socialist party—this was the party on which all hopes were laid, toward which all eyes were turned.

When Lenin read the news that the Social Democrats had voted war credits in the Reichstag, he simply refused to believe it. He had not expected the International to be able to prevent war, but he had never doubted that they would reject responsibility for it. They would suffer, and the people would suffer, but in the end they would be justified and, out of the ruins of war, lead the people to revolution and socialism. He had doubted that "Franz Josef and Nikolasha will give us that

pleasure," but he had never doubted that the great socialist parties would meet the issue with loyalty to their pledges
and principles. The news dispatch, he declared, had been invented by the German Government to deceive its enemies, and
to sow confusion in the ranks of the socialists. Even when he
saw the report in the *Vorwaerts,* he concluded that that entire
issue of the paper was a forgery of the German General Staff.
Then he learned that Plekhanov in Paris had turned recruiting
agent. "Can Plekhanov be a traitor, too?" he asked again and
again, and tried to explain it by the fact that Plekhanov in his
youth had served as an army officer. But the blow that was
hardest to bear was to learn that Karl Kautsky, the man he
had revered most after the founders of Marxism, had coun-
seled abstention from voting, but had followed his advice with
sophistries to explain and apologize for, if not justify, the treason of the majority. At this his fury knew no bounds.

First gloom settled over him; then anger seized him; then
the steel trap of his mind closed on the new situation. Many
a time he had stood alone against all the leaders of his party.
Many a time he had split away, and started from scratch to
build anew on his own foundation. Now he would stand
alone, if need be, against the leaders of the entire International. He had read Martov and Axelrod and all the other leaders
out of his party. Now he would read all the pro-war leaders,
and all who had truck with them, out of the International.
More than once he had declared that he, and those few who
stood with him, were the Party. Now he, and those few whom
he might recruit, would be the International. Even as he fled
from Cracow to Vienna, from Vienna to Zurich to Berne, he
was turning this huge, monstrous news over and over in his
mind, reducing it to a series of ordered explanations, propositions, slogans, theses. By the time he reached Berne in neutral
Switzerland and called together a half-dozen or so of bewildered, frightened, but still faithful friends and comrades, he
had it all worked out in his mind, and read off to them *Seven*

Theses on the War. The date was September 6 or 7. Present were Lenin and Krupskaya, the Safarovs, Duma Deputy Samoilov, Mokhov, Shklovsky, and possibly Inessa Armand. According to Krupskaya, the meeting was "held in the woods," but this is improbable and is contradicted by Shklovsky, who records that it was in his apartment. Later, when Lenin tried to rally more Bolsheviks, groups and individuals, objections would rain upon his head. But those gathered that day found little to object to.

> The European War—said the first thesis—has the sharp and definite character of a bourgeois, imperialist, and dynastic war.
>
> The conduct of the leaders of the German Social Democratic Party of the Second International (1889-1914) [the dates of birth and death were included in the second thesis!] who have voted the war budget and who repeat the bourgeois chauvinist phrases of the Prussian Junkers and of the bourgeoisie, is a direct betrayal of socialism. [Such was the second proposition.]
>
> The conduct of the leaders of the Belgian and French Social Democracy—continued the third—who have betrayed socialism by entering bourgeois cabinets, deserves the same condemnation . . .
>
> The betrayal of socialism by the majority of the leaders of the Second International (1889-1914)—continued the fourth inexorably—means an ideological collapse of that International. The fundamental cause is the actual predominance of petty-bourgeois opportunism . . .

The fifth thesis noted and branded as deceptions the various justifications for their part in the war given by the participating countries.

> The task of Social Democracy in Russia—read the sixth—consists in the first place in a merciless and ruthless struggle against the Great-Russian and tsarist-monarchist chauvinism, against the sophistical defense of this chauvinism by Russian Liberals, Constitutional Democrats and the like, and by some of the Narodniks. [No mention of the Mensheviks, for he had learned that the entire Social Democratic delegation to the

Duma, Bolsheviks and Mensheviks alike, had voted on August 8 against the war credits!]

From the point of view of the laboring class and the toiling masses of all the peoples of Russia, the lesser evil would be the defeat of the tsarist monarchy and its army, which oppresses Poland, the Ukraine, and a number of other peoples of Russia . . . [This was the most important sentence in the whole document.]

And the seventh thesis:

> The slogans of Social Democracy at the present time should be: a thorough propaganda—to be spread also in the Army and the area of military activity—for a socialist revolution and for the necessity of turning weapons not against one's brothers, hired slaves of other lands, but against reaction in the shape of the bourgeois governments and parties of all countries—to carry on such propaganda in all languages it is absolutely necessary to organize illegal cells and groups in the armies of all nations . . . It is imperative to appeal to the revolutionary conscience of the working masses . . . against the leaders of the present International who have betrayed socialism . . . Agitation in favor of German, Polish, Russian and other republics, along with the transformation of all the separate states of Europe into a Republican United States.

These rough-hewn but massive propositions were discussed briefly by those present, and then, with a few changes, launched as best they could be upon an unreceptive and unpropitious world over the signature of "A Group of Social Democrats, Members of the R.S.D.L.P." The principal changes were:

1. The addition of an attack upon "the so-called 'Center,' which has cravenly capitulated before the opportunists" and which should be "resolutely and irrevocably uprooted from the future International."

2. An acknowledgment that not all workers had been immune to the war fever but that "in most cases the workers were hostile to chauvinism and opportunism."

3. The addition of a final group of slogans for Russia:

A struggle against the tsarist monarchy and Great-Russian, pan-Slavist chauvinism, the preaching of a revolution in Russia, the liberation and self-determination of the nationalities oppressed by Russia—on the basis of the immediate slogans: a democratic republic, confiscation of the landowners' lands, the eight-hour day.

The second amendment was apparently forced upon Lenin by someone else present who pointed out that it was not only the leaders who had yielded to the general patriotic fever but also the masses, and even many Bolsheviks. But Lenin would not compromise except to add the evasive words, "in most cases," because already he was envisioning his strategy in terms of rousing "the masses" against "the leaders," imputing to the former, at most, occasional error, to the latter deliberate, systematic treason. The first amendment was doubtless Lenin's own, by way of paying respects to his erstwhile theoretical leader, Karl Kautsky. And the third amendment is a characteristic Leninist formulation of the needs and slogans of a democratic revolution in Russia.

ACKNOWLEDGMENTS AND SOURCES

A complete bibliography of all the books, pamphlets and magazines I have consulted during the ten years of my work on this book would be itself of book length. Wherever possible, wherever the reader might be inclined to doubt or the interpretation appears most novel, I have included the source right in the text. Here I wish only to make certain general acknowledgments of indebtedness.

First, I am indebted to those Russian men and women whom fate has thrown on our shores, and whose souls are irreplaceable human archives of all they have lived through and experienced; and to those who have so kindly read my manuscript in whole or in part, and given freely of their information, suggestion and criticism:

To Solomon M. Schwarz, who read every word of the manuscript twice over.

To Vera Alexandrova, who was my guide in the Russian tongue, Russian literature and the Russian spirit.

To Michael Karpovich, who read the historical section.

To Boris Nikolaevsky, himself a living archive, who read the chapter on Roman Malinovsky and several others.

To Rafael Abramovich, who read the sections concerned with his own personal experience.

To Sidney Hook, who read the chapter on "Lenin as Philosopher."

To Angelica Balabanoff, who read a number of chapters, particularly those concerned with her own experience.

To Leo Borochowitz, who offered many useful suggestions.

To countless Russians, here and in the Soviet Union, who must remain nameless, who answered freely all questions put to them.

To the Slavonic Division of the New York Public Library and all its staff for their patient and friendly cooperation.

To the Hoover Library, Stanford, California, and the Library of Congress for making available valuable material.

To Leon Kramer and George Telberg, specialists in Russian books, who ransacked the libraries and Russian colonies of the world from Shanghai to Prague in an effort to secure for me obscure and out-of-print papers, pamphlets and books which might enable me to set the "outmoded truth" and the "truth of the defeated" alongside of the "official truth," in order to extract from the array of versions a truth closer to the ultimate verdict of history.

To Edmund Wilson for lending me the library of Leniniana he collected for his own *To the Finland Station.*

It goes without saying that all of the above are exempt from responsibility for any errors, interpretations or use made of the material they have so kindly provided.

The interpretation of Russia's history offered in the first chapter is my own, but I must acknowledge a large debt to many Russian historians and thinkers, to Klyuchevsky and his school, to Karpovich, Vernadsky, Berdyaev and Mavor, and to the sudden flashes of profound self-knowledge that abound in the literature of the Westernizer-Slavophile controversy and the Russian novel.

The chapters on Lenin are based primarily on his writings, on the notes thereto provided by the Marx-Engels-Lenin Institute in the Third Russian Edition of his *Collected Works,* on the memoirs of his wife and his sister Anna, his letters, and innumerable memoirs concerning him. In addition I have threshed the sparse grain from official biographies and hostile ones, and from all the legends which have grown up naturally or on command about his person. Special acknowledgment is due to Leon Trotsky for his careful analysis of the available sources in "The Youth of Lenin," pathetic fragment of what gave promise of being a truly great biography.

The chapters on Trotsky draw heavily on his *Autobiography* and other writings. These have been supplemented by Max Eastman's *Leon Trotsky: The Portrait of a Youth* and G. A. Ziv's *Trotsky.*

The chapters on Stalin owe much to Boris Souvarine's groundbreaking biography and to the unfinished biography of the same protagonist by Leon Trotsky. With these critical accounts I have collated all the official works published in the Soviet Union and elsewhere, setting contradictory versions and sources side by side in the text so that the reader may draw his own conclusions as to the disputed facts. I am also indebted to Charles Malamuth, translator of Trotsky's *Stalin,* for making available to me unpublished documents and for securing valuable material in Europe.

For the period leading up to the First World War I owe a special debt to Gankin and Fisher: *The Bolsheviks and the World War,* Bunyan and Fisher: *The Bolshevik Revolution,* and F. A. Golder: *Documents of Russian History, 1914-17.* Other sources are largely indicated in the text.

ON TRANSLITERATION AND PRONUNCIATION

In transliterating I have followed generally the system used by the Library of Congress, but have not hesitated to modify it wherever 1) a name has already become familiar to the American reader under a different spelling; 2) a change (as from *ii* and *yi* to plain *y*) might make matters easier for the reader who knows no Russian. The two Russian letters *dzh* I have rendered by the simple English *j* which is its true pronunciation, except in the case of Djugashvili (Dzhugashvili), which has become more familiar in the above forms.

The reader need have no hesitance about pronouncing Russian names with an American or English accent. It is as legitimate to say Trotsky as Trutsky, just as we give so well known a name as Napoleon an Anglo-Saxon pronunciation.

The problem of accenting, which gives so much worry because there are no set rules in Russian, is best met by giving all syllables equal value. A Russian may misunderstand you if you put the accent on the wrong syllable, but will always understand you if you put the accent on no single syllable at all. Thus it is wrong to say Lenín and right to say Lénin, but you will be indistinguishably close to the right pronunciation if you give both syllables equal value.

The vowels which may give the Anglo-Saxon reader most trouble are *e,* normally pronounced *ye* as in Enukidze, pronounced *Yenukidze,* and frequently spelled so in transliteration; the letter *ya,* which is a single letter in Russian; the letter *yu,* to be distinguished from *u* which is pronounced *oo.* The vowels *a, i* and *o* (and sometimes *e*) are in general pronounced as in other continental languages.

The troublesome consonants are chiefly the large array of letters that in Russian are single letters and in other languages must be rendered by two or three consonants: *zh,* pronounced like our *z* in azure or like the French *j; kh* (Russian *x*) pronounced gutturally with a slight throat-rasping like the German *ch* or the Spanish *j* or *x; ts,* a single letter, the transliteration of which is self-explanatory; *sh,* another self-explanatory transliteration of a single letter; and *shch,* a single letter which, given its full value, would sound like the starting of a locomotive, but in actual speech is usually only a prolonged and slightly softened *sh.*

The general reader who is not striving for pedantic perfection can pronounce the names for his own inner ear and for fellow Anglo-Saxons and even Russians by avoiding the accenting of any syllable, by following the transliterations provided, and by using his common sense. Even Krzhizhanovsky looks harder than it is, for Russian is a highly phonetic language.

INDEX

Abramovich, Rafael, II: 60, 172-173
Adler, Alfred, II: 196
Adler, Victor, I: 261; secures Lenin's
release, II: 358-361; aids Trotsky,
II: 365; at Brussels Conference, II:
377-378
Adoratsky, I: 88; II: 285
Aesop Language, Slave Language. *See*
Censorship
Agrarian question: military state
farms, I: 15-16; Decembrists and,
I: 19-20; Lenin as specialist on, I:
276; Lenin's *To the Village Poor,* I:
281; Lenin abandons *otrezki* for
nationalization, I: 377-379; Stoly-
pin's agrarian reform, II: 29-33; its
success likely to deprive Social
Democrats of agrarian program, II:
31-32; debate at London Congress
(Plekhanov's warning on binding
peasants to new state), II: 35-39;
Stalin's proposals carried out, 1917,
reversed in thirties, II: 167-169;
state ownership of land, and peasants as foundation for total statism,
II: 35-39, 169
Akhundov, R., II: 142
Akimov (Vladimir Makhnovets), I:
271, 290-293, 304
Alakaevka (Lenin's landed estate), I:
95-96
Albania, II: 339
Alexander I (1801-1825), I: 15, 18-19,
20, 204
Alexander II (1855-1881), I: 15, 21, 28,
62-64, 204, 224
Alexander III (1881-1894): reaction to
father's assassination, I: 62-63;
character of reign, I: 62ff., 74ff.; on
Lenin's brother, I: 71; industrialization under, I: 75; and Jews, I:
204ff., 224
Alexinsky, G. A., II: 33-34, 59, 234;
jest on Jewish Menshevism and po-

groms, II: 169-170; on Elizabeth K
and Lenin's poem, 170n.
Algeciras, II: 4
Alliluev, Sergei (Stalin's father-in-law),
II: 120-122
Allilueva, Nadezhda (Stalin's wife),
II: 122
Amsterdam, Saul (Henrykowski), II: 233
Anarchists, I: 258-259; in Tsarist and
Bolshevik Siberia, I: 160
"Angels." *See* Liberals
Anna. *See* Ulyanova, Anna I.
Antid Oto (pen name of Trotsky, Leon
q.v.)
Anyuta. *See* Ulyanova, Anna I.
Apostolic succession, I: 85, 169
Arakcheev and military state farms, I:
5, 15-16, 18-20
Archduke Francis Ferdinand of Aus-
tria, II: 353
Arefeev (Lenin's opponent in lawsuit),
I: 98
Argunov, II: 374
Armand, Inessa, II: 349-350
Armed bands, I: 408-409; II: 45-79
Armenia, II: 142
Asia: and Asiatic Russia, I: 6-7, 9-11,
192, 333; Lenin and Stalin on, II:
88-89
"August Conference," "August Bloc,"
II: 249-250
"Auntie." *See* Kalmykova, Alexandra
Austria-Hungary: Lenin moves to, II:
292-293; and Poles, II: 293-295;
and national question, II: 295; and
Balkans, II: 294-295, 338ff.
Authoritarianism: root in patriarchal-
ism, I: 22-23; authoritarian party
necessary to authoritarian state, I:
320-321; in Lenin's thought, II:
219ff. *See also* Autocracy; Centralism; Democracy, Marxism and
Populism; Thought, Russian; To-
talitarianism

A NOTE ABOUT
THE PRODUCTION
OF THIS BOOK

The typeface for the text of the special edition of *Three Who Made a Revolution* is Times New Roman, designed by Stanley Morison in 1932 for the London *Times*. The text was photocomposed at Time Inc. under the direction of Albert J. Dunn and Arthur J. Dunn. The book was printed and bound by J. W. Clement Co. of Buffalo, New York. The cover was printed by Livermore and Knight Co., a division of Printing Corporation of America, in Providence, Rhode Island.

x

The paper, TIME Reading Text, is from The Mead Corporation of Dayton, Ohio. The cover stock is from The Plastic Coating Corporation of Holyoke, Massachusetts.